COCKPIT COMMANDER

COCKPIT COMMANDER

A NAVIGATOR'S LIFE

THE AUTOBIOGRAPHY OF WING COMMANDER
BRUCE GIBSON

Pen & Sword
AVIATION

First published in Great Britain in 2013 by
PEN & SWORD AVIATION
An imprint of
Pen & Sword Books Ltd
47 Church Street
Barnsley
South Yorkshire
S70 2AS

ISBN 978 1 78159 089 8

A CIP catalogue record for this book is
available from the British Library

Printed and bound in England
By CPI Group (UK) Ltd, Croydon, CR0 4YY

Pen & Sword Books Ltd incorporates the Imprints of Pen & Sword Aviation,
Pen & Sword Family History, Pen & Sword Maritime, Pen & Sword Military,
Pen & Sword Discovery, Pen & Sword Politics, Pen & Sword Atlas,
Pen & Sword Archaeology, Wharncliffe Local History, Wharncliffe True Crime,
Wharncliffe Transport, Pen & Sword Select, Pen & Sword Military Classics,
Leo Cooper, The Praetorian Press, Claymore Press, Remember When,
Seaforth Publishing and Frontline Publishing

For a complete list of Pen & Sword titles please contact
PEN & SWORD BOOKS LIMITED
47 Church Street, Barnsley, South Yorkshire, S70 2AS, England
E-mail: enquiries@pen-and-sword.co.uk
Website: www.pen-and-sword.co.uk

CONTENTS

PROLOGUE

*L*ife is full of light and shade, good news and bad news, joys and sorrows, and the year 1936 was no exception.

But this is to be a happy book, and although we can acknowledge the sad events of that year such as the deaths of King George V, and one the most famous poets, Rudyard Kipling (who was never to become Poet Laureate), I want to concentrate on the successful events that also happened.

This was a buoyant year when England beat the All Blacks at Rugby for the first time, filling the nation with joy. Golden Miller won the Cheltenham Gold Cup for the fifth time in succession and made us all happy, and the Spitfire aircraft made its maiden flight, lightening our hearts and creating a feeling of great pride among the impending gloom.

But above all, the most joyful occurrence, and one which was to completely change my life, was when the Air Ministry announced the formation of the Royal Air Force Volunteer Reserve (RAFVR).

1

I remembered what my Uncle Chris told me about what he had endured during the First World War, when at one time he was standing up to his waist in mud and water in the trenches for a fortnight.

By the time he was relieved his feet had swollen to twice their normal size and he was sent to the Sick Quarters, diagnosed with Trench Foot. I was determined that I was going to have none of that and so, in 1937, I joined the RAFVR. This was a triumph in itself as the Medical Officers did their absolute best to fail me but, against all odds, I was accepted and my life was never the same again!

So, 'if you are sitting comfortably', I'll begin............

* * *

1

1913

I was born in Plaistow, in the Borough of West Ham, on 28th May 1913, at 20 Redriffe Road, Plaistow, E13.

The name 'Plaistow' means Play Place, and many moons ago it was spelt 'Pleystow'. By the time I was born, the pronunciation had become 'Plarstow', but that was in a time when most houses were rented out to the working classes and who were relatively poor.

By then the whole area was largely built up and formed a part of the Greater London sprawl. In my maternal Grandmother's day however, it was completely rural and she lived in an area known as Stratford, and was a village approached from all sides by large Elm trees.

In her day the main wealth of Plaistow was derived from the grazing land in the area on which stock was fattened.

Some very wealthy men had large houses and estates in Plaistow, one of whom was a Mr. Foot who was a former Lord Mayor of London and was buried in the West Ham Churchyard.

The word 'Hamme' is an Anglo Saxon word, recorded in the Doomsday book, and means 'home' or 'residence', and it is from this that the names West Ham and East Ham are derived.

As what can only be presumed a testimony to love, it was here that King Henry VIII ordered the construction of the Anne Boleyn Tower, from where it was possible to see the Thames, which today is over a mile away. Ironically, it was also from this Tower that she was taken to the Tower of London prior to her death.

Stratford was renowned as the Slaughter House of London, and my Grandmother 'Nan' often mentioned the cries of sheep as they were taken to slaughter.

Many noteworthy events occurred in the year of my birth.

The Suffragettes stepped up their military campaign – and Mrs. Pankhurst was a very naughty lady in her efforts to get the votes for women and, although she was for ever in and out of prison, this did not deter her followers. Mrs. Emily Davison, a fellow Suffragette, flung herself in front of the King's horse at the Derby that year and died the following day without regaining consciousness.

Police in London seized a woman for simply wearing a split skirt!

Germany launched the first flight of the largest Zeppelin Airship, which was later to explode with the loss of all who were on board.

French aviator Roland Garros gained fame for making the first non-stop flight across the Mediterranean from Fréjus in the South of France to Bizerte in Tunisia, a distance of 558 miles, and which took 5 hours and 53 minutes, even against strong headwinds. The French also set a new air speed record of 118 mph.

Sir Amroth Wright, a British bacteriologist and immunologist, was either tired of living or just stupid and wrote an anti suffrage book claiming that women were inferior to men!!

On the day of my birth, King George V and Queen Mary, as honoured guests of the Kaiser, were present at the annual review of the Troops of the Potsdam Garrison by the Emperor of Germany, and from whom later they took a cordial farewell.

Whilst all of these exciting things were happening, the most important event in the Gibson family was my mother going into labour and finally succeeding in evacuating me! During the previous nine months she must have been constantly talking to me, as one of the very first phrases I can remember is my mother saying, "Votes for women – rats on the men"!!

Redriffe Road was one of three short roads leading from Plaistow Road to Stratford Road and as far as I can remember had about 30 houses on either side of the road. The houses were numbered even on one side, and odd on the other. They were built at the turn of the century and were of solid construction with yellow bricks (which harden with age) and grey-slated roofs.

When I was born my parents already had two children – my big sister Jess, who was 4 years and eleven months older than me, and my brother Cyril, who was just eleven day's short of his second birthday. We lived in an upstairs flat above Mrs. Mason and her family.

In the house opposite was a family with two girls who appeared to me quite ancient, being about six and eight years of age respectively. When I was about 18 months old, one of those girls had a birthday party, and we three Gibsons were invited. Young as I was, I can remember having jelly, blancmange, cakes and orange squash to drink, followed by a grand singing session around a piano.

Everybody was in a happy, party mood, wearing paper hats that we had 'won' from pulling crackers amidst great excitement! The songs we sang that day were the first I had ever heard, and I was later to learn that they were all from the First World War, songs such as: 'Are we downhearted? No!'; 'It's a long way to Tipperary'; 'Keep the homes fires burning', and 'How're you gonna keep them down on the farm after they've seen Paris'! Our repertoire was so limited that we had to sing the same songs over and over again – by the end of the party I knew all of the songs and words by heart and in my nostalgic moments I remember them with great affection to this day.

It was whilst we were living above the Masons that my brother Cyril was taken ill with Poliomyelitis, which we kids called Infantile Paralysis.

At the time on-one told me that he had been ill, and I didn't find out until later when we started to play team games with other boys and I discovered that he could not run as fast as the rest of us as he had no calf muscles in his left leg.

However that did not stop him from insisting in playing with the rest of us.

When I was about twenty-one months old we moved less than half a mile from the Masons to an upstairs flat at 107 Stratford Road, Plaistow, E13. Mrs. Mason's three boys were growing up and they needed more living space.

Our new home was a two bedroom flat with a kitchen come living room and scullery, with an outside toilet that we shared with the tenant downstairs. We had not been there long when Cyril became very ill with measles. As this was considered to be a childish ailment, my mother decided to put me in the same bed as Cyril in the hope that I would contract it also, and we could get it over with together.

Whilst I did catch measles from my brother, I only had one spot on my forehead and I did not feel at all unwell, and so I was constantly getting up and rushing round like a mad thing, much to the annoyance of my mother who would rush to get her 'weapon of discipline' (her punishment cane) – however I was always too quick and nimble for her and I cannot ever remember her catching me!

My next recollection was, as if by magic, we had moved to the downstairs flat, and must have taken place while I was asleep! This meant that we now had an upstairs neighbour and no stairs to climb or keep clean.

Our landlord had an Ironmonger's Shop in Stratford Road, and he was a sanctimonious old 'hay bag'. He was not very tall but was red of face with a large beer belly and a perpetual grin on his face as if he had played a practical joke on someone and was just waiting to see what happened if they found out!

Every Monday without fail he called to collect his rent – he knew that if he left it until the Tuesday the money would have been spent and he would have no chance of getting two week's rent on the following Monday.

Rent collecting was one of his happier chores. He would listen to complaints from his tenants, his face reefed in smiles whilst he made copious notes, knowing full well that he had no intention of satisfying his tenants' requests and keep his property in a reasonable state of repair.

Every Sunday he was to be found in his pew in church, praying with other worshippers for the forgiveness of his sins, which gave him the inner strength to start the week all over again. In the words of our mother, 'he was an old skinflint'.

Again we had a two bedroom flat with a large kitchen that we also used as a living room, and a scullery with a built in copper standing in one corner. Also in the scullery was a large sink with cold running water. The kitchen had a bay window on one side and a range on the other side, which was set into the wall, and was known as a "Kitchener". This had a coal fire on one side and an oven on the other for baking, and an iron top with a round removable plate above the fire for refuelling the first, and for heating a 'flat iron' for ironing the laundry.

The front bedroom also had a bay window, outside which was a six-foot space giving access for window cleaning and also where the dustbin was kept. That space was determined by a brick wall, four feet high, and had short railings on top to separate the property from the public pavement and at the same time supporting the cast iron front gate.

The kitchen-come-living room was the only room to have a 'Veritas Gas Mantle', which was fastened on the wall above the top and to one side of the Kitchener, and was used for lighting.

All of the interior walls were decorated with pink distemper, and the ceilings were off white, mainly due to age! Once again we had an outside toilet, which we shared, with our upstairs neighbour.

Our short row of houses had cellars stretching underneath most of the house, and which went with the downstairs flat, and was the main reason why we moved downstairs.

My father was a Cabinet Maker and furniture designer and would work down in the cellar in the evenings, making furniture that he had designed, to test the feasibility and practicality of his work. There was gas lighting in the cellar and plenty of room to work and also store seasoned timber. There was a large carpenter's bench and many racks fastened to the walls filled with tools ready to hand. At weekends I would watch him work. I was fascinated to see how a rough piece of timber could but be cut and planed and finally dove tailed and joined up with other pieces (no nails used), to make the finished article.

As I grew older there were times when I was able to help, and one of my most enduring memories was the horrible smell of the glue, which had to be heated on the Kitchener in a special glue pot. The stench was truly revolting!

My father never spoke to me when I was helping him. If I were holding one end of a large piece of timber, he would make signs to turn the wood over etc. But he never gave a verbal instruction! He was a chain smoker. His large hands were rough and covered in corns obtained through manual labour lifting timber, and also covered with nicotine stains.

On one occasion when he was doing an intricate and small piece, he was using a tenon saw and was concentrating so hard that he cut through a corn on his hand and a spurt of blood shot out – he had started to cut through his thumb! The expletives he used did not make any sense to me, and are not to be found in the Oxford English Dictionary, but he made me laugh. He quickly stopped the bleeding however by dabbing some glue on the cut!

When he realised what a fool he had made of himself in front of his young son, he joined me in laughing, stuck a shaving on the cut, and carried on working

There were many thousands of houses of that design to the north, south, east and west of London, and when maintained properly were quite habitable. They were not considered slums, as they were houses where proud, working class families lived, who kept their premises spotlessly clean, with a door step whitened with Hearth Stone and a cellar flap cleaned with black lead.

The scullery had no furniture in it as such, just the copper in one corner which heated the water by a coal fire which was only lit on Mondays, which were wash days, and a sink in the other corner used for washing up and personal hygiene. It had a stone floor, which was scrubbed at the end of washday after the copper fire had been put out and the ashes cleared away. There was a window in one wall, which gave light and was able to be opened to let the steam out on washdays.

One nasty odour suffered by many families in the early part of the 20th Century was the smell of boiled clothes. I used to dread coming home from school for our mid-day dinner on a Monday of cold meat (left over from the Sunday's joint), boiled potatoes, cold rice pudding, and the awful stench of boiled laundry.

The kitchen was sparsely furnished, with a large kitchen table, which fitted into the bay window and could seat eight people – three at each side and two at the ends. My father had made it especially for that kitchen, and I came to learn that all of the furniture that he made for us was massive. We had a fireguard around the Kitchener, which always seemed to have tea towels draped on it to dry. There was a dresser with shelves loaded with crockery. The three drawers and two cupboards underneath always seemed to be packed with goods which were controlled by my mother, and she was the only one who knew what was in those drawers!

The front bedroom, occupied by my parents, was packed chock-a-block with furniture - all of which had been made by my father and was, of course, massive. He only used the finest quality mahogany, and the finished product was french polished fit for a King. There was a large wardrobe and a dressing table, which, my father told us, had a secret drawer, and he was the only one who knew where it was! There was also a king sized wooden bedstead, a washstand with marble top, and a baby's cot. The chest of drawers that went with the suite was located in the second bedroom where we slept, as there was no room for it in the first bedroom. We three children slept in the same iron bedstead, two at the top and one at the bottom. There was also a large piece of furniture that my father had made for private sale or special order. All of the bedrooms were lit solely with candles.

As my father used to get home between 6.30 and 7.00 p.m., my mother would pack Jess, Cyril and myself off to bed by 6.00 p.m. so that she could have some time on her own with him during his evening meal.

Our bedroom had a dark green roller blind to the window, which was always pulled down so that the gas light from next door did not keep us awake. However by 6.00 p.m. we were never tired, and Cyril, who slept nearest the window, would skew the curtain round to allow some light in, and would proceed to tell us stories which he had concocted from his very vivid imagination. They were naturally always about a clever, handsome boy called Cyril, and which often caused arguments, bringing my mother into the room who would give us all a whack with the punishment cane. Then, with the roller blind back in place, we ultimately fell asleep.

Lino covered the floors of all the rooms and passageways, with the only rug in front of the Kitchener. The outside garden was shared with the neighbour upstairs, and we each had one side.

On the wall of the outside lavatory we had a flourishing rambler rose tree which received much tender loving care from my father who regularly deadheaded it, and as a result always seemed to be in prolific bloom during the summer months. The rest of our patch was an herbaceous border, full of perennial plants.

My mother loved Thrift (sea pink) and had several clumps of this in the border. On one occasion, in my efforts to be helpful, I decided to do some weeding, and pulled up all of the Thrift as I thought it was grass. Needless to say I was not the flavour of the month, and I hid until things cooled down!

Being one of a large family has its joys as well as its sorrows. One quickly learns that it is not always popular to want all of your own way, especially when the responsibility has been left to one's mother to bring up the family to be decent citizens as one's father is a member of the Royal Flying Corps and away in Egypt mending broken wooden aircraft. Looking back I am amazed how well she coped. With the help of our Grandmother Nan, who we saw every day, our mother did a good job. If we fell by the wayside it wasn't her fault. It was because we had not conformed to the rules, which were etched in stone.

We had many friends – therefore Rule One was to 'Share Everything'. Rule two was 'Play Fair', and Rule Three was 'Clear up your own mess'. Those tenets were drummed into us and woe betide the one who stepped out of line.

These rules we thought were reasonable and we learnt quickly, but others, such as 'wash your hands before you eat', and 'say you're sorry if you hurt somebody' I thought were quite sissy and would go to some lengths to avoid applying them.

However the sight of the punishment cane always had the desired effect!

My father was a chain smoker. He used to smoke Will's Wild Woodbines, 10 old pence for 20 cigarettes. He would get up to go to work just after 6.00 a.m., and the first thing he did was light a cigarette and start coughing. He had the most atrocious smoker's cough and it was so loud it used to wake me up. That was it – as soon as I awake I have to get up. My mother used to send me back to bed again, but I could not go to sleep, and I would fidget so much I would wake everybody else up, and so ultimately my mother would give me some breakfast and I would join her in seeing my father go off to work at 7.00 a.m., and I would go and stand just inside Sawyer's shop to wait for my friend, Arthur Sawyer, to join me which he never did because he was far too sleepy. But Mr. Sawyer had no complaint; he just let me stand there watching him get up the newspaper rounds.

While this was going on, my father was walking down Maud Road towards Plaistow Railway Station, coughing his heart out, and making so much noise he would wake up Maud Road inhabitants, who ultimately complained so much my father had to take a different route to the station.

One morning one of the paper delivery boys did not turn up. Mr. Sawyer said, "Bruce – you know where Mrs. Northeast lives, don't you?" "Yes", I said. "Well, be a good chap and take her paper, will you?

On my return to the shop, Mr. Sawyer did a repeat performance, naming the customers. The same thing happened for the rest of the week; in fact, the absent boy never returned, and at just seven year's of age, I became a delivery boy.

My father was never without a cigarette in his mouth and would light one cigarette from the end of another. My mother used to nag him rotten, but it made no difference – my father completely ignored any request for him to ban the dirty, filthy, costly habit. Our whole house smelt of stale cigarette smoke, and we always had a fug of smoke in any room he was occupying.

He was a very selfish man. Never at any time did he ever buy anyone a Birthday or Christmas card. He only ever gave my mother enough housekeeping money to provide the bare necessities of life, and yet, besides packets of cigarettes, he always had in his pockets a bag of sweets and spare cash.

On Saturdays at lunchtime I would meet him at Plaistow Railway Station and we would walk to his mother's house where he always gave her money as if he were still a bachelor. In effect he was keeping two homes going. His mother – my grandmother – could never reconcile the fact that my father was married because she could not do without the money.

Because of this, and the fact that she would spread untrue stories about how our mother carried on while he was at work, she was banned from our house.

On one occasion, my younger brother Percy complained to our elder brother, Cyril, that he had heard that our father was not his father. Brother Cyril adopted his most superior attitude as he took Percy by the arm towards a full-length mirror, and said, "Pubby, just look in that mirror. You are the spitting image of your father."

At that time our mother had five children with another one in the oven, and I can remember her saying, "It's over five weeks since I put my foot outside this house."

In other words, she was fully employed!

* * *

12

2

Growing Up

L ife is one long learning process and I started to learn the minute I could play games.

One of the first games I became involved in was when big sister 'Jim' (Jess's nick name) would rope me in to play with her friends in their favourite game of 'Doctors and Nurses' with me as the patient. I was only about three at the time and can remember being constantly mauled about, with the 'nurses' looking in my ears and mouth, and I always ended up with no trousers on, lying across Doris Sawyer's lap, having my bottom smacked. The smacking was only light taps and at that age it didn't worry me a bit running around with no trousers on because it gave the girls some amusement and it met with Jim's approval, and that was O.K. by me.

From then on I was interested in all games, especially if there was a ball involved. Being naturally a right-footed player, I used to practise for hours kicking and controlling a ball with my left foot until ultimately I became equally proficient with either foot.

Boxing, a physical contact sport, has always been a favourite of mine, but my mother persuaded me to stick to athletics or ball games because, she said, "Only rough boys went in for Boxing", despite the fact that the Queensbury Rules were strictly adhered to, and boxing was taught as the noble art of self-defence.

In 1918 Joe Beckett knocked out Bombardier Billy Wells and became the Heavyweight Boxing Champion of Great Britain, whilst in the same year Jack Dempsey overpowered the giant cowboy, Jess Willard, in three gruelling rounds to become the Heavyweight Champion of the World. Jess Willard never fought again.

One of our favourite games was pretending to be Dick Turpin, the infamous Highwayman who had been a terror in our district, but to us kids he was a popular hero. Apart from his violent crimes he was also accredited with many acts of kindness. He was admired more than he was blamed – and this we could understand because he was possessed of those qualities of Daring, Do, Endurance and Resource on which we English set such a high value. He was executed in York on 7th April 1739 for horse stealing. Had he been alive today he would have been sent on a Safari Course at public expense!

Before the declaration of war by Great Britain against Germany on 4th August 1914, civilian populations had been mainly spectators during any previous wars. However, with the advent of the Zeppelins and fixed wing aircraft, the most likely source of violence against ordinary citizens was not by land forces but by assault from the air.

The first air raid on London by a Zeppelin was in August 1915.

At the time civilians did not realise what havoc bombs could cause and would watch those huge sausage shaped machines caught in the searchlights spellbound –and one particular lady remarked that it was the most thrilling and wonderful sight!

I know my mother didn't think much of being bombed as I can remember being pulled out of a nice warm bed and stuck under the kitchen table. Although the table was of very strong construction it would have been no protection from the bombs, but it was different and I found it quite good fun.

Mobile anti-aircraft guns used to be stationed in our street but I cannot ever remember them being fired. On 3rd September 1916, during a Zeppelin raid on London, Second Lieutenant Leefe Robinson shot down a Zeppelin and was given an instant Victoria Cross. The dreadful sight of part of the Zeppelin containing the gas as it caught fire with its roaring flames of blue, red and purple so affected one spectator, Sybil Morrison, that she became a life long pacifist.

In total there were 57 airship raids on Britain and some 14,000 tons of bombs were dropped, and, although they caused much damage, they were met with the same fortitude and endurance that was to be displayed 25 years later.

14th June 1917 – German Aircraft bombed London for the first time; 20th October of that year eight Zeppelins bombed London, four of which were subsequently shot down over France on their homeward journey.

On 10th January 1918, The Representation of the People's Act, which gave the vote to women over the age of 30, was approved by the House of Lords. I remember my mother repeatedly saying "Women's rights; rats on the men": so that's what it was all about!

13th March 1918 saw the school leaving age being raised to 14 years of age. The British MP's meant well, and it was a step in the right direction for everyone to have a basic education, but looking back in retrospect, with the nation still at war and teachers in short supply, we were being trained to be factory fodder.

My mother, who had been trained to be a teacher, insisted that we learn the three 'R's' and inspired us to have ambition, self respect and always be polite, but the two elements of true politeness are grace and self denial and have to be worked at as they do not come naturally to the human race.

My mother was an excellent cook and produced the tastiest meals cooked in the Kitchener. She used to cook the most beautiful meat pudding in a basin with a thick suet piecrust on top, which was covered with a cloth and tied on and then placed in a large cast iron saucepan to cook.

One day when I was playing with brother Cyril in the garden just after we had eaten our pudding, I had indigestion, and some of the pudding I had eaten repeated on me and came back into my mouth. Brother Cyril told me to "spit it out" but I swallowed it again, and later when I was relating this occurrence to my mother, I said "Cyril told me to spit it out, but I did eat it; it were luvly!"

That anecdote was repeated so many times as I was growing up that I remember that happening as if it were yesterday.

Roly Poly Pudding was one of her specialities. It was delicious and, although it is still on some Pub menus today, it is not like our mum used to make, and that at a time of First World War food rationing. I remember once my mother was emptying her bag after a shopping trip, and she produced a bag of sugar, and said, "That's your sugar ration for the week". I immediately grabbed it and was going to put it away for safe keeping, but was prevented from doing that and was assured it would be used with all of the other rationed food, and that I would get my share.

Jam was not easy to get; it was either too expensive or in short supply; but as a substitute with bread and margarine for tea time we would have a spread of Nestlé's milk with a sprinkling of sugar on the top. There was a little ditty Nestlé's used at that time to advertise their product, and it went:

> *"Skimmed milk unfit for babies, not good enough for cats,*
> *Nestlé's milk is what you want, leave skimmed to mice and rats"*

At that time the health of children was a cause for great concern. Some 500,000 children were ill fed and diseased due to the effects of a poor diet. More than half needed dental treatment and a third were unhygienically dirty. One child in ten had serious eye defects, and several had hearing problems, and food rationing did not help. Hindsight can never be wrong.

Four premises away from our house at 107 was a shop, 115, which was on the corner of Stratford Road and Maud Road. This was Murphy's, the Ironmonger, and next door to that was Sawyer's the Newsagent. It was a double fronted shop with Billboards outside on which were displayed on a daily basis posters advertising the news of the day.

I used to play cricket with several friends in the street, chalking the stumps on a lamppost, with one of our gang posted as a lookout to warn us of the approach of our local policeman. We always used to have a great time until we were warned by the lookout's whistle that trouble was approaching.

On one occasion I was just hiding our bat and ball behind Sawyer's billboards when I found myself sitting on my bottom and, as I looked up, there was old 'Fat Belly' (our local Bobby) on his beat, who whacked me with his rolled up leather cape. It was my pride that was hurt more than physical pain, but old 'Fat Belly' frightened the life out of me when he said, "Don't ever let me see you doing that again, young Gibson, or I'll tell your father."

I leapt up and rushed home which was only three doors away, scared out of my wits. It was not the fact that he had discovered our hiding place, which worried me but that he knew my name and where my father lived! That terrified me!!

Today, ninety years later, in the last 25 years since living in our village of Ripple, I have only seen a Police car drive through our village, at approximately 20 miles per hour, on just three occasions. It's not that today we are better behaved, we just don't have the Bobbies, and those we do have spend most of their time writing out reports. Coppers like old 'Fat Belly' kept the peace, and so he didn't have to write about it!

Opposite Maud Road and across Stratford Road was Park Road which, as the name suggests, led to West Ham Park. The Park had a long history. Dr. Fothergill, the great botanist, had owned it previously and he had developed the gardens by introducing rare plants from all over the world to such an extent it was regarded as second only to Kew Gardens. The next owners of the Park were the Gurneys, a family of Quakers, and they lived in a house called 'The Cedars' which adjoined the Park, and was where Elizabeth Fry (née Gurney) had once lived.

An area was allocated within the Park for cricket, and there were also six tennis courts. The cricket pitch was beautifully maintained and was known as the Billiards Table. There was also a Pavilion, complete with changing rooms and refreshment facilities.

The tennis courts were hired out at one shilling (five pence!) for one hour, and we used to act as runners to collect the tennis balls for the players, for which we were paid one penny. That was considered good money because our pocket money was a half penny per day, and we could double that in one hour!

There was also a Maypole, which the girls monopolised, and a paddling pool which our mother forbade us to use for fear of getting our feet cut from the broken glass thrown in by vandals.

It seemed the sun always shone during the summer holidays in those days, and big sister Jess was always in charge of her siblings until Cyril and I were old enough to play cricket in our next door neighbour, Bert Coates, cricket team. Bert was a bit older than both of us and was a good fast bowler, and he taught Cyril how to bowl. However in those days I was considered too young and they made me play Long Stop.

'The Cedars' was separated from the park by six-foot high iron railings, and the property had a large, unkempt garden which Cyril and I decided to investigate. We dug a hole underneath the railings and climbed under. It had once obviously been a very fine garden with numerous small trees, shrubs and clumps of herbaceous border plants, indeed ideal territory for playing Hide and Seek, and plenty of places for ambush when playing Cowboys and Indians!

Located within the grounds was a large concrete shelter, at least 20 yards long, with a door at each end and completely empty. We would regularly investigate the building but were never able to work out why it had been constructed – although it was just after the war, there was nobody living at the house and Air Raid Shelters hadn't yet been thought of.

Whenever Jess decided it was time to go home to our next meal we would always replace the soil to cover our tracks of entry and exit, and not one of the three Park Keepers ever discovered our exploits. Needless to say we made ourselves filthy but we did not notice this until we returned home when a very cross mother would point that fact out to us, when she would say "You filthy beasts, where have you been to get in that state? You'll get nothing to eat until you've cleaned yourselves up, and remember to wash your knees."

It was always Knees! Knees! Knees! And if it wasn't knees, it was "Have you washed the back of your neck?"

By the time we had nearly scrubbed our skin off we were so hungry we could have eating our mother's apron! Come the next day, all had been forgiven and we were ready to get ourselves filthy all over again.

We made a point of always being at 'The Cedars' every Wednesday afternoon during our holidays as this was when the West Ham Police Tug of War team would turn up for practise.

They had a very large galvanised container filled with brick bats and rubble, which weighed about two tons. The Tug of War rope was fastened to the container and thrown over a very large branch of a tree, and then the team proceeded to pull the container into the air under the instructions of their coach.

Quite a lot of talking went on before the team took up the rope, and it all seemed very friendly until the container was about six foot in the air, at which point they would be ordered by their coach to 'Hold!' The coach then went down the line and his language was very different from what we were used to hearing at Sunday School, and the general impression was that he did not like the members of his team at all! Mostly it was because their feet were not in the right position, and when that error had been put right, the head or body was wrong.

During all of that time the two-ton container was being held six feet off the ground. Apparently the holding of the container in the air was most important and was to build strength and stamina until it was gently lowered, inch by inch, to the ground. We kids who were watching from the other side of the railings were always terrified of the Coach's attitude, but surprise, surprise, it completely changed as he congratulated the team on a good workout.

It was noticeable how the team alternated by being either to the left or right of the rope, and how important it was to keep the rope straight, and the team to always stay in balance. The coach would then take up the rope and demonstrate, with much hilarity, the errors made by the team. He stressed making full use of the weight of the body – the head being the heaviest part, and how to make use of that at the moment of pull. He would get three members to take up the rope, and he would demonstrate at the moment of pull to throw back the head as the leg is raised by going up, down and back.

In demonstrating this movement the coach, who was well over six foot and weighed about 18 stone, would quite easily pull the other three members who were trying their best to prevent that from happening. We never gave it a thought that it was a Police tug of war team as in civilian clothes or sports gear they looked quite normal and friendly – but in police uniform we used to give them a wide berth!

In the park there was an excellent Bandstand and which had an ample supply of chairs around it. On the odd summer evening my mother would take the three of us there to listen to the music played by various military bands. Jess and Cyril would sit with her, but I could never sit still. My mother used to call me a 'fidget arse' as I would slink off and quite often earn an extra penny at the tennis courts.

The gardens, which were all at different levels, were superb, and every year West Ham Park won the competition of all LCC parks for the best display of Rhododendrons. Some of the blooms were twice the size of my head! There were large seats permanently fixed at strategic points in the gardens, and it became my job, when the weather was fine, to take a blind gentleman neighbour to one of those seats, where he would sit and enjoy the company of like-minded friends.

I was never without a tennis ball, and if I had a few minutes to spare, would control with my feet and dribble and aim at some pre-determined spot to gain accuracy, but mainly with my left foot as being a naturally right footed player, I was determined to be able to play on either wing of a football field.

When I was four years old my mother took me to see Miss Shrimpton, the Headmistress of Holbrook Road Infants School. By now this was a familiar chore for her to do as she had already performed it twice with Jess and Cyril.

As a result of our visit, the following Monday, with Jess and Cyril each holding one of my hands, I remember crossing the tramlines in Plaistow Road and I was on my way to my first day in Miss Ewing's class at the school.

On that first day, at the age of four, I soon discovered some words had double meanings.

Being of an inquisitive nature I was trying to find out how everything worked in my new environment and I was touching everything I could lay my hands on, much to the exasperation of my newfound friend, teacher Miss Ewing.

Clearly she had had enough as suddenly she picked me up and plonked me in a chair, and said, "Sit there for the present." I don't know how long I sat there, but I never did get the present!

From that day on it gradually occurred to me that words have to be chosen very carefully to prevent ambiguity if one is to make a statement that is incapable of varying interpretations. As every member of the acting profession knows, with the spoken word, inflexion of the voice can be used to make a single word have many different meanings, ranging from the world of fact to mere fantasy.

In this connection, politicians, union officials or business negotiators use words incorrectly at their peril!

The freedom of speech is the basis of democratic life and political promises can be made in party manifestos, which, if studied carefully, have a proviso which can lead to a compromise. Speakers and Writers who have studied the effective use of language make sure that the words they use are chosen to convey the point or argument they wish to make and rarely fall into the trap of having to publish a disclaimer or apology.

The word 'NEVER' should always be avoided as once it has been used, it is then impossible to compromise without losing face, and this can be disastrous to the persuasive reputation of the user. The use of simple words of one syllable, and which the majority of people should be able to understand, should be preferable at all times.

For example, I was giving a lift to a hitchhiker once when we passed a sign that said 'Equestrians Only'. My passenger said, "'Equestrians Only' – what does that mean?". I replied, "Horse Riders only". My friend said, "Well, why doesn't it say so"! The moral is obvious and I have tried to remember it ever since.

School hours were 9.00 am to 12.00 noon, and 2.00 pm to 4.00 pm, five days a week.

On my second day of being the new boy I sat on teacher's lap. Mostly we played games, and with square bricks with letters on she taught us our alphabet. With a bead frame that we played with, in no time at all we could count up to ten, which I thought was great fun.

One of the games we played was called 'In and out the windows', with someone playing the piano. It consisted of half our number forming a ring with the rest of us forming up, boy girl, boy girl etc and dancing in front of or behind the members in the ring alternately as we made progress around the ring. I thought this game was soppy!

We also had wooden trays of sand and, with our index finger, we copied letters that our teacher had written on the Blackboard. We were taught the chorus 'Ring a roses, usher, usher, we all fall down'. I liked that game, as there was robust movement and could sing and make a big display of ourselves when we fell down.

Every afternoon we were meant to put our head on the desk and rest for a while. Rest? I didn't want to rest! I was not tired and kept fidgeting and disturbing all of the other little dears who were knackered and needed to rest. Miss Ewing soon cottoned on to this and would have me on her lap, and would read me nursery rhymes, which I quickly learnt.

I stayed in Miss Ewing's class until I was seven years of age when I went upstairs into the Big Boys School. By that time I could read, do simple sums, spell all of the words in my limited vocabulary, and express myself in written compositions.

At the same time I joined the Cubs which Cyril had done two years previously. I was so proud of my green Cub's jersey that I wore it every day to school. Up until then I had always worn the clothes that Cyril had grown out of, but the green jersey with my Cub's badge on was all mine and very special.

In the Big Boys School my teacher was a Mr Griffiths, a Welsh gentleman, and he was my teacher for the next five years.

On the signing of the Armistice at 1100 hours on 11th November 1918, there were universal spontaneous demonstrations.

By that time our family had grown in size and I had two brothers and two sisters. I was five years old at the time and my mother, to celebrate the victory, took me out for a walk just before my bedtime (which was usually 6.00 p.m., but never later than 7.00 p.m.). We walked down Maud Road into Plaistow Road, took the next turning right into Redriffe Road and back into Stratford Road. These four short roads formed a square, which took about 15 minutes to talk around.

Big sister Jess, who was 10 at the time, had been left to look after Cyril, Percy and Nell, and as we approached our house, Henry Sawyer, who was the eldest of the Sawyers, set off a firework which he had placed in the centre of a concrete manhole cover in the middle of the road. The firework must have ignited gases in the sewer underneath because the bang was enormous and the explosion so intense it lifted the manhole cover three feet into the air before coming to rest on the curb.

My mother however was completely unperturbed and as we walked by, she simply said, "Stupid boy", but Henry laughed so much he cried. I said, "What's he crying for?". My mum said "He knows what will happen to him when his mother finds out!"

For many years after that, no matter what one was doing at 1100 hours on 11th November of every succeeding year, everything stopped for two minutes silence to commemorate the ten million lives that had been lost as a result of the Great War which the politicians claimed at the time to be the war to end all wars. Of course we didn't know then what was in store for us 21 years later when we would be at it again. When will we ever learn?

* * *

3

Such Discipline!

With such a large family and still growing, discipline was strict and severe. My father was in Egypt with the Royal Flying Corps, and so it was all down to my mum with the help of her mother, our Nan. We were ruled by Edwardian standards. At mealtimes our table was never properly laid until my mother had produced the punishment cane.

We learnt at a very early stage the way of transgressors is hard. Rule Number One was 'Children should be seen and not heard'. Rule Number Two was 'If one did not clean up their plate, what was left over one had to eat at the next meal'. If one complained because they didn't like cabbage – a whack with the cane was the answer because Rule Number One still applied. Sinners got whacked first, and they found out what it was all about afterwards.

I was always amazed how many rules my mother had made, but were possible to break! It made us think quickly, and I accepted it as a challenge to see if I could get through a meal without being whacked.

My mother was very intelligent. She had been trained to be a teacher at a Church of England School which had cost her parents one shilling per week.

When it was time for her to start work however, her father decided that teachers were poorly paid, and so he got her a job as a waitress at the ABC chain of restaurants in London as, with tips, one could earn more money than being a teacher.

She had a wide vocabulary, and her knowledge of the English Language was excellent. Woe betide the sinner who made a grammatical error in speech – whack!

"What was that for?"

"You'll find out what it was for!"

Then Jess or Cyril would say "It's different from – not different to" "Oh! But that hurt!" "There's plenty more where that came from – but remember, it's different from!"

The whacks hurt our pride more than anything else, but it sure made us quick learners. We were all treated the same with no favourites; it made it easier to accept. In fact, we became little sadists and we used to laugh at the transgressors who had just received the whacks.

That of course was the greater punishment.

Opposite our house at 107 was an Ebenezer Chapel and on Tuesday evenings Cyril would go where he joined the Band of Hope, and signed the Pledge to be a total Abstainer from Alcohol. That cost half a penny a week out of his pocket money, and I used to pull his leg about it, and tried to find out what went on at their meetings. Cyril however was quite smug and would not divulge, saying it was top secret. Therefore if that was the attitude he wanted to adopt he could get on with it; it was his pocket money he was spending, and that was the end of the matter.

My younger brother, Percy, had the most wonderful sense of humour and there were times when we would be romping and playing games amidst boisterous laughter and for some unknown reason my mother would always say, "Stop that – it will end in tears". Of course we could not stop just like that, and so she used to wade in with the punishment cane, whacking everyone indiscriminately until we did stop, crying our eyes out. She was never wrong, it always finished in tears – she made sure of that!

The main roads, such as our road, were laid with cobblestones, but the side roads were sandy. During the long summer months we used to have lovely sunny weather and the sandy roads would become very dusty. To lay the dust the Council would send water carts, which were pulled by the most beautiful Shire horses, and the spraying of water was one of the sweetest smells on a very hot day, and which still lingers in my memory.

Situated behind the Ebenezer Chapel were the stables of the local funeral director where he kept his pure bred black Arabian horses, together with the Hearse and Carriages. The Hearse was of the most elaborate form of coach building, with the four glass side panels deeply etched, and a concave roof. The final turnout, with horses perfectly groomed fit for a dressage competition, and with deep purple side valances and superb harness, they were fit for a state funeral.

The professional Pall Bearers were immaculately dressed with black mourning dress and black silk top hats. We kids hardly recognised them from the men we used to see grooming the horses and mucking out the stables.

Before the coffin was put into the Hearse, wreaths and floral tributes would be put on display in front of the neighbouring houses, and the superstitious ones among the neighbours believed that the house they started with would have the next funeral.

Bolsheviks were in the news in those days, and although we did not know what a Bolshevik was, it sounded evil, and so they were always the enemy in our games.

The most popular boys' game was Cowboys and Indians. On one occasion Pip Kent, a neighbour, was a Cowboy and threw a large granite chunk at an Indian – me – and split my eyebrow open. It caused quite a commotion because I ran indoors and my mother (who became covered in blood) staunched the bleeding with some cotton wool and took me to St. Mary's Hospital where I had 7 stitches put in the cut under anaesthetic. The rest of our mob was left in the capable hands of our little mother, big sister Jess ('Jim').

My mother had to leave me in hospital, and so she returned home to find the rest of our mob all spruce and cleaned up under Jim's orders, awaiting to hear if I was going to live or not. In the evening when my Dad returned from work, he collected me from hospital and carried me in his arms because although I had 'come to' I was still a bit squiffy. My mother made a great fuss of me and made up a bed on two chairs in front of the dresser.

Although I was starving I was not allowed to eat, but after a while I was given some warm milk. Whoops! That did it. I brought everything I had eaten that day up, but I felt O.K. afterwards. The next day I was back to normal and my clever devil brother Cyril remarked, "That's one way of attracting attention to yourself!"

The following week Jim took me to the hospital Out Patients department and I had my stitches out and didn't feel a thing, but I have the scar to this day.

On 19th January 1917 Colonel Samuel Franklin Cody (nick named Buffalo Bill) was killed in an air crash at Farnborough, Hampshire. He was a legend in his own time. He was an aviation pioneer extraordinaire. Over a period of just 18 months he was accredited with killing 4,820 buffalo to supply meat for the workers on the Kansas City Railroad, hence his soubriquet.

He toured America and Europe with his Wild West show and he is still remembered at Farnborough where there are the remains of a tree at the airfield to which it is claimed he tied his aircraft.

In our childish eyes he was a hero and was so popular in our games that we used to have to take it in turns being Buffalo Bill. His death was greeted with the universal grief reserved only for true heroes.

50,000 people, including Heads of State and Royalty, attended his funeral at Aldershot Military Cemetery. Every serving member of the embryo Royal Flying Corps escorted the gun carriage bearing his coffin.

He is remembered in the Royal Air Force to this day.

On Saturday afternoons, Jim used to take us along with some of our friends to the Park Cinema, which cost us a penny each. She was like the Pied Piper because usually there were 13 of us. That happened every week and Jim would regularly produce 13 pennies, but she had the intuition that the ticket collector at the entrance did not count how many of us entered.

One Saturday our finances were not in a very good condition (today it's called a cash flow problem!) and she took 14 of us in, but only paid for 13. Eighty-five years later, even though this had only happened once, she related that instance to me and told me she was still praying for forgiveness for having turned the Park Cinema over for one old penny!

When we went to the pictures we had two favourite actresses, Mary Pickford and Pearl White. Pearl White was always in a serial, and the ending each week featured her in some dire strait with the villain about to cut her in half with a circular saw or some other diabolical weapon (poor cow!). Those endings scared the living daylights out of us kids, but they had the desired effect because we were always first in the queue the following Saturday.

Charlie Chaplin was our favourite comedian. His films were of about 30 minutes duration, and were silent films in black and white. In some of his later films we now know that he wrote the script, produced and directed them. Most of his films were 'one take' and made on a shoestring budget.

Charlie Chaplin was born in 1889 in Lambeth, and when he was 14 he became a member of Fred Karno's circus who were under contract from the Keystone Studios. He dressed as a tramp with baggy trousers, bowler hat and cane, and no matter how he tried everything would go wrong. His antics were hilarious, and we laughed until we cried. It was pure, basic humour, and today are considered classics in the film making world. One of the first songs I learnt was:

> We are Fred Karno's army
> Fred Karno's Infantry
> We cannot shoot, we cannot fight
> So what darn good are we?
> But when we get to Berlin
> The Kaiser he will say
> Hoch hoch mein Gott
> What a bloody fine lot

Fred Karno's Infantry.

After 8 years in Hollywood, when he was only 22, he returned to London and he was completely overwhelmed by the reception he was given. The crowds were so great he had difficulty reaching his hotel. Our Park Cinema together with many other London cinemas cashed in on his visit with re-runs, much to our enjoyment.

My best friend at that time was Johnny Sawyer who lived opposite me and next door to the Ebenezer Chapel. His garden overlooked the Funeral Directors and from his upstairs window we used to watch the grooms brushing the Arabian horses, and doing the mucking out.

He went to Balaam Street School and I never was able to work out why as it was much further to walk than my school, and, he did not have the advantage of having Mr. Griffiths as his Sports Master and so he really missed out there. However, he had a natural tendency to play games, and so he was considered one of us.

Johnny's mother already had a grown up family of five children, and there was such a huge age gap between him and his elder brother, he was either an afterthought or an accident, but his mother worshipped him and she insisted in making Johnny wear his hair long in curls. His nickname was 'Curly', and he would have fitted into the 21st Century whereas I had my hair cut short back and sides (with no clippers please Mr. Barber!), which cost 3d.

We were very sorry when Johnny's mother died when he was just aged 7, but Johnny kept his hair in curls in her memory right up to the time he started work.

Johnny's eldest brother was a very superior person, and was employed at a tailor in Saville Row. Although he was a member of our Scouts Group, we never saw much of him because he was a Rover Scout and he did not mix with us rough kids. He ultimately started his own firm in Saville Row, and Johnny joined him when he started work. When we moved to Seven Kings we lost touch with one another and sadly I haven't seen him since.

On the corner of Maud Road was an Ironmonger, which was owned by Mr. Murphy, a bachelor. I was about 10 at the time and I used to work in his shop on Saturday afternoons weighing up soda into two-pound bags from a two hundred weight sack of the stuff. Quite often he would check the bags I had weighed to make sure I had not put in one lump too many which kept me on my toes, and I became quite adept at the use of the scales. I was also given the job of serving paraffin, which was a smelly job from the splashes, and I was ostracised by my brothers and sisters when I returned home until the smell of the paraffin had worn off.

Two of his customers were a pair of old ladies (who must have been at least 50 years of age!) who used to shop together, and they would each buy a gallon of paraffin. They lived on the other side of West Ham Park and the paraffin was too heavy for the poor old dears to carry, and so I would give them about half an hours start, put on my roller skates and deliver to their door. They would each pay me 1d with much grateful thanks, and for weighing up the soda and serving the paraffin, Mr Murphy would pay me 3d.

Despite the fact that my mother had six mouths to feed she agreed to make a cooked lunch for Mr. Murphy. She – working on the premise 'if you want anything done, ask a busy person' – got me to take him his lunch every day, nestled between two plates. That led him to ask me to get him some supper each day. So at 7.00 p.m. each evening I would go to the cooked meat shop or fish and chip shop to feed the ungodly gut of our neighbour!

The reward for that was the princely sum of one shilling per week.

At the age of 10 I was selected to play for the YMCA Table Tennis team. I was so excited that after I had finished my two evening paper rounds I dashed off to play my game, totally forgetting about Mr. Murphy's supper. The next day when I took in his lunch I said that I was sorry and explained the reason, to which Mr Murphy responded, "I expect that was more important than my supper", to

31

which I made no reply, as I didn't want him to tell my mother in case the punishment cane came out. The sequel to that was on Saturday, instead of my usual shilling for that chore, he gave me sixpence and said "Here you are Bruce, treat yourself".

I thought at the time that he had genuinely made a mistake, and as I was earning money from other sources I forgot about it. However, some months later, I was again chosen to play Table Tennis in the YMCA team, and for the second time I forgot the mean old devil's supper! The next time I took his lunch nothing was said by either side but Mr. Murphy had not forgotten.

On my next payday he once again gave me sixpence and said, "Here you are, treat yourself". I believe it was Philip Smith who said "Nothing is perceived more clearly by little children than injustice".

I thought to myself, "Right monkey" and that was the last time I took Mr. Murphy his lunch or bought his supper, and although Cyril was made to take in Mr. Murphy's lunch, he could not get anybody to buy his supper.

Many a time at 7.00 p.m. I would see Mr. Murphy going to buy his supper, and I would make it my business to let him see that I was not doing anything in particular, but he knew me better than to leave himself open to a refusal, and or course he had to weigh his own soda and serve his smelly paraffin which served the miserable curmudgeon right!

My grandfather on my mother's side would sometimes take me for a walk. He had once been a Ships' Chandler and whilst working in the docks he had an accident when his right foot was crushed and he was invalided out with a small pension.

For a time he took to drink and was very sociable with lots of drinking pals who, true to form, disappeared as soon as his money ran out.

We always walked the same way, and he made it a habit of calling on some distant relations who had a baker's shop. One of the most pleasant smells is that of newly baked bread and cakes, and the expression of delight on my face was always rewarded with a glass of fizzy lemonade and a cream cake. My Granddad had to settle for a coffee. We would then make our way down Queens Road alongside which were some allotments.

All of the owners knew my grandfather, and they were always ready to stop whatever they were doing to pass the time of day. He always introduced me to his friends in such a way to make me feel special and a bit of a favourite. That feeling didn't last long when returning to the bosom of my family when I was always told to "take that silly grin off your face and go and wash your knees"!

As a little boy I learned very quickly the importance of keeping out of the way of grown ups as if one failed, neck and knees always had to be washed!

My mother, with a babe in arms and four children to keep clean, feed, and 'bring up', was fully employed, and without the assistance of her mother she would never have been able to cope.

Every day after we had eaten breakfast, our grandmother Nan used to call to find out what shopping had to be done.

Down at the end of our road there was a group of shops on either side of the road, forming a mini market.

Each shop had a stall in the gutter and with the shop's roller blind down which linked with the awning of the stall, it formed a covered way for customers to keep dry when shopping in inclement weather. There was a Provision Merchants who had two shops with stalls in the kerb displaying the whole range of bacon, ham and cheeses, which gave off the most beautiful aroma. Next door was the Ironmongers, smelling or bundles of firewood.

No smell was competition however for that of Tilly Turtles wet fish shop which displayed every imaginable type of fish!

Then there was the Greengrocers with two shops and stalls which provided the most colourful and best decorated shop of them all with its highly polished apples reflecting the lights of the incandescent lighting, and the colourful distribution of oranges, pineapples, grapes etc. It always did look a picture.

There were also the various subsidiary shops such as the newsagent/confectioner/tobacconist, and a shop selling cat's meat. On the other side of the road was a butcher who occupied four shops with stalls, two of which sold beef products and the other two specialised in pork. There was also an off-licence and a bookshop.

The Greengrocer's wife was a short lady who was as wide as she was high. This prevented her from making quick movements, and it always took her a second or two before she could get under way. She was however always very polite as in those days 'the customer was always right'.

One morning my Nan took me shopping and we stopped at the Greengrocer's stall where they had on display a huge pile of freshly picked peas.

The lady greengrocer waddled over to us and said, "Good morning Mrs. Studd".

My grandmother replied, "Good morning Ada. How much are the garden peas, Ada?"

"Three ha'pence a peck Mrs. Studd".

"I'll have a peck of peas Ada".

Ada duly scooped up a peck of peas, topped right up it was impossible to get another pea in the container.

"Do you call that a peck of peas Ada?"

"Yes, Mrs. Studd".

Whilst Ada was gathering up the peck of peas, my grandmother must have changed her mind because she said, "Right Ada, you keep your peas and I'll keep my money – Good day Ada" and off we went.

I was only a little boy but I was so embarrassed that I blushed as red as a beetroot and to such an extent that my Nan said to me, "Are you alright?". It never occurred to her the reason for my blushing.

My father's name was Irving John Gibson, the Irving bit referring to Sir Henry Irving, who was a famous stage actor at that time. To his friends and contemporaries however he was always known as Jack.

He was a wonderful storyteller, and his stories were always accompanied by dramatic facial expressions and arm actions. Although we kids had heard his stories many times and could join him in the punch line, he never failed to make us laugh. Some of his service exploits were outrageous, and later on in life when I became a Royal Air Force Officer I realised his stories had very little truth in them, but even if they had, they depicted the acts of a rotten soldier, and in any outfit of mine he would not have lasted five minutes!

As a result I decided that it was to be in the air for me – if I am going to die during a war, I want it to be quick. Or to quote Andy Warhole, "I'm not afraid to die – I just don't want to be there when it happens."

Just after the war my father, like many other men just demobilised, was unemployed, and it took quite a while to revert from wartime to a peacetime footing. At that time mass production methods were being developed which was not much good for a cabinetmaker, but he eventually got a job as a cabinet fitter. That meant as the different parts came off the machines, the fitter had to assemble them into the finished product. For this he was paid one and nine pence per hour, which was much less than he would have earned had he been able to use his skill producing hand made furniture. However, it was still more than his brother earned working the machines to mass produce, which was one and five pence per hour.

One of the stories about my father worthy of recording was: before the war he would habitually go to work wearing a morning coat and silk top hat and all the regalia as if he were a city gentleman. On arrival he would change into his working clothes, and dress up again after work for the journey home - he travelled to and from work on the District Railway.

One evening on the train as he was travelling home in all of his finery, he had the feeling that the girls sitting opposite him were having a little joke at his expense, and were tittering, staring in the direction of his feet. He followed their eyes to where they were looking and to his horror realised he had forgotten to change his boots - he was sitting on the train with a mass of wood shavings and sawdust stuck to his working boots. That was the last time he wore a top hat and tails to work!

It would seem that Jack was a bit of a practical joker. Customers would visit the Firm's Showroom to buy furniture and in some cases they were taken into the workshop for them to see the furniture being produced. There was one customer who frequently visited the works and on one occasion he was uncomplimentary about the piece he was being shown. So, my father made a little boat with a piece of wood with a paper sail and, having put a dab of glue on the bottom of it, surreptitiously dropped the boat on the top of the customer's bowler hat as he walked by in close proximity to the staircase. That customer made no further complaints as he was never seen again!

Working for this firm was a Hungarian cabinetmaker who was my father's special friend. He was always referred to as Barty, and I cannot recall him having any other name, which of course he obviously would have had.

They were both very interested in bodybuilding, and they would both go to a gymnasium to practise muscle-building exercises, which they took quite seriously, and had many photographs taken to show off their muscles.

Although Barty had immigrated to this country many years before World War I, when war was declared, he was taken into custody as he was still considered to be an alien. However he did not waste his time in captivity and used his talents making gifts for his captures, and so he had a relatively easy time.

Barty never really mastered the English language, but he had the most attractive way of making himself understood. He married a dour Scots girl who had a private income; in fact she was loaded! It was her money which bought a beautiful four-bedroom house, and it was Barty's skill which kept it in immaculate condition.

Barty and his wife would take long holidays in Scotland and before he was married my father, used to live at Barty's house in their absence as Caretaker. On one occasion my father on entering Barty's house thought he could smell gas. With the front door still open, he struck a match, and the next thing he knew he was floating through the air, and was deposited with a thump outside the house on the pavement, sans hair, eyebrows, and with the front of his clothes smouldering!

After the war Barty was released, and he started working on his own account. As well as being a talented Cabinet maker, he was also a skilled interior designer, and his customers would go abroad on holiday, and return to a completely newly decorated house from top to bottom. He would clear each room, send the soft furnishings and curtains to the cleaners, french polish all of the furniture, paint and wallpaper the walls, so that when the holiday makers returned, a seemingly brand new establishment was theirs.

At one time my father worked for two Jewish gentlemen called Sugarman and Markovitch. Sugarman did all of the buying and controlled the workshops, and Markovitch was in charge of the accounts.

On one occasion Sugarman had purchased a shipment of marbles which in those days were used for the tops of washstands on which stood water basins and jugs. The story goes that Markovitch came storming into the workshop with an invoice for the marbles in his hand, and said to Sugarman, "Look at the price they are charging for these marbles!" and Sugarman completely smoothed the situation by saying, "What does it matter what the invoice says if you don't intend to pay!"

There were occasions when my father was made redundant, and the first visit he would make was to his friend Barty, and this is where Barty proved what a good friend he was as he would always find work for my father to do until he could get another job.

At least once a month my father would visit Barty on a Sunday morning, and he usually took me with him. We used to walk from our house to the Wanstead Flats, where we would then take a Number 96 bus to the George Hotel in Wanstead which was very near to where Barty lived.

At this time my parents had five children, and we were living in a two bedroom flat, whereas Barty was living in the country in a four bedroom detached house. But what impressed me most was the large conservatory that he had in which there was a grapevine, and in the summer huge clusters of black grapes used to hang from the roof. Barty always made sure my father never went home without a large bunch of grapes. They were delicious, especially as they were far out of our income bracket – so much so that we never even thought about acquiring such things.

On one of our visits it was obvious that Barty was very upset, and although I was too young to realise what was wrong, Barty completely communicated his distress to my father, Jack, who in this case was a good listener.

Apparently Barty's daughter, whom he idolised, had got herself a boyfriend who was a market porter with no skills – in fact a complete ignoramus – and despite much parental pressure, his daughter would not give him up. They eventually married and a few weeks later Barty became a Grandfather! My father went to the wedding; my mother, although invited, could not leave us five kids, and when I related to Cyril, who was two years older than me, the circumstances which had led up to the wedding, Cyril said, "You stupid clot, of course he had to marry her. He'd put her in the Pudding Club!"

Once again Barty in his magnamity took his new son-in-law in hand and taught him how to become a painter and decorator.

After the armistice of the Great War, all school children were given a day's holiday.

Street parties were arranged and we children were entertained at tea parties, sitting at long trestle tables in the middle of Park Road, with jelly, blancmange, and all of the trimmings such as cakes, paper hats and things, and with our parents doing all of the chores.

It was a glorious day, the sun shone and we all made complete pigs of ourselves.

On another day, our church had a party for us children in the grounds of the Vicar's house at St. Mary's Vicarage. I was given a colourful jacket to wear with bags of sweets attached, and had to run and be chased by all of the other children, and when they caught up with me they were able to snatch a bag of sweets as their reward.

Brother Cyril could not run, but as I was running in circles, on one circuit he managed to trip me up and claimed his bag of sweets.

As I have said before, although he was lame, he never missed out. He was as artful as a cartful of monkeys and by any subterfuge, even if he had to tell lies, he always got his share.

In later life he admitted that he told lies and would boast about it!

When Pip Kent moved to the USA, Bert Coates and his family moved in to become our next-door neighbours. Bert had three sisters, all of whom were old enough to go to work, but one had to stay at home as she suffered epileptic fits which would occur without any warning. Bert's father was a specialist engineer and was seldom at home as he spent most of his time travelling abroad.

When I used to play in our garden with my four siblings, we could become quite boisterous and make a lot of noise, but Mrs. Coates never complained. Bert was a fine cricketer as a batsman, but more especially as a bowler. In those days we always had sunny weather and during the summer school holidays we would go to West Ham Park and play cricket. With Bert's help Cyril became quite a useful bowler and many were the times we accused him of throwing the ball. That of course he denied, but we took no notice of that because we all knew that he told lies.

I found it quite strenuous to bowl but, as in any game that I used to play, I had to be fully involved, and so I chose to become a wicket keeper. With the dint of much practise I became quite a useful player in that position, and I was always chosen to play there in any team I was picked to play in.

My school teacher, Mr. Griffiths, was also our Sports Master, and at the age of eleven he picked me to play wicket keeper in the school's senior team where I was playing with boys of thirteen and fourteen years of age. Immediately after school hours he would give me quite a lot of private coaching in the school playground and although I say it myself, I became quite good.

On one occasion Mr. Griffiths was umpiring a game we were playing against another team when the ball was thrown towards me to run a batsman out, but in my haste to stump him I broke the wicket without the ball in my hand. I gathered the ball and Mr. Griffiths yelled, "Break the wicket again!", which I did by pulling a stump out of the ground before the batsman could regain his crease, and so he was still run out.

Because of my ability to kick a football with my left foot I was chosen to play outside left in the school's senior football team, and from then on Mr. Griffiths always called me Bruce. Up until then, although I had been in his class and one of 63 boys for four years, he had always called me 'little green jersey' as I always wore my cub's jersey to school; in any case I didn't have anything else to wear.

At that time, with five kids living in a two bedroom flat, we were overcrowded, and my big sister Jess began to sleep at my grandmother's house at 96 East Street which was about 200 yards away from where we lived.

A gentleman by the name of Almeroth had bought the Sawyer's Newsagents Shop, and arrangements were made for me to sleep at their shop. That suited me fine as I was doing two paper rounds for them, and two for Hammonds Newsagents in Plaistow Road.

Before I started sleeping at the Almeroths my mother had only had to call me to get up on one occasion. The previous night I had been out until very late, playing table tennis for the YMCA team, and the next morning I had overslept, and my mother had to come and wake me up. I was so tired I said, "Oh No!! I can't get up!" 'Bash', was my mother's immediate reaction as she whacked me round the face, "You said you could do it – you didn't have to – get up this minute!" she yelled. Needless to say, it was the first and last time I ever tried to break a promise, and I was out of the house like a shot.

After I started living at the Almeroths, old man Almeroth used to call me at 4.40 a.m. and, after some breakfast, I would start my first round at 5.00 a.m. delivering newspapers to all of those artisans who wanted to read the news before starting work at 8.00 a.m. That round was quite far flung and I used to do it using Fred Almeroth's bicycle. Fred was about 3 years older than me but he was my friend.

I don't know how it happened, but I used Fred's bike so much that ultimately it was recognised as my bike and Fred bought himself another one for his own use.

After I had done my two rounds for the Almeroths I would arrive at Mr. Hammond's shop at 7.00a.m. sharp and woe betide if I was a minute late. Hammond would welcome me with "Come on Bruce, pull your socks up," and I would be given my first round which consisted of - up Morley Road which was opposite to Hammond's shop; into Holbrook Road, and then back into Morley Road and down the other side which would normally take about 20 minutes.

Hammond always awaited my return with my second round which took longer, and consisted of zig zagging down Corporation Street, into Napier Road, and then into Harcourt Road to finish, and then back into Plaistow Road and back to the shop where I would finish at 7.55 a.m. I would then go back to 107 for a second breakfast, and on to school by 9.00 a.m.

At midday we had 2 hours off when we had our dinner. I would rush home, scoff down whatever there was to eat, and rush back to school where I would play football until 2.00 p.m. when once again we started lessons until 4.15 p.m. After a quick tea I would do my 2 evening paper rounds, one for the Almeroths and one for the Hammonds.

On Saturday mornings I used to collect the paper money for Mr. Hammond, and my weekly wage working for him was three shillings and six pence, most of which I put into my Post Office account.

I never did find out what arrangements my mother had made with the Almeroths, but I was never given any pay for the work I did for them. However I worked out that in return for providing me with my bed and breakfast, it cancelled itself out. Anyhow, I quite enjoyed myself living at the Almeroths as I was treated as one of the family, and it was good.

The Almeroths were a large family. There was 'Mum' and 'Dad', Ethel, Andy, Jack, Albert, Will, Fred, Lily and Violet. The 5 boys were all good footballers and they all played for the same team, Holbrook Athletic. Dad was a Freemason and worked as a Foreman at King George V docks. Then, as now, it was not what one knew but whom you knew that counted. Mr. Almeroth, like any other Dock Foreman, would go daily to the dock gates to select the workmen he required for that day.

In those days it was well known that those workmen who were favourably disposed towards the Foreman would always get preference. 'Dad' had got 3 of his sons regular jobs in the docks, and using his personal influence, had got another son a job as a sheet metal worker on the railways.

William, who loved to travel, was working as a Steward on one of those large shipping lines, but my friend Fred, who was a very strong character, did not need 'Dad's' help to get work, and got himself a job as a Van Driver's mate delivering mineral water.

When Fred was 19, 'Dad' decided to get him a proper job, which resulted in Fred becoming a waiter at the Swan Hotel in Stratford, Broadway. Fred, all dressed up in black tie and tails, looked the part and was soon earning good money with the tips.

He had every afternoon off and we frequently met up and would either go to the Broadway Cinema, or play snooker at the local Billiard's Hall.

Lily, who was then 14 years of age, would help 'Mum' serve in the shop. The shop was open from 6.00 a.m. to 9.00 p.m., seven days a week, and sometimes after I had done my evening rounds I would also serve in the shop with Lily. After the shop closed I would help with the cashing up, and after a little bit of supper, I would go upstairs to bed. Bed consisted of the top of twin bunks, which had been procured from the Royal Docks.

We had many itinerant sales persons who regularly perambulated our streets selling their wares and which reminded me of the old Cries of London. There was a gentleman with a wooden tray on his head selling muffins and crumpets, and who rang a large bell to attract attention as he paraded during his peripatetic rounds.

Every Sunday afternoon a purveyor of molluscs, selling Oysters, Whelks and Winkles etc never failed to put in an appearance. Winkles for Sunday tea (when we could afford it) were a delicacy worth waiting for.

Our knife cleaner was a gentleman who had suffered a stroke, which had left him, crippled down his left side, but despite that handicap he was able to work his machine efficiently, and as a result he had built himself a profitable business.

We were also regularly visited by a group of male dancers who performed to the tunes from a barrel organ. They could not dance for toffee but they had rhythm and their antics were hilarious and they never failed to earn themselves an honest penny or two.

One of the most popular street traders made an appearance in about 1923 when an ice cream vendor appeared on the scene selling Wall's ice cream. It was a pedal drawn vehicle with a uniformed cyclist, with the slogan on the side 'Stop me and buy one'. That was something quite new, and during the hot summer months did a roaring trade.

Working on the maxim that 'competition is good for trade', it spurred Lyons, the Restaurant and Catering Group, into action, and it was not long before many local shops had been provided with refrigerators and were selling Lyon's ice cream.

Mrs. Almeroth also started making ice cream and it became one of my chores to turn the handle which caused the container to revolve in a barrel of ice until it was the right consistency to sell in wafers or cornets. That used to take me about two hours and was quite strenuous, but the most pleasurable reward when finished was to lick the finished product off the wooden blades on completion.

After I had licked the blades completely clean, I was ready to start all over again.

43

One morning, Fred had got my first paper round together, and as I left the shop, I experienced for the first time black ice. As I stepped out of the door my first step trod on the ice and I finished on my bottom sliding gently down the slope of the pavement into the gutter. Fred came rushing to help me and did the same thing, and we both finished side by side in the gutter, laughing our heads off!

As a newspaper delivery boy I got to know quite a number of men and their wives who were seeing their men off to work. Everybody seemed to be so kind and appreciative for having their paper delivered before breakfast. On very cold mornings there was always a cup of tea waiting for me at one particular house.

On Saturdays I used to collect the paper money. On one particular Saturday morning one of my lady customers noticed I had some warts on the back of my left hand.

"How long have you had those warts?" She asked.

"I can't remember, but I've had them a very long time", I replied.

"I'll buy them off you, I'll give you a penny for them," she offered.

"Done!" I said.

She then took off her wedding ring, wet it with her tongue and proceeded to rub the ring on my warts.

"Right," she said, "they are mine now – here's your penny, just forget all about them."

This I did, and the next time I can recollect looking for my warts, as if by magic they had all completely disappeared.

When I was about seven years of age, Cyril asked me to go shopping with him because our mum had heard cabbage was a penny a pound at the Greengrocers in Pelly Road. The owner and his wife ran the shop, and it was a thriving business, and they were far too busy to look after their baby son who was about three years of age at that time. Cyril noticed that the little boy as a consequence was always running around the shop with holes in his trousers, and so Cyril nicknamed him 'Bum Holes'.

About 50 years later when I joined Cyril's business in Covent garden, Cyril pointed out to me a smartly dressed Greengrocer customer and he said to me, "You see that gentleman over there – do you know who it is?" Of course the answer was "No". "Well", Cyril said, "That's 'Bum Holes'". And although the gentleman in question had a small chain of Greengrocer shops, no matter what exulted position he might have ultimately achieved, he would always be known to Cyril as 'Bum Holes'!

At a very early age, I started to collect cigarette cards. Each packet of ten cigarettes would contain one card, and normally they were in sets of fifty cards. All of the Almeroth brothers smoked and they used to give me their cards.

It was quite difficult to get a set because the manufacturers would hold a certain number of each set back to encourage smokers to continue with a certain brand to complete the set.

Cigarette packets were not sealed with a cellophane wrapper in those days, and it was possible to open a packet to see which card was contained in the packet before purchase. Therefore, in the evenings when I was helping Lily Almeroth serve in the shop, I used to look inside packets, and if it had a card which was new to me, I used to swap it with one of my duplicates, and so I was able to get sets quicker than most collectors. I had large albums to hold my sets of cards, and I was very proud of my collection.

My father possessed two or three smaller albums of sets of cards he had collected in his youth, and when he saw what I was doing he gave me his collection, which because of their age were quite valuable, and I finished up with about ten albums full of sets of cigarette cards, all in pristine condition. I guarded my albums like a miser, and my brothers and sisters were only allowed to view them under my supervision.

My brother Percy, nicknamed 'Pubby', was a scallywag. He had his own set of friends of his own age group and none of them joined in our team games, such as soccer or cricket, but he always wanted to get at my cigarette card collection. I would have none of that, and used to hide them away in my secret hiding place. Over the years as we were growing up, Pubby used to pester the life out of me to let him play with my collection, and despite the fact that I offered to give him my duplicate cards so that he could start his own collection, No! That was not what he wanted – he wanted to play with my albums.

One day Cyril and I returned home from playing cricket and there was Pubby, sitting on the floor, playing with my cigarette albums. He had detached several cards so that he could read what was on the backs of the cards, and of course I went berserk. Apparently he had pestered my mother so much because he was bored and had nothing to do, to keep him quiet she had divulged my hiding place to him. By the time I sorted out the sets and replaced them back in the albums, my lunch was stone cold, but I ate it because I was starving hungry and I knew that if I didn't eat it then, it would be dished up for my tea. This I considered however to be a small price to pay to restore my prized possessions.

Another time I arrived home, filthy dirty from some team game or another, only to find my mother had once again given Pubby my cigarette card collection to play with, but that time, remembering the threats I had sworn to dish out to Pubby, he had not dislodged any of the cards. I immediately gathered all my albums together and was about to put them away when my mother tore such a strip off me for being a selfish beast, and told me it was against one of the basic principles of a large family where one had to share everything.

And that I was a 'dog in the manger' as I did not play with cards myself and would not let anyone else play with them.

And that I was a kleptomaniac, and that I was developing into a miserly creature, and that people would not want to know me unless I changed and started to share things with my brothers and sisters, and until I changed my ways I was going to have a rough time.

I was so crest fallen at the tirade of abuse that I received from my mother, and seeing the grinning face of Cyril laughing at my displeasure, I felt like hitting him over the head with one of my albums, but my big sister Jess came over and, although she did not say anything, she helped me gather my things together.

That simple act of kindness was a great comfort to me, as I knew she was on my side. Therefore, I agreed to share anything I owned, but in the case of my cigarette cards, only when I was present.

However, I found a new secret hiding place for my albums and for several weeks I was so busy doing other things my albums did not see the light of day until one day, lo and behold, I found Pubby underneath the kitchen table with my albums all over the floor.

"What are you doing with those?" was my first demand.

"Mum said I could have them," he said.

"Oh!! Did she!!" I exclaimed.

"Yes!!!" said my mother returning from the scullery, "I said he could have them to play with – it's been weeks since you last looked at them: in any case, you're too old for those things now, and I'm not having them cluttering up the place if you're not going to use them."

Therefore, for the next few weeks with my mother's agreement, Pubby played daily with my Albums of cigarette cards.

One Saturday I was returning from my job of collecting newspaper money and I saw Pubby with his snotty nosed friends and they were playing skating cigarette cards to see who could skate the farthest. That was a game Johnny Sawyer and I used to play with my duplicate cards, but as I got nearer I noticed the cards they were skating with were in pristine condition. I rushed home and there I spied several of my albums underneath the kitchen table sans cigarette cards.

I went to my mother and showed her my empty albums and told her, "Pubby and his friends were playing with my cigarette cards", and she replied, "I said he could have them – he can put them back when he has finished with them." "But they will not be in pristine condition fit for collectors items."

I was heartbroken and I broke down and cried.

My collection had taken five years to get together, and five minutes of Pubby's time to destroy. After a bit my mother clouted me around the ear and said, "Stop making a fool of yourself", and I noticed that brother Cyril had adopted his superior attitude, and I slowly managed to control myself, and as far as I can remember, that was the last time I ever cried.

Being a Gemini, ever since then I have always been able to switch off from unpleasant situations and carry on as if nothing untoward has happened.

Mrs. Mills who lived next door to us at 109 Stratford Road was a cat lover. She lived on her own with five cats that occupied her full time. She had a wire fence, eight feet high, all around her garden, with the top 18 inches sloping inwards at an angle of 45 degrees so that it was impossible for the cats to get out of her premises. Other than that, the cats had the run of her property, but if any of them ventured into the garden, Mrs. Mills was always there to supervise any feline activity! My sisters thought she was a very caring person, but my brothers and I thought she was 'bonkers'.

Next door to her at 111 lived Mrs. Manders who was very popular with us boys as she had a parrot with a very wide vocabulary, including many swear words. When the weather was fine, Mrs. Manders would hang the parrot in its cage outside in the sunshine, and we boys would talk to it across the gardens to encourage the bird to talk.

One of the parrot's favourite phrases was, 'Mrs. Manders, you're an old bugger' which we thought was hilarious, and couldn't stop laughing, which encouraged the bird to show off his vocabulary even more. Mrs. Manders would then come out and ask us to stop talking to the bird, and, as if the parrot knew what she was saying, he would repeatedly say, "Mrs. Manders, you're an old bugger."

There was a joke going around about that time which I have not heard repeated for over 80 years:

> 'The local vicar had a parrot, and he was in the habit of taking the parrot to church on a Sunday and park it near the pulpit. Every time the coalman called at the Vicarage, the parrot would

say, "One cwt, please." After a while, the coal store could hold no more, and so the vicar said to the parrot, "If you order any more coal, I'll pull every feather out of your head." The next time, the coalman called, the parrot once again ordered another one cwt of coal, and so true to his word the vicar pulled every feather out of the parrot's head. The following Sunday in church, as the visiting Clergyman (who was as bald as a badger's arse) went into the pulpit to deliver his sermon, the parrot said, "Another poor sod has obviously been ordering coals".

St. Mary's Church was about half a mile from where we lived, and at the age of 7 Cyril joined the 25th Scout Group as a Cub. Two years later when I was old enough I joined too, and Cyril helped me become a good Cub.

I soon got in the Cub's football team and we used to play on a ground owned by Beckton Gasworks. In that team I was made left half, and on one occasion, I had to mark the outside right of the opposing team, a boy named Rees. He was a very fast winger and good at dribbling the ball, and on one particular day he was giving me the run around, and I was furious. I noticed a bad pass intended for Rees was coming straight towards me, and as Rees was approaching, I kicked the ball as hard as I could, straight at him. It hit Rees on the knee and then came straight back at me, striking me with additional force on the face. I had never seen so many stars before temporarily passing out.

The Referee was a Mr. Stoop who was the Scoutmaster of St. Andrew's Church Scout group. He knew me as only a week before he had tested me for my Cub's First Aid Badge. He revived me, and when he realised I was not really hurt, tore such a strip off me for ungentlemanly conduct, and finished up by saying, "That was poetic justice, Gibson; you won't do that again will you?" But there was no answer to that as I was feeling very sorry for myself, in fact I wanted to cry!

The 25th Scout Group had a band with four boys who played the flute, a big bass drum and two side kettledrums. Once a month we would have a Church Parade and afterwards would parade through the local streets, which was a very good public relations exercise. Mr. Ted Cowey was our Scout Master, and he was also a very good drummer. His father was our Church Verger, and when he died, Ted took over.

When Jess was about ten years of age, she was put in charge of her three younger siblings, and off we would go to the 9.30 a.m. Sunday School, where we were told bible stories and learned hymns, which we sang to the echo. After that we would go to the 11.00 a.m. service in St. Mary's church, but were allowed to leave when Communion for the grown ups had commenced.

In the afternoon we would go to St. Mary's Sunday school, and in the evenings we would go to the 7.00 p.m. service where we sang hymns and had further religious education. That way of course we not only received a good basic knowledge of religion, but it gave our mother a break.

At St. Mary's Church we had a Curate who tried so hard to please everyone that the Parishioners put upon him. No matter what task he was invited to do, he would try. He was a very intelligent Curate, but his one weakness was he could not say 'No'. He was no good at athletics or ball games as he could not run or kick a ball, but when invited he always did his best, but he was useless. He would have been better off if he had refused gracefully.

On the Pastoral side of his duties however he excelled. On one occasion he called at our home to meet our mother, and a good time was being had by all over a cup of tea, when Percy (the wag of the family) said, "My mum thinks you're soppy". With no punishment cane to hand, my mother was non-plussed and had no defence, but I laughed so much I became the centre of attention and my mother thought I was going to have an apoplexy. However, it broke the tension, and the Curate left making all the right noises of how he had enjoyed meeting my mother, and that he would call again, making a mental note to make sure his next visit would be during school hours.

While Fred was courting Jess, he used to spend every spare minute of his time at our house. When they ultimately got married and he became our brother-in-law, it did not change anything as Cyril, Percy and I had always considered him as a brother, and Fred had always acted as such.

I will always remember one particular Christmas Day. We had eaten our Christmas Dinner and Christmas tea, and were all sitting around our large kitchen table. At that time, the Wireless had just been invented, and programmes were sent out from 2LO London. We could not however afford such luxuries, and so Fred started a singsong. We started with all the old favourites until we reached,

'California, here I come, back to where I started from, where flowers and bowers bloom in the sun. Each morning at dawning birdies sing and every thing, the sun kissed me and said don't be late, that's why I can hardly wait, open up those golden gates, California here I come.' Bombardy, Bombardy, Bombardy, California here I come and so on to Bombardy, Bombardy, Bombardy, California etc.,

And although we tried to stop Fred and change the tune, he would have none of it and we carried on singing it until it was our bed time, when our mother took over and that put paid to that.

Although that took place over 85 years ago, I still remember Fred thumping on the table as he said "Bombardy, Bombardy, Bombardy, California", as clearly as if it were yesterday.

* * *

Bruce Gibson

4

Education, Education, Education!

E ducation in 1917 was primitive in the extreme compared to
what we have today. Our compulsory school leaving age had
just risen to 14 years of age. Teachers were in short supply,
and there were 63 boys in our class to prove it. The teachers we had
were either too old to fight or had been invalided out of the army.

Our forces were bogged down in the Flanders mud, and London
had experienced its first aeroplane-bombing raid.

Politicians had other things to think about besides education;
President Woodrow Wilson had just signed the Declaration of War
against Germany committing the USA to make the world safe for
democracy.

Holbrook Road School was of the three-floor type and was built
around 1900. At that time elementary education was conducted
similarly to Church schools, and it was not until 1922, when I was
nine, that all secular education was made the responsibility of West
Ham Borough Council, which included sports, such as football,
cricket, boxing, Cumberland wrestling, netball, swimming and
athletics. It was here that Mr. Griffiths came into his own as,
although he had been organising sports in his own time on a
voluntary basis, he was now officially appointed Sports Master.

With the exception of Boxing and Wrestling, which he delegated
to Mr. Pack, and netball, and a lady teacher, the rest was down to
him, and working with the School's Sport Association, and the
Juvenile Organisation Committee, schools formed teams and played
against one another. It was a wonderful innovation.

The only thing was the basic learning curriculum interfered with
our games programme! But, Mr. Griffiths made sure if one slacked
off in history, geography or the three R's, one did not get picked for

52

one of the teams. That didn't affect Mr. Park who taught us Boxing as the art of self-defence under the Marquees of Queensbury Rules and even the good boxers were hot allowed to hit one's opponent too hard, as it was not the object of the exercise.

My mother did not like the idea of boys hitting one another, and so to please her once I had learned the basic rules of boxing, I concentrated on the games in which Mr. Griffiths specialised.

In 1920, when I went up to the Big Boys', I was always in the top ten of the class without trying too hard. I used to share a desk with the class bully, Albert Stovold, and whenever I answered a verbal question correctly, Albert would to pinch my backside, but when playing practise games at soccer I always made sure I was on the opposite side of Albert to ensure that at some stage in the game I would be able to make physical contact with him in retaliation.

Mr. Griffiths was my teacher for the next five years, and took us in all subjects, but concentrating on the three R's. He was an ex service man, and he made history lessons most exciting. He told us about his experiences during the Great War, and the appalling conditions of trench warfare. He forecast that tank warfare was here to stay, and that how the ground staffing by the Royal Flying Corps had played a significant part of the destruction in the final push at Amiens by British, American, Canadian, Australian and French troops which had caused the German collapse.

During those lessons time just flew, and were over all too quickly. However it was always impressed on us the futility of war, and that world politicians should find a better way of solving world problems.

Every morning, school would start the same way. Mr. Griffiths laid down rules, and woe betide anyone who stepped out of line. Immediately after religious assembly we would go to our classroom where we would have to sit in perfect silence, and on his entry we would have 30 minutes of mental arithmetic. He would call out 3 consecutive numbers that had to be added together; he would then tell us to add, subtract or multiply other numbers, and then say, what's your answer, e.g. 8. 9. 10, add on 3, divide by 2, multiply by 5, and then add on 5, what's the answer? This was delivered at about 150 words per minute, and at first nobody bothered to work it out because we did not think there was an answer, until one of our classmates, who was known as 'Monkey' Collins, said, "80, Sir". "Right Collins – go home ten minutes early!" WELL, that was the dreaded end. If Monkey Collins could solve the mental arithmetic problems, so could we all.

From then on, two or three of us who got the answer right first would go home ten minutes early.

Mr. Griffiths, being a Welsh man, had a wonderful singing voice and he taught us as a class how to sing. On one occasion we were practising the Welsh National Anthem when suddenly he went into a rage, waving his arms about, and was temporarily speechless. After he had cooled down, we had our first elocution lesson. He said, "You London cockney boys must learn how to pronounce your vowels correctly – it's not 'Wiles, Wiles' – its 'Wales, Wales'", and for ever after, when starting an English lesson, we always started by pronouncing our vowels correctly – A, E, I, O, U...........

Around the walls of our classroom we had posters displayed on which were the names of pupils who had achieved success in various degrees of scholarship. On one occasion I volunteered to produce the current list of pupils when Mr. Griffiths discovered I had an artistic talent. As a result I passed a scholarship examination to go to the West Ham Municipal School of Art. I was thirteen years of age at the time, and so in September 1926 I started a six-year course of training in my new surroundings. That meant, having left Holbrook Road Elementary School, I had six weeks holiday before commencing schooling in a totally different environment. I couldn't wait to dash to the Department Store to buy my new school cap which I wore with great pride.

To get to the Art School, I had to walk down Park Road, across West Ham Park and into Tavistock Road, which lead into Romford Road where the West Ham Municipal College was. The distance was about one and a half miles, but after Holbrook Road School, which was less than half a mile from where I lived, at the age of 13 it seemed an awful long way.

In the next road to us, where my Nan lived, there was a girl who was a year older than me named Irene Love. During the school holidays she had seen me wearing my new school cap, and so on the first day at Art School she was waiting for me just inside West Ham Park to welcome me to my new school, and to walk with me, and which she proceeded to do for the next three years.

There were 25 students in our class; 24 boys and 1 girl, Margaret Butler, which was a very good thing as the tone of our general behaviour was reflected in how we carried on when she was present.

Lessons did not start until 9.30 a.m. and went on until 12.30 p.m. when we had an hour for lunch, and finished at 5.00 p.m. My fellow students were a totally different bunch of individuals from those of my elementary school days, and I loved every minute of the time I spent there.

Apart from English, Arithmetic, History and Geography, all of our other subjects were to do with Art of Trade training, which in my case was carpentry. In that connection, I discovered I would never be as good as my father, and that it was much harder work using the tools than watching my Dad perform, and so that decided me against any form of manual labour.

Twice a week for a whole morning we used to have animal drawing when live cats, dogs, rabbits, hamsters etc were provided for us to draw. Still life painting, Architecture and Measured Drawing were my favourite art subjects, and once a month on a Friday we used to go to the Victoria and Albert Museum in South Kensington to study Illustrated Manuscripts and do measured drawing.

One picture, illustrating 'The Raping of the Sabine Men and Women', was most impressive and full of action, and although at the age of 13 I did not really know what Raping was all about, it sounded wicked.

Today, however, children at the age of 6 and 7 have lessons on the subject.

I used to greatly admire the antique furniture and could appreciate the skill and workmanship of such craftsmen as Chippendale and Hepplewhite. In one room there was a bed with a descriptive label saying 'Queen Victoria slept on this bed', and so just for devilment to amuse some of my fellow students I decided to lie on the bed. Unfortunately, I went to sleep and was rudely awakened by a Porter who kicked me up the backside before I could run away.

The No. 96 bus from Stratford, Broadway took me via Aldgate East, down Leadenhall Street, past the Bank of England and Mansion House, the official residence of the Lord Mayor of London – into Queen Victoria Street, down Cannon Street, and past St. Paul's Cathedral – down Ludgate Hill into Fleet Street – past the Law Courts into the Strand, past Charing Cross Station, which we reckoned was the centre of London from which all distances were taken, into Trafalgar Square to Pall Mall – up the Haymarket into Piccadilly Circus which was a sight for sore eyes with all of the electric light advertising signs – down Knightsbridge, past Harrods and Brompton Oratory where all of the posh catholic ladies got themselves married, and finally to the Victoria and Albert Museum where the entry was free.

The bus fare used to cost 8d (3 and a bit new pence) and the journey itself was about 8 miles, and, if we were lucky and did not get bogged down with too many horse and carts, took about an hour, and was an education in itself.

The buses had solid tyre wheels and were open topped. If it was raining, there was a rolled up thick waterproof canvas fastened to the back of the seat in front which we held over us to keep dry.

It was a wonderful experience driving along 8 miles of London's main streets – there was so much going on, there was never a dull moment.

During our lunch break we would explore the other museums in the area. The Science Museum, with all of its working models, was favourite, but the Natural History and War Museum were often visited, the latter before it moved down Lambeth Way. The Albert Hall and Kensington Gore, where Mr. Churchill had an abode, were quite familiar to us, as was Hyde Park and Rotten Row. The Lido at the Serpentine and the round pond in Kensington Gardens were also frequently visited. Little did I know then that some 30 years later I would be taking my son, Stuart, and his friends, to sail their boats on the round pond at Kensington!

Sometimes on my way home from Kensington I would break my journey, and on one occasion I was wondering around Trafalgar Square into Leicester Square when I came across the Statue to Edith Cavell. Mr. Griffiths had told us about her once during a history lesson on World War I – she was a nurse, inspired by Florence Nightingale, who had set up a nursing school in Belgium.

She was a strict disciplinarian, and insisted on her nurses being immaculately dressed in bright blue cotton dresses with white collars, aprons and caps. She demanded absolute devotion to duty, saying nursing was not easy, but was worth the sacrifice.

She had also been responsible for building an underground escape route, which enabled over 200 English, French and Belgian soldiers to escape to Holland.

In 1915 she was finally caught by the Germans, and at her trial, she told the Court that "It was her duty as a nurse to save lives."

As a result the German Judge pronounced her sentence to be executed by a firing squad. Mr. Griffiths, my welsh teacher, had emphasised the bravery of Nurse Cavell with such feeling and emotion, and as I stood before her statue all those years later I had the greatest respect, knowing that I was in the presence of someone who had been truly great.

The college had three floors and a basement where the students' bicycles were stored during the day. The ground floor was used for training girls in Dressmaking. The first floor was the Art School, and the second floor was the Science School.

There were several porters whose main job was to keep the place clean, and with over 300 students plus staff it was an on-going occupation. We got on well with most of these gentlemen, but there was one officious porter who had seemingly forgotten that he had once been a boy, and made it very apparent that he did not like us. We did not give him any encouragement to change that opinion however and were always playing games with him.

When he was washing the corridors one of us would attract his attention, and later he would find that someone had nicked his mop and hidden it. His resultant language and what he was going to do to the culprit when he found him caused much ribald humour.

That particular porter lived in Tavistock Road in a house with no front garden, and on his door he had a doorbell with a sign, 'Please Ring'. Well, every time we passed his door on our way to school we would obey that order, and continued to do so until he took the sign down.

There was a row of shops along the side of the college where we used to buy fruit in very strong brown paper bags. On joining the school as a new boy, the boys in the senior class made us go through an initiation ceremony that entailed dunking our heads three times in a lavatory wash basin that was full of water.

No harm was done, apart from our loss of dignity.

To retaliate, in collusion with two or three of my classmates who would watch out for one of our seniors entering the toilets, and then would tip me off. I would creep into the lavatory, fill one of my fruit bags up with water, and throw it over the top of the lavatory door. I would then rush out, and a few seconds later, re-enter the lavatory to use the urinal to see the victim drying himself off.

That was great fun and was hugely enjoyed by my confederates, especially as we were getting our own back.

One day, one of my friends came rushing up to me to say a senior had entered the toilets. I got a brown paper bag out of my satchel, crept into the lavatory, threw the bag of water over the occupied toilet, and rushed out.

My friend advised me not to go and see the results of my naughtiness and led me well away from the vicinity of that corridor, as he told me that my latest victim had been the Headmaster!

58

Strenuous efforts were made to find out who the culprit was and, although several boys in our class were in on our water escapades, no one split.

It was however the last time I threw a water bag!

Twice a week at Art School we had Physical Training, each session lasting for one and a half hours. Our teacher was a retired Army Sergeant Major Pritchard. He was always immaculately dressed, all in white with a vest, long white flannel trousers, and white plimsolls. His last few years in the army had been spent teaching Sergeants how to become Physical Training Instructors. He really did know his stuff, and during rest periods, after putting us through strenuous exercises, he would demonstrate his personal prowess, but he never tried to teach us anything other than the basic routine work exercises.

We had a modern gymnasium, which was well fitted out, complete with wall bars, parallel bars, a vaulting horse, etc., but apart from routine tumbling exercises and vaulting over the horse, he never tried to extend us to the more dangerous pursuits in case we hurt ourselves.

The last thing he wanted was a visit from our mothers with rolled up umbrellas!

During rest periods, he would enthral us with life in the army and his thrilling exploits, but I was later to discover when I became an officer in the Royal Air Force that these exploits were a load of bullshit, and we would have been better employed doing drill!

He taught us a game, which he called 'Whip the Gap'.

We all had to stand in a circle facing inwards with our eyes shut and hands behind our backs. He would then walk round the circle and place a knotted handkerchief into the hand of one of us. They would then strike the person to his right (who would still have their eyes closed) with a resounding whack with the knotted handkerchief, and then commence to chase the victim round the circle, with the aim of striking him as many times as possible.

The secret was for the striker to always get a good first strike in as if the victim was fleet of foot, that might be the only strike the striker would make. It was a game we loved as it appealed to the sadistic nature of us schoolboys who were at liberty to whack a fellow student without any recriminations.

It was a game I went on to teach P.T. Instructors in the RAF who used it with good effect against airmen who needed to be taken down a peg or two!

It soon became general knowledge that Irene Love used to accompany me to school, and there were times when other members of my class would go out of their way to join us which was good as we were then able to kick a tennis ball across West Ham Park and 'Rene' (who was a proper tom boy) would join in.

During the winter months, the park used to shut at 4.30 p.m. which meant over a two mile detour around the perimeter. Most nights however we would climb over the gate and walk across the park as usual. On one occasion, when London was enveloped in its infamous pea soup fogs which were so dense that visibility was nil, we had to walk around the perimeter of the park, trailing our hands along the railings so that we did not get lost.

Rene's father was a top Civil Servant who worked from 9.00 a.m. to 4.00 p.m., and he got to know me quite well as there were times when he would accompany Rene to our meeting place in the park to check on the company she was keeping.

There was another senior civil servant who lived in the same road as Irene, to whom I used to deliver newspapers to, and who was a language translator. He gave me an antique Elephant Gun to play with, which had a very long barrel and was over six feet long. It took both Cyril and me to operate it and create a spark from the flintlock mechanism, and we had many hours of fun. However, it did take up a great deal of room in our bedroom, and alas one day when we went to play with it, there was no gun to be found. After diligent searching we discovered our mother had given it away to the local rag and bone man, as she had decided that she was not going to have that cluttering the place up. On another occasion that same man, a Mr. Maurice Norman, gave me a barbell and a set of weight lifting discs – they however did not last as long as the Elephant Gun and were gratefully received by the gypsy rag and bone man on his next visit. My mother was one of his best customers!

Sometimes, when the newspapers were late, I would be late home for breakfast, which meant rushing to school. On those days I would go by roller skate, and on the way home would teach Rene how to skate. This took longer than I thought was necessary, but after all she was only a girl, and with time and a few tumbles she made it. This was a good thing as at one stage it looked like it would ruin a beautiful friendship.

There was no romance between us as I was only 14 years of age and I much preferred my footballing friends with whom I had a robust relationship, and besides, she had a boyfriend from West Ham Church, so that suited me fine.

One day I was so late reaching school that I did not bother to take my skates off, but continued to my classroom, and was skating down the corridor when suddenly the Headmaster, Mr. Barnes, grabbed me as I passed his office. This brought both of us down with a crash! I bounded up like a newborn baby, but it took Mr. Barnes (who was pushing at least 50 at the time) a little longer, but with my help, he made it, which made me laugh.

That however increased his rage to a fury.

"Don't touch me", he said, "Come to my office in half an hours time."

When I told my school friends what had happened, they said I was for the high jump. The least I could expect was to be expelled, at which I responded, "I could do with a holiday." This however was the not the result for when I reported to his office, the Headmaster tore such a strip off me, and told me,

"You are the most unruly pupil I have ever had the misfortune to come across!"

He was trying to teach me how to behave, and how to lead an academic life, but all I could think about was rushing here, there and everywhere as if there was not a minute to breathe. What was I doing skating down the corridor?"

I said, "I am sorry sir, but the newspapers were late, and I was trying to get to my class on time."

"Newspapers?! What newspapers?"

I related that I did a paper round every morning and there had been a strike, which made the papers late. In view of what he had previously said, the last thing I wanted him to know was that I did four paper rounds every morning before breakfast.

"That's no excuse", he said. "Have on my desk by 9.00 a.m. tomorrow morning an essay of 250 words regarding punctuality."

Of course, Mr. Barnes did not know that I was fully employed with four paper rounds every morning, two in the evening, and collecting paper money on Saturdays and Sundays, and that at some times I was rushed to do my homework. However, next to drawing, I loved writing, and before I knew it had dashed off 500 words about time keeping. How reasonable people were after 10.00 a.m., but how cross they were if their newspaper was not delivered before they went to work. How the sheet metal workers at the Railway Yard increased my vocabulary when they found the entrance to their workplace was locked sharp at 8.00 a.m. and was not opened again for 10 minutes which meant they had lost an hour's pay.

At 8.50 a.m. my epistle was on the Headmaster's desk and I heard no more – I made sure however that I did not knock Mr. Barnes head over apex again and kept a low profile!

We had a female teacher for English subjects, a Miss Dolly White, who was such a refined person and far too gentle for such a rough and tumble pupil as I was then. She was excellent at blackboard work, but there was no fun in pelting her board with a pea shooter as she completely ignored my capers, carrying on as if nothing had happened, and to such an extent that my fellow students took her part and rounded on me, so I had to desist and start paying attention. As a result, I was amazed how interesting I found her subjects.

Dolly's attitude was that if any of her pupils were foolish enough to want to play about that was entirely up to them, but if we wanted to learn, she was prepared to teach us.

Throughout the term, each one of us had to give a lecture on a subject of our choice during one of the lessons. When it came to my turn I gave a lecture on the distribution of evening newspapers, starting from the gathering of all of the newsvendors at Plaistow Railway Station. This gave me the opportunity for some ribald mirth, and I had everybody, including Dolly White, laughing their heads off.

We were making so much noise at one time that Mr. Barnes put his head round the door, but when he saw Miss Dolly was in charge he left us to it. My audience just did not know such happenings took place.

At question time afterwards I made my answers just as humorous as in most cases the questions were stupid, mainly because everything I had told them was so foreign to them they thought I had made it all up.

Dolly's criticism was that she thought the content of my lecture was good, but by speaking in the vernacular, my sentence construction left much to be desired. She did think however that my presentation was excellent, and I got full marks.

* * *

5

"Friends, Football and other activities!"

The five Almeroth brothers with whom I lived were all good footballers, and were all members of Holbrook Athletic Football Club. On Saturday afternoons, if I was free from my other chores, Ernie Marks, the Almeroth's brother-in-law, used to take me to watch the brothers play. I went so often that I was considered the Club mascot.

In 1923, West Ham United Football Club got into the final of the FA Cup and were due to play at Wembley Stadium which had been built to show off Britain's splendid sports arena.

The whole of West Ham went football crazy, and Holbrook Athletic Football Club arranged to take a busload of spectators, and, as their mascot, they wanted to take me. The bus was completely full with people standing upstairs and down, and when my mother saw such a motley crew she wouldn't let me go.

Her decision turned out to be right as no-one had a ticket, and being a new Stadium, the organisation had not been tested because 126,000 tickets were sold at the turnstiles for a ground capacity of 100,000, and by another serious oversight another 75,000 managed to scale the walls and gain free admission. Naturally the swollen crowd spilled over onto the pitch and it was feared the match might have to be cancelled, but Police Constable George Storey, mounted on a white horse, patiently and with good humour, managed to persuade the trespassers to leave the pitch and let the game commence. Sadly Bolton beat West Ham 2-1 but, as my mother said, that was no place for her 10-year-old son to be.

When I was 16 I got into the Club's second eleven team. We used to play on a pitch on the Wanstead Flats which was hired out. We had a dressing room underneath the railway arches in close proximity to the Flats, and where our goal posts and nets were also stored.

Once we had changed we used to carry our posts and net across the Flats to our pitch, erect them, play our game, and then the same in reverse back to our dressing room, and would think nothing of it.

On one occasion Ethel Almeroth, who was older then her five brothers, was watching Holbrook's first team play along with her husband, Ernie, and me. There was a 2-year age gap between each of the five brothers. Andy was playing at centre forward, Jack at centre half, Bill at left back, Albert at right half, and Fred, who was only 18 at the time, was playing his first game for the First Eleven at left half against a team who were Holbrook's arch rivals.

In those days football was a physical contact game and this one was getting rough, when suddenly a player on the opposing team fouled Fred. The culprit did not know what had hit him as in no time at all Albert had him by the throat, shaking the life out of him with the four other brothers in support. Ernie said to me, "Bruce, that's typical of the Almeroths, if you hit one, you hit the lot!"

After three years in the junior section of the Art School I was on my summer holidays and quite prepared to commence the next three years in the senior section. Cyril had left school at the age of 14 and was employed as a clerk in a firm of wholesale fruit and vegetable merchants in Stratford Market. Through his good offices, our family was able to move into a four-bedroom house at Seven Kings, which was owned, by one of the Directors of the firm where Cyril worked.

As a family we were in heaven. Not only had we enough sleeping accommodation, but also on top of that we had a bathroom. Seven Kings was 4 miles away from Plaistow where we had been living, and that had meant I was no longer living with the Almeroths and had also given up my paper rounds and other jobs. That was a completely new environment.

All of the houses in the road were of a similar size, and in a road not far away there were triple fronted houses with six bedrooms.

I was in the process of negotiating concessionary travel arrangements to go to the Art school when a friend of mine, Frank Hillier who had left Art School the year before, called on me and told me there was a vacancy in his Firm's studio, and would I like the job. My mum thought it was a wonderful idea, and I was duly interviewed and got the job.

It was only a small studio specialising in retouching photographs but it had a weekly wage, and so my father agreed for me to become an apprentice at retouching photographs.

The Firm had its own photographic studio and my friend Frank was employed as a Commercial Photographer under training. The studio was in an office block in Stonecutter Street, just over 100 yards from Ludgate Circus. It was 8 miles from where I lived and the fare by bus was 8d each way, which made a large hole in my wages of 12 shillings and 6 pence per week, and so it was agreed for me to journey each way by bicycle. That suited me fine because by nipping in and out of the traffic I could do the journey in half an hour, whereas the bus took over an hour.

The hours were from 9.00 a.m. to 1.00 p.m., and 2.00 p.m. to 6.00 p.m., Monday through Friday, and 9.00 a.m. until 1.00 p.m. on Saturdays, making a 44 hour week. There were four re-touching artists including Mr. W. J. Scott, the boss, and a Mr. Bingham who kept the accounts and also acted as the Firm's representative to get new work and was in an adjoining office

A Retouching Artist requires a basic art education covering the form of things, light and shade, and the skill to operate an airbrush no larger than a fountain pen. My main job to start with was as a stooge to my superiors, and so long as I kept them happy with frequent cups of tea, and perform any other chore too degrading for them to contemplate doing for themselves; life was uneventful.

Our studio was on the fourth floor, and next door was a bijou café with just two tables, which could each seat up to four people, but catering mainly for take away cups of tea or coffee and sandwiches etc. There were 81 stairs up to our studio, one on entering the building and 20 between each floor. My work mates were very thirsty individuals, and with a tray of six cups of beverages, I traipsed up and down those stairs many hundreds of times.

On the ground floor there was a large office labelled 'Accounting House', in which were employed about 30 male clerks. At the end of the office and across the whole width was a glass partition, behind which the Company Secretary worked, who kept a watchful eye on his dour workforce. Sharing his office was the most attractive young lady who was secretary to the boss – a Miss Perkins, who was just over 20 years of age. I often used to pass her on the stairs as she came out of the ladies toilets where she had been to wash her hands. We never got beyond saying 'Good Morning' or 'Good Afternoon' but she said it with such a lovely smile that she made me feel good.

I got to know some of the younger clerks because sometimes I would help John, the café owner, carry refreshments which had been ordered by the clerks into the Counting House.

One day I saw Miss Perkins come out of the ladies toilet and instead of going into her office, she went straight out into Stonecutter Street. I went into the Counting House and said, "I've just seen Miss Perkins going down Stonecutter Street with her skirt tucked inside her knickers!" I did not realise the impact my statement would have as I nearly got trampled in the rush as several of the young clerks rushed by me to see Miss Perkins improperly dressed.

One of the clerks was so chuffed he bought me a cheesecake!

One of the first things Mr. Scott taught me was how to mount photographs on to a 16 sheet cardboard before the photograph could be retouched. The photograph had to be soaked in water to make it stretch, and special photo mountant paste was then applied to the back. This had to be rubbed in thoroughly before being put on to the cardboard, and then it had to be pressed totally smooth, and with no bubbles, by placing a piece of paper over the photograph and with the use of a pencil or similar object, pressed to eliminate any surplus paste. The mounted photograph then had to be washed using cotton wool to remove fingerprints etc, and then washed again with ammonia to remove any grease.

I also discovered that if any small grease spots persisted, nothing would remove them better than one's spittle. After the photograph had been retouched, it was my job to cover the face of it with tracing paper, which created a very good presentation of the finished work.

My next job was to deliver the finished product to the customer and take instructions if there were any alterations to be made.

Most of our customers were within walking distance from the studio, but anywhere over a mile away I would go by public transport. This gave me an excellent opportunity to learn about that part of London.

One of our biggest customers was Citroen Motor Cars, who had a showroom at Hammersmith, and we did such a lot of work for them we knew their requirements and seldom had to do any alterations.

I was also shown the construction of an aerograph, how it worked, and how it had to be cleaned. We had several spares and these I used to practise on until I became an expert at the manipulation, but more especially how to keep the needle in perfect working order.

I repaired one of the discarded spares by cleaning the needle, and commandeered this for my own use, and with which I could spray a line of paint as thin as one's hair. I was always told to retouch a photograph as if the light was coming from right to left, and it was not long before my fellow artists were complimenting me on the progress I was making.

We used to do all of the retouching work for Berry's Electric Fires. The Advertising Manager was always most charming and it was always a pleasure taking instructions from him regarding any alterations he would like. Every time I went to see him he was always in his office sitting at his desk, and I would have to go to him to get the details of any alterations he required. That was fine, and he always looked quite normal, but on one occasion he stood up and, to my surprise, he had very short legs and I, at five feet seven inches tall, was taller than he was.

Our photographic department used to do work for Jaegar's and the Advertising Manager was a frequent visitor to our studio. On one occasion he called on his return from the USA where he had attended, as a guest, a mannequin parade of the next season's swimsuits. While he was there he had surreptitiously photographed the proceedings using a hidden camera, and he brought the results on 3 rolls of film for us to develop. He stressed the secrecy and urgency and our photographic department got cracking. Having developed the films, our photographer put them through a dish of methylated spirits to dry the films off quickly, and hung them out to dry in front of an electric fire, which was about four feet away.

I was in the photographic studio at the time having a coffee with my friend Frank when suddenly the fumes from the methylated spirits reached the fire and WHOOSH!!!, the three rolls of film went up in flames. Instantaneously everybody, including the photographer, burst out laughing until it was realised the catastrophe it had caused, and I was ordered back to my studio as I was considered a disturbing influence so that the photographer could adopt a contrite attitude before confessing to our boss what had happened.

When our boss was finally told the result of the efforts to expedite the processing of the films, his first remarks were, "Shit! Shit! Shit!, now what are we going to do?" Of course it was a case of poetic justice, but that was not the moment to mention such things.

It was decided to come clean, and when the advertising manager called for his films, he was taken into the photographic studio and shown the charred remains of his films, which rendered him speechless, and he just sat looking aghast, listening to what had happened. It was some little while before the friendly relationship returned to normal and the catastrophe was never mentioned again.

But the irresponsible Frank and I thought it was a good laugh.

Several times a day I would go to John's café for refreshments and John never failed to remind me to return the cups.

He would say, "Bruce, remember to bring the cups back because Johnny, he got no cups; I ordered six/seven dozen cups the other day, but they haven't come in yurt."

There were times when I used to accompany one of our photographers on outside work to fire the flashlight. One day we were in a very large room with about 30 nuns who were packing up food parcels to send to the poor. It was a beautiful room with shelves all around displaying various religious icons and furnished with tables on which were the hampers in the process of being filled.

We had a whole large sized plate camera on a stand, and we were perched up in a corner with a very wide angled lens to enable us to include the whole room with as many nuns as possible. The photographer had everything in focus, and when he removed the cap off the lens it was my job to fire the Flash.

I was wearing a bowler hat to protect against the possibility of the flash coming down instead of up, and with the flash tray held well above my head, as the lens cover was removed, I fired. There was a loud explosion and a WHOOSH.

This brought down dust off the icons that had been building up for centuries.

All the nuns screamed, but I couldn't stop l laughing as the dust hanging in the air was like a London pea soup fog. The photographer immediately thrust the black velvet cloth he used for focussing over my head and pushed me down in the corner while he apologised for the mess he had caused, and offered comfort to the nuns who were scared out of their wits.

Incredibly the final photograph was excellent and showed the nuns smiling, totally different from the looks we had seen just seconds later after the flash had been fired.

I had reached the Journeyman stage in my training and I was quite competent at retouching photographs. I had learnt all of the secrets of the trade, but due to inexperience, I was lacking in speed; my boss assured me however that this would come with time.

Everything in the garden was lovely. I had finished my apprenticeship; I had got myself a rise, and at home my mother had produced another sister, Betty, who was just over two years of age and the most wonderful gift for her brothers and sisters that could ever imagine.

Another young artist had joined our firm, Robert William Turnbull Hogg, and who became a good friend of mine. He was a Scotsman from Dunnoon who had been working in London for some time and had been looking for somewhere to live so that he could bring his newly wedded wife to join him. Suitable premises to let were not easy to find, and so he bought himself a three-storey house with a basement in Penge High Street.

Once he was settled, he invited me to stay for a weekend when I met his younger sister, Margaret, who was the same age as me, and we got on like a house on fire.

Robert was in the process of furnishing his new property and it was obvious money was no object. The main items of furniture had come from Maples in Tottenham Court Road, and the soft furnishings from Harvey Nichols and Harrods. To someone like me who could recognise good furniture because of my father's talent, I could see Robert had done his wife proud.

She was a charming lady who was quite at home in her new luxurious house, but there was no sign of affluence in her dress as she appeared as a homely Scottish lady, and was an excellent hostess.

On my first night at Robert's new home he took me out to his local pub while his wife and sister were preparing the evening meal, and he bought me my first half pint of lager, which I thought was revolting! I did not like the smell, the taste was horrible, and I simply could not drink it. Robert knew I was not used to visiting Public Houses, and he thought it was quite funny when he asked what drink I would prefer and I said, "Please may I have a Coca Cola."

71

Life was good; I was doing well at work, and when I went home there was our baby sister Betty to play with. I remember trying to increase her vocabulary when she was first learning to talk. She could not say 'donkey'; she kept saying 'gonkey'. I said, "It's not 'gonkey', it's der – donkey." I kept on making her say 'der','der,'. She repeated after me 'der' 'der' and then said 'der gonkey'. It was great fun and we loved her all the more for it. When all of her brothers and sisters were at home, our mother had very little to do with Betty's up bringing as we took over and we commandeered her presence.

On one occasion however when Betty was just over two years of age, our mother went to chastise her with the punishment cane.

This made me see red – I grabbed the cane, broke it into many pieces, and said to my mother, "Don't you dare hit her – you're not going to bonk her like you used to us", and I threw the cane away. That was the last punishment cane we ever had. That very act usurped my mother's disciplinary powers and Jess, being 20 years older than Betty, acted as the mother figure, and with Cyril, Percy, Nell and me, we took over and brought Betty up – and we didn't make a bad job of it either.

They were very exciting times. At Hornchurch aerodrome, the RAF would practise aerobatics in their Hawker Hart aircraft, which was thrilling to watch.

Amy Johnson flew solo in a second-hand Gypsy Moth aircraft 10,000 miles to Australia, and I went to Broxbourne and had my first aeroplane flight with Roger Frogley for air experience, as the only thing I wanted to do at that time was join the Royal Air Force.

My mother, who knew nothing about aviation, thought it was far too dangerous, and so to put me off she said,

"You don't want to do that – only the riff raff join the Royal Air Force."

The business world was beginning to feel the effects of the Wall Street crash, which had happened two year's previously. Mr. Montague Norman, Manager of the Bank of England, persuaded the Government to go on to the Gold standard, which meant for every bank note printed, the Royal Mint had to have enough gold bullion to support it. Firms were going bust in profusion.

When businesses are facing a recession, the first thing they do is reduce the advertising appropriation, and as a result my firm went 'Belly up', and I became one of the 2,000,000 unemployed. However, I was able to get another job with Briggs Blockmakers in their studio with 36 other artists, but after a few months the recession began to bite deeper, and on the principle of 'last in, first out', I was out of work again. I signed on at the Labour Exchange and after a while I got fourteen shillings a week.

During that time I did a bit of freelance work. Fred's firm had also gone broke, but he managed to get himself a job with the London Co-operative Society as a milkman and was employed at their Canning Town Depot. He started work at 4.00 a.m., seven days a week, and if I had no freelance work on I would cycle the five miles to where Fred worked and help him do his milk round.

I used to meet Fred at his Depot at about 4.30 a.m. by which time he would have loaded his milk pram, and together we would push it along Barking Road to Cumberland Road, where we used to start delivering. We would deliver to the whole of Cumberland Road, and then turn into Wanlip Road, into Prince Regent's Lane where we would have a break and breakfast at a Transport Café, after which we would reverse our steps back to the Depot for the second delivery, which was to top up with milk, eggs and butter, and collect the cash on a daily basis.

On that second delivery, I would deliver the top up requirements and Fred would do the booking, and take the cash. The system worked well and it reduced Fred's working time considerably. Fred, being of a very sociable nature, would get involved with some of the 'old dears' when their kids were at school and would listen to their troubles. I got used to the nattering bit, but on the Wednesday second delivery, no money was taken, and quite often Fred would get button holed by a talkative customer at the beginning of Cumberland Road and, as I knew Fred's customers' second round requirements, I would carry on with deliveries on my own, finish the round and pick up Fred on my return to the Depot with Fred still talking to the first customer!

Fred was everyone's friend and was well liked by the other milkman at the Depot. Two of them owned an Austin 1927 Tourer motorcar, but they wanted to improve on that, so Fred bought their car off them for £25.00. They delivered it to where Fred and Jess were living at the time, and it was my pleasure to take Fred out and give him his first lesson.

There were not many cars on the roads in those days, thank God! But Fred was an apt pupil and within 2 hours he was changing gears, double-declutching up and down like a veteran. Reversing the car and parking he took in his stride, and it was not long before he was driving me back home for tea. I then went home to Seven Kings and later Fred brought Jess in their car on a family visit.

After a while he said to my father, "I've got my car outside, would you like to come for a drive?" My father, who had never travelled by anything other than public transport or his bicycle, accepted with alacrity, and so Fred demonstrated his driving skills all around Ilford.

On his return to our house my father was truly exhilarated, and after a bit over a cup of tea he said, "But Fred, I didn't know you could drive!!" and Fred replied, "I couldn't this afternoon!".

"Bloody hell", my father said, "and I put my life in your hands!!"

The transport café, where we would sometimes have a mid morning break of a cup of tea with a cheesecake, (which consisted of a pastry base with pseudo cream with coconut on top, in those days obesity never bothered us) was owned by a gentleman who had been a steward on a ship of the P&O Line.

At the time the first Queen Mary ship was under construction and which was intended to be the largest liner in the world, and we used to talk about the PR guff that had been broadcast on the wireless regarding its size of 83,000 tons and the number of decks it was going to have. But our Steward friend, the owner of our favourite café, convinced us it would never sail as in his opinion it was far too big and would break its back as soon as it was put to sea.

That statement coming from the voice of experienced was to us the Gospel Truth, and we awaited the demise of the vessel with bated breath, but happily on one of its first trips it won the Blue Riband for crossing the Atlantic to New York in record time.

* * *

75

6

Know which side your bread is buttered!

E verything continued to go from strength to strength. I would go home with Fred after we had finished his milk round and help him eat his lunch, and sometimes afterwards we would go and play Billiards at the local saloon. Fred always played well, and we were thoroughly enjoying ourselves, but that didn't suit big sister Jess, and she took me to task over it, saying, "Bruce, you can't waste your talent like this, you should be looking for work to use your talent. Besides, Fred is a married man now, and I've got things for him to do."

As those words of wisdom had no immediate effect on me, she got her old boss, a Mr. Turner, to use his good offices for me to keep an appointment with a business firm of his acquaintance, as a result of which I got a job in the advertising department of H T Greenlaws, a firm which made 'Grenville' shirts and ties.

Here that I learnt how to do silk screen-printing, and on one occasion I designed a show-card advertising 'Grenville neckwear' in seven colours, which meant cutting seven stencils to print the colours depicted as a bowl of Polyanthus, for which the firm paid me a bonus. I was also sent on a course to learn how to operate a Rollaflex Lithographic Printing Machine.

In no time at all I was designing printed matter in three and four colours, which was most difficult because I had to allow for the limitations of the machine's registration as the machine was designed to print only in one colour, and the manufacturers would only guarantee registration within one millimetre.

The Sales Director of Rollaflex heard what I was doing, and he called to see how I was getting on with the new machine, and was so impressed that he offered me a job selling Rollaflex machines. I remembered how Jess's old boss had got me my job, so I politely declined the offer. However, the Director persisted and offered me twice the salary Greenlaw's were paying me, but I explained it was not a matter of money, but of principle. Mr. Turner had got me my job when I was out of work and when I needed it, and the only way he could get me to work for him was to buy H T Greenlaws, and so we had a good laugh at this, and that was the end of the matter.

The Rollaflex machine made quite a lot of noise, and so it was put in a special room against a party wall, the other side of which was the ladies toilet, which was used by the factory girls who made the shirts and ties etc.

I was still a teenager at the time and was playing football for the local Seven Kings team at weekends, and most evenings I took part in roller skating races at the Forest Gate Roller Skating Rink, and one way or another I had no time for girls.

But, the things those girls spoke about in their toilet would so embarrass me it would make me blush, and I would have to leave my printing room and go into the studio. I was the laughing stock of the more mature artists when they saw me blushing with embarrassment, but all I could say was, "They're at it again".

The Sales Director of Rollaflex telling me I could earn more money selling his machines than Greenlaws were paying me unsettled me for a bit until I saw an advertisement in the Daily Telegraph for an artist, to which I responded and forgot all about it. Several weeks later, out of the blue, I received a letter inviting me to attend an interview at Smith's Advertising Agency in Fleet Street. I was thrilled. I made arrangements to have the morning off, washed my neck, grabbed specimens of the work I specialised in, and trotted off to the City.

There I met Mr. Muir who turned out to be the advertising Manager of Chivers and Sons Limited of the Orchard Factory, Histon, Cambridge. I found Mr. Muir most charming and he appeared to be more interested in my sporting and social activities than in my ability as a Commercial Artist. He told me that Chivers made jams and marmalade, and canned fruit and vegetables, and that they owned 8,000 acres of fruit orchards, and asked would I like to go and work in the country? To which I replied, "I cannot wait to get there!"

That concluded my interview, and Mr. Muir said I would hear from him again in the near future. Weeks went by, and I had forgotten all about Mr. Muir, when once again I was invited to attend another interview at Histon, Cambridge.

Despite the fact that I was early for the interview, I reported to the office where I was met by the Sergeant Commissionaire who knew all about my appointment, but as I was early he made me a coffee and took me to a private office where he chatted to me until it was time for my appointment. He made me feel quite at home, and after the interview when I was once again told to go home and wait for a further communication, he escorted me off the premises, but before doing so he gave me my travelling expenses.

It was not long before a further communication arrived, telling me I had got the job, and to report to the Histon Office the following Monday week. By the same post I received a letter from Bill Toms welcoming me to the firm and asking me if I would like him to fix up lodgings for me, and if so to let him know whether I would like to live in Histon Village or Cambridge Town. I replied by return of post stating I would like to live in Histon Village.

I duly reported to the Office at Histon where once again I was greeted by the Commissionaire Sergeant Blake, who took me up to the advertising studio, where I met my immediate superior, Bill Toms. After a cup of coffee I was taken into Mr. Muir's office, who welcomed me to Chivers, and expressed the hope that I would be happy in my new village environment. For the rest of the morning Bill Toms (who was also a Londoner) spent the time of day getting to know me before taking me to my new lodgings, which were right opposite where he lived.

Working in the English countryside in a small village of some 2,000 souls was out of this world.

To start work in the country with the gorgeous smell of strawberry jam being made at the factory on a British summer's day was to experience English weather at it's best.

At the age of 20, this was the first time I had left the bosom of my family, and my initial feelings of apprehension in starting a new job 50 miles from home were soon allayed, especially by the kindness of Bill Toms who knew how I was feeling, and did his best to make me feel wanted.

The cost of my digs for 7 days a week, including laundry, was £1.00 per week. As I was earning £5.00 per week I had no unemployment stamp to pay, and after my contribution to the Chivers' Pension Fund had been deducted, I had nearly £4.00 per week pocket money. I had never been happier.

I had not been working in the country long before I noticed the effect of the clean country air as opposed to the filthy air conditions of London. The shirts that I had brought with me changed colour from off white to pure white. My landlady duly confirmed this.

My digs were a mile away from the factory. We worked a 44 hour week, 9.00 am to 6.00 pm with one hour for lunch Monday to Friday, and from 9.00 am to 1.00 pm on Saturdays. Bill Toms and I were the only outsiders employed by Chivers with all of the rest of the 3,000 staff from the surrounding villages.

Chivers was a family concern that had started in 1876 in their kitchen making home made jams. They were a very religious family and attended the local Methodist Chapel regularly, and as a result their business was conducted with the highest of basic principles.

In the evenings after work I used to go to the Firm's Social Club, called the Histon Institute. Here all indoor games were available. There were two full size Billiards tables, Darts facilities, a card room, and a large Table Tennis room, and this was where I spent most evenings and where I reached County standard. The Club's premises were formerly a Chapel, and the main building had been converted into a Badminton court.

If I take part in anything, I have to be fully involved, and it was not long before I started to organise competitions, which took place every Monday evening. The aim was to get Billiards people to play Darts and Table Tennis, and Darts players to play Billiards and Table Tennis, etc. It was therefore necessary to handicap the better players in each pursuit to make the competition more attractive.

It was limited to 32 players, and each contestant had to pay an entrance fee of 3d. It started each Monday at 7.00 pm with the aim to finish by 10.00 pm, which we always managed to achieve. The competition consisted of one game of each activity, 501 for Darts, 21 for Table Tennis, and 11 for Billiards.

Unskilled Table Tennis players could receive up to a maximum of 15 points as their handicap, meaning the skilled player had to score 36 points against an unskilled player with the maximum 15 point handicap, who would only have to score 6 points to win. Due to the handicap system people were always keen to have a go, and every Monday we always had 32 competitors to play, with the chance to win 5 shillings – the rest of the entrance fee was ploughed back into the Club funds.

I also organised Badminton tournaments, and on one occasion I was playing a match in the semi final and in endeavouring to play a shot close to the net to get it to just trickle over alas, I failed. My shot went too high and my opponent smashed the return straight back at me, resulting in the leather part of the shuttle going straight into my eye! It was so painful it literally made me sick, and I could not continue.

I could not see out of my eye for a fortnight, and I later discovered that a shuttle, on its return, turns in one 25th of a second – it was a painful way to learn, but that's life!

The firm also provided several hard tennis courts, and an excellent football pitch with a small stand. I took part in all of those games according to the season, and so it was impossible to get bored as teenagers claim to be these days.

Bill Toms, my immediate superior, was a much better artist than me, and he was also an excellent photographer. He would take photographs of work going on in the factory and farms, and I was able to use my photographic retouching skills to make the prints suitable for reproduction in our advertisements or works magazine.

We were a good team; we liked one another, which went to create a very pleasant working environment, and each day I looked forward to going to work.

During our normal course of work Bill decided to teach me how to become an ideas man, and how to write copy. On one occasion he set me the task of thinking up a new approach to advertising Chivers Olde English Marmalade. After quite some thought, I produced a scheme, and as I was presenting my idea by means of thumbnail sketches to Bill, I said, "The only was to do this........." Before I could proceed further, Bill said, "Stop". I said, "What have I done wrong?" Bill said, "you will never make an ideas man if you say 'the only way' – in every scheme there are many different ways – there is the right way, the wrong way, the best way – there are always dozens of ways to promote advertising schemes and so NEVER, and I repeat, NEVER, use the phrase 'the only way' to present an idea."

Such wonderful advice has stood me in good stead for over 60 years, and I have been able to pass on such wise advice to others when the time was right.

Working in such a friendly atmosphere was idyllic, and I loved every minute of it. The most important thing Bill taught me was that if I wanted to become something more than an ideas man and commercial artist, I had a lot to learn. Coming from Bill I took this comment to heart. No one had spoken to me like that before; I was a Londoner and knew it all! However, I started attending evening classes at the Cambridge Technical College, where I learnt about printing and type setting by hand composing, and art classes to improve my watercolour technique.

One evening, a Mr. Samson joined our still life class and told our teacher he wanted to learn to paint. He had no previous art experience. He did not want to accept the teacher's advice and learn how to draw first, he just wanted to paint. Our instructor realised he was not getting anywhere with Mr. Samson, and so he plonked a pot of Geraniums down on a stand and said, "Very well, paint that", and walked away. The rest of us experienced students thought, 'we'd got a right one here', and got on with our work.

However, at the end of the evening we went to see what our strange new member had done, and we were amazed, for although his ellipses were all wrong and his pot would not have stood up, anyone could recognise that he had painted a pot of geraniums.

He was immediately accepted as one of us, and he joined and made wonderful progress in our still life class. Mr. Samson's day job was as a scientific toolmaker at Pyes in Cambridge. I got to know Samson quite well for he was a budding genius!

One Saturday morning I was wandering around the Petty Cury Market and there was Samson, serving at a second hand bookstall. He was delighted to see me and told me that the stall was his father's business, and he was holding the fort while the old man went for a coffee.

On his father's return, he took me to his flat, which was quite near, for a coffee. There I saw some of the most exquisite model ships, all in full sail, which I discovered Sammy had made as this was his hobby. All the sails operated up and down by the use of the tiniest of pulleys, which had been made on a miniature lathe. This skill had come from his experience of being a scientific toolmaker. "Sammy", I said, "you've missed your vocation, have you ever tried to sell these?" He replied, "Bruce, if I were to charge a farthing an hour for my work on that Battleship, it would be worth over £1,000".

During my visit I noted some violins, which, of course, Sammy had also made. He picked one up and played a tune. I said, "Where did you learn to play like that?" He said, "I've had no lessons, I'm self taught".

On another occasion we cycled from Cambridge to a small village just north of Newmarket where there was a watermill that Sammy wanted to paint. Sammy had previously made the acquaintance of the owner of the Mill, and it was quite obvious to me that these two gentlemen were on the same wavelength.

The owner of the Mill escorted us around, and I was absolutely amazed at the intricate and complicated system of wooden gear wheels, all of which had been made by the owner. Sammy said to the Mill owner, "I'd like to make a model of your Mill, have you a set of blue prints I could borrow?" The Mill owner said, "Blue Prints? I don't have any Blue Prints or drawings to go by, I just get a piece of wood and get cutting!"

Sammy was absolutely amazed at the skill involved in cutting all of those complicated gear wheels of various sizes which all messed together to turn the water mill, and all created off the top of his head without any draughtsman's drawings.

While I was sketching the outside of the Mill, Sammy was painting the working parts of the inside of the Mill in watercolours. Subsequently after several visits, Sammy finished his picture and had it framed. At the Art School's annual exhibition, which was opened by the Principal of the Slade School of Art, the Principal was commenting on the artistic attainments of the students' artwork for the year and, when he came to Sammy's picture, gave an excellent critique of his picture, which pleased everyone. Sammy however could not stop laughing, and so I hung back with Sammy to let him cool down, and said that I thought the Principal's comments were good, and that I didn't see anything to laugh at. Sammy said, "Bruce, see those large wooden brackets on the floor? Well, they are the brackets supporting the roof – they have hung my picture upside down!" I said, "I hadn't noticed that, and I still think the Principal's comments were good", which started Sammy laughing all over again!

When I first started working at Chivers, I used to go home every weekend, but it was not long before I was so involved at work and playing football for the Firm's team at weekends that my home visits became intermittent.

My 'happy go lucky' way of life began to be disturbed by the serious news in the Press, and I started to listen to the BBC news at 6.00 pm each night. In 1935, storm clouds were gathering over

Europe, and Mr. Churchill was making speeches in Parliament warning us of the dangers of not being prepared for war. Adolph Hitler had been made Chancellor of Germany, and by his rhetoric he was gaining power.

Later that year Germany ordered Conscription and it was obvious we were heading for trouble. Until then I did not have a care in the world, but as the BBC News got worse, I started to read the daily newspapers and realised that I had to do something about the deteriorating situation because if there was going to be a war, I did not want to be 'a poor bloody Infantryman.'

I remembered the tales my Uncle Chris used to tell me about the time when he had been standing up to his waist in mud in the trenches for a fortnight, and when he was relieved, his feet had swollen to twice their size, and had to be treated for Trench Foot. As I have said before that was not for me; I am an Andy Warhole man and 'I'm not afraid to die, I just don't want to be there when it happens!'

So, I decided to join the Royal Air Force.

I had already had some flying experience with Roger Frogley, (whom I used to hero worship as a West Ham Dirt Track Rider) at his Flying Field at Broxbourne, Hertfordshire. Once Roger had got us airborne and gaining height, he would hand over the controls, and I would be in heaven. Those trips were in the hope that one would sign up for a course of flying lessons to get an 'A' Pilot's Licence, but at that time I could not afford it. However, Roger gave me a taste for flying, and it was the RAF for me – but how!! ?

By 1935 I had saved up enough money to buy a motorcar, and I bought a 1931 Singer Saloon. This was a wonderful investment as I was able to get home at weekends from door to door in half the time it took by public transport. I was also able to take other members of Chivers' Table Tennis team to play the Away fixtures.

It was strange that now I was mobile I did not get home to London at weekends as often as before. There were villages to explore, and I was not lost for friends to accompany me.

Some Sunday mornings I would go out walking with my country friends, most of whom were members of Chivers' Football team. Our self appointed leader on those walkabouts was a local village boy named Len Toates, and he had a Staffordshire Bull Terrier, and we used to alternate our activities; some days we would go rabbiting, others to catch rats. Len's Bull Terrier was very intelligent; if we were going ratting the dog never looked at a rabbit, and vice versa, if we were rabbiting the dog totally ignored the rats. Being a Townie, I was amazed at what my village friends knew about the countryside, and it gave them much pleasure to point out my ignorance.

One day we were in a chickens' run. Len had blocked up all of the escape holes and was pumping gas down one of the rat runs. I was in a stooped position due to the lowness of the chickens' run, when suddenly a rat burst through the soft earth and sprang up into the air right next to me. My instantaneous reaction was to catch it, but when I realised what I had done, I threw it against the wall and the Bull terrier made short work of it. I had never seen a rat before, let alone handled one, but Len tore such a strip off me for being so stupid as the rat could have bitten me, and I would have had to have a Tetanus injection, and that would have finished our morning's ratting. For every rat's tail we produced, the farmer gave Len 9d. Often we caught 12 to 18 rats in a morning.

On another day when we were out to catch rabbits, Len had his dog and was carrying the gas equipment and I was carrying the spade. We went straight to the rabbit warren, and after I had blocked off all bar two of the bolt holes, Len started pumping gas down the entrance and I was sitting astride the exit hole, holding a net in one hand and the spade with the other in an upright position with its handle on the ground. Suddenly, the ground underneath me shook and a large rabbit hit my net. My instantaneous reaction was to bring down the spade and stun the rabbit.

Alas, the stupid Townie had done it all wrong again. Did I not realise that we would be paid a shilling for every rabbit, but not if the flesh had been bruised by hitting it with a spade? The other members of our party couldn't stop laughing at my ignorance, and I was once again in the doghouse.

Another of my village friends was Cyril Goldsmith. His parents owned the village fish and chip shop, and Cyril was always trying to get me to go fishing. I however could not envisage myself sitting for hours on end waiting for a fish to bite, for if I am not sketching, writing or reading, I cannot sit still. My mother used to call me a 'fidget arse'. I have always had an active brain, and my mother would say, "You'll never go mad Bruce, you change your mind too quickly!" However, one Sunday, Cyril and his friend talked me into going fishing. So, off we went in my motorcar, and we sat all day by the River Ouse, and by 4.00 pm we had not had a bite or any sign that there were any fish in the Ouse.

We had a lovely picnic lunch that Cyril's mum had provided, and of course I had nothing to do but watch, and so I just kept talking. Talking I have always found easy, and Mum used to say, "Bruce likes the sound of his own voice." Be that as it may, as we were packing up to go home, I said, "Well is that it, sitting by the Ouse all day without the sign of any fish?". Cyril replied, "Joe (Cyrils' friend) and I have had a very restful day listening to your exploits, but don't think you are going to catch fish with you gabbling away – fish can hear you know!"

About this time the River Ouse was perilously close to overflowing its banks, and Chivers' farming employees had been constantly patrolling the river banks to see if there were any tell tale cracks, which were the warning signs that the river was about to burst its banks.

A notice was circulated round the office staff asking for volunteers to patrol the banks at the weekend to give the overworked farming employees a break. There was no shortage of volunteers and a bus load of us were taken to one of Chivers' farms through which the river flowed to do an eight hour stint looking for cracks in the banks.

The weather was overcast, with a strong breeze blowing. I noticed the farm workers we were taking over from wore dungarees and Wellington boots and walked peculiarly. I was wearing a brown three piece suit as if I were going to the office, and Cyril Goldsmith had lent me a pair of Wellington boots.

The river had been rising for several weeks, and the banks had been raised by adding a heavy blue clay, which was still soft and sticky. As I patrolled my section of the bank, I noticed the blue clay had stuck to the sides of my Wellingtons, and I must have brushed my feet together as I walked for after I had finished my eight hour shift, I noticed the clay had worked its way up inside my jacket, and had become adhered to my waistcoat, penetrating it right through to the lining which I found impossible to move, and so my three piece became a two piece!

It was then I realised why the local farm employees walked peculiarly with their feet wide apart so they did not brush their feet together. Their Wellingtons were relatively clean, whereas my waistcoat was a write off. This Townie' still had a lot to learn.

Working as a Clerk in the Laboratory Section was a man who ultimately became one of my best friends; his name was Francis Clifford Latimer Richardson, who was known to everyone as 'Richie'. Clifford, as I chose to call him, had a hobby as a Lay Preacher at the Methodist Chapel, and was a very good rhetorical speaker. His immediate boss was the Technical Director in charge of the Laboratory, who was also a member of the Plymouth Brethren.

Our Advertising Manager was also a member of the Plymouth Brethren, and through this connection Richie had heard that our Exhibition Manager was shortly to retire, and Richie wanted that job. It was therefore arranged that Richie would take his tea break each day with Bill Toms and me to get to know what went on in the Advertising Department. Richie had been an excellent tennis player and had represented Cambridge County, but due to a motorcycle accident, which left him lame, his athletic prowess had been curtailed, but his interest in all types of games had not been diminished. So, he and I got on like a house on fire.

One Saturday afternoon, I was playing football for the Histon Institute team, when during a break while one of the players was receiving medical attention, the outside right of the opposing team who I was marking said to me, "What went wrong in your factory last week?" I said, "What do you mean?" "Well," he said, "I work in the Sewer Pits, and five tons of liquid sugar came down the tube", at which point the game restarted and nothing more was said.

At Monday tea break, Richie came to tea and Bill was taking a phone call in the Manager's office, and I said to Richie, "What went wrong in the factory last week?" "Same as usual", Richie said, "Why do you ask?" "Well", I replied, "Five tons of sugar went down the tube into the Sewer Pits last week!"

If I had blasphemed to Lay Preacher Richie, he could not have looked more astonished.

"What are you talking about – how do you know?!"

I then related to Richie what had happened on the football pitch.

"Well I never", Richie said, "Have you told anyone else?"

"No Richie, its none of my business, I would not have mentioned it to you except I know you are responsible for keeping the statistics. It was just a throw away line for a teatime chat". I replied.

"Disciplinary action has been taken internally by the Technical Director, and the matter is now closed. Please Bruce, promise me that you will never repeat that story again", Richie said.

"As far as I am concerned, it never happened," I responded.

Apparently a foreman had turned on the wrong tap, and instead of the liquid sugar going down to the Jam Filling Machines, it went straight down to the Sewers, and five tons of sugar was lost before the error could be corrected. The Foreman had been reprimanded and the Directors did not want the matter to go any further to save embarrassment.

I used to enjoy the tea time sessions with Richie. He was a character after my own heart, and so different in his outlook on life compared with Bill Toms. Bill was careful about money to the extent of meanness, and he would regularly save money, whereas Richie lived up to the hilt of his income, and didn't save a penny. The friendly arguments that developed were often quite funny, but if ever I was losing an argument with Richie, I would get my own back by closing with the phrase, "Oh! Sugar to you!"

Richie was well sought after as a Lay Preacher, and many were the times I would go with him to other Chapels to hear him Preach.

One Sunday we went to Papworth, which in those days was known as a Lunatic Asylum. One of the inmates was a friend of Richie's because he came from the same village where Richie was born.

The inmate was an ex farm labourer, over 6 feet tall and broad with it. He had been acting a little strange for many years, and, to use a Cambridge expression, he was considered 'Half Sharp'. He was as strong as an Ox, and the final straw was when he had been given the job of clearing a Spinney. With no one to help him, he was given an axe, and he cut down all of the trees. He then stripped the branches and started to burn them in huge bonfires. This went on for several weeks, and, come the winter, he started taking branches home to burn on his open grate fire.

He lived in a semi-detached village cottage, and the heat from his fire was so great, it could be felt in the neighbour's cottage next door. Village communities are very close-knit affairs, and everybody knows each other's business, and the neighbour decided to keep a close watch on his friend next door.

One night, the heat generated from 'Half Sharp's' fire was so intense the neighbour called to see what was happening, and to his amazement, 'Half Sharp' had built such a huge fire, the floorboards had started to burn. By the time the Village Fire Engine arrived, the living room was alight, but they soon had it under control. The outcome was that it was decided it was not safe for 'Half Sharp' to live on his own, and so he finished up at Papworth.

Due to his farm labouring experience he was given a large allotment. He did not grow anything, but each day he dug the huge plot over, and this got rid of his surplus energy. He had to be taken off that job because, once he had finished digging his own plot, he started digging the plot next to his, which upset the owner of that plot as he dug up everything including vegetables which were coming to fruition!

On one when Sunday Richie was going to preach at Papworth, I was amazed to see the Chapel crammed with inmates – or patients (as they are now called), and also the high number of male and female Warders, or 'Carers' as they are called today.

Before the Service I was introduced to Richie's friend and he volunteered the information that he no longer had an allotment, but was now an indoor 'Agricultural Worker'. Apparently he would scrub the floor of a ward on hands and knees in the morning, and in the afternoon he would polish it.

Richie's guests for that morning's Service had to sit in the choir stalls well away from the inmates. The hymns chosen were all of the most popular ones and were sung by the congregation with great gusto and volume. Any one of them would have made a great Lead Singer in today's Pop groups; they shouted to the echo. They didn't need hymn books as they knew all the words.

During Richie's Sermon I noticed quite a number of people present were not paying attention, when suddenly a little old lady stood up, turned round, and started bashing the lady sitting behind her with an umbrella. Several attendants quickly surrounded the fracas, and the little old lady was led quietly away. I had never seen anything like that at a religious service before, and couldn't stop laughing. Richie, who had witnessed this sideshow, didn't bat an eyelid and carried on with the sermon as if nothing had happened.

Since my Sunday School days, which I started at the age of 4, I have listened to many very dreary sermons – some of which needed a little old lady with an umbrella to liven up the proceedings!

After the Service Richie and his guests had to leave before the congregation, and some of the inmates tried to shake my hand, but this was not allowed because, as one of the Warders explained, some of the male inmates did not know their own strength and could easily cause an injury.

7

As the Storm Clouds Gathered...

At our tea time sessions, Bill Toms and Richie would discuss current affairs, and sometimes we were joined by Stanley Banyard, who was a Statistician in Chivers' Sales Department.

Stanley was a very bright young man. He had won a scholarship to Cambridge University, from Soham Grammar School, and obtained a 1st Class Honours Degree in Mathematics in just two years instead of three, and so the third year he stayed on and took a Degree in Organ Music.

As a listener of those sessions I started to learn the ways of the world. How the Communists were causing trouble in Spain by joining up with anarchists, but far more important were the changes which were taking place in Germany. Hitler had become Chancellor of the German Reich, and had started to make outrageous demands. Sometimes my opinion was sought, but my attitude had always been to let them get on with it, because with all of my other activities, I had not had time to think about such things, but now I realised I had to get up to date.

Therefore I started to read newspapers and listening to the BBC news. I was more concerned at that time about the fuss the Australian Cricket Team were making about Harold Larwood's Bodyline Bowling. Their tears would have filled an Olympic Swimming Pool because, they said, 'It was not Cricket'.

Also at that time there was a mystery fire, which gutted the German Reichstag. Hermann Goering was the first Minister to arrive at the fire, and he blamed the Communists and shouted that every one of them should be shot on the spot. These were very troubled times, especially as Japan left the League of Nations which was a talking shop just like our present United Nations is today.

Mr. Ramsey MacDonald was our Labour Prime Minister at the time, and on his return from a visit to Italy, he told us he had met the Il Duce Mussolini where he had been discussing his plan for removing the causes of War. His Government had run down the Armed Forces to a point where we were unable to defend ourselves.

That did not please Mr. Churchill who delivered a bitter attack on the Prime Minister's Foreign Policy because it had made us weaker, poorer and more defenceless than at any time in our history.

But Mr. Churchill was a voice in the wilderness, for nobody in Parliament took any notice of him, but I liked what he said and told my friends at our tea time soirees that I was a Churchill man, but that was put down to my youth and inexperience.

Hitler's Nazi excesses, especially against the Jews, caused great concern. He banned all Opposition Parties and had huge bonfires of all books which did not support His Regime. By 1934 Hitler had done away with all forms of Democratic Government, and had become Dictator with the title of Fuehrer.

The death of President Hindenburg cleared the way for Hitler to take full power, when he stated he wished to be known as 'Fuehrer' and 'Reich Chancellor'. He also styled himself 'Supreme Commander of all the Armed Forces', and made all officers and men swear a sacred oath of unconditional obedience, not to Germany, but to himself personally.

Churchill, in Parliament told us we were now in real trouble, and it was then that people started to take notice of him. Jews were being put into Concentration Camps, and Himmler had been put in charge of those.

Stanley Baldwin planned a massive expansion of the Royal Air Force by boosting it by 41 new Squadrons, as we were way behind France, Italy and Russia. In 1936 there was a massive Civil War going on in Spain, and idealists from all over the world flocked to Spain to help. Germany took advantage of this war to try out various war machines as well as aircraft flown by Luftwaffe pilots to gain war experience.

Churchill again warned Parliament that our weak defences could lead to Britain being "tortured into absolute subjection" in a war with Germany, with no chance of ever recovering. Germany's munition factories were practically working under war conditions, and it was obvious that her Air Force would, in the very near future, be twice the size of the RAF.

In 1935, the League of Nations had condemned Hitler's rearmament of Germany, and as a result Great Britain had increased her defence spending. Hitler ordered his Nazi troops to re-enter the Rhineland, which had been taken from them under the Treaty of Versailles, and this brought German troops 100 miles nearer France. However, no action was taken to drive them back.

It was in this environment that the Royal Air Force Volunteer Reserve was formed (RAFVR), and Mr. Churchill continued to warn us about German rearmament and the dangers of a future war.

Being 23 years of age, I knew if war was declared, I would have to go, and so I jumped at the opportunity of joining the RAFVR as a pilot.

Richie had a nice three bedroom detached house in the village of Histon, with a garden 250 feet long. It was split in two by a hedge; the front half for flowers, and the back portion was used to grow vegetables. He was an excellent gardener, and sometimes I would go and help him, when he taught me the basics of growing things.

One of Richie's neighbours had been left a large house with six acres of land attached. He was only a young bachelor in his early 30's but he objected to paying rates, and so he took the roof off a large part of his premises so that he did not owe the Council anything! Everyone in the village thought he was 'half sharp'; he had no job to go to, he was of independent means, he didn't interfere with anyone, and so he was accepted as the village idiot.

The local developer, who was a 'Wide Boy', bought 4 acres of 'Half Sharp's' land at a ridiculously low price to build houses, and everyone in the village thought Half Sharp had been 'turned over.' However, when it came the time to build, the Developer discovered that the services, such as the laying of sewer pipes, gas, electricity and water etc, it was necessary to go across Half Sharp's land.

Half Sharp had heard the tales about how the Developer had pulled a 'fast one' over him in the original sale of the land, and his first reply to the Developer was a refusal, as that was not part of the original deal.

That refusal put the cat among the pigeons because not only had the Developer been refused; Half Sharp was refusing to talk to him. After some considerable time a deal was struck but the Developer had to pay an exorbitant price. Our village idiot was not half sharp after all!!

The international situation was deteriorating. Mussolini, the Dictator of Italy, had come to an agreement with France for them to turn a blind eye on what his ambitions were regarding Ethiopia. Germany was re-arming at a rapid pace, and Winston Churchill was making speeches warning the Government of the dangers he could foresee.

On 1st March 1935 Saarbruck was transferred from France to Germany, and German troops marched in for the first time since the end of World War I. This was another act of appeasement, trying to stop Hitler's expansionist demands. Hitler addressed the celebrants as 'My Saarbruckers', which was received with rapturous applause. All over the world armaments were increasing. Hitler renounced the Versailles Treaty and ordered conscription of German forces. Mussolini, Italy's Dictator, followed Hitler's example and conscripted Italian Forces. Ramsey MacDonald, our Prime Minster, issued a White Paper stating that because of Hitler's aggressive spirit, British defence needed bolstering.

In 1936, an announcement was made to triple the Royal Air Force, resulting in the formation of the RAFVR.

I joined as a Pilot, and started training at Marshall's Aerodrome in Cambridge. The permanent members of the RAF were very anti Volunteer Reserve applicants, and having completed the Application

Form which had been sent to me by a gentleman who stated that he had been 'directed to send me the Forms to complete', and who finished the letter by saying he was my 'Obedient Servant' – which I thought was very charming – I did not hear a thing for several weeks. In fact, I thought they had forgotten all about my application, when out of the blue, I received an instruction to attend an interview at the Royal Air Force Volunteer Headquarters at Cambridge.

I was a keen cyclist in those days and had a Racing Bicycle that had been hand made to my specification, and I could not wait to present myself for my interview.

The Cambridge Headquarters of the Volunteer Reserve was in a large country house off the Trumpington Road in Cambridge. On my arrival, I was greeted by a Sergeant Commissionaire who appeared terribly old to me (after all I was only 23 at the time), and he escorted me to a Drawing Room where there were several other volunteers waiting to be interviewed.

When my turn came, I was ushered into a large room with a Board Room Table at one end, behind which sat three RAF Officers. I was invited to sit, and one officer, who noticed that I was very tense, asked me simple questions based on my Application Form, which I found simple to answer, and before very long I was enjoying myself. It was obvious they wanted me to speak and express myself, and when they asked me about my job, I was away and in my element!

They were very interested in my sporting activities; soccer, badminton, tennis, and that I was County Standard at table tennis, but they seemed a little disappointed that I did not play Rugby. The officer in the middle of my three interviewers was an aged gentleman who was more interested in my parents, but when I told the Panel my father was a Cabinet Maker and designed his own furniture, they realised where my artistic temperament came from in advertising. The interview ended with my telling the Panel that in the evenings I helped organise competitions at Chivers' Social Club, which seemed to go down well.

I was then sent to another room where I was examined by an RAF Doctor who did his best to fail me. He obviously did not agree with the Air Council's decision to expand the RAF with weekend flyers, but after testing me physically, my heart and blood pressure, he told me I was in good shape and that my blood pressure was that of an athlete, and that I would never have a heart attack. Now that I am a nonagenarian, he has been right so far!

After my medical, the Commissionaire took over and told me I would be contacted in the due course of time. Weeks went by and, although I was raring to go, nothing happened. Bill Toms, my immediate superior, thought I was crackers to want to volunteer, and he did his best to convince me my future was with Chivers. However, I agreed with everything that Mr. Churchill was saying in Parliament, although his was still a voice in the wilderness. Then surprise, surprise, I received another letter from my Obedient Servant, directing me to present myself at the RAFVR Headquarters to sign certain papers.

After I had completed this chore under the watchful eye of the Commissionaire, I, together with other members who had similarly been summoned to attend, congregated in an adjoining ante room where we were welcomed as Volunteer Reservists in the Royal Air Force by the elderly gentleman who had been present at my Selection Board, and who was in uniform and turned out to be Air Vice Marshal Sir Tom Webb-Bowen.

He was a charming gentleman, and had been brought back out of retirement to form the Cambridge Branch of the Royal Air Force Volunteer Reserve. He told us we were expected to attend lectures three times a week, and be available to fly at the weekends. He showed us all over the Headquarters building where there was a large drawing room - which we were to call the anteroom - a dining room, games room, and two large lecture rooms.

The Air Vice Marshal was such a friendly gentleman, more like a father figure, that I did not realise at the time what an exalted rank he held in the RAF. It was not until 1942, after I had been mobilised for three years, that I met anyone above the rank of Group Captain.

The first lecture I attended at Cambridge was given by the Air Vice Marshal and dealt with the history of the RAF and the traditions which had been built up. He informed us that he was justly proud of what had been achieved in less than 20 years since the RAF had been formed, and he stressed that each one of us must consider it a challenge to reach and maintain that standard of excellence.

Sir Tom's part in our training was RAF Administration and Honours and Awards. He explained the lowest rank in the RAF was Aircraftsman II, who after a satisfactory period became an Aircraftsman I, and after passing an examination in the Airman's particular trade would become a Leading Aircraftsman. That was the rank we were starting at, and we would have to prove ourselves worthy of that rank if we were to become Aircrew.

Sir Tom had the most wonderful way of making us feel good, and that we were the chosen ones. The way he passed on the information he had to impart was so differently presented that we hung on every word, and we left each lecture he gave feeling special.

One of the volunteers attending those lectures was the son of the local vicar at Histon. His name was Don Kingcombe, and he was able to get leave of absence from his firm so that he was able to spend six months with the RAF at Duxford Aerodrome, so that by the time war was declared, he was a fully trained Fighter Pilot.

We had lectures on Airmanship, Flight (what makes an aircraft leave the ground), Navigation, Air Reconnaissance, Air Photography, Bombing and Gunnery, etc., but of all of those subjects the one I found most absorbing was Navigation. I bought books on the subject and learnt fast, and became far advanced in the lectures we were being given and left the rest of the class standing.

The Air Marshall told us we were being trained as Officers, and what it was like to live in an Officers' Mess and that certain procedures had to be learnt. He invited us to Dine at the Headquarters at least once a week to get the feel of how to go on in an Officers' Mess.

Among the many subjects we were introduced were 'Bombing' and 'Gunnery', and although they were totally different from my previous artistic life in advertising, I took to them like a duck does to water.

I fully understood the theory of Bombing, with all its complexities, and on the Gunnery side, I found it so easy it was like being given a new toy. We had guns which we had to take apart, which was called stripping, and each part had a name, which we had to learn. Some parts had peculiar names, and I still remember to this day, over 70 years later, the name of the 'Prolongation of the left inner side plate'.

We had to familiarise ourselves with these weapons, and our instructor would hold competitions to see who could strip a gun and put it back together again the quickest. This was great fun, and taught us how to handle a gun with great dexterity.

One evening when I was cycling to the V.R. centre, a motorcar came out of a side turning and knocked me down. The noise was so great it brought people out from the nearby house and, when they discovered I was not seriously hurt, the lady of the house brought me a cup of tea, which was very welcome. Just then the lady's husband appeared, whom I quickly realised was Mr. Fife, the Secretary of Chivers, who was most concerned about my welfare and started questioning the driver who had knocked me down who turned out to be a member of Chivers' Sales Department.

I thanked Mrs. Fifie for her hospitality, and said that I must be on my way to the VR Centre, and although they did their best to persuade me to delay and rest a while, I was adamant, and after straightening my handlebars, I was on my way.

I had to put on a spurt as I hate being late, but I arrived at the VR Centre just in time. The next day Mr. Fife came upstairs to see how I was. He was most interested to learn I had joined the VR and he wished me well. Mr. Fife had recognised the man who had knocked me down as a Mr. Smith, a member of the Chivers' Sales staff, and after he had seen me, he had a word with him also. As a result, Mr. Smith also called on me to see if I was OK.

A couple of days later I was summoned to the presence of Mr. William Chivers who was the Chairman of Chivers. He was delighted to know I had volunteered be become a pilot in the Royal Air Force as a Volunteer Reserve, and he wished me every success in my new venture.

My first visit to Marshalls' Aerodrome at Cambridge was most awe-inspiring. Parked around the airfield were Tiger Moths, Fairy Battle and Hawker Hart aircraft, all with the RAF Roundel markings. It was a wonderful feeling to be so near such spick and span machines.

It was obvious that the RAF had been planning flying tuition through civilian organisations for some time because Marshalls main business was selling motorcars in Cambridge, but the airfield was an off-shoot interest with Marshalls' son who was in charge and who was a qualified flying instructor.

The Chief Flying Instructor was a Flight Lieutenant Peter May, and he let us know in his welcoming address how honoured we should consider ourselves to be in having taken the first steps to become a Royal Air Force Pilot. He was terribly proud of his Service, and he told us, even if we qualified as Pilots, it did not mean the RAF would take us as they did not take any Tom, Dick or Harry, and we had a long way to go before we could meet the RAF's high standard of excellence!

Marshalls had spent a great deal of money developing their airfield, and we were the first RAF trainees to use their brand new flying facilities. There were lecture rooms, a crew room where one waited in flying kit for their turn to fly, and a parachute room. One of the first things we were taught was how a parachute is packed. We were told how many panels of real silk a parachute had, and that if we were unfortunate enough to have to use it, the breaking strain of the cords, which supported a body, was 2240 pounds!

We were allowed to help pack a parachute and then release it to prove it had been packed properly. Next, the parachute was hung up to air in a purpose built, ventilated section of the room, and this was done as a matter of routine to every parachute once a month.

Having helped pack a parachute, the pulling of the handle and see it spring into action was a thrill.

We were told should we at any time have cause to bale out, in order to ensure that one is clear of the fuselage, one should count to three and then pull the handle, but what usually happens in such dire circumstances, one jumps and says, "Oh my gawd", and then pulls the handle!

They are such magic words, and have never been known to fail! Practical lectures given in such a light hearted and humorous vein were very impressive, and one remembers them for the rest of their life.

The first weekend at the aerodrome was very windy, and with overcast skies and intermittent rain, it was not possible to get anyone airborne, but nevertheless we were all issued with flying kit which consisted of a flying suit (known as a Sidcot), an inner suit, flying boots, leather gauntlets with silk linings, a leather flying helmet, and we were each allotted a key to a locker in which to keep our gear, and told that we would be charged for any item which we lost. This warning was given by an ex RAF Officer who was now a civilian in charge of Stores. He made us sign for everything, and it was obvious he did not like us, and he gave us the impression that it was his own personal property he was dishing out, and that we were not worthy of it!

As there was no flying involved we were left to our own devices to get to know each other. This was when I got to know Don Kingcombe, and we arranged to cycle together from Histon to Cambridge for our evening lectures.

Quite a number of our group were from Marshall's Garage in Cambridge. Some were Apprentices, and others were Motor Mechanics, and they all considered themselves special as they were going to fly from the Firm's airfield, but Peter May treated us all the same with no preferential treatment for anyone.

There were several Flying Instructors, who were all members of the RAF, and it was obvious to me that as we were being taught by RAF Instructors, using RAF aircraft, some complicated Contract had been worked out with Marshall's as we were using their Airfield and Ground Training facilities.

After several weekends of bad weather, I finally met my Flying instructor, a Flight Lieutenant Grace, who appeared to me to be a very ancient gentleman, and had a belligerent attitude! He told me I should consider it an honour and privilege to be taught to fly by the RAF, and that as I was a member of the Volunteer Reserves, I was not a member of the RAF and probably never would be. It was however his job to teach me how to fly, and I was about to commence my ab initio Pilot's Course. He continued that, just because the RAF were expanding and I had joined the Volunteer Reserve, I had so far had it easy, but unless I achieved the RAF's high standard of excellence for all Pilots, I would find it just as easy to leave.

This down to earth language I fully understood, and it was typical of the attitude of the regular members of the RAF who did not agree with the formation of the Royal Air Force Volunteer Reserve, which was so different from the Head of the Cambridge Centre, Air Vice Marshal Sir Tom Webb-Bowen.

My Instructor knew I had attended lectures on the theory of flight, and so he commenced by showing me round a Tiger Moth Aircraft, and how the controls worked. By standing on the wings and leaning inside the cockpit, he showed me how the control column operated by pulling it back to make the aircraft climb, and by pushing it forward to make the aircraft dive. Also, the effect the rudder bar had on the tail of the aircraft, and in conjunction with the control column, how to make the aircraft turn.

Of course this all fitted in with the lectures I had attended, and the fact that I had held the controls during my air experiences with Roger Frogley (which Grace was unaware of). He then showed me how to start a Tiger Moth by turning the propeller to suck in petrol vapour and, after putting the switches in the 'Up' position and giving the propeller a final swing, all things being equal, the engine should fire into life, but before doing this, always make sure that the wheel chocks are in position before the final swing.

101

And so, when my instructor asked me if I fully understood my first practical airmanship lecture, I was able to answer in the affirmative.

"Right", he said, "Let's go and get our flying gear on and we will take a flip round the top sides."

There has to be a first time for everything, and putting on my Sidcot I was most uncomfortable. It was far too big for me, and when I zipped it up to my throat, I could hardly move my head.

Worse was to follow for when I put on my leather gauntlet gloves with the silk inner gloves, I had very little feeling in my hands, and it was impossible for me to put my flying helmet on, and so I had to take my gloves off to do this.

Having finally overcome my difficulties, I slung my parachute over my shoulder, and went out to the aircraft where Flight Lieutenant Grace was waiting for me.

"Where the hell have you been Gibson?", he said, "I thought you'd chickened out".

"Sir", I said, "this is the first time I have dressed like this, and it took longer than I thought it would."

"I expect there are lots of things I am going to try and teach you which will take longer than you thought Gibson", was my instructors reply.

To use a northern expression I said to myself, "Right Monkey", and started to put on my parachute.

"Who showed you how to do that?", Grace said.

"When I was being shown how to pack a parachute I was shown how to wear a Pilot's harness – Sir", was my reply.

"Right", said Grace, "Jump in the aircraft and I'll show you how to strap yourself in".

After he had done this I said, "OK Sir, I give in, I'll go quietly".

"Go quietly, go quietly, what the hell do you mean?", asked Grace.

"Well", I said, "with my flying clothes on I was dressed up like dog's dinner, and now you have imprisoned me in this cockpit so that I find it impossible to move, there must be a better way to learn how to fly than this."

"Don't be impertinent Gibson, we'll take off and just do a familiarisation trip, and I'll decide how we go on from there", said Grace.

"OK Sir", I said.

And then it happened.

The engine burst into life as if by magic, and I heard Grace say 'chocks away', and we started to move over Marshall's grass airfield which was so bumpy I though I was on the Cake Walk at the local Fair Ground. It was so rough I had to laugh; I thought Grace was getting his own back, but that wasn't so as after a bit I heard Grace say, "I am turning into the wind, Gibson, prior to take off".

If the taxiing of the aircraft was rough, for the next few seconds, despite being trussed up like a Christmas turkey, I was tossed around so much I found I had a little freedom.

I thought it was strange that the taxiing and take off at Roger Frogley's airfield was not rough like this, and then I remembered, Roger used to keep sheep, and his airfield was as smooth as a Billiard's table.

I was now perfectly relaxed, but Grace had to spoil my reverie by asking "Are you still there Gibson?"

"Sir!" I replied.

"You still want to learn how to fly don't you Gibson?", was my Pilot's next comment.

"Yes Sir, but I am most uncomfortable" was my reply.

"If you continue in this vein, we are not going to get anywhere Gibson, and you will find flying a fighting aircraft can bring you into the most uncomfortable positions, but right now, all I want you to do is pay attention."

This remark upset me a bit; I was 23 years of age and, working at Chivers, was not used to being spoken to like that.

Grace then explained the most important thing to learn was to keep a good lookout. I was told to look around not just in front, but left, right, and above, and as this was a flight to gain air experience, he would demonstrate the action of the controls.

The word 'Look' was the executive word to be as I remembered Mr. Griffiths, my elementary school teacher, saying, the most important word in the dictionary was the word 'LOOK', and so as ordered I started to look to the left, to the right, and all around, and when my instructor suddenly screamed at me, "Stop taking the piss Gibson; I said look around you, not waggle your head around like a strangulated turkey!".

Of course, there was no answer to that, and then I noticed for the first time Grace had a rear-facing mirror and could see what I was doing in the rear cockpit.

"Right, Gibson, I've had enough of this, notice how I bank the aircraft to the left, which we call 'port', as I return to base."

"OK Sir" I said, and the remainder of the trip was carried out in utter silence.

As soon as we touched down, if I had not been strapped in, I would have been tossed around like pennies in a moneybox. Grace got out of the aircraft and stormed off, and it was some seconds later before I found out how to release myself. I found it quite difficult to get out of a Tiger Moth wearing a pilot's parachute, and I must say I was most clumsy, and it wasn't a pretty sight.

Grace was waiting for me on my return to the crew room, and I noticed he was not wearing a Sidcot flying suit, but a huge tweed overcoat, much more comfortably dressed than a Sidcot.

The first thing Grace said to me, "Well – that was a bit of a disaster wasn't it; do you usually wind people up like that?" Before I could reply, he carried on, "I will forget that trip ever happened and we will start afresh next time." I said, "OK Sir," "And by the way Gibson, when you want to talk to an officer, it is 'Yes Sir' or 'No sir', not 'OK Sir."

I just stopped myself in time from saying 'OK Sir', when I replied 'Yes Sir!", and off he flounced!

One of my colleagues came over to me and said, "What was all that about?". I said, "I don't really know!" "Oh, come off it Gibby,

104

you obviously upset your Instructor", he replied. "Well, maybe I didn't hit it off with Flight Lieutenant Grace, but as you heard, he is going to give me another chance", I said. "Consider yourself to be a lucky bastard; if you carry on like that it will be a Bowler Hat for you". "A Bowler Hat, what do you mean" I replied, "It'll be back to civvy street to you", he said. "Well, we'll see about that" I said, and got changed in a very sombre mood.

The weather was bad the following weekend, so there was no flying.

My next flight with Flight Lieutenant Grace was like chalk and cheese; he was absolutely charming and I responded accordingly. He helped me into the rear cockpit of the tandem seated aircraft; he helped me strap myself in, and, surprise surprise, he asked me if I was comfortable.

This time I noticed Airmen hovering around, checking the position of the chocks against the wheels of the undercarriage to prevent it from leaping into the air when the engine was started. I remembered to connect my voice tube into the intercommunication system and waited, and then I noticed how easy Grace made it look getting into the front cockpit. He showed great dexterity and made it look easy. Grace then said to the ground crew, "Switches off", and the airmen started to swing the propeller to suck in petrol vapour, after which Grace said, "Switches on", and the airmen gave a final swing of the propeller and the engine started first time.

Grace waved to the airmen who then pulled the chocks away, and he then started to taxi out.

He said, "Can you hear me Gibson?",

"Yes Sir, loud and clear" I replied.

"Well, that's a good start, let's keep it that way".

I said, "I will do my best, cubs' honour!"

As we were taxiing out, Grace said, "See the wind sock Gibson, what do you think the wind speed is?"

"30 knots Sir" I replied without any hesitation.

"Knots?" said Grace, "Who's been telling you about knots?"

"In our navigation lectures Sir, we always deal in knots".

"Well, look in front of you Gibson, and you will see an airspeed indicator which is in miles per hour, so lets stick to mph."

"Very good Sir, estimated wind speed is therefore 33 mph."

"OK", said Grace, "I'm turning into wind."

I thought, it's alright for him to say OK, but I can't!

"Always look around you Gibson before turning into wind to make sure it's clear for take off", he said.

At that he opened the throttle, and bumpity bumpity bumpity we went, with my cheeks wobbling due to the vibration, and before I could say I wish I had never joined, we were airborne, and – oh what joy to look around and see Terra Firma from the air.

Grace then said, "We will climb to 3,000 feet, but always keep a good lookout because, remember, we are not the only ones flying. Look at the panel in front of you Gibson, and you will see it shows an airspeed indicator to show you your airspeed, an altimeter to show you your height, and an artificial horizon to show you whether you are flying straight and level; are you with me Gibson?" "

Yes Sir" I said.

"You're not looking around you Gibson!".

Oh Gawd! I thought, he tells me to look at the aircraft panel, and he expects me to look around at the same time!

"Do you see that instrument with the two pointers? That is your turn and bank indicator. It tells you how steeply an aircraft is banked in a turn, and whether you are slipping in or skidding out of the turn. Pay attention and I'll demonstrate."

We then did a steep turn to port, and Grace said, "Don't touch anything, just watch. You will see that one pointer shows the degree of turn which we call banking, and the other pointer stays in an upright position. Therefore, the banking pointer shows we are doing a rate one turn, and the upright pointer shows we are doing a perfect turn, neither slipping in or skidding out; have you got that?"

I was then shown what an aircraft did when the turn was not perfect, and Grace continued, "That's all for now; we will deal with it in greater detail at a later stage."

That remark cheered me up, and I was hoping it was not just a figure of speech and that there would be a later stage in my training to become a pilot when 'you know who' said, "Are you looking around?" I was looking around, and I was told to look on my compass and tell him how far we had turned. It was a nice, sunny day and I could tell him from the direction of the sun, we were going back the way we had come, and so I said, "180 degrees Sir." "That's good Gibson; now on our way back you can handle the controls. Put your feet on the rudder bar and take hold of the control column, and try to keep flying straight and level."

This was not the first time I had done this as Roger Frogley let me fly straight and level, and so, although my attempt was not bad, he yelled, "Relax Gibson! Don't hold the control column as if you are going to fall out!" As a consequence things started to go wrong, and Grace said, "OK – I've got her", and I thought, 'thank God for that because I don't know where we would have finished up.'

"We are now going to do a circuit and landing; pay attention and I will talk you through what is happening". I was looking around and suddenly, dead ahead, I saw Marshall's Flying Field.

"Keep a good look out and make sure all is safe for us to land. I am throttling back to lose height to 500 feet – I am now flying cross wind – I am now turning on the down wind leg, and now onto the cross wind leg, and finally into wind to do a glide in approach and landing," Grace explained.

We touched down, and then bumpity, bumpity, bump, I was again being shaken to pieces and thought the Tiger Moth was going to fall to bits, but it was not long before we came to a halt and taxied back to within close proximity of our crew room. Airmen were waiting, and they put chocks under the wheels of the undercarriage.

Grace was out of the aircraft and walking back to the crew room before I had even unstrapped myself.

My colleagues, who remembered the contretemps I had previously had with my Instructor at the end of my very first flight were waiting to know how I had got on. I told them I thought it was a little better, and one of my friends said, "I think you're right, because Flight Lieutenant Grace came into the crew room smiling, and that doesn't happen often!"

It was quite some time before I flew again as I was only able to fly at weekends, whereas quite a few of my colleagues worked for Marshall's Garage in Cambridge and could get time off work to fly during the week.

At that time a film was showing in London which featured a breakfast scene, and a Public Relation's exercise had been arranged with the cinema circuit in London for a display of Chivers Olde English Marmalade to be erected on a Friday in the forecourt of the cinemas, and for several weekends a Chivers van used to take me around to put these displays up, and take them down again the following Monday. Therefore, I used to spend the weekend at home in Seven Kings. It seemed also that the weather at weekends was unsuitable for trainee pilots; however I was amassing loads of information from the evening lectures at the VR Centre, especially in the subjects I was really interested in, such as: Navigation, Bombing and Gunnery, Air Photography etc.

On this latter subject I will always remember the Sergeant Instructor's definition of Infinity. His definition was, "To the west of Blackpool there is a small island called Isle of Mann, and to the west of that is a larger island called Ireland, and to the west of that there is a large rock, called Rockall, and beyond that there is 'Bugger All', and that's Infinity." Of course, we all roared with laughter, and I learnt at that early stage in my Air Force career, if one can bring humour into the instruction, the chances of remembering certain details are enhanced.

Apart from my efforts to learn to fly, I was busy at my job as a Commercial Artist. It was a fascinating job. There were just two of us on the production side in the Advertising Department, and my superior, Bill Toms, told me that there had been 160 applicants for my job, and I couldn't believe my luck, but in the due course of time I worked it out. Bill did the first selection after seeing specimens of my work. He had given me preference firstly because I was a Londoner, and secondly because I had served my apprenticeship at Retouching Photographs, and this was a skill he was keen to learn! Also, Chivers' Advertising Manager was a Scotsman, and as my name - Bruce Stuart Gibson - was very Scottish, and in Dundee the name Gibson is as common as Smith, and he thought I was Scottish!

Weather permitting, at weekends we would do Circuits and Bumps, during which, very early on, Grace had demonstrated the effect of stalling and spinning, and as a result my Airmanship was improving.

Despite the fact I never seemed to do anything right when flying a Tiger Moth, after only 8 hours Grace sent me solo. My take off, circuit and approach was passable, but when I touched down, it was so bumpy, I opened up and went round again. My second landing was just as bumpy, but after a bit I came to a halt which I thought was alright, but Grace gave me such a bollocking I was thoroughly demoralised. As I was unable to fly as often as some of my colleagues, I had only clocked 8 hours flying time while others had amassed 50 hours plus, and were flying Fairy Battle aircraft. Apparently my going round again had scared the living daylights out of Flight Lieutenant Grace. He thought I was going to 'prang', but as soon as I had made up my mind to go around again, I trimmed the aircraft for take off, and so all was well.

But I was completely incompatible with my instructor. Nothing I did was right. Even when I seemed to fly straight and level, or performed any other manoeuvre satisfactorily, he would 'Ball me out' for not looking around. There was just no pleasing him, and as soon as the Observer Branch of the VR was formed, I did an immediate transfer to this new branch. Soon after this, I was in the VR Centre's anteroom waiting for friends to go into dine, when who should come in but Flight Lieutenant Grace.

He came straight up to me and said, "I hear you've transferred to the Observer Branch".

"Yes Sir" I replied, "I think I will make a much better navigator than pilot".

"Be that as it may", said Grace, "And I wish you well, but I think you've chickened out".

This confirmed to me our incompatibility, which made me more determined than ever do to well as an Observer.

* * *

8

War is declared

For the previous six months before war was declared, I was working on the finished drawings for the 1940 Chivers' jelly advertising campaign in India. I was so concerned about Hitler's aggression that, try as I did, I found it impossible to concentrate, and I never did finish the scraper board sketches of the various jelly recipes for India.

In March 1939, Mr. Chamberlain gave a solemn undertaking to defend Poland in the event of an attack by Germany.

In April 1939, Chamberlain vowed to go to the aid of Holland, Denmark and Switzerland if they were attacked.

In May 1939, Chamberlain warned Hitler that if force were used in Danzig, it would mean war.

By many acts of appeasement, Mr. Chamberlain had done his best to curtail Hitler in his inspirations, but, he had failed.

On 1st September 1939, German troops invaded Poland, and I was mobilised.

I had to report to my Chairman, Mr William Chivers, that I had been mobilised, and he was surprised to learn that I had become a trained Navigator in the Volunteer Reserve, and he wished me well.

I said good-bye to all my friends at Chivers, especially Bill Toms, my immediate boss, and Clifford Richardson who, being a Lay Preacher, said he would remember me in his prayers.

On 3rd September 1939 Mr. Chamberlain announced we were at war.

I was ordered to report to Marshall's aerodrome in Cambridge and, although I was a Leading Aircraftsman in the RAF, I was still in civilian clothes. My first job was guarding Marshall's Aerodrome.

Marshall's was a civilian organisation taken over by the RAF. I was one of a patrol of six airmen whose duty it was to patrol the Aerodrome boundaries from 8.00 am until 8.00 pm daily, when we were relieved by a night patrol, until we returned at 8.00 am the next day.

I was later to find out these guard duty hours were not allowed in the RAF, but we were still acting like civilians. The proper guard duty hours, I was to learn, were two hours on guard duty and four hours off, around the clock.

September 1939 was a month of glorious sunshine all day, every day, and apart from a few Tiger Moth aircraft parked around the perimeter of the airfield, there was nothing to guard. On the far side of the airfield was a haystack, and after patrolling the boundary of the airfield once, with one of our patrol left as a lookout, the rest of us used to climb on top of the haystack and play Solo Whist all day.

It was during that time I got to know a man named Lodge. Lodge had previously served a four-year short serviced commission and was a trained pilot on reserve, and therefore he had been mobilised like the rest of us. However, while on reserve, he joined the RAFVR as an Observer.

Lodge was a mature gentleman, and his peacetime job was as a Special Detective at Scotland Yard. One of his jobs was to protect the Prince of Wales. This was an arduous task as he always had to be in close proximity to the Prince, but at the same time be invisible, which was not easy.

Lodge had a fund of stories about the difficulties of guarding the Prince, and he was always glad at the end of a day escorting the Prince to his place of abode and locking him up for the night. The squad protecting the Prince had sleeping quarters near to the Prince, and many were the times in the middle of the night their telephone would ring with the message, "Your Prince is at our night club again getting drunk, please come and take him home!" They never did find out how the Prince 'broke out' and eluded them!

After a few weeks guarding Marshall's Aerodrome, I was posted to

Northampton Technical College for a RAF Navigation Refresher Course. During that time I was kitted out with my uniform displaying the badges of rank of a Leading Aircraftsman. We were billeted out in private accommodation, and nothing of note happened.

Our practical air navigation was done in Anson aircraft flying from Sywell Aerodrome. In the evenings and at weekends, my fellow Observers would tour the pubs in Northampton, usually finishing up in the 'Black Boy'. That didn't suit me because I don't like the smell or taste of alcohol, and so I used to drift off and spend my time at the Roller Skating Rink.

From Northampton we were posted to Squire's Gate Aerodrome to do a six-week Sea Navigation Course, where I learnt the art of 'Dead Reckoning Navigation'. We boarded the train at Northampton at 0830 hours and arrived at Squires Gate at 1500 hours.

There were six of us Observers on this course from the Cambridge Centre, one of whom was my friend Joe Brayley. It was pouring with rain as we approached Blackpool, and I said to Joe, "I'm not walking in this weather," and Joe said, "Let's take a taxi". You see, we were still thinking like civilians. But this Air Force had other ideas. We were met at Squires Gate Railway Station by a Warrant Officer and two Sergeants, who said, "You lot – get fell in!". It was not only raining 'cats and dogs', but there was a gale force wind blowing, and we were all wearing our brand new Greatcoats. It was only about a quarter of a mile from the railway station to Squires Gate Aerodrome, but by the time we got there we were soaked to the skin.

It was about 1520 hours when we arrived at the Airman's Mess, soaking wet, and remember we had not had anything to eat since our breakfast in Northampton at 0700 hours, and we were starving. We were the first RAF contingent to arrive at Squires Gate, which was run by civilians, and we were about to have our first RAF meal in uniform. I was ravenous, and the soup provided was piping hot and delicious. This was followed by what looked like onion gruel, but it smelt good, was hot, and as I was still hungry, got stuck in, and it was gorgeous!

By the time I had devoured a huge portion of whatever it was, I noticed that Joe had not touched his meal, and I said, "Joe, aren't you hungry?". Joe said, "I could eat a horse, but I can't eat that stuff!" I said, "But Joe, its lovely", and Joe replied, "I can't eat tripe and onions". That was a dish my mother disliked intensely and therefore had never cooked it for our family, so I replied, "but I don't like Tripe and Onions, but that was lovely!", and so I ate Joe's dinner as well much to his amazement.

We were still wearing our Greatcoats which were sodden. It was so hot in the Airman's Mess that our greatcoats were steaming, and after our meal we were marched to a billet which was a wooden shed, because Squires Gate was what the Air Force called a 'Hutted Camp'.

There were 32 of us airmen, and we were each given a canvas sack (which we found out was called a palliase) and this we had to fill with straw to make a bed. We were each allocated a bed space and, with 16 of us each side of the shed, this was to be our living space for the next six weeks.

So, with a bed space, by the side of which was our kitbag with our sole worldly possessions, we were issued with a pillow case, which again we had to fill with straw; 2 sheets, and 3 blankets, after which we had to make our bed. We were then 'Stood Down', and were free until 'Lights Out' at 2200 hours. That meant we had about 5 hours to kill, and so Joe and about six others decided we would walk into Blackpool.

By this time the rain had stopped, but it was still blowing a gale. We walked down to the front, but the waves were so high that, as they hit the sea wall, the spray of water was about 30 feet high and came right over the width of the road, soaking us still further. We were like drowned rats. If our mum's could have seen us, we would have been given a hot bath and put straight to bed!

When we got to the centre of town the wind was still blowing a gale, but there was no sea spray. The shops were still open along what we were to discover was the 'Golden Mile', and the first shop

Joe made for was a fish and chip shop where he had a meal to staunch his hunger. We slowly made our way back to camp which was about 3 miles, and with no rain or sea spray but with a gusty wind, by the time we returned, our Greatcoats and trousers were completely dry.

Then came new adventures; to sleep in a wooden shed ('Hutted Camp'), with 31 other men, many of whom I had only known for a few weeks. Each bed space was about three feet apart, and I discovered the RAF provided only the bare necessities of life, and for the first time I had to sleep in my under pants. Up to this time, whenever I went to bed, I would sleep the sleep of the just, and for all intents and purposes I was dead to the world for at least six hours. But, from my first night's sleep in communal circumstances, apart from finding it difficult to go to sleep, at the slightest sound or if anyone changed their mind, I would be wide-awake and raring to go. Alas – it has been like that ever since!

One of our colleagues was Acting Corporal. It was his job to receive instructions and pass them on to the rest of us. It was also his job to see lights out at 2200 hours. That first night I found it impossible to sleep on a straw sack, and I was not alone, for although those of us who had braved the storm and had walked a distance of 7 miles to the centre of Blackpool and back were completely knackered, we still could not sleep. Therefore, we did the next best thing - we talked.

Most of my colleagues were 18 or 19 years of age, and I was 26, and so it seemed quite natural for me to have more to talk about than the others. It was several nights before we got our Palliases to sleep on to our liking, and it became quite normal for talking to take place before we drifted off into the unknown.

Being young men, most of the talk consisted of dirty stories, of which I seemed to know more than any of my colleagues. There were two stories in particular which had universal appeal. The stories were so popular that I was called upon two or three times a week to do a repeat performance, but no matter how many times I told those stories, my bed mates always joined me in the 'punch line', and it always got a laugh. The first went as follows:

> *A newly married couple in bed, and Joe says, "Do you know, Lisa, your breath smells like new mown Hay?". "Does it really Joe, does my breath really smell like new mown Hay?" "Yus, Lisa, your breath really does smell like new mown Hay, after it has passed through a horse!"*

The second story was about the Salvation Army, and went:

> *"There was time when I used to go out every night with the boys, and get drunk – go home – beat the living daylights out of the wife, and then make her cook a full English breakfast, and then I wouldn't eat it. But since I joined the Salvation Army all that has changed. I no longer get drunk and beat the wife up and as I stand here beating this Drum. I feel so bloody happy I could kick this F****** Drum in!"*

Another popular ditty was

> *"Sister Susannah will carry the Banner"*
> *"But I carried it last week"*
> *"And you'll carry the Bloody Banner this week!"*

with everybody joining in with the punch line.

Our Course attended lectures on most days, but every third day we would do practical Navigation in Anson aircraft. These aircraft were piloted by civilian pilots, most of whom were ex RAF pilots, but they all had a sound knowledge of Navigation and were able to make sure we were doing our job properly so that they didn't get lost. For these exercises there were two Navigators per aircraft, and we used to share the aircraft's Navigation Table.

There were about six Navigators from Cambridge on this course, and it was noticeable how much further advanced we were than some of our colleagues. This necessitated some of our backward students staying on after working hours to catch up, but Joe and I decided to see the pleasures of Blackpool.

On one occasion we saw a poster advertising Ballroom Dancing Lessons, and I said to Joe, "I'd like to have a go at that", and so we joined a Ballroom Dancing Class. That gave us female contact which Joe and I thoroughly enjoyed. These classes took place in Blackpool, and we always stayed until the end which made us late getting back into camp. When that occurred, instead of going past the Guard Room on our return, we would climb over the perimeter fence and break into camp to avoid being charged with being absent without leave after 2200 hours and 'lights out'.

We were doing this one night, and as we were walking back to our barrack room, a voice suddenly said, "Where do you think you are going?" To our amazement we were being challenged by one of our Flying Instructors who had recognised us, and I said, "We are going back to our Barrack Room Sir". He said, "No you're not, come with me". He took us to a room that had been specially prepared with just two beds. The Officer said, "You two will have to sleep here for a bit, because while you have been gallivanting about in Blackpool, one of your colleagues has been taken ill with Meningitis, and the rest of your Course are to be kept in isolation. On no account are you to return to your barrack room." Joe said, "Well, that's a turn up for the book", and on looking around our new quarters we discovered all of our personal belongings had been brought to our new bed space.

This changed everything for us as we were the only ones of our course who were allowed to go to the Airman's Mess for breakfast. Our colleagues were kept in strict isolation and had their meals taken to them.

But there were bigger problems to follow.............

Squires Gate was a civilian run organisation with civilian Teachers and Pilots. There were enough aircraft to get the whole of our 32 members of our course airborne, but there was only Joe and I able to fly, and so while those in isolation were having lectures on navigation in their Barrack Room, Joe and I were kept airborne. We got so far advanced doing our practical navigation, sometimes doing the same exercise two or three times, we left the rest of our course far behind in their flying exercises.

Joe and I were given a précis of the lectures we had missed, and these we studied in the evenings, which curtailed our dancing lessons for a bit, but meant we had the best of both worlds. Not only were we kept up to date with the theory of Navigation, we also had an abundance of flying experience in which to practice those theories. This went on for a whole month during the Isolation Period when Joe and I were fully employed in the evenings swotting away, but Joe had made friends with his dancing partner and he would keep the dates they had made.

When the one-month Isolation Period was up, Joe and I returned to our billet and were welcomed with open arms. Apparently the one thing they had missed most were my funny stories.

When Joe returned from his dates in Blackpool after 'lights out', he would creep into our Barrack Room and back to his bed space without alerting our Corporal or disturbing the rest of us, and all would be well.

One night, with the cooperation of my roommates, I decided to give Joe a little surprise on his return from his date. I laid a staggering line of kit bags from the Barrack Room door to Joe's bed space, and after 'lights out', we all waited with baited breath for Joe's return. Sure enough, Joe crept into our room in the pitch-black darkness and fell, arse over head, into the second obstacle. Joe's language was not what one would expect during polite conversation! He made such a noise that the Corporal switched the lights on, much to the delight of our roommates witnessing the chaos. I was not able to take part in the hilarity as I knew Joe would accuse me for his unceremonious entry, and so I made out I was asleep. When Joe recovered his equilibrium, he said, "I know who did that, it was Gibson the bastard!" My friends said, "No it wasn't; Gibby's asleep." Joe didn't believe that and he came and sat on my bed, but I was able to concentrate with such effect, I ultimately drifted off into the lap of the God's with Joe still sitting on my bed, nursing his embarrassment.

I am proud to admit that my colleagues never broke rank, and no one ever divulged to Joe that it was me who set that trap for him.

At breakfast the next morning nothing was said about the previous night's incident, but everyone who came face to face with Joe just smiled or burst out laughing. At our mid morning NAAFI coffee break I went up to Joe and, with a dead pan straight face, said, "Did you enjoy your date last night Joe?". Everybody except me, who had a look of amazement on my face, burst out laughing at which Joe joined in.

Before the war most people led a parochial life and did not travel much. I had read about Blackpool and its 'Golden Mile', and what a wonderful seaside resort it was, but I had never been there. To be able to investigate the Tower and the other attractions in my off duty hours was most exhilarating, and although the Navigation course was quite arduous, I was really enjoying myself.

One of the most important factors Sir Tom Webb-Bowen used to impress upon us with was to always tell the truth because the life of a comrade might depend on it. Truthfulness came to my rescue on one navigation exercise. It was on a Sunday, and the whole course was sent on a Radius of Action exercise. This meant flying out into the Atlantic on the first course, after a given length of time doing a dog leg, and on the final course to intercept the Flying Scotsman travelling from Euston to Edinburgh on the long straight stretch from Preston to Lancaster.

We had been told at our briefing the time the train would be on this stretch of railway track. All went well, but when I arrived at the time I was expecting to intercept to achieve my aim, there was no Flying Scotsman. I was doing this exercise with my favourite Pilot, a Sergeant Cook, and with his co-operation, we flew up and down the railway track. Although we saw many other trains, alas, there was no Flying Scotsman. I was completely crestfallen. Sergeant Cook said to me, "What are you going to do, Gibson, because this thing doesn't fly on air?!" I said, "I don't know Sergeant." "Right", said Cook, "but I know - give me a course for base!. This I did, and because Cook had helped me flying up and down the railway line searching for the bloody train, we were the last ones to land back at Squires Gate.

I reported to the Operations Room to hand in my log and to attend the debriefing only to find I was the only one who had not found the Flying Scotsman. My colleagues started to take 'the piss', but I had no answer to their comments.

The debriefing was taken by our Chief Flying Instructor, and I knew him well, because during the isolation period I had navigated for him on many exercises.

He questioned each one of us in turn, and being the last to land, I was the last one to be questioned. So, when it came to my turn he said to me, "And what time did you intercept the Flying Scotsman, Gibson?" Utterly miserable, I had to admit I had failed.

There was much laughter from my colleagues at my incompetence, but the debriefing officer continued to question those who had claimed success, and when the banter at my expense was getting out of hand, the Chief Instructor said,

"Steady on now, I don't know who sent you on this exercise, but Gibson is the only one telling the truth because the Flying Scotsman doesn't run on a Sunday!"

I went from utter despair to total exhilaration, and I felt very smug. My friend Joe Brayley told everybody to shut up by saying,

"You want to watch our friend Gibby; he's a cunning old bastard!"

That night in our straw beds after the dirty jokes period, I sang my party piece, which goes as follows:

When I was young and seventeen I found I had a thing
I stood before the looking glass and put one finger in
But now I'm old and seventy seven my thing has lost it's charm
For I can put five fingers in and half my bloody arm!

Many were the times I had to sing this ditty with my colleagues joining in the 'punch line'!

* * *

9

All Navigators is Bastards!!

Joe and I very quickly caught up with our colleagues on the theory of navigation that we had missed due to the Meningitis scare, but we still had the advantage over them, having flown all of the flying exercises many times.

The art of navigation is to be able to solve the triangle of velocities. This triangle consists of 6 forces, which are Course and Air Speed, Wind Direction and Wind Speed, and Track and Ground Speed. That is the most simplistic of affairs.

Get any one of those wrong and one is in trouble.

When an aircraft gets airborne it moves within a column of air, which is moving at a certain speed, and also varies with height. That is why a navigator's job is to continuously check that his track and ground speed is correct. To do this, alterations to course have to be given to the pilot, which sometimes starts an argument.

That is why a Pilot's definition of a Navigator is

"All Navigator's is Bastards!".

It is essential that pilots and navigators work as a team, and are happy with one another. Otherwise either one can make things very difficult for the other.

To quote a case in point, whilst we were flying over the Atlantic my pilot instructor suddenly said, "Gibson, I want to check you out on your map reading. Take this map and map read me to Banyard Castle, which I have marked on the map."

The Castle he wanted me to map read him to was in the Peak District.

I duly gave my pilot the course to steer together with the ETA

(Estimated Time of Arrival). Five minutes before my ETA, I went up to the front of the aircraft to look out, and surprise, surprise, the whole area was covered with a layer of snow, and bore no resemblance to the map I had in my hand. However, I had studied the map, and the Castle I was looking for was near a railway siding.

As my ETA approached, I recognised the railway siding, but there was no Castle there. I asked my pilot to circle the area while I checked my position, but my original ETA had been correct, and so I had to admit I could not find the Castle. Of course, I was looking for a large building with turrets etc, but after we had been circling for a few minutes, my pilot said, "Our map reading is not very hot is it?! What are you looking for Gibson?" "I'm looking for a Castle", I replied. "Well, Gibson, do you see that large bungalow near that railway siding down there – that's it!", he responded. "But that's not a Castle; how do you know?" I asked. "Because that Castle is owned by a friend of mine, and I'll be there this weekend" he said, and burst out laughing.

And of course when I realised he had pulled a fast one on me, I joined in on the hilarity.

"Right, Gibson, give me a course back to base, and we will have some lunch, and remember things aren't always what they seem," he continued.

I thought, 'Right Monkey!!', but all the way back to Squires Gate he was grinning like a Cheshire cat – he had got one over the bastard navigator.

It was nearly Christmas 1939 when our course had finished, after which we were entitled to wear the Observer's Brevet, but because Civilians were training us, there was no Brevet Parade; in fact we had to buy our own.

Because we were entering the Festive Season, a party atmosphere developed in our billet and a certain amount of horseplay was going on. At that time I was sporting the most disgusting moustache, and one of my colleagues, who had just won a game, was asked what he would like for his prize. Without hesitation he said he would like 'half of Gibby's moustache'. I said, "Not on your Nelly", but before I knew what was happening, I was being firmly held by my friends and, although I struggled, when a Cut Throat razor appeared, I realised it was a 'put up' job, and I allowed the one with the razor to do his duty, and cut off half of my moustache – of which I had been justly proud!!

On my return from ablutions, Joe Brayley said, "Bruce, you look quite handsome clean shaven, and remember it is the first sign of conceit when a man lets hair grow on his face." I immediately knew it was Joe's idea that my facial adornment be removed, and he was just getting his own back, which was fair enough, but I took Joe's comment to heart and have remained clean shaven ever since.

In addition to having earned the honour of being permitted to wear the Air Observer's Badge, we were all promoted to Sergeants, and it was quite fun sewing on our Sergeant's Badges of rank. This sorted everybody out, and those of us who had been taught by their mothers to sew had the pleasure of helping the others, some of whom could not even thread a needle!

The next stage of training for our course was to go to Number 3 Bombing and Gunnery School at Royal Air Force Station Aldergrove, which was in Northern Ireland. We took the ferry from Heysham to Belfast, across the Irish Sea, which took about 8 hours. We got friendly with an Irishman, and by plying him with Guinness, he sang Irish songs to us for the whole of the 8 hours! On arrival we were met by RAF transport, which took us straight to the Sergeant's Mess at Aldergrove.

This was a great improvement on Squires Gate Airman's Mess, but it still did not match the Cambridge Volunteer Centre's Mess where Air Vice Marshal Sir Tom Webb-Bowen reigned supreme, and where he had taught us how to conduct ourselves in an Officer's Mess.

As far as the War was concerned, we were in the doldrums, and apart from the odd leaflet raid we made on Germany, and the odd bit of haphazard bombing Germany made on this country, nothing

124

happened.

As far as Aldergrove was concerned, there was no sign that there was even a war on. In the Sergeant's Mess peacetime standards were being maintained. The sleeping quarters were much better (no straw beds), and the food was good. We had a full English breakfast, a cooked lunch, and tea was available at 1600 hours. At 1900 hours we had a four-course meal, and for those Sergeants who were still feeling a bit peckish, before retiring to bed there was always a joint of beef, lamb or pork, with cheese and biscuits left on the sideboard for any Senior NCO to help themselves.

When we awoke after our first night away from Blackpool, we were amazed to read at breakfast time that there had been a very heavy fall of snow, and Squires Gate had 14-foot snowdrifts. In Blackpool itself the snowdrifts were as high as double decker buses. Where we were in Northern Ireland there was no snow.

We couldn't believe our luck!

It must be remembered that on 1st September 1939 we had just been mobilised as Leading Aircraftsmen, and in less than four months, we had become Sergeants. This caused quite a bit of disquiet among the Senior NCO's at Aldergrove, and Sergeant Soloman (the only Jew I ever came across in the RAF), took it upon himself to sort us out. "You are not Sergeants", he said, "Do you see these?" (pointing to his chevrons), "It took me 18 years to get them, and you have been in 5 minutes, and yet you join me and my mates in our Mess. I'll show you during the next 6 weeks (the length of our course) you are NOT true Sergeants, so watch out!!"

Being the Spokesman for our course I said, "Sergeant, it is because we are Aircrew and hence are liable to be shot down and taken prisoner, that is why the Air Council, in their wisdom, have decided that we should be made Sergeants, because SNCO's, when taken prisoner, are treated with greater respect and are not given fatigues, and also it is to give us the rate of pay that is demanded by a Navigator's job." "Bollocks to that", said Sammy, which broke the tension and we all had a laugh.

But, Soloman was so riled by what he considered was the unfairness of it all, he decided to teach us a lesson. He picked on 6 of us, and reported us to a Warrant Officer for some trumped up misdemeanour. The Warrant Officer then appeared in our classroom just at the end of one of Sammy's lectures, and told us to remain while the rest of our course went to tea. Sammy repeated his complaint, and the Warrant Officer said, "Right, you 6, report back here at 1800 hours, and scrub all of these tables and chairs", and walked out. Sergeant Kidger, who in civilian life had been an Assistant Bank Manager, said, "He can stuff that, I'm not coming back."

It was left to me to reason with Kidger, after which we all reported back to our class room, and scrubbed the tables and chairs, and thoroughly enjoyed it for if I have anything to do with water, everybody has to have some, and I was surreptitiously splashing water around until I got caught and got thoroughly soaked.

But, it was fun, and this was witnessed by Sammy who was most perturbed because seeing us enjoying ourselves was not the object of the exercise.

Sammy, who had been chewing gum while supervising our work, went to inform the Warrant Officer our work was complete, while we returned our cleaning materials to the ablutions. The Warrant Officer inspected our work and, lifting up one of the tables, found a piece of chewing gum stuck underneath it. He said, "You haven't scrubbed underneath the tables; you will come back tomorrow night and scrub these tables and chairs from top to bottom – and do it thoroughly next time." I said, "Sammy, you bastard, you planted that chewing gum there", which he hotly denied, but none of us believed him.

Of course, we were still acting like airman students and it was later we discovered that Sammy had taught us a lesson because firstly, the Warrant Officer had no power to discipline us, and secondly, Sergeants cannot be punished by giving them fatigues.

When Soloman found out we had discovered our rights, he said,

"But I proved my point; if you lot had been proper Sergeants you would have known that!". We all had a good laugh and the matter was never referred to again.

When Joe and I found out that the Warrant Officer had no disciplinary powers over us I thought, "Right Monkey", and I decided to play a practical joke on him. His office had recently been fitted out with new telephone equipment, and so I went back to the Sergeants' Mess when there was no-one about and telephoned the Warrant Officer. I put a handkerchief over my mouth and told the Warrant Officer I wanted to check the newly installed equipment, and would he repeat after me, '1, 2, 3, 4, 5 – 5, 4, 3, 2, 1'

I said, "That's fine, now will you do a verbal check, and repeat after me, 'I cannot eat my currant bun'". After the Warrant Officer repeated that phrase I said, "Well, stuff it up your arse then!", and I put the phone down. I dashed back to where my course were having a coffee break and it was only Joe who had missed me, and he said, "Where have you been?" I said, "I've been to the toilet – I was caught short."

The Warrant Officer, try as hard as he did, failed to find the telephonist, mainly because he was interrogating the wrong people, namely members of his own staff. I don't know if he suspected any of our course. All I know is he gave us a wide berth for the rest of our stay there.

The theory of Bombing and Gunnery had been dealt with at our Volunteer Centre, but when we were able to drop bombs and fire guns, everything came together. The dropping of 11lb practice bombs on a target in Lough Neigh from 6,000 feet I found most exciting and, despite the possible pitfalls, such as height error, airspeed error or wind speed and direction error, I got above average results. In fact, applying the Theory of Bombing, I found a lot of it was common sense.

The Theory of Relative Speed and Apparent Speed when firing at a moving target was just as obvious, and I got excellent results firing on a Drogue, which was being towed by another aircraft over Lough

Neigh.

It was going to and returning from the Firing Ranges that I discovered what a beautiful country Northern Ireland is. We had to do these exercises very early, and our aim was to be in the target areas by 0600 hours as by 0800 hours the cloud would lower, and although we could continue with Gunnery exercises, High Level Bombing was out.

The low cloud would appear so regularly we used to call it 'Duty Cloud'. Our instructors used to take it in turns to organise these flying training programmes, and one particular Flight Sergeant Quinnell always blamed me when 'Duty Cloud' appeared. He said, "It's your fault Gibson, you are a Jonah!" He really believed this, and he would set me tasks which I had to do in the classroom, or he would send me on 'fools errands' to get me away from the Crew Room. This of course was stupid, and I was only able to perform my practical airborne work when Quinnell was not organising the flights.

One day, when a more sensible instructor had sent me to do some high level bombing, I had only dropped 4 bombs when 'Duty Cloud' started to appear, and my pilot, whose name was Pilot Officer Gibson, decided to abandon the exercise and return to base. It was only a few miles from Lough Neigh to Aldergrove Aerodrome, but 'Duty Cloud' raced us, and my pilot, in attempting to land, overshot, and suddenly a hangar came into view. My pilot yanked on the control column, and cleared the hangar, but the Fairy Battle Aircraft could not maintain that rate of climb and stalled before going into a flat spin and crashed from 600 feet.

I had already opened my cockpit and was flung clear. But my Pilot was trapped, and so I climbed onto the wing and together we opened the cockpit and got him out.

During this time our Practise Smoke Bombs decided to go off, and the aircraft was covered in smoke, and everyone thought the aircraft was on fire, but it wasn't so, and we were able to stagger out of the smoke zone, by which time the Fire Engine and Ambulance had arrived.

My Pilot had a gash on his forehead, and was a bit stunned, but I was OK, but still the medics in the ambulance insisted on taking both of us to sick quarters for a check up.

This was the first time I had received first aid treatment from RAF medical staff, and I was amazed at the care and attention I received, and I was having a cup of tea and chatting up the nurses when, who should visit me but Flight Sergeant Quinnell. When he found out I was alright, he said, "It wouldn't have happened if I had been on duty – two Gibsons in one aircraft is inviting trouble!"

We both laughed and I thanked him for his concern. But I still had the impression he really thought I was a Jonah.

The medics insisted we both lie down, but when no one was looking, I crept out and went and joined my course who were having a lecture. The Instructor, who knew about the crash, said, "What are you doing here?" and I replied, "You are my favourite Sergeant, and I did not want to miss your lecture." This was good for a laugh, and my colleagues all wanted to know the gory details of my crash, and that was the end of the lecture.

We were making such a commotion it attracted the attention of our Chief Instructor, a Squadron Leader who, when he found out I was OK, said "Well done Gibson – let's all go off and have a coffee break."

The stripping of automatic machine guns I found easier than stripping off to have a bath, and the name of each part and what it did presented no problem; even long names such as 'The prolongation of the left inner side plate', to be found on a Lewis Gun. I took to Air Gunnery like a duck to water, and I could strip a gun and put it back together again quicker than any of my colleagues.

After we had got the hang of it, we were left to our own devices to practise the handling of guns; therefore I treated it as a game, and organised competitions to see who was the fastest. I passed the Bombing and Gunnery Course with flying colours, so much so my next posting was to the Empire Air Armament School at RAF Manby in Lincolnshire, to become an Air Armament Instructor.

Whilst I was waiting for my clearance from Aldergrove, because I was always organising things, I was put in charge of the next course of 30 Observers to take them in 7 lorries to Belfast Docks to pick up five hundred 100 lb Bombs. This was a new experience for me because I had never been in charge of anyone before. I had only had myself to look after, rushing around like a mad thing, and here I was in charge of 30 airmen with a job to do.

I reported to the Armament Officer, who gave me two airmen experienced in handling bombs, and then off to the Transport Officer who had the lorries ready with experienced drivers, all of whom had done this job before and knew just where to go. I then went to brief the 30 Observers, and I was surprised to find among them two mature airmen, both about 30 years of age, and so I decided to find out more about them. One was an ex army man who had transferred from the army to the RAF to become a Navigator, and the other one was a Journalist who had joined the RAF to make himself more useful.

I collected the paperwork which authorised me to pick up my load and, having split the airmen up among the 7 lorries, off we went. The Transport Officer had detailed the drivers to drive in convoy, and I had told the drivers I would be in the last lorry should we meet any problems, and I settled down to relax for the 20 mile journey.

During this trip I discovered from my driver that my journalist student was nicknamed 'Mogg the mad photographer'. Apparently during his navigator training he was supposed to take 6 hand held oblique air photographs. His F23 Camera had a magazine of 125 negatives, and whilst airborne, instead of taking 6 shots of the surrounding countryside, he used the whole magazine and took 125 pictures, hence his nickname, 'Mogg the mad photographer'.

We arrived at Belfast Docks without incident, and I made my number with the Warehouseman who was expecting me, and I was taken to the storeroom where the bombs were being kept under lock and key. Each lorry had a sack truck especially adapted to carry bombs, and I got the Corporal Armourer to supervise the loading of the bombs on to the sack trucks, and 2 airmen wheeled the trucks to the lorries, where the other Armourer supervised the loading of the bombs from the sack trucks to the lorries.

All was going well when, at about 1330 hours, the Warehouseman approached me and said, "I am of the opinion that your Airmen are stealing food from the warehouse." As it was a Saturday, we were the only people in the warehouse. I was amazed at this information and said, "I am sure you must be mistaken as my airmen are honest, and they would never do such a thing."

Whilst I was defending the integrity of my airmen, I looked past the Warehouseman, and, to my horror, saw Mogg standing on a sack truck, and Lane, the ex army man, receiving items from a couple of my airmen and stuffing them into Mogg's uniform! I don't know how I did it, but I kept talking to the Warehouseman whilst walking back to his office.

As soon as I got rid of him, I dashed back to Mogg, who was still standing on the sack truck with Lane still stuffing things into his uniform, and said, "What the hell do you think you are doing? Get back to work!" Mogg said, "Don't ask me to move Sergeant; I've got oranges here", pointing to a bulk in his uniform, "and apples here", at which Lane interrupted, saying "Serge, it's nearly 1400 hours, and we haven't eaten since breakfast at 0700 hours. We're feeding the airmen; you go and make sure the Warehouseman keeps in his office."

This I did until we had finished loading the bombs, and I couldn't help thinking how right Sammy was – I wasn't a Sergeant – I still had a lot to learn.

Having checked the lorries were properly loaded, and that none of my airmen were missing, I found Lane sitting in my seat in the last lorry, and before I could turf him out, he said, "Sergeant, when we get back to the guard-room, they might want to inspect our load, but if you occupy the front seat and report, and tell them what we have been up to, it will save a lot of time."

That made a lot of sense, and as we were driving back to Aldergrove, I thought Lane should have been in charge of this chore.

On our return, I went into the Guardroom and told them that the convoy of 7 lorries, of which I was in charge, had returned with 500 bombs, and could I have permission to report straight to the Armament Officer. This permission was freely given, and off we went to the Armoury. As I was getting out of the lorry, Lane was at the door to open it for me, and he said, "Well done, Serge, we didn't want the Guardroom to find that case of butter you've been sitting on did we?!" "Lane", I said, "Don't get me involved in your nefarious activities, I am going to report to the Armament Officer, and I expect you to have the lorries clean on my return!"

The Armament Officer thanked me for helping him out as his Sergeant had gone on a 48-hour pass. I went back to my billet and told Joe Brayley what had happened, and he laughed his head off, but he reiterated what I had been thinking when he said, "You know Bruce, Sergeant Soloman was right about us, we've got a lot to learn."

That night at dinner in the Sergeants' Mess, the Warrant Officer in the Armoury congratulated me on a job well done, but Joe said to me, "If only he knew what really happened!"

I was 26 years of age at the time, and people today will find it strange when I say I had never been outside the UK before, not even to the Isle of Wight. Having crossed the Irish Sea, things were different and it was like being overseas. For example, there were certain roads in Belfast that were out of bounds to us in RAF uniform, and another thing that amazed me were the advertisements for domestic staff in the local newspaper which said 'Only Protestants need apply.' There is something sick about people who think like that. Here we were at war with Germany. I knew Sergeant Samson was a Jew (and you do not find many of them in an Air force), but so long as he did his job properly, the Service didn't care if he was a Plymouth Brethren or any other denomination.

Individually, the Irish are lovely people. On our first day in Aldergrove, four of us Sergeants, after we had settled in, went for a walk. We were walking through a village called Crumling and as we passed one house, we saw a little girl playing in the garden, and she rushed up to us and said "Hello". As we were chatting to her, her mother approached, and I thought she looked a little sad, and I asked her "Are you alright?" She replied, "Yes, my husband is a Colour Sergeant in the army on Reserve, and he had to report for duty today."

Naturally we commiserated with her, and she invited us in for a cup of tea, which we found delicious. She was a lovely lady with lovely big brown eyes, a typical Irish colleen.

* * *

10

At the Empire Air Armament School

I duly arrived at the Empire Air Armament School at Royal Air Force Station Manby in Lincolnshire. This was a permanently built Station, constructed of brick, and purpose built to teach Armament to all of the air forces in the British Empire.

The main instruction block was massive and was called 'Tedder Block', after our Marshal of the Royal Air Force. It was a square building with classrooms and offices on four sides, with a grass quadrangle in the middle. One of the lecture rooms was large and could accommodate 100 people. It had a blackboard the whole width of the room, and seats on rising levels. The wooden corridor floors were highly polished and gave the appearance of a prestige building.

It was only a three-week course that we were on, where we were taught how to teach Bombing and Gunnery subjects. The Station Commander was a Group Captain Ivans, who had been a Colonel in the Scots Guards and had got himself transferred to the RAF. He ran his Station as if it were an army unit, with strict army discipline. This was quite foreign to RAF personnel, and it was here that I had the chore of being Sergeant in charge of the Guard Room from 1800 hours until 0600 hours the next morning.

On arriving at the Guard Room at 1800 hours, the Sergeant I was about to relieve said, "Corporal 'So an So' is on with you. I'll see you at 0600 hours tomorrow", and left.

The Corporal soon realised I did not know what I was doing, and so he swung it on me, and said, "Sergeant, can you take over from me booking out these civilians, it's time for my supper break".

I was surprised how many civilians I had to book 'in' as well as 'out', but it was no problem, but after a bit an airman came up to me and asked if he could make some toast. I said, "Who are you?" he said, "I'm your prisoner, the Corporal let me out to go to the toilet."

There was a large cast iron round stove in the centre of the Guard Room with the chimney going up to the roof, and the heat generated was intense, and I said, "OK, make yourself some toast."

After a while, there was a smell of toast, and so I knew my prisoner was OK. A little while later there was a break in my booking in and out duties, and so I decided to see how my toast maker was getting on. To my surprise I found two airmen sitting, eating toast.

I said to the second airman, "Who are you?" and the airman replied, "I'm your other prisoner." I said, "Why have you got no shoes on?" and he replied, "The Corporal took them from me so that I can't escape." I said, "You had better get back to your cells", and as I was following them down the corridor, the one with no shoes asked, "Aren't you going to lock us in?" I replied, "Yes", and the first airman said, "OK, I'll show you where the keys are"

Just after I had locked my prisoners up, the Corporal arrived back from supper, and I related to him my episode with our prisoners, and he replied, "I'm sorry Serge, I forgot to tell you about them; by the way, have we still got two?" I answered, "Yes – why?" "Well", he said, "the one with no shoes has escaped three times". I said, "Corporal, go and see if we've still got two prisoners." The Corporal soon returned and said, "We've still got two", and then he told me that he had asked the one with no shoes why he had not escaped, and he had replied that I seemed to be a decent Sergeant as I had let them make toast, and he didn't want to get me into trouble!

I had to laugh to myself, and I thought, 'What a Fred Karno's Army'!

The Armament Instructor's Course was quite straight forward; there were specialist Instructors on the equipment about which we were going to teach, but the most important man was an ex army officer who taught us the best way to present a subject. He was very good. He showed us how to use the Blackboard, and how to illustrate lectures by the use of diagrams etc.

The Course ended with an examination where we each had to give a lecture lasting 20 minutes, and the piece of equipment I was given was a Detonator. I have never found it difficult to express myself verbally, but be that as it may, I went into Louth and bought some Poster Colours and Cartridge Paper, and made some coloured sketches of various different types of Detonators, and to cut a long story short, I returned to Aldergrove with the highest Instructors' Category of A1.

Gunnery was my favourite subject, and I was becoming an expert at teaching about automatic weapons. When I was teaching the Course who had done the fatigues at the Belfast Docks, there was a different spirit in the class, and I got the impression they had really enjoyed their day out from the usual routine.

I found out that Lane had served 12 years with the Royal Artillery before transferring to the RAF, and he was a proper 'old lag'. He knew the ropes of Service Life, and if any naughtiness was taking place, you could bet that Lane was the Ring Leader. Lane, Mogg, and two or three other airmen clubbed together and bought an old banger of a motorcar for £7.00. Today it would not pass an MOT, but it had a good engine. Mogg the Journalist was the only one who could drive, and these five airmen became quite well known visiting the local village pubs.

One day, a Blenheim Aircraft did a 'wheels up' landing and finished up on the far side of the aerodrome. After the dust had settled, Lane and company waited until it got dark, and milked the Blenheim of fuel and put it in their old banger. The petrol was High Octane, and when they started their car up, it nearly took off! The old engine had never been fed with anything like that before!!

After duty hours I used to go into Belfast to Albert White's Ballroom, and after a few visits, Albert White became my friend. He was a Yorkshire man, the salt of the earth.

He had a large Ballroom, and he only catered for the young. He had a Soda Fountain, and only soft drinks were served. The

Ballroom was on the first floor. At the street level entrance he had two doormen whose job it was not to allow anyone who was under the influence of drink to climb the stairs.

Halfway up the stairs was a platform where there were another two doormen who took the entrance money, and acted as a long stop to prevent any unwanted customers from entering.

Albert had a private bar behind the Bandstand, and in between dances I would join him and we would natter. He introduced me to a girl named Ida Parkinson who was a good dancer and I got to know her quite well.

She was a lovely Irish colleen, and on Sundays I would spend the day with her family. Her father owned a corner Grocery Shop, and her mother was an excellent cook and would produce wonderful meals which were a lot better than those in the Sergeants' Mess. Ida had three brothers, and all were strict Methodists. On Sunday evenings, I would join them at their Chapel where I was treated as one of the family.

Ida had a boyfriend whose father owned a gentleman's outfitters, and he became quite jealous of the way I was accepted by Ida's family.

One Sunday, I arrived at Ida's abode, and everything was different. Ida's father had a Bowler hat on and was wearing an Orange Sash, and with a rolled up umbrella over his shoulder, and was marching up and down the kitchen. I said to Ida, "What goes on?". Ida replied "It's the Battle of the Boyne celebrations; Dad always marches." I said to Ida, "But Ida, that was over 300 years ago!" Ida replied, "I know, but that doesn't stop them!". The change that had come over Ida's father was amazing; from being an ordinary, hospitable gentleman, he had become an 'Orange Order' bigot.

On one special occasion I was invited to the birthday party of one of Ida's brothers. All the family were there, including Ida's boyfriend, and it was noticeable that Ida was paying me far too much attention when Ida's boyfriend suddenly blurted out – "What goes on here?", and Ida's dad replied, "Bruce is a friend of the family and is welcome here at any time."

It was usual that after Chapel I would go back home with Ida, and have a coffee before returning to Camp, but on this occasion I made my excuses and got the early bus back to Aldergrove. The last thing I wanted was to cause trouble with Ida's Catholic boyfriend.

One day as I was walking from the bus stop to Albert White's Ballroom, when who should I bump into but a giant of a man in army uniform who I immediately recognised as Frank Swift, England's International goal keeper. I stopped and said to Frank, "I know you - what are you doing in Belfast?" He said, "I'm at a loose end; I'm a member of the Army Football team, and tomorrow we are playing Northern Ireland Football team in a friendly match." I said, "Let me buy you a drink, I'm on my way to Albert Whites – come and meet him, he will be delighted to meet you."

I introduced Frank to Albert, who immediately took us behind the Band Stand for refreshments, when Albert discovered the whole team had been given Railway passes and accommodation, but had been left to their own devices to amuse themselves until the match was to be played. This wasn't good enough for Albert, and he invited the whole team back to his country residence and put them up for the weekend!

Breaking my ties with Ida's family left me free at weekends, and I often stayed at Albert's house, where he had a full size Billiard's table, and we would play for hours on end.

Albert's policy of running a non-alcoholic Ballroom was a tremendous success as Mums allowed their daughters to attend, and, of course, where girls congregate, boys seem to follow, and the Ballroom was filled to capacity with 300 dancers, 7 nights a week.

Back at work I was gaining good experience teaching Bombing and Gunnery which I found quite easy and satisfying. Lecture periods were of one-hour duration; the first 40 minutes I passed on the 'Gen', and the remaining 20 minutes were spent answering questions or discussion. I became quite an expert on teaching the Browning Gun, and I could speak on this subject for 8 hours without repetition!

In March 1940, the IRA prisoners in Dartmoor Prison rioted, and over the Bank Holiday, Aldergrove was under threat of invasion. The Station Commander, in his plan for the defence of the aerodrome, employed every available Officer, Senior NCO's and airmen on this exercise. The only ones exempt were the Guardroom staff.

Every strategic point was manned, and machine gun posts were established every 50 yards around the perimeter of the Station. Aircraft used for Air Gunnery were placed on hard standings as additional deterrents to defend against would-be attackers.

We were all employed 24 hours a day, 2 hours on and 4 hours off. I was employed with my friend, Joe Brayley, manning an aircraft fitted with a Vicker's Gas Operated Gun. During the first week of this exercise I noticed in close proximity to where Joe and I were employed were the Accountant Officer and his staff.

In those days, the Airmen were paid every fourteen days at a Pay Parade, and I said to Joe, "The airmen are not going to get paid this Thursday." Joe said, "Why?" I said, "The Accountant Officer and his staff have been manning the section next to us and have been for the past ten days, and they have not had enough time to work out the airmen's pay, so they are not going to get any." Joe thought this was hilarious, and for the want of something better to do, we started to spread this rumour. We only did it for a bit of fun, but the effect was instantaneous. It had a domino effect, and spread through the camp like the bubonic plague, and mutiny was even suggested.

Within 48 hours the Station Commander had us all lined up on the Parade Ground and announced that "Some scurrilous individual has spread a rumour that there will be no Pay Parade this coming Thursday. You can take it from me that this is not true, and there will be a Pay Parade as usual, and if I find the perpetrator of this rumour I'll have his guts for garters!" Joe was standing next to me and, out of the corner of his mouth, said "Gibson – so there!"

So, everybody was happy and we all returned to our guard mounting duties. The IRA did not attack our aerodrome, but we maintained 100% defence of our Station until one week after the Bank Holiday. Joe and I had often spread rumours in the past, but none of them had had any serious effect, but we learnt for future reference never to start a rumour which effects Airmen's pay!

After duty hours I used to organise football matches between the various Wings, and Table Tennis matches in the Airmen's mess, and this became known to the Station Commander who in recommending me for a Commission, mentioned that I was an excellent Armament Instructor with good organising ability.

By the end of 1940 our morale was very low.

The French had capitulated, and our expeditionary force had been evacuated from Dunkirk.

Our Station Commander cleared the hangars of aircraft, and army personnel who had been evacuated from France were sleeping rough.

Most were unkempt, with parts of their uniform missing, and some without boots etc, and when not feeding at the Airmen's Mess, they were allowed to rest.

This went on for about two weeks until Mr. Churchill (who had just become Prime Minister), made an amazing declaration that:

> *"Even though large tracts of Europe, and many old and famous States have fallen, or may fall, into the grip of the Gestapo and all the odious apparatus of Nazi rule, we shall not flag or fail. We shall fight in France, we shall fight in the seas and the oceans, we shall fight with growing confidence, and in growing strength in the air; we shall defend our Island whatever the cost may be. We shall fight on the beaches, we shall fight on the landing-grounds,*

we shall fight in the fields and the streets, we shall fight in the hills; we shall never surrender!"

Up until that time, if Mr. Churchill had said we were going to pack up in the war against Hitler, we were ready to do so. But after that speech, everything changed. We were all raring to go.

The Station Commander had all of the army personnel on parade and everyone was individually inspected, and lists were made of the equipment needed to kit each soldier out.

RAF Physical Training Instructors started to get the men fit; parades were held, morale was high, and we knew with Churchill in charge, we were going to win the war.

The atmosphere was electric.

We all went about our duties with fresh vigour, when out of the blue I was posted along with a friend of mine, Maurice Hodget, to Number 9 Bombing and Gunnery School at Penrhos, North Wales.

We reported to Warrant Officer Smith who was in charge of Administration. He was delighted to see us as he was very short of Armament Instructors. Royal Air Force Station Penrhos was in the Tremadog Bay area, and we had firing ranges and bombing targets for our students to do their practical work.

Arriving in the Sergeants' Mess as Armament Instructors, we were accepted as Sergeants without the animosity spread by Sergeant Soloman at Aldergrove.

The Chief Instructor of the School was a Wing Commander Wray, nick named 'Hoppy', as he had a 'game-leg', which was the result of an aircraft accident. Hoppy was as brave as a lion, and everyone looked up to him. He had attended a six-month course and had become a Senior Armament Officer, and his supernumerary job was as a General Duties Officer. Every GD Officer had to have a supernumerary job as flying was not considered a full time occupation. Observers were always on a six-week course as they had to learn how to drop bombs as well as gunnery, whereas the Air Gunners' course lasted only three weeks.

Penrhos was a hutted camp, but quite comfortable. Here I learnt that there is nothing more difficult than working to a syllabus. The allocation of time for ground instruction was no problem, but to get students to drop the required number of bombs or fire the correct number of rounds of ammunition in our unpredictable weather was not so easy.

Lectures were from 0900 hours to 1700 hours daily; with a 36-hour break at weekends. I was sent to Boulton & Paul's factory in the Midlands on a fortnight's course to learn how to operate their 4 gun electric turret, and I returned as the 'Gen Kiddy' on B.P. Turrets.

There were 20 of us on this course from various units, and we had a coffee break in the mornings and a tea break in the afternoons where we were able to relax and be sociable. At these breaks, a charming young lady would join us who was about the same age as we were, and her company was well sought after.

During the course we did a tour of the factory, and it was noticeable that all female employees wore pretty overalls, but our lady visitor was always very smartly dressed in expensive clothes.

At one tea break I was chatting up our lady friend along with several others, when I said to her, "How come you don't wear a pretty overall like the rest of your staff?" She was drinking a cup of tea at the time, and she nearly choked. She put down her tea and rushed out of the room. The Instructor came up to us and asked, "What was all that about?" One of the group replied, "Gibby asked her why she was not wearing an overall." The Instructor replied, "Because she is a member of our executive staff, and she is a mathematician, and works out the stresses and strains of the aircraft we build etc,. Her salary is about six times greater than mine!" I put on my gormless look and said, "Oh!!", much to everyone's enjoyment.

Back at Penrhos, each course was allocated a Sergeant whose duty it was to attend to the welfare of those students. I was going through the formal details of one course I was responsible for, which contained the personal information, next of kin etc, when I noticed one student had annotated that his civilian employment had been that of a Funeral Director. So, during the next break, I got him to tell the course about his previous job.

I was absolutely amazed at what he told us.

The firm he worked for had all the local 'layer outs' on their books, and they were kept informed whom they could expect to be their next customer, so that they could have a coffin ready made. I asked, "Don't you take measurements?" He replied, "the 'layer out' provides those details, and" he added, "never provide an expensive shroud, because when we are sure no one else wants to see the corpse, just before we screw the lid down, we whip off the expensive shroud and substitute it with a cheap one!" He had the whole course in an uproar, laughing so much that we overran our coffee break, but it was worth it, as it is much easier to teach in a happy environment of smiling faces.

He also told us two jokes that I consider worthy of mention:

"A lady had died in bed upstairs. This house had a difficult staircase, and as the coffin was being brought downstairs, it hit the newel post, after which there was a knocking heard coming from inside the coffin. They opened it up, and the lady sat up, and she lived for another two years. As the undertakers were carrying the coffin down the stairs for the second time, the husband said, "Mind that newel post – remember what happened the last time!""

The second is about an Irishman who went to bed and died, and one of the many friends he had was being shown the corpse, and she remarked how well he looked as all of his wrinkles had gone, and that he was smiling. The man's wife said, "He died in his sleep dreaming, and he doesn't know he's dead yet, and when he wakes up and finds he's dead, it'll kill him!"

At another time when I was checking the details of a student, for his previous civilian occupation, he had put down 'Burglar/Pickpocket'. I tackled the man about this, and said, "Even if this were true, you could not put that down." He said, "In your welcoming comments, you stressed the essential quality of always telling the truth, and when I do just that, you want me to alter it!"

Shortly after this, during a short break for any questions, I heard my burglar student ask a colleague if he knew the number on his Identity Card. Of course, he got a negative reply, but then I was asked if I knew my ID number. I rattled this off, because if there was anything I once was good at, it was remembering numbers. My burglar friend then asked me, "Can you prove that?" I dived into my pocket but there was no ID card. I searched in all of my pockets and exclaimed, "That's strange, I know I had it when I left for work this morning!" Immediately my pickpocket student responded with, "Hey presto!" and, producing my ID card, said "Now do you believe I'm a pickpocket?"

This gave me an opportunity to stress the importance of trust between service men, and that the most serious crime a serviceman can commit is stealing from a comrade!

I found teaching Bombing and Gunnery the easiest job in the world, and of course my supernumerary job was the organisation of games on a Wednesday afternoon. I found team games, such as Rugby or Soccer got rid of 30 or 40 players in one go, cross country running was also popular, but those clever sods who put their names down for Golf, I sent to the Drill Sergeant, and it was strange how after just one session of physical exercise, how quickly their preference changed to a team game.

At 0730 hours one Monday morning, an enemy aircraft paid us a visit and bombed our aerodrome. I had just finished breakfast and, together with several other sergeants, I went to the nearest air raid shelter. It was a JU88, and it made several bombing runs over our aerodrome, and during a lull I noticed my friend, Gerry Stockwell, was not in the shelter, and so I ran back to the mess to find him. There was Gerry, shaving in the ablutions! He was suffering from a hangover, and he looked terrible. I said, "Gerry, we're being bombed!" but Gerry interrupted me saying, "Don't Panic!! Don't Panic!!" and so I stayed with him while he continued to shave.

Fortunately after the raid we had suffered no casualties, and only superficial damage had been done to the Aerodrome, which was quickly repaired. Some of the bombs did not go off, and Hoppy had these stored in a place of safety and out of the way.

At this time I was in charge of the Flying Programme. I had a large crew room where I used to keep my students who were waiting their turn to get airborne, with a desk just inside the door so no one could escape without going past me. As a result, I never lost a student trying to skive off to have a N A A F I break.

My Crew Room was part of the armoury, and one day I noticed all of the Armourers including the Sergeant rushing out of the Armoury.

I stopped the Sergeant and said, "What's the panic?" and he replied, "Hoppy's in there dismantling one of those Gerry bombs." Sergeant Hodgett was helping me with the Flying Programme, and so I got him to take the students out of the crew room on to the airfield, while I went to investigate, and there was Hoppy, dismantling a 'Gerry bomb'.

He asked me, "What are you doing Gibson?"

"I am an armament instructor and I heard you were dismantling a German bomb, and I would like to see how it's done." I replied.

"Right", he said, " Well I've already made it safe and it only remains to remove this electric fuse, so get back to your duty and get your 'Jeeps' airborne."

I had to smile because all of us Instructors called our students 'Jeeps', but I didn't know Hoppy knew that's what we called them.

As a result of our airfield being bombed, all airmen and Senior NCO's were billeted out into the surrounding villages. I was billeted out in Pwllheli with one other Sergeant and five airmen. We had a large room with RAF beds and equipment, and although we were not overcrowded, the lighting was poor with just one 40-watt bulb in the centre of the room. It was impossible to read, and so when we returned from work on the second night, the first thing we did was to replace the 40-watt bulb with a 100-watt lamp. Everything was fine, but when we returned the next night, our 100-watt lamp had been replaced with another 40 watt one. Our landlady was being paid to house seven airmen, but she was so mean that she deprived us of decent lighting.

Of course it is not conducive to good air force discipline for NCO's to share sleeping quarters with airmen, and within a day or two I was moved to a new Billet at Llanbedrog, which was a very large house owned by three Irish ladies. This was heaven on earth. I shared a room with two other Sergeants with all mod cons. We had our own bathroom and toilet, and our hosts could not do enough to make us comfortable.

The house was called 'Pernawell', which means Five Springs, and it was built on high ground with many acres of land with a ravine running through part of the garden. At the top of the garden was a small pool, which was fed by five springs, and the overflow water ran down the ravine into a much larger lake.

The three Irish ladies were sisters; two were spinsters, and the third was the widow of a Bishop, and she had a 12-year-old son who was away at Public School. Housing us Sergeants was their war effort, and during our 36-hour weekend breaks we were free to roam in the grounds or use the summerhouse as we pleased.

Each Sunday we were invited to take tea with our hosts, and if the sun was shining, this took place in the summerhouse. Tea was made in a George III silver teapot, and this was replenished by a silver tea kettle, which had a methylated spirit burner to keep the water hot. Bone china cups and saucers and side plates made our tea and cucumber sandwiches taste all the better, and a tray of cakes bought especially for us Sergeants were a delight we looked forward to.

When the Bishop's widow's son came home for holidays, he would go fishing in a rowing boat from our hosts' private beach, and would come back with a dozen or so mackerel, which were then served for tea. I had never had soused Mackerel before or since, but they were delicious.

We were encouraged to wear civilian clothes by the ladies, and on one occasion I was relaxing, waiting for tea to be served, when who should call by but Hoppy Wray, who was a friend of the ladies. He was invited to join us for tea, and when he saw me in my civilian clothes, he said, "What are you doing improperly dressed, Gibson?" Before I could reply, one of the ladies jumped to my defence and said, "Hoppy, you do not speak to one of our guests like that; now simmer down and join us for tea!" and that was the end of the matter.

The Flying programme always started at 0800 hours, and so I was always in my office by 0730 hours to await the arrival of my first 'Jeeps'. The air gunnery was done from the rear turret of a Whitley aircraft, and the 'Jeeps' fired bullets with red tips so it was possible to count the score by the marks made on the drogue, which was towed by a Henley aircraft in Cardigan Bay. Six 'Jeeps' were taken up per exercise and each one had to fire 200 rounds of ammunition.

In most cases, this was the first time these airmen had been airborne, and I noticed on this first trip many of them were airsick. I put this down to the fact that waiting in the fuselage of the Whitley before it was their turn to fire from the rear turret was worrying them because they did not know what was going on. Therefore, I made the suggestion that an air gunner's first flight should be an airmanship trip, so that they could stand behind the pilot and see what was happening.

All our pilots were either too old to fly on an operational squadron, or they were with us for an operational rest. We had one Flight Sergeant pilot who was very experienced, and on an airmanship flight he would do a bit of low flying, and on approaching the airfield he would fly straight at a lighthouse, and just when it appeared that he would hit it, he would just lift one wing up and just clear the lighthouse. This caused much merriment, but to cap it all, when he was on his final circuit prior to landing he would put on a pair of spectacles and of course land quite safely. This scared the living daylights out of some 'Jeeps', until the Instructor on with them explained it was just the pilot's little joke, there were no pebbles in the spectacle frames!

Bruce Gibson

We had an American Squadron Leader Medical Officer on our station, and also an American Leading Aircraftsman on the three-week gunner's course. They became quite friendly, and any spare time they had, would meet up. I mentioned to the Medical Officer the problem I was having with students' airsickness, and he said he would make a pill to combat it. After a few days the MO came to me and said he had made some pills which he thought would cure airsickness, and could I arrange a flight for him to test them? We had a fighter pilot on an operational rest break on our station named Bugs Hugget, and I told him what the MO wanted to do and would he like to take the Doctor up and fly the aircraft around a bit to test the pills?

Bugs jumped at the idea, and said that he'd love to. The American airman was present while this was happening, and he immediately said, "If the 'docs' getting airborne I must go with him", and so that was agreed. Bugs took the aircraft up to about 6000 feet over Pwhllheli, and then turned the aircraft inside out. I was told everyone in Pwllheli stopped to watch the aerial display, and after about 30 minutes, Bugs landed and taxied up to my crew room. Bugs jumped out and said, "Thanks Gibby, I enjoyed that". The American airman got out of the aircraft, but there was no sign of the Medical Officer. After a while however he slowly reached the ground, and he looked awful; he was green, and he said to me, "Do I look as if I've been sick?" Before I could say anything, the American LAC said to him, "No, but you do look as if you've shit yourself!"

Everybody present roared with laughter, not only because of the apt statement, but coming from an airman to a Squadron Leader, it was outrageous, but all the more funny for that.

One of the most interesting courses I was put in charge of consisted of 25 Polish Officers, only one of whom spoke English. He was a Polish Prince, and had been educated at Eton and Oxford, and he spoke beautiful English with a very wide vocabulary. All I had to do

148

was teach him which I found very easy. He then proceeded to teach the remaining 24 officers.

I explained the theory of gun sighting on the blackboard with diagrams etc., and then watched the Polish Instructor explain these to the others, and although it took a little longer due to the number of questions they wanted answering, I could tell they understood what I was trying to put across.

When it came to stripping the guns and putting them back together again, I could see whether they were going about it the right way.

These discussion periods conducted by the Prince were hilarious. Sometimes I thought they were coming to blows, but suddenly all would go quiet, and the Prince would say, "Its OK Sergeant, they've got that."

The acid test of course came after they had fired their 200 rounds of ammunition in the air on the drogue, but they all got pass marks.

When it came to the time for their practical test to demonstrate what each part of the guns did, I would examine the Prince, and he would examine the rest of the course, and I was able to see if they knew what they were doing or not. However the Prince, having had the advantage of teaching his colleagues, passed the final examination with flying colours and got high marks. Although all of the other officers passed, I got the impression he was a little bit harsh in his assessments, but that was none of my business; I had done my job – and surprise, surprise, I was thanked by the Polish Prince for my patience and toleration!

As soon as I was posted to Penrhos, I was put in charge of organised games which took place every Wednesday afternoon. I had arranged a special soccer match between the staff and students, and this gave me the chance to play. However on the Friday before the Wednesday when we were due to play, a Low Pressure System settled itself right over North Wales, and was stationary.

Visibility was nil, and it rained as it only can in Wales. It came down like 'stair rods' all over the weekend, and it looked as if it were going on for ever. In my youth I would have relished playing under those conditions, but in my old age (I was 28 at the time) I did not fancy getting soaked, and so on the Monday I started the rumour that our game had been cancelled.

It continued to pour down all day Monday, and by the next day, Tuesday, my rumour seemed quite reasonable and was spreading like wild fire. By the Wednesday, with rain still coming down 'in buckets' my rumour had become fact, and an indoor session with a Physical Training Instructor had been arranged by our Administrator Warrant Officer Smith.

By Wednesday, my rumour had also reached our Chief Ground Instructor 'Hoppy' Wray.

Five minutes before 1500 hours, Hoppy arrived, completely kitted out for wet weather, and walked to the football pitch, and stood in the pouring rain for 10 minutes before going to Warrant Officer Smith's office to demand where the footballers were. WO Smith said, "But Sir, the game's been cancelled". "Cancelled! Cancelled?" said Hoppy, "who cancelled it? I'm the only one who can cancel a football match!" Of course, WO Smith did not know the answer, and so the matter was closed, with Hoppy saying, "In future there can never be an alteration of programme without my say so." I thought to myself, I'd have to be more careful in future with any rumours that I might start!

Sergeant Huggard (Bugs) was a wonderful companion in the Sergeants' mess. I had acquired a number of 78 rpm playing records, and Bugs would amuse everyone present in his antics, according to his impression of the scenario the music depicted. On flying duty however he always seemed to get on the wrong side of his immediate boss, O C Flying.

In 1940 there was no Air Traffic Control as we know it today. There used to be a small caravan near the perimeter of the aerodrome, which was manned by a 'Duty Pilot', who would give pilots' permission to take off or land.

Also, in those days, aerodromes were laid with grass with no runways, and quite often the position of the caravan was such that the Duty Pilot could not see the far end of the airfield, and when pilots asked for permission to land, the answer would be "Land if the aerodrome is clear".

Our OC Flying was a very staid gentleman, and he could not cope with Bugs' exuberance, the result of which was Bugs seemed to be the permanent Duty Pilot.

On one occasion for some misdemeanour, Bugs was doing a 14-day stint of Duty Pilot, when a Flight Commander needed to have an aircraft air tested after it had had some repairs, and the only pilot available was Bugs. Therefore, the Flight Commander explained the position to OC Flying and because Bugs had done 10 of his 14-day punishment, it was agreed to let Bugs do the air test.

Bugs was a fighter boy, and he had not flown for a fortnight. He climbed to 10,000 feet and started his air test, and suddenly everybody on the aerodrome stopped work, and all movement in Pwllheli came to a standstill, while they watched a Fairy Battle aircraft perform manoeuvres no one thought it was possible for an aircraft to do. Of course, one of the watchers was OC Flying, and he was livid. But, all good things must come to an end, and Bugs duly landed and taxied up to the dispersal point, and with his parachute over his shoulder, he started to walk to the Flight Office, only to be met by OC Flying who said, "Huggard, what the hell do you think you've been doing?" and Huggard said, "I've been testing 'A' for Apple Sir, it flies left wing low". OC Flying was nonplussed; all he could say was "See me in my office in an hour's time!"

One hour later, OC Flying had had time to cool down, and when Bugs presented himself, smartly dressed in his best blue uniform, he was reminded that Fairy Battle Aircraft were not designed to be thrown about all over the sky, and he thought it was time for Huggard to return to his squadron, which of course was just what Bugs wanted!

One of the Sergeants sharing our room at Penarwell was a Robert Gore, who was a mature Observer, older than we other two, and before the war had been an engineer. He was a mathematical wizard who did not have to remember mathematical formulaes as he could always work things out from first principles.

Despite the fact he had a brilliant brain, he was dyslexic and he couldn't spell for toffee. His spelling was so appalling I bought him a birthday present, a 'Teach Yourself' spelling book. When I gave it to him, he went berserk!

"How stupid can you get Gibson. Don't you think I have tried to overcome my inability to spell?".

To stop him raving, I said, "I was only trying to help"

Gore's reply was, "Don't!".

In navigation there are many times when one has to do mental arithmetic. I could beat Gore at this hands down, but Gore always carried in his pocket a small slide rule. One day we were walking along and Gore was talking, and during the conversation, he said, "That's 15 divide it by 3," and here he brought out his slide rule and quick as a flash, said, "2.99, call it 3" which made me chuckle, and to this day Gore never knew what I was laughing at.

But, he was a very good navigator and had given up his Engineering Consultancy to do his bit in the services. He never flew as a navigator however without being airsick. It was something he was never able to master, but he was always prepared, and after a few minutes of this temporary indisposition he would be as right as rain. Lots of less strong willed people would have thrown in the towel.

Every Tuesday and Saturday evenings, I used to organise a dance in the Abersoch Village Hall which was made available to me free of charge, with the local ladies supplying the refreshments. Only soft drinks were allowed, and the music was supplied by a record player, using my strict dance tempo records. Costs were kept to a minimum and a token entrance charge was made. It was a social event for the locals and the evacuees from Manchester and Liverpool who turned up regularly, and the Penrhos airmen had their pick.

There were some very wealthy ladies from the Midlands towns who had taken refuge in the safe area of Abersoch, most of whom were lacking in male social activities, which our airmen were able to provide.

There was one lady who was the wife of a man who had a chain of shops in the Midlands, and she had a large car and two teenage daughters, Barbara and Pauline, who were 15 and 17 years of age respectively. I nick named her 'Mama Jones', and she had an escort, an RAF Corporal in the Provost Branch (a policeman) and he drove the family around, and with 'Mama' generally chaperoning the two teenage daughters.

These weekly dances were informal affairs, but every three months, I used to organise a formal dance in Pwllheli where the airmen wore Best Blue uniforms, and the ladies wore long Ball gowns. Mama and her daughters always attended these formal Do's, but on one occasion at one of our dances at Abersoch, Mama said she would not be able to attend the next formal dance but that Barbara and Pauline would be there and would I keep my eye on them. I told Mama it would be a pleasure, in fact I would take them in my taxi and return them home afterwards.

Come the night, Barbara and Pauline were thoroughly enjoying themselves when, just before the last waltz, who should turn up but Mama and her Corporal. This annoyed me no end, because I thought Mama did not trust me to look after her daughters. So, I approached Mama and said, "How nice to see you; by the way Corporal, you've got lipstick on your face." The Corporal's immediate reaction was to wipe his face, but of course, there was no lipstick – but it did show a guilty conscience. When Mama realised I had caught them out, she said "You naughty man, Bruce," I replied, "Mama, next time you ask me to look after your daughters, don't check up on me!"

We had an airman who had just returned from six month's detention in the 'Glass House' at Colchester. This belonged to the

Army, and everything was done at the double, and a very painful experience it was. Here all of the inmates are given a very close haircut, which at the beginning of the 21st century is now is all the vogue, but in 1940 was sign of disgrace.

This airman was a braggart, and he used to boast about his exploits at Colchester, and to his contemporaries he was a bit of hero. He turned up one Tuesday to one of my dances, and started to dance with his hat on, because he was actually ashamed of his Colchester haircut. I called him on one side, and told him he was quite welcome to come to our dances, but he would not be allowed to keep his hat on. He said, "I'm not taking my hat off", I said, "In that case, you'll have to leave" and I showed him the door.

It was several weeks before he came again to Abersoch, and I welcomed him at the door, and told him he could stay, but if he intended to dance, he would have to take his hat off. By this time his hair was beginning to grow, and so that was the end of the problem.

He continued to swagger about Penrhos Station, enjoying the hero worship he received from the other airmen, and of course it had to happen; for some minor misdemeanour, he was put on charge. The Station Commander, who was a wise old airman, (and would have been retired had it not been for the war) had heard via the grape-vine, the general behaviour of this airman, and having found him guilty of the charge, spoke to him like a 'Dutch Uncle', and explained to the airman that unless he changed his ways, he would be sent back to Colchester for another spell. This was the last thing this airman wanted, and at the mention of Colchester, his swaggering attitude collapsed, and he cried like Trafalgar Square Fountains! And this, in front of his airman escort and witness!

That was the end of the hero worship; in fact, some of his former mates started to make life difficult for him, but our Station Commander came to his rescue and had him posted to a different Command where he was able to make a fresh start.

One of our trainee air gunners was an airman named Christopher Columbus.

I was out in the airfield supervising students into their various aircraft when my telephone rang, and who should answer it, but Christopher Columbus. The person ringing could tell that it was not me who had answered the 'phone, and asked, "Who is that?", and the reply was "Christopher Columbus". The other voice then said, "This is the Station Commander – tell Sergeant Gibson to report to my office immediately!"

Having received the message, I handed over to Maurice Hoddgett, and off I went to the Station Headquarters. The Adjutant ushered me into the Group Captain's office, and he was livid! He recounted what had happened on the telephone, and was about to tear a strip off me when I interrupted, and said, "But Sir, Christopher Columbus is the airman's proper name!" "Poor sod," said the Group Captain, "And I thought it was a case of insubordination! Anyway, what I rang you about was the Bridge party you are organising between the Officers' and Sergeants' Messes; I understand one of your Observer students is Captain of the North of England Bridge Team, and I would like you to invite him as a guest, and he can play for your team."!!

We were not firing enough rounds of ammunition on the 25 yards range, and therefore not meeting our syllabus requirements, and so I was transferred from the flying programme to organise the Range work.

We had Browning guns fitted on to portable mountings, and each 'Jeep' had to fire 200 rounds of ammunition, and learn how to clear gun stoppages. Browning Guns fire at 20 rounds per second, and there is quite a lot of vibration when the gun is being fired. Therefore, the gunner has to hold the gun very firmly to hit the target allocated to him,

Firing ranges are dangerous places, and strict discipline is the order of the day. I had not taken over long before it became Christopher Columbus's turn to fire. I gave him the usual instructions to fire in short bursts, and he started to fire, but he was not holding the gun firmly enough, and had let the gun tilt upwards, and was shooting over the top of the range. I immediately slammed on the safety catch, but the damage had already been done.

Air force language is not appropriate after the event, but I stressed to Columbus the target he was supposed to be aiming at, and then pointed at the bullet marks up the wall of the range to prove to him that some of his bullets had been fired over the top of the range. I had to cancel firing for the day and report to the Station Commander what had happened. I did not tell the group Captain it was Christopher Columbus who was the culprit, because that might have caused more trouble, but the Commanding Officer said, "Of course, Gibson, it was your job to see that things like that don't happen; thank you for reporting your misdemeanour – keep it to yourself, don't broadcast it, and we will see what happens."

Each night when I went to my billet I bought a local newspaper, and after a fortnight, there was an article stating that a farmer had found one of his beef cattle dead as a result of a bullet wound. I reported it to the Station Commander and showed him the article, and he said, "Well, that's a turn up for the book, we know how the animal got shot, don't we Gibson! That's the end of the matter, keep it to yourself!"

I had previously instructed Columbus to keep his mouth shut about what had happened on the firing range, and on the day he finished his air gunnery course, I threatened him with the dire consequences to his RAF career should be blab about what he had done on that day, and as far as I know, he kept his word.

I reorganised the Firing Range procedure so that it was possible for anyone in charge of the 25-yard range to meet the syllabus requirements, and I was ready to return to the flying programme. Before doing so however, I was instructed to be in charge of a training party of members of the Local Defence Force in rifle shooting one evening per week. This put me in a dilemma for, although I was an expert at firing automatic firing guns at 20 rounds per second, I did not know the first thing about rifle shooting; in fact, I had never handled a rifle.

I mentioned this to my buddy Maurice Hoddgett, who said, "It's what you might call HARD LUCK!! The best thing you can do is find out!"

Therefore, I drew a rifle, ammunition, and a manual of instruction from the Armoury, and that evening Maurice and I went to the range to learn how to fire a rifle. The Manual gave very good directions and illustrated the many positions from which a rifle can be fired. Therefore, under Maurice's supervision, I chose to fire from the lying down position. All was well and I fired my first single shot from a rifle; the noise was so shattering and I was so surprised that, still lying on the ground, I burst out laughing. I laughed so much that Maurice started laughing as well. He then said, "What's the joke, why are we laughing?" I said, "It was the surprise at the noise of the rifle shot so near to my ear that made me laugh, you try it!", which of course Maurice did. Although he laughed, the surprise element was gone, and so we got on with training one another in rifle shooting.

Come the night when the Local Defence Force was about to arrive, I asked Maurice, "Would you like to join us?" Maurice replied, "This is going to be funny, I wouldn't miss it for the world!" and so Maurice went to the Guardroom to do the 'meeting and greeting', and I went to prepare the range.

Bang on time, 12 civilian gentlemen arrived at the range, complete with a pickaxe handle each. Their ages ranged from 35 to 65 years of age, and one of their number was obviously in charge. I made myself known to him, and confirmed that rifle shooting was the object of the exercise, and to my utter surprise and delight, when I asked, "Have you done this before?", the answer was "Yes. I am a retired Sergeant Major, may I have your permission to take over?"

Maurice noticed the expression of relief that came over my countenance, and I said, "That's OK, I'll supervise the safety regulations, and you carry on with the instruction." Maurice sidled up to me and exclaimed, "Jammy bastard Bruce, you've robbed me of a laugh!"

The instruction given was first class, and in no time at all, the Instructor was saying, "That's all for this period; same time, same place, next week, and we will progress from there."

I invited the trainees back to the Sergeants' Mess for refreshments, and the Sergeant Major thanked me, however they had to return to their headquarters to be dismissed. And, off they went, with pick axe handles at the slope, a proper 'Dad's Army' – but it was the start of The Home Guard who were to do such wonderful work when the bombing raids ultimately started.

After completing my temporary stint on the ranges, I returned to work along with my 'Oppo' Maurice Hoddgett on the Flying Programme. I had made it part of the routine for me to fly as the Instructor on the first gunnery exercise every morning.

Each Whitley aircraft had six student gunners on board, each of whom had to fire 200 rounds of ammunition, in turn, from a Frazer Nash turret in the tail of the aircraft.

We had to fly about 10 miles over land to reach the target area, and during that time, the gunners were expected to practise turret manipulation with the guns on safe.

On one trip, we had just got to height and were still flying over land when, suddenly, the guns in the rear turret started to fire! I was sitting in the Second Pilot's seat. I looked at the pilot, absolutely amazed, disconnected my intercom, and dashed down the fuselage, and there, calmly rotating the turret and completely oblivious of what was going on, was the student gunner. I bashed on the turret doors, and when the gunner opened up, I said, "What the hell are you doing?!" He replied, "Turret manipulation, Serge!" "You stupid sod!", I exclaimed, "Can't you smell the cordite? You've fired all of your ammunition over land!" "No I haven't", the student replied, "I've just been following that winding village road down there" "But your guns aren't on 'Safe', and all of your ammunition has gone! Get out of there, you've done enough damage for one day!"

I told the pilot what had happened, and told him to return to base. Once again I had to report to the Station Commander. The Group Captain said, "Not you again, Gibson!" "I'm afraid it is, Sir", I responded, and made my report.

I pointed out on the map the remote village road where the firing had taken place, and my Commanding Officer said, "We will just have to wait and see, but remember, silence is golden."

Fortunately, no damage was done, and that was the end of the matter, but I added to the instructions for screen gunners that they should ensure the safety catches were on to both guns before practise turret manipulation started!

* * *

11

As the war continued......

One of our Instructors was posted, and in his place yet another Sergeant Gibson arrived from a Bomber Command Squadron for an operational rest! He was an experienced Air Gunner, but not a trained armament instructor, and so he was employed on administrative duties, or he could act as a screen air gunner on flying duties, and so he was sent down to me so that Maurice could resume lecturing.

He was quite useful, and was capable of 'holding the fort' whilst I was airborne. One day, he asked if he could do the first trip in place of me, and that was fine by me, and so he got into the aircraft, fully briefed, to fly with our new Wing Commander Flying as a pilot.

During the exercise there was an engine failure, and the aircraft had to ditch. Everybody got into the dinghy except for Sergeant Gibson, who was tragically drowned.

The flying programme was cancelled for that day, and all Whitley Aircraft were grounded for a check up. This only lasted for 24 hours, when all of our Whitleys were cleared for take off, and so our flying programme recommenced.

This was the only accident we had during my six-month's tour of running the flying programme.

We also did air firing in Fairy Battle aircraft, when we could only take up two 'Jeeps' at a time. In these aircraft Vickers Gas Operated Guns were fitted. Firing at 600 rounds per minute, part of the exercise was for the air gunner to clear any stoppages that might occur when airborne.

However, one aircraft landed with a stoppage that the 'Jeep' couldn't clear, and so an armourer took the gun out of the aircraft to clear the stoppage. There is a laid down procedure how to do this, but the armourer, in trying to cut this procedure short, put the gun on its end on the ground and tried to free the stoppage by stamping on the 'cocking handle'. He was wearing gum boots which were wet, and as he stamped on the cocking handle, his foot slipped off, but also released the stoppage, causing the gun to fire and the bullet went straight up and went through the side of his face, leaving a nasty gash. I saw this take place and rushed to the armourer's assistance and found, apart from a lot of blood, the airman had had a miraculous escape. The Warrant Officer in charge of the airman, when he knew he was relatively unharmed, was furious, and slapped the airman on a charge. The result of this was the airman had to spend several days on fatigues in the Guardroom whilst repairs to the airman's facial wounds were treated in sick quarters.

A vast amount of equipment is needed at a Bombing and Gunnery school, which is all methodically recorded in an Inventory. Each piece falls within a Section, and within that Section every item has a reference number.

Just after I arrived at Penrhos, the officer in charge of the school Inventory was posted, and he handed over the Inventory to a Flight Lieutenant Officer of the Administrative Branch, who was an Egyptian. The present holder had not held the Inventory for long, and he showed the date that he had taken over from his predecessor to the Egyptian, and related that a 100% check had been made and everything was OK. So, on that assurance, the Egyptian Officer took charge of the Inventory without personally checking it.

The Egyptian Officer was a very popular member of the staff, particularly as he always seemed to have a surplus of petrol coupons, which he would either sell or give away for favours received. One of his best customers was a Pilot Officer in the Equipment Branch, but, somehow, these two officers fell out, and the

Egyptian Officer refused to sell any further petrol coupons to his fellow Officer, although it was known there were plenty available.

After a few months, the Egyptian Officer was posted, and he was detailed to hand the Inventory over to a Flight Lieutenant Gunnery Officer who had come up through the ranks, and who demanded a 100% physical check. Everybody who had been billeted out had been issued with two RAF blankets, and these were on the Armoury Inventory. After the Inventory had been checked to the Gunnery Officer's satisfaction, apart from some small items which came under the classification of Class 'C' stores and could be written off, the missing items were: 1 Mark IX Bomb Site, and 600 RAF blankets! Was everybody in Wales sleeping on RAF blankets??

When this was reported to the Pilot Officer Equipment Officer, he demanded the lost items be recovered, but failing that, the Egyptian Officer would have to pay for the missing items or face a Court Marshal. The Equipment Officer was acting with malice because he had been refused petrol coupons, and so when the Egyptian asked me if I could help - as a grateful previous purchaser of petrol coupons – I said I would do my best.

On looking at a list of shortages, I noticed the Section and Reference number given was for a lost Bomb Sight Spirit Level, and not a Bomb Site, and so I was also able to produce the missing item with the intrinsic value of a shilling or two, as apposed to a Mark IX Bomb Site, valued at over £1,000! Apart from the blankets, that was the costliest item on the list of shortages, and in the case of the Blankets, it was because the billeted airmen were moved around to various addresses, and the blankets went with the airmen, and that was why not all of the blankets could be traced. However, the Provost branch was given the job of trying to trace the missing blankets.

Disciplinary action was ultimately taken by the Commanding Officer who reprimanded the Egyptian for failing to do a 100% physical check before taking over the Inventory, much to the chagrin of the Equipment Officer!

Later, when I was doing a routine check on the Inventory for the current holder, I discovered there were three additional hand grenades, which were not on the Inventory. Having checked they were unarmed, I said to my assistant to gather them up and take them back to their proper place, which was the main Armoury. My assistant was quite nervous and asked, "Supposing one of them explodes!!" I said, "Not to worry, I'll say we only found two surplus!!"

Before the war the Pilot Officer Equipment Officer used to teach Bridge at Selfridges in Oxford Street. He would make up a four and charge £1.00 per hour, and one shilling per point scored for the instruction he used to give. He had been making a fortune! Bridge was played in the Officer's Mess every night, and the Equipment Officer would invite the Observer student, who was Captain of the North of England Bridge Team, as his guest and to be his partner. Needless to say, they always won, and took everyone to the cleaners!

In 1940, the RAF Gunnery Schools had produced a large number of Air Gunners, and a new classification was introduced, that of Gunnery Leader. We had a Flying Officer who was on the Station Headquarters' Administrative Staff, and he wanted to transfer to the General Duties Branch and become a Gunnery Leader. He was attached to an Observer Course that I was teaching for me to teach him Gunnery. He was a very rich gentleman, and a good administrator, but it is sad to relate that as a Gunner he was dim! He was keen to pass and become a Gunnery Leader so that he could join a squadron, and take an active part in the war, but despite the fact that I gave him quite a lot of personal tuition, he just could not grasp the basic principles of Air Gunnery.

The Flight Lieutenant Gunnery Leader who was with us was on an operational rest, and had a lot of common sense. I approached him and explained the position because I did not want to fail my officer student as it would reflect on both of us, and, to cut a long story short, my officer student was persuaded by our canny Flight

Lieutenant Gunnery Leader to withdraw his application to become a Gunnery Leader, and stick to his paperwork!

At the end of each Course, the 'Jeeps' would hold an end of Course Party in Abersoch, and I was always invited to attend. However, as I am a Coca Cola man and do not enjoy watching other people getting under the influence of drink or getting drunk, I always politely made my excuses saying that, as a non drinker, I had made it a point of principle never to attend any end of course parties. This I religiously adhered to, until one Observer's Course, where one of the students was a member of the Wedgwood family of the Stoke on Trent fame.

He was a mature student, older than the other members of his course. He had a large 16/50 Wolseley motorcar, and he invited me to be his guest at his end of Course Party. Of course, I declined his offer, but then he twisted my arm by saying he was inviting me for two reasons: firstly he would like to take me in his car with his other guests; and secondly, he would like me to drive him home after the party, because he would be under the influence of drink and not safe to drive! If I still refused, he would have to decline also.

Against my better judgement I agreed, and thoroughly enjoyed myself! Come the time to drive everyone home, I did not feel like my normal self, in fact, I was a bit light headed, and so I took extra care. When I ultimately went to bed I slept like a log!

Next morning by 0800 hours I had got the first details airborne, and by 0850 hours, no bombs had been dropped and no guns fired, and I said to Maurice, "What's happening?" Maurice said, "You're pissed!! You've got the bombing aircraft on the firing ranges, and the gunnery aircraft on the bombing ranges; if I were you I would go back to bed and leave this lot for me to sort out!"

By this time I had the most dreadful headache, and was feeling really ill. So I said, "Maurice, if you think you can do better, DO IT – I'm going back to bed!"

It was a 20 minute walk back to my billet, and I was nearly there when I heard the guns firing, and so I knew that Maurice had put things right. After a short rest, I returned to my office, still feeling very groggy, and as Maurice was doing better than me, I let him get on with it. By lunchtime I did not want anything to eat, but I was fit enough to relieve Maurice, and as he went back to the Mess, he said, "You do realise that someone spiked your drinks last night?" I never did find out what I had drunk the previous night to make me feel so ill, but it made me even more determined to never accept invitations to end of Course parties.

My Commissioning procedure which had started in January 1940 somehow had got lost, and so it was started all over again in 1941. In doing this, it was discovered that since May 1941 I had been promoted to a Flight Sergeant, but nobody had told me. However, I got a lump sum of back pay, which regularised the position, but I never was able to display the Crown above my chevrons because I was discharged on 13th September 1941 on appointment to a Commission, under Kings Regulations, Paragraph 652.

Group Captain Williamson, Station Commander of Royal Air Force Penrhos, in his 'Brief Statement of Trade Qualifications, Character and General Conduct' wrote,

"This NCO has proved to be above average as an Observer Instructor, and has shown exceptional organising ability. His character and general conduct has at all times been very good."

The result of this was I was sent on two week's leave with £234.00 to buy myself some officer's clothing. I was given a list of the bare necessities, and Jess and Fred went with me to Simpson's of Piccadilly to do some shopping. Before I left Penrhos, I had to return the service equipment I had received and, joy to behold that was the last time during my Service Career that I had to have a kitbag!

We had lunch at Simpson's, and Fred was so chuffed, anyone would think it was he who had got the Commission. He said to me, "We've come a long way since pushing milk barrows Bruce," which helped me to keep my feet on the ground.

I was to learn on my return to Penrhos that I now filled the established post of Gunnery Leader, and, as I had been teaching officers to become efficient at filling such appointments, that made sense.   Since Sergeant Soloman had said to me, "You're not a Sergeant", I had never stopped learning, but now I was a member of an Officers' Mess, a whole new world opened up to me.

For the first six months as an Acting Pilot Officer, the first thing I was to discover was that I was the lowest form of animal life in the Royal Air Force! I was 27 years of age, and as a child, my mother had taught me that children should be seen but not heard, and woe betide anyone who broke that rule.   I was therefore quite experienced at 'Watching Silence', which helped me become a member of the Officers' Mess – I was there if needed, but otherwise I tried to be invisible.

The basic principles of living in Mess had been taught to me by Sir Tom Web-Bowen, but applying that etiquette was all new to me, and so I kept my eyes open, and it wasn't long before I was passing on information to the other two Acting Pilot Officers who had joined the mess at the same time as me. I was the only APO who the Penrhos Station Commander knew by name. I had stood before him in his office so many times confessing misdemeanours in armament training that I considered to be my fault that I felt I came under the classification of 'Once seen, never forgotten', but as it was his final recommendation that gained me a Commission, I knew where I stood!

Most lunch times, and in the evenings after dinner, Bridge schools would develop, and I was often invited to make up a four which I enjoyed, but I didn't like the inquisitions that went on after a hand when someone had boobed.

At weekends, if a certain Flying Officer Barber was present, drinking parties seemed to take place and I noticed it was always the same group of officers who were involved, and he was the life and soul of the party, and the high jinks that followed were hilarious.

Drinks in the Mess had to be ordered from a Batman, and had to be signed for as it was considered infra dig for an officer to pay cash as the mess was considered to be the Officer's home. These books were examined monthly by the President of the Mess Committee to make sure no-one was drinking too much or getting beyond their means.

Barber's monthly bill was staggering. He was a sociable gentleman, and the PMC knew it was not possible for Barber to have consumed the amount he had to pay for each month, but it was also evidence that he had been in the Mess on the date he had signed for the drinks. At many of his parties, furniture would get broken, or damage done to the fabric of the Mess, and he was frequently summoned to the Station Commander's presence to account for what had happened.

He was a big fellow, and a superb member of the Station Rugby Team. After one particular weekend party, the Group Captain had Barber on the telephone and, using the usual excuse that was trotted out of the drinking fraternity, that he could not remember being in the Mess at the weekend, he was told to report to the Mess immediately, where he was met by the Group Captain.

Barber at that time had a 1927 Austin motorcar, and there, in the Billiard's room, was Barber's Austin car wedged under the Billiard's table, and written at least a dozen times all over the table with Billiard's chalk was the name 'Pissy Barber','Pissy Barber'....

There were four steps up to the Mess, and there were tyre marks on the polished floors of the Mess, showing where the car had been driven

The Group Captain said, "Now do you remember what happened?"

"I woke up this morning Sir, but I had to walk to work, because I could not remember where I had left my car.", responded Barber.

"Don't give me that bullshit Barber; I'm going to charge you six times the value of the damage you have done, and so let's not have any more of this nonsense – get back to work!"

Barber was the most senior Flying Officer in the Royal Air Force, and would remain so while he continued with his drinking sessions.

After the war he left the Air Force and went to live in Cheshire. One day he was driving into Chester when he came across three youths assaulting a Policeman. That was right up his street. He stopped his car and laid into the three youths with such gusto the policeman was able to summon reserves and, with Barber's help, the Policeman was able to arrest all three.

Barber had to go to the Station to give evidence of the occurrence, and forever after that in the eyes of the Police, Barber could do no wrong. He could park anywhere, and he became quite a local celebrity.

One Saturday, I arrived in Abersoch a bit early to arrange a Dance when I met Helen, who attended our Dances regularly, and so I took her into the local Café to have a cup of tea.

There were three ladies sitting at the next table to ours, gabbling away in welsh, when suddenly Helen got up and started such an altercation with the ladies in welsh, I thought they were going to come to blows. Helen returned to me and said, "Come on Bruce, we won't have anything here".

Outside the café I said, "What was all that about?" Helen replied, "Those ladies were Welsh nationalists, and they started to criticise the Air Force, but I wasn't going to have any of that, and so I gave them piece of my mind!"

We had a Flight Sergeant Pilot at Penrhos who proudly wore an Air Force medal on his chest. This was most unusual because these have to be earned, and so I made it my business to find out what he had done to earn such distinction.

Apparently early in the 1930's he had been the Wireless Operator Air Gunner in a Blenheim aircraft. On one occasion for some unknown reason the pilot lost control and baled out without warning his crew members, leaving the aircraft spinning to earth. The WOP could not get to his parachute but managed to get to the Pilot's controls where he corrected the spin, and flew back to his aerodrome, where he managed to land, albeit a little bumpy.

For that act of courage and good airmanship, he was awarded an Air Force Medal, and a Pilot's course.

When this story was related to me I remembered reading about this exploit in the newspapers, and here I was serving on the same station as this gallant airman. Remarkable!!

He was a good pilot and loved to do formation flying. On one trip, having completed our exercise in a Blenheim Aircraft, we were flying in sixth-eighths cloud, when he saw another Blenheim Aircraft, and started to formate with it. We were in and out of cloud, and suddenly I noticed a Swastika on the side of the aircraft. I switched on my intercom and said, "You're trying to formate on a Junkers 88!" The look of astonishment on his face made me laugh as he did a steep diving turn to port, and ultimately back to base!

One of our armament instructors was an ex Flying Officer who was employed as a civilian. He was a charming Irishman living the life of a bachelor in a caravan parked on the airfield. He had a wide experience with a fund of stories and he would try to convince his listeners that he still believed in fairies!

For most of the time he was as sober as a judge, but if he met an old colleague, it was a cause to celebrate, and he would go on a drinking spree lasting several days. He was such a popular colleague that the rest of us used to cover for him until he sobered up. On his return, he would say he was going to be a monk in a monastery. No more drink – nothing stronger that cocoa.

In the late 1920's as a qualified Airship Pilot, he was accused of flying his Airship straight at his Commanding Officer whilst still in the hangar. At his Court Martial, he was completely exonerated because he claimed he did not see his CO!

One of his appointments was to be in charge of the Bombing Range at Calshot, and one day he was towing a moving target with a motor launch, and pilots were practising their skills at dive-bombing when one aircraft failed to pull out of its dive and sank in the Solent. 'Andy' and his assistant dived in, both fully clothed, and rescued the pilot who had been trapped in his cockpit. For that he and his partner received the highest award granted for gallantry in peace time, that of the 'Albert Medal of the First Class'.

In 1946, Andy had to attend an investiture at Buckingham Palace to receive a George Cross in exchange for his previous award, the Albert Medal, which had been superseded by the George Cross. Of course, it had to happen, he met up with his 'Oppo' who was at the Investiture for the same purpose, and they both got stinking drunk. At the Palace, Equerries lined up all recipients of awards in the correct order of precedence. Andy, while waiting in the queue, became so thirsty he took some flowers out of a vase and drank the water, before replacing the flowers. Nature however took its toll and Andy had to go to the toilet, but he was gone for so long that he missed his turn to get his award, and after him, everyone got the wrong decoration and which had to be sorted out afterwards.

Whilst he was in charge of the Bombing Range at Calshot, on checking his inventory of equipment for which he was responsible, it was discovered that a Motor Launch was missing, and several thousand gallons of fuel could not be accounted for. But as someone with the luck of the Irish, he got away with it!

We had a Czechoslovakian Spitfire Squadron dumped on our Station. The German Luftwaffe used to use Liverpool as a Trainee Bombing run. Their navigation consisted of flying coast wise down the English Channel until they reached Land's End where they would turn right, and fly along the coast to Liverpool. But, if the defences of Liverpool were too strong and they were unable to bomb their Primary Target, they would fly a reciprocal course back down the west coast of England, and haphazardly drop their Bomb Load on any target of their choice, and so the Czech Squadron had been sent to stop this happening.

One day they were ordered to 'Scramble', and the whole Squadron got airborne except one aircraft which was about to take off when it hit something, and the Spitfire did a complete cart wheel and finished upside down on the far side of the Airfield. Before the Ambulance and Fire Engine could get to the scene, I saw the pilot get out of the cockpit and run across the aerodrome, where he got into another Spitfire and took off, and flew to join his mates. All of the pilots of this Squadron were Officers and outstandingly brave, but they lacked the charm of the Polish officers and the Welsh girls did not go for them.

In the spring of 1941, an Air Ministry Order was published asking for volunteers for SNCO's to become Parachute Jumping Instructors.

I immediately banged in an application, but was turned down because being an Observer Armament Instructor, I was too well qualified.

About the same time, one of our Armament Instructors who was living in Married Quarters was posted overseas. In the Sergeants' Mess he was cursing his luck as he was well settled in and did not want to go Overseas. Mind you, he did not know where he was to be posted, and so I offered to swap and go in his place. Once again my application was turned down for being over qualified, and GUESS WHAT?! The posting was to California, USA. I could have enjoyed that!

When I reported back to Penrhos dressed in my Officer's finery, my Chief Armament Instructor Wing Commander 'Hoppy' Wray sent for me, and congratulated me on my promotion, and as I was the Instructor training Officers to become Gunnery Leaders, he told me that I was to fill the vacant Gunnery Leaders post under his command. He then referred to the recent applications I had made to leave his unit, and he asked, "Are you not happy here?" I replied, "Under the present circumstances I could not be more happy, but as more officers were being posted to our unit for an operational rest, my first preference would be to be posted to an Operational Command where I can start earning my keep as a Navigator." 'Hoppy' was a man's man, and said, "In that case I will see what I can do for you." True to his word, by November 1941, I was posted to the Number 3 School of General Reconnaissance at Squires Gate to do a Sea Navigation Course.

My second visit to Squire's Gate Railway Station reminded me of my first arrival two year's previously when I was marched in the pouring rain with a kitbag wearing airman's uniform, but this time I was dressed in officer's uniform with a suitcase, and taking a taxi to the aerodrome.

Squires Gate was still under civilian control, and had no Officers' Mess, and so I was accommodated at a 3 Star Hotel, which had been commandeered by the Royal Air Force. The main occupant was a Fighter Command Fighter Squadron with 'Defiant' aircraft. These were of a unique design in that they had a 4 Gun Boulton Paul Turret. This enabled the pilot to fly alongside his target and attack from the Beam. It was a wonderful idea, but it failed because the engine did not have enough power to catch its quarry.

I was given a nice large room to myself with a very comfortable bed as opposed to sleeping in a Barrack Room with 31 other airmen and on a paillaisse filled with straw – an experience I will never forget!

My daily routine never varied. I used to breakfast at 0700 hours, and report for work by 0800 hours. I had a snack lunch at the aerodrome canteen, and I was ready to dine back at the hotel by 1900 hours.

As a Navigator I was the odd man out among the Fighter boys, because their sorties rarely lasted more than an hour, and it was their Ground Controller who gave them a vector to get to their target area, and, after their Combat, the same man would again give them a vector to base. The thought of flying for 12 to 15 hours over the sea with no Ground Controller to tell them where they were or what course to steer to get back to their aerodrome was something they did not want to know about. They did not mind how far or how high they flew, but the action was the important thing, so 'let's get it over as soon as possible', was the attitude.

One night after carrying out a night flying exercise, I arrived back at the hotel just after 2200 hours. As I entered the foyer, I could tell from the noise coming form the Ballroom that there was a party going on, and so I peeped through the glass door of the Ballroom, and there were 20 plus naked officers acting as Roman soldiers. They had torn down the blackout curtains, which were being worn by the Emperor and His Court as Cloaks, and the inebriated officers were thoroughly enjoying themselves. The light pouring out into the street attracted the attention of the local policeman, but when he saw what was going one, he exclaimed "Good God", and beat a hasty retreat.

One of the first lessons I learnt as an officer was never to get involved in incidents which did not concern me, and I decided that this was no place for a stone cold sober Navigator, and so I crept upstairs and went to bed!

Apart from the Anson aircraft, which was ideal for navigation purposes, we had several Bofor aircraft, which had been especially designed for Coastal Command. Their main feature was that in the event of an engine failure at sea, the aircraft would float. Aviators need their aircraft to keep airborne, but if they do have to ditch, they prefer dinghies, which they know how to handle. These Bofor aircraft were therefore most unpopular with pilots, and there was one Flight Lieutenant Jones who was scared stiff of the aircraft and in his pre flight checks, if it were at all possible to declare the aircraft unserviceable, he would so do. He had earned himself the nickname 'U S Jones'. When navigators were detailed to do an exercise with Jones as the pilot in a Bofors aircraft, they knew the chances of it happening were slim.

There was one pilot who was an aged civilian with a world of experience, and he took the chances of ditching in his stride, and would boast that he was a 'sail, steam and Bofor pilot', much to the amusement of his contemporaries.

Quite often at Blackpool a sea mist would develop, and aircraft would be diverted to other inland aerodromes, but our hero had his own blind landing approach. He would fly to the Blackpool Tower which normally had its top sticking above the sea mist, and he would fly out to sea, count up to 20, and then turn to port, count up to 15, turn again to port and start losing height, and there was the aerodrome straight ahead. He claimed that by using this method, he never had to be diverted.

The General Reconnaissance Course I was on presented no difficulties, but consisted mainly of Plotting Exercises on Mercators Charts which, because they expand the Secant of a Great Circle can be represented by a straight line. It was on this course I was introduced to Astro Navigation where I learnt that 'man is not lost if he can navigate by the stars.' It was a six-week intensive course, which, with homework reading, meant there was not much time for social activities, but there was always the odd occasion when I managed to get to the Winter Gardens and dance with the local girls, who were most charming!

From Squires Gate I was posted to an Operational Training Unit at Thornaby on Tees for three weeks on a Hudson aircraft. After that I joined 53 Squadron who were engaged in shipping strikes in the North Sea. Here I met Pilot Officer Michael Hunt. He was the most naïve officer I had ever met, but was exceptionally brave. He had developed his own special attacking method to sink ships. Having sighted his prey, he would start his attack from a height of about 3,000 feet. He would then dive down to sea level below the height of the enemy's gun power, and when almost up to the ship he was attacking, he would yank on the control column and literally throw his bombs at the target whilst climbing away and just before his Hudson went into a high speed stall, he would correct the stalled position, gain some height, and then stand off and watch his quarry sink. This was a highly dangerous manoeuvre, which scared the living daylights out of his navigators, but Michael knew no fear, and his crewman had to admit the system never failed.

Every night in the Mess after dinner when everyone was well oiled with alcohol, we used to play mess games. The most popular was a Bombing Run from start to finish. This consisted of two large leather Club Sofas laid down on their backs, and joined together. This was the fuselage of their aircraft and from where the crew operated. Michael was always the pilot, with three experienced aviators as crew.

Briefing was conducted at one end of the anteroom by a senior officer and would go something like this: - "The target tonight gentlemen is Berlin" – Question: "Is that in Germany?" - Answer - "It was yesterday!". This sort of banter went on during the briefing and continued during the pre flight check. Take off was imaginary but formal. The Navigator gave the pilot the course to steer, height to fly, and airspeed to maintain, together with the ETA.

As they crossed the enemy coast, a certain amount of Flak was experienced - here the audience who were being amused would throw lighted matches into the make believe aircraft, which caused quite a bit of consternation to the crew in extinguishing the Flak, but which Mike sitting as the Pilot completely ignored.

As the aircraft supposedly got nearer the target area, the odd lighted match was again thrown at the crew, until the navigator took over on the bombing run when instructions were given to Mike, such as: target dead ahead, left, left-steady, right-steady – bombs gone, after which violent evasive action was taken by Mike, and much more Flak was thrown into the crew area, when one crew member would announce the aircraft was on fire, at which a piece of lit newspaper would be thrown at the crew.

This really put the cat among the pigeons, but another onlooker was ready for any emergency, and the conflagration was brought under control with a fire extinguisher. And of course everybody in the vicinity had to have some foam. Mike then ordered his crew to bale out, and this is where the onlookers took over when they literally threw the crew out of the aircraft, but left Mike in the Pilot's position.

At this stage there was usually such a commotion with everybody trying to sort themselves out, and on one occasion when Mike announced that he could do with a beer, this was immediately poured over him by one of the supporting cast. After such episodes as this everyone would settle down to some serious drinking.

Mike was awarded a DFC for his successes at shipping strikes and he had to attend an investiture at Buckingham Palace. He got to Piccadilly and was having a quiet drink when of course he met other

175

officers who were also to be decorated, and a party soon developed where Mike came into his own. With everybody buying drinks all round, Mike noticed a Flight Lieutenant had joined the party, and that there was something not quite right about him. Therefore, Mike started chatting him up.

The Flight Lieutenant had a DSO and DFC, and whilst Mike was getting a drink for his suspect, it suddenly stuck him that the Flight Lieutenant was wearing his DFC the wrong way round. However, to make sure, Mike started mentioning names of well-known officers, and his newfound acquaintance knew all of those, and so Mike said, "Well, you must know Bunny Currant". "Bunny", was the reply, "She's a great friend of mine." Right monkey!! thought Mike, because Bunny Currant was a gallant Battle of Britain pilot, and so Mike excused himself, and went out into Piccadilly. There he met two members of the RAF Provost Branch to whom Mike reported the doubt he had, and that he thought the Flight Lieutenant was an impostor. They followed Mike back into the Pub, and the last Mike saw of the phoney officer was him being escorted out of the Bar by the two RAF policemen, under arrest.

Mike Hunt was one of the nicest people one could meet. He was everybody's friend, innocent to the point of being naïve, and he was a soft touch for anyone with a thirst!

After his little contretemps with the impostor, Mike had some drinking to catch up on, and he noticed some ladies had joined the party. It was not long before one of the ladies got hold of Mike and was hanging on to his every word. She invited him back to her flat in Shaftsbury Avenue, and after many more drinks, he finished up in bed with his newfound friend where he passed out.

He was awoken the next morning by the smell of a delicious cooked breakfast, which he thoroughly enjoyed before being reminded that if he did not get a move on, he would be late for his 1100 hours investiture.

On his return to Thornaby-on-Tees, with a pint of beer in his hand, he was relating his adventures to all of his fellow officers, when he came to point of his departure after breakfast at his girl friends' flat, he said to his Squadron Leader Flight Commander, "But Sir, she wouldn't let me pay!" amidst much communal laughter.

To the pure, all things are pure.

* * *

12

On the move again - and into action.......

T his was my first introduction to be associated with operational aircrew, and I knew immediately this was the life for me.

Since leaving Number 9 Bombing and Gunnery School I had only myself to take care of. I was free from working to a syllabus and the responsibility teaching 'Jeeps' Bombing and Gunnery to the correct standard. But before I was able to be employed on a shipping strike with 53 Squadron I was posted to Number 58 Squadron Bomber Command and, I was instructed to report to RAF Station St. Eval as the squadron had been transferred to Coastal Command.

That of course made sense because that is what the six-week course I had just completed at Squires Gate was all about, navigating 10 to 15 hours over the sea. I do not remember how I got to St. Eval, but I finally finished up at Travalgie Hotel where 58 Squadron was domiciled, which was about 3 miles from Newquay.

During 1940 and 1941, St Eval had been badly bombed, and all of the local hostelries had been commandeered for living accommodation. Travalgie was a little different from other buildings that had been taken over insofar as the owners were still in residence to see fair play; in fact they still operated the bar. Otherwise, 58 Squadron used it as an Officers' Mess.

I shared a room at the Travalgie with a young pilot (but then most aircrew seemed to be young to me) As I was 26 when I was mobilised, and had spent 2 years as an Observer Armament Instructor, I was not so light hearted as some of the other members of the Squadron; in fact, I was a little mature. Before I got to know my roommate well, he went missing, and I was given the job of making an inventory of his personal belongings and put them into store. It was the most morbid job I had ever been given, but, being a Gemini, I was able to switch that side of me off which prevented me from acting emotionally, and was able to get on with my Squadron duties.

Due to my previous Armament experience I was immediately made Squadron Bombing Leader, as my Squadron supernumerary job. As soon as the Squadron were settled into their new quarters, we started operating. It took some of the crews a little longer than normal because being transferred from Bomber to Coastal Command, the navigation was different, and as I was one of the few navigators who had been trained in Dead Reckoning Navigation, my first job was to act as a screen navigator to some of the other crews.

The 'A' Flight Commander was a Squadron Leader Lawson who was a mature Squadron Leader as he had come up through the ranks, and because of his onerous duties at running a Flight he only operated once a fortnight. However, when he did, he had all the Leaders of the Squadron as his crew, which included the Squadron Navigation Officer, Squadron Wireless Officer, Squadron Gunnery Leader, Squadron Engineer Officer, and myself as Squadron Bombing Leader.

My first operational flight therefore was with him. We had on the Squadron a Flight Lieutenant Terry Earp who had finished his tour in Bomber Command and was awaiting posting on an operational rest, but Terry agreed to fly on as second pilot to Squadron Leader Lawson to see what Coastal Command work was all about.

We took off from St. Eval and flew the 67 nautical miles to Bishop's Rock, and set course on our ante submarine patrol. Lofty Lawson took off from St. Eval and after about two hours handed over to Terry Earp. Terry had just settled in when I decided to check the wind by the 'Wind Lanes and White Cap method'.

About 5 miles dead ahead I spotted a fully surfaced U Boat. I called up on the intercom to Terry, and we went into an attack. We were at 2,000 feet: I reported that I had put on the Master Switch and I told the Wireless Operator to make his first sighting report to 19 Group Headquarters. Terry continued his dive to the target and said, "I've got her – I'll drop the bombs" and this he did.

Unfortunately, our stick of 8 Depth Charges slightly overshot, and by this time the U Boat was submerging, and on our return run, all there was to see was a large oil patch showing that we had damaged our Target. The photographs taken by our camera as we went into our attack confirmed this.

Coastal Command Policy at that time was, that the attacking aircraft should stay in the vicinity of the attack until relieved by another aircraft to ensure that the damaged U Boat could not come to the surface to charge its batteries. After a few hours circling the oil patch, another aircraft relieved us, and we returned to St. Eval.

After we landed and taxied to our dispersal point, who should be waiting to greet us but Wing Commander Squadron Commander, who was really chuffed at our success, and afterwards in the Mess he discovered that I was a Coca Cola man, and did not need alcohol to celebrate.

The whole crew were summoned to attend a debriefing at Coastal command Headquarters which was conducted by the Commander in Chief Coastal Command, Air Marshal Slessor, who wined and dined us at a Luncheon party afterwards.

Our Squadron policy for all crews was to operate one day, rest the next day, get our aircraft ready to operate on the third day, and operate every fourth day. This was an excellent procedure because all aircrew knew where they were, and what was expected of them, but as my Flight Commander could only operate once a fortnight, this was no good to me.

However, being a Senior Navigator, this left me free to fly as a screen navigator with our crews, and share the navigation, which suited everyone fine.

One of the crews I operated with had a Captain who was a Warrant Officer, whose name was W H A Jones. The rest of his crew were all Senior NCO's, and in my opinion at that time, 'Jonah' had the best crew in the Squadron. Jonah had a Canadian navigator, who went sick, and so I volunteered to become Jonah's navigator until his man returned. However, he never did return and, although I still flew with the Flight Commander once a fortnight, I became the permanent navigator in Jonah's crew.

Warrant Officer Jones was a Welshman, and he normally spoke at 200 words a minute, but if he became excited, he would speak at 300 words a minute which was so fast no one could understand him.

Before the war, Jonah had been a steeplechase jockey, and it is well known to all aviators that the best pilots are equestrians or sailors, and Jonah was one of the best. He had excellent balance and virtually flew 'by the seat of his pants'.

Travalgie Hotel was about three miles from St. Eval as the crow flies, but about ten miles by road due to the hilly terrain and sharp hairpin bends. Sadly on the first day our Squadron arrived in Newquay, two of our Airmen went swimming and got caught up in the strong currents and were drowned. Therefore, from day one, many beaches were out of bounds.

As the war progressed, new and better bombing equipment arrived, and as the Bombing Leader, it was my job to train the other aircrew members how to operate this. Also, having previously trained gunnery Leaders, I made it my responsibility to keep Jonah's crew up to date and in full practise. I was therefore considered to be a very experienced navigator, but a bit bossy. This of course was the result of having bossed Observers about for two years while teaching them Bombing and Gunnery from scratch. It was also quickly discovered that I knew all about inventories and airmen's welfare, and was considered a 'Gen Kiddie'.

There came the time when we were being briefed to patrol our first convoy.

The Intelligence Officer briefing us was a Squadron Leader Shackleton, whose grandfather had been the great Antarctic Explorer.

As far as we could be told, the convoy was just this side of the middle of the Atlantic. For the past fortnight, the convoy had been sailing in the middle of a Low Pressure System with a cloud base of no more than 100 feet. Due to a strict rule of silence being maintained by the convoy, no one knew its exact position. Squadrons of Coastal Command had been searching for it for over 10 days to no avail. In fact, as far as Shackleton was concerned, the convoy was lost. He knew it was in the middle of the Atlantic somewhere, and that was the best he could do for us.

Therefore, the only facts I knew were that: the Atlantic Ocean was a vast place; and, that convoys always travel at the speed of the slowest vessel. And so, I asked the Intelligence Officer two questions. One – what speed had the convoy been travelling at before it became lost, and two – what was the Latitude and Longitude of its last known position. Having obtained this information, I took Jonah into a huddle in the map room and drew a large circle on my chart, and said to my Captain of Aircraft, "Jonah, I think the convoy is somewhere in the middle of the circle", which he agreed with. And so it was decided to fly to the middle of the circle that I had drawn on my chart and off we set.

It was brilliant sunshine for the first one hundred miles, flying at 2,000 feet, but as we entered the Low Pressure System we were forced to fly lower and lower to keep contact with the sea, until we were flying in the base of the cloud at 100 feet.

We ultimately reached the point where I thought the convoy might be, but all we found was acres and acres of dirty, dark green ocean, which looked most inhospitable.

Jonah said, "What do we do now?"

The visibility distance was about five miles, and so I said that we would do a 'creeping line ahead search'. I drew a line from my position towards St. Eval, and gave a course to steer 20 miles to Starboard, and then turn to Port for 10 miles, after which another turn to Starboard for 40 miles etc. Jonah had all hands on deck; some crewmembers were looking to Port, and others looking to Starboard with Jonah looking dead ahead.

Jonah had the most wonderful power of concentration. Whenever we were airborne he never stopped looking, and low and behold, after we had been doing a Creeping Line Ahead Search for about an hour, who should spot the Convoy but our Jonah. He immediately ordered the 1st Wireless Operator to send a Recognition Signal with the Code of the Day by Aldis Lamp to the Cruiser Somerset who was in charge of the Convoy, which was formally acknowledged.

It must be remembered that this convoy had been covered by cloud for over a fortnight, and so their navigator had had no means of getting a fix by Astro Navigation. Therefore, the first message we received from the Cruiser Somerset was "What is my position?" Jonah called me up on the intercom, and said, "Gibby, the Convoy Commander wants to know his position. Personally I think it's bloody awful, but will you please give the 1st Wireless Operator our position to transmit."

However, the 1st Wireless Operator was able to send our Latitude and Longitude by Aldis Lamp, which was received with grateful thanks. We were then given instructions to patrol around the Convoy doing an ante Submarine search. It was then that we realised the size of the Convoy, which was travelling at 7 knots, and was spread over an area of over 20 square miles. We patrolled for several hours until our Prudent Limit of Endurance, and on leaving the Cruiser Somerset, we sent a signal saying that we were leaving, but that they could expect further patrols by the RAF in the near future.

On our way back home, Jonah climbed up above the clouds, and it was a joy to behold the brilliant sunshine again. I was also able to check our wind speed and direction and amend our ETA.

By this stage in my career I had become a Flying Officer, but what I liked about flying with Warrant Officer Jones was that he was definitely the Captain of his aircraft, and we all knew it. He had trained his crew to keep a good lookout, and in this connection he set a wonderful example.

After a patrol of at least 10 hours, Jonah's eyes were like 'organ stops'. There were 8 members in his crew; they were the Captain, 2nd Pilot, Navigator, Flight Engineer, 1st Wireless Operator, Mid Upper Turret Wireless Operator, Air Gunner, Tail Turret Wireless Operator, and a spare Wireless Operator Air Gunner.

Of the 4 W/Ops Air Gunners, they alternated between the three positions. They changed positions every 40 minutes, with one always at rest while the other three positions were manned.

When flying over the Ocean on look out duty, it is very easy to become lethargic and think, 'We're not going to see anything today', because one bit of the Ocean looks very much like another, but with Jonah's method of changing positions every 40 minutes the crew members had only just settled in before it was time to move again. Hence, lethargy was never a problem.

At the debriefing after finding the convoy, Squadron Leader Shackleton informed us that another aircraft was on its way to take over the ante submarine patrolling around the convoy, and that the Navy had sent their grateful thanks for passing on the Latitude and Longitude of their lost convoy.

Our Squadron Commander was quite chuffed in the knowledge that it was one of his Squadron's aircraft that had made the discovery, but our Irish Rear Gunner said, "That's OK Jonah, if the convoy had not been there in the first place, we would not have been able to find it!"

Such Irish logic kept our feet on the ground, and we all went off to our various messes and had a good meal.

I can recall one particular incident of note when I was 58 Squadron's Operations Officer and working in the Operations Room. At this time, Number 61 Squadron from Bomber Command were seconded to St. Eval for an operational rest. The Coastal Command Squadrons at St. Eval thought this was an insult, as the Bomber Command Navigators were completely incapable of performing Dead Reckoning navigation, and in all cases had to have a Coastal Command Navigator operating with them to make sure they carried out the Patrols they were ordered to do.

On 17th July 1942, a 502 Squadron Whitley aircraft was detailed to fly a 3-legged Patrol lasting about ten hours from start to finish. 30 minutes later, a Lancaster aircraft from 61 Squadron, with Flight

Lieutenant Hunter as Captain and a 502 Squadron Navigator to supervise the navigation, took off to fly the same patrol down the same tracks as the 502 aircraft. However, as the Lancaster carried more fuel than the Whitley, they flew further on the outward leg, but returned down the same track as the 502 aircraft on the homeward leg.

The 502 aircraft, flying at 2,000 feet, flew right over a U Boat without seeing it except for the rear gunner who reported to the Captain that they had just flown over a U Boat.

At that time U Boats were not submerging and had army gunners on board with 37 mm cannon to protect them. However, the 502 aircraft carried on as if it had not seen the U Boat, dropped down to sea level, did a dog leg, and then returned, dropping a stick of eight Depth Charges right across the U Boat and damaging it so badly that the U Boat could not submerge, and all it could do was go round in circles.

The 502 aircraft however could not continue to circle the U Boat until another aircraft had relieved it as it had reached its Prudent Limit of Endurance, and had to return to St. Eval.

Now, due to the expert navigational skill of the 502 navigator who was in the 61 Squadron Aircraft who were returning by same track as the Whitley aircraft, they saw the damaged U Boat circling, and dropped another stick of Depth Charges right over the U Boat, and blew it out of the water.

All aircraft on Ante Submarine Patrols were fitted with Forward and Backward facing Cameras. When Flight Lieutenant Hunter's negatives were developed, they showed 67 bodies floating in the water.

Then the fun started.

Bomber Command made an immediate award of a DFC to Flight Lieutenant Hunter. Coastal Command was completely confounded. DFC's were not dished out with the NAAFI rations when the crews were only performing tasks for which they had been trained. However, after a fortnight, Coastal Command also awarded a DFC to the 502 Squadron Pilot.

And then I 'blew my top'.

I was a mature navigator of 29 years of age, and I took my Squadron Commander Wing Commander Wilfred Oulton to task, stating how unfair this was.

I pointed out the U Boat had been sunk because the rear gunner in the 502 aircraft was the only one to sight the U Boat, and his name had not even been reported in the Form Orange (the debriefing form). Wing Commander Oulton, to his credit, agreed with me, and ultimately the 502 Rear Gunner was awarded a D F M.

Honour had been satisfied, and Coastal Command reverted to its standard procedure. Crews had to bring back either photographic evidence or prisoners on the wing tips before anyone received congratulations from the management.

In 1940, St. Eval was bombed, and the Station Headquarters was severely damaged, and all of the Accountancy records were lost. At the next fortnightly Pay Parade, airmen, on presenting themselves to the Pay Table, were asked their name, rank, number, and trade.

There was one clever airman who realised what had happened.

When this airman presented himself, he gave his name, number, rank and trade - Fitter IIe – drew his pay, and went home. He did this every fortnight for the next 18 months.

In the Accountancy Office there was a bright young WAAF who, on examining the accountancy records, noticed that this airman had not had any leave for 18 months. She reported this to her Boss and said, "Sir, I know there is a war on, but there is an airman here who has had no leave for 18 months." The Accountancy Officer rang his opposite number, Wing Commander Teck, and said, "Have you an airman 'x'", (and he gave the name, number, rank, and trade of the airman), "working for you?" Wing Commander Teck replied, "I've never heard of him."

An the next Pay Parade, when Fitter IIe presented himself for his pay, a Military Policeman confronted him and said, "Got yer!". Of course, the Station Commander wanted to Court Martial the airman, but when the Manuals of Air Force Law and King's Regulations were studied, it was discovered that as the airman had only been absent for 14 days since the last Pay Parade, he could only be charged with being absent without leave for that period.

When the Station Commander was taking the Charge, he asked the airman why he had done it. The airman replied, "No one gave me any work to do after I was paid, and so I went home." The airman was living in a hiring with his wife and children. The maximum punishment the Station Commander could give was 14 days detention as the airman had only been absent since the last Pay Parade. The Station Commander got some redress because he sent for the airman and said, "I think you have become rather set in your ways, and so after your detention, you will be posted to India."

Before World War II, there was an Auxiliary Air Force of women who became the Women's Auxiliary Air Force, and were called up to serve.

St. Eval was one of the first stations to receive a contingent, but there was one snag. Stations were built for men only.

However the Station Commander solved the problem by choosing two huts far away from the men's accommodation. He was showing the WAAF Officer the site he had chosen, and said he would have it surrounded by barbed wire for greater safety.

The WAAF Officer said, "There's no need to do that Sir, my girls have got it up here!" pointing to her temple.

To which the CO replied, " Flight Officer So-and-so, it doesn't matter where they've got it, my boys will find it!"

Every fourth normal operational rest day, most aircrew would relax in Newquay or on the beaches, but I could never waste time laying about in the sun, and so, as the Bombing Leader, I would busy myself checking that the navigator/bomb aimers were au fait with the use of the equipment, or I would make myself useful helping the Adjutant.

I often noticed that on lovely sunny days, many airmen would be walking about the camp with a piece of paper in their hands while enjoying the sunshine. Therefore I asked myself, if it was necessary to walk about when the sun was shining, why was it not necessary to do the same when it was raining? Of course, it was a way of skiving, and no one is better at skiving than the AC Plonk.

In this connection I was up to my old games. On a beautiful sunny day with at least 80% blue sky, I would get an 'Oppo' to join me in looking upwards, occasionally pointing, and within a minute or two it was possible to bring a Station to a standstill, with everyone looking skywards. There was never of course anything there, and so we used to skulk away, leaving everyone looking at nothing!

On one particular day the weather was atrocious, and we 'stood by' all day, waiting for it to improve, and eventually it was 1700 hours and Jonah's crew was 'stood down'. After dinner that night, I walked into Newquay to a dance. The usual crowd was there, and I danced nearly every dance. Just as I was leaving, I got dragged into a party with some of the other members of our Squadron, and it was nearly 0200 hours before I was walking back to Travalgie Hotel. When I was about 400 yards from the hotel, I could see an aircrew coach waiting, and I said to myself, 'Some poor sod's got an early start!'

As I got close to my sleeping quarters, I noticed Jonah and his crew waiting outside the coach. When Jonah saw me, he said, "Come on Gibby, we're on 'Ops'. "But we were stood down," I said. "I know" was the reply, "but the weather improved, so I volunteered." I suddenly felt a little weary, but I went to my room, got my flying gear, and by 0300 hours we were being briefed for a 12-hour patrol.

As soon as I started to navigate, I was wide-awake. If a navigator does his job properly, he is fully employed. There is always something to do. We were on the final leg of our Patrol when Jonah broadcast on the intercom, "Scillies, Dead Ahead." I went and stood beside the 2nd Pilot, and there, in the brilliant sunshine, was Bishops Rock, and beyond, the Cornish Coast, and I knew that Jonah did not need me any more as the aircraft knew the way to St. Eval without my help!

Apart from debriefing, my job was over, and I suddenly felt a little tired again. I always carried some Benzedrine Tablets in case any of the crew needed pepping up, but if any were issued, an entry had to be made in the Log. I had never had to issue any before, but on this occasion I thought I'd try one. It was the worst thing I could have done. If I had thought about it I should have taken one four hours earlier, because when we landed 45 minutes later, I was raring to go! I asked the rest of the crew, "What are you doing tonight?" They said they were going to a dinner dance. "Right, I'll see you there!!"

Once again, I danced all night. After the dance, although it was only two miles back to the hotel, I took a taxi, and by the time the driver had stopped at the Hotel, I was fast asleep and he had to wake me........!

One day when I was Bombing Leader I had some work to do at RAF St Athans and, luckily for me, Squadron Leader Lawson also had cause to go there. I was therefore able to cadge a lift with his crew, and off we went.

At that time the Squadron Navigator had become a member of Lawson's crew, and so I decided to take a back seat and went to sleep. It was on the same day that I had organised a Station Dance, and it was most essential I return to St. Eval as soon as possible.

St. Athans was only about 30 minutes flying time from St. Eval, and I had no idea how long I had been asleep, but it was not long before I was awakened by the sounds of the wheels going down and the normal revs of the engine's change, and in no time at all we were taxiing to the dispersal point.

I looked out and saw it was very overcast, and Monty, who was Lawson's Rear Gunner, came up to me and said, "It's OK Gibby, we're there. It has taken a little longer than usual because the cloud base is down on the deck. We won't be able to take off again in this, and so we have got permission to stay the night." I said, "Don't be bloody silly Monty, I can't stay the night here. You know I've got the Station Dance to organise tonight. I'm not getting out of this plane!"

By this time, Squadron Leader Lawson had joined us, and had heard our conversation, and he said, "Gibson, we're staying here tonight, and so get out of this aircraft - that's an order!" I reluctantly obeyed, and was quietly mumbling to myself that I would do my business and get my Pilot, Jonah, to pick me up. Lawson's crew however completely ignored my protestations, and were grinning at my discomfort.

The aircrew bus ultimately arrived, and the WAAF driver got out. When I saw who it was, I said, "Hello Mary, what are you doing here?" She answered, "I've come to pick you up." "I know that," I said, "but what are you doing at St. Athans?" "St. Athans? This isn't St. Athans, this is St. Eval!"

Lawson's crew were laughing their heads off, and then the penny dropped. Because of the low cloud base at St. Athans, while I was asleep they decided to return to St. Eval to make sure I would be able to run the Station Dance. "You rotten sods!" I said, which caused more laughter when I realised I had fallen for yet another of Monty's pranks......

After I had been with 58 Squadron for about six weeks, we had a new Squadron Commander, a Wing Commander Ferguson-Stewart, who was Coastal Command trained as opposed to our Bomber Command trained 'Wing co', which made sense. But even before he had got to know his aircrews, his Squadron was posted to Stornaway.

I helped the Adjutant to write the operation order to move the Squadron, and one day we operated from St. Eval, and the next we operated from Stornaway, and in so doing, we did not lose a nut or bolt, but more importantly any airmen. Everyone departed from St. Eval except me. As I was the Inventory Holder of the Officers' Mess at Travalgie Hotel, I had to stay behind to hand over the Inventory to an American Squadron who had moved in. This took all day, and so I decided to stay the night and move to Stornaway the next day.

After dinner, the Yanks insisted on entertaining the 'Limey' to thank me for the help I had given them, and the best way they thought they could do this was for me to join them in a game of Poker. I tried to get out of this by saying I didn't know how to play Poker, but one of the American Officers said he couldn't play because he was expecting a telephone call from America, but he would sit with me and 'hold my hand'.

All I had on me was £5.00, and so I decided to play until I had lost that, and then call it a day. However, with the help of my newfound friend, I kept on winning. There were seven of us in this 'school', and five of the players thought it was great fun, and were happy to call it beginner's luck. One of the players who kept losing however was getting really nasty. He just did not like losing, especially to an ignoramus like me.

Each of the Americans had over £100.00 in their shirt top pockets, and I had such a pile of money in front of me that I went and got my peak cap and put my money in that. A different dealer dealt the cards for each game, and when it came to the turn of the man next to me, he announced, "Five cards, three's and nine's are wild". Just then, the telephone rang and my guide went off to take his call, and so I was on my own. I was dealt with two threes, an Ace and a nine, and a rubbish card, and so I decided to change the rubbish card, and in its place I was given another nine. I was, therefore, stuck with two threes, two nines, and an Ace.

In my ignorance I thought I had two pairs and an Ace, and so the bidding went on, and I just kept putting money in to the kitty which was just fine because I was getting rid of my ill gotten gains, until there was only me and the horrible type left in the game. Ultimately the horrible one said he would 'see me', at which time my advisor returned, and when I turned my cards over, all hell was let lose, and I didn't know why. I asked my friend, "How come? Three's and nine's are wild, whatever that means?" My friend said, "You bloody fool, you've got five aces!" I thought that the horrible one was going to put a knife in me because he had four kings!

There was over five hundred pounds in the kitty that had been pushed over to me, and by this time it was way past my bedtime, so I took my original £5.00 out of my hat, turned it upside down, and said, "I'm off to bed now, thank you for the game; have a drink on me".

The sequel was they all got drunk on their own money, and at breakfast the next morning I was the only one without a hangover.

The greeting I got was, "Stupid Limey!!"

Having made my farewells to the owners of the Travalgie Hotel who were still in residence, the Americans gave me a lift into St. Eval where I completed my clearance and got myself a Rail Warrant for my 600-mile journey to Stornaway.

On arrival, the first thing I noticed on Daily Routine Orders was that all personnel had been confined to camp. Apparently the Squadron who we were relieving had not enjoyed the Stornawegien's hospitality and so, on being posted, they had bombed the town with streams of toilet rolls, which did not agree with the Scottish sense of humour!

That meant 2,000 officers and airmen with just 1 Flight Officer WAAF (who was the Cipher expert), because of the previous Squadron's prank, were all confined to Camp.

The Station Cinema was most popular and was filled to capacity each night and, therefore, in an endeavour to prevent the airmen from getting bored, the programmes were changed every 48 hours. At one time one of the secondary films being shown contained a long drawn out romantic scene with the hero in old-fashioned Cavalry Uniform telling his sweetheart that he had been ordered to join his Regiment. This scene went on and on, until one airman lost patience, and yelled at the screen, "Get in – you're posted!" which broke the tension with everybody laughing.

For the airmen, the Salvation Army provided facilities for indoor games such as Table Tennis and Darts etc, and also excellent food.

Every night, the Hall was packed while the NAAFI, although open, was empty. The "SallyAnn" as it was called was run by a Salvation Army lady with the rank of Major, and she could not do enough to please the Airmen. Needless to say, the Airmen knew when they were well off, and there was never any trouble.

Somehow or other in the Officers' Mess a party developed every night. We had a large anteroom, at one end of which was a Bar where all of the 'Pissy' types congregated, and at the other end was a very large open brick fireplace where logs were burnt continuously throughout the evening. That was where the sober types sat, in a semi circle of leather armchairs, drinking their refreshments. The 'Wag' of the Squadron was the Flight Lieutenant Gunnery Leader who, after a few beers, would stand with his back to the fire and, in his own words, 'try to liven up the sober Bastards'!

One evening he joined us, with a glass of beer in his hand, and took a spare seat. Our Flight Officer WAAF Helen was standing with her back to the fire, drinking an Orange Juice. Beside her was our Wing Commander, who was drinking a beer and partaking in polite conversation. The Wag Roberts started teasing Helen, and after a bit, he said, "Helen, I've never noticed before, but do you know you're bandy?" "Bandy!" exploded Helen, "Don't be so stupid!" That was just the reply our Wag wanted because he managed to draw everybody's attention to Helen and her legs. He bent down on his knees before her and said, "If I were to put my hand between your ankles, I could go right up your thighs without touching your legs!"

By this time our end of the anteroom was in uproar, so much so that the drinkers had joined us to see what the hilarity was all about. That was too much for Helen, and she said, "Roberts, I know I'm not bandy, you ask the Wing Commander". 'Wingco' was non-plussed, spluttered in his beer and said, "Helen, don't bring me into this – how would I know?" Somebody poured beer over Roberts who retired to clean himself up, leaving the rest of us laughing uncontrollably. Helen joined in our hilarity because she realised she had fallen prey to Roberts' sense of humour, and that, being the only female on the camp, there was safety in numbers!

Wing Commander Ferguson-Stewart was an officer and a gentleman, and prior to becoming our Squadron Commander, had been with a Sunderland Flying Boat Squadron. That alone told us a bit about our new 'Wingco' because only the best aviators were posted to 'Boats'.

Soon after our new CO took over, we heard we were going to be converted on to the 4 engine Halifax aircraft, and that our CO would convert the pilots himself. As soon as the first two Halifax aircraft arrived it was decided to train one new Officer crew, and one SNCO's crew.

As Jonah was the Senior NCO, his crew was chosen, and Squadron Leader Lawson's crew was selected for the officers' crew. There were no flies on our Jonah, and before the Halifax's had arrived he had acquired a copy of the 'Pilot's Notes', and after a few circuits and bumps with the CO, Jonah was declared fit to operate a Halifax aircraft.

A new crew member was posted to join Jonah's crew, a Flight Engineer, which we did not have in Whitley aircraft, and so Jonah got us all airborne for a familiarisation exercise, and in particular to get to know his new Flight Engineer whose job it was to keep a check on petrol consumption, and change the fuel tanks etc. Jonah's new crew now consisted of: Captain, Navigator, Flight Engineer, 2nd Pilot and 4 Wireless Operator/Air Gunners.

Searching for U Boats was Jonah's highest priority when on ante Submarine Patrols, and no one set the example better. He knew that searching thousands of acres of Air force could become very boring. The four wireless operators had three positions to man, with the fourth W/op always on rest. Therefore, to overcome boredom, Jonah rotated his four W/ops every 40 minutes; therefore before they could start going to sleep, they had to change position again. This system worked, and it meant we always had an alert crew on lookout.

The first thing I noticed about Stornaway was that there were no trees. We never had less than a 30 knot wind blowing - and that was the reason – high winds, no trees. We carried on as normal with our ante submarine patrols but we were now covering the area from the Outer Hebrides to Iceland, and the Northern Approaches.

On my first patrol, after I thought we were about half way to Iceland, I thought I would check my wind speed and direction by the three-course method. I dropped down to the Bomb Aimers' position and looked forward and, surprise, surprise - there was Iceland dead ahead.

I dashed back to my navigation table and checked all of my calculations, but my ETA Iceland remained the same.

Therefore I looked dead ahead, and there was Iceland, apparently just as far away. The reason for this clear visibility I worked out was because the air was so clean and pure, one could see forever.

It was like breathing champagne....

* * *

13

All Aviators are characters!

A
ll aviators are characters, but the more extravert they are, the more noticeable they become. At Stornaway, we had two Flying Officer Pilots on the Squadron who were both named Hartley – one was Eric, the other, Fred.

Fred was into everything, even things that had nothing to do with him, and quite often he would make a 'cock up' of whatever he was supposed to be doing. He would then be told to pull your finger out'. Hence, his nickname became 'Fingers', and no one ever called him anything else.

Eric was totally different. He was only 19 years of age with a youthful outlook on life. He had a good crew, was a Captain of Aircraft, and was doing a man's job, and I became quite friendly towards him.

Another one of our pilots was a Flying Officer Tom Stoney, a Southern Irishman, with a beautiful Irish brogue, and all of the charm that goes with the Irish race. Piloting aircraft came easy to him. He treated aeroplanes as toys for grown ups.

He was an exceptional pilot, and on one occasion his crew were ordered to do a practise bombing in a Whitley aircraft. As the Squadron Bombing Leader, I went along to make sure his crew knew how to work all of the bombing equipment.

Our Squadron Commander, who was new to the Squadron, had heard of Tom's ability, and decided to act as 2nd Pilot to witness Tom's powers at first hand. All went well, with the Navigator/Bomb Aimer working all of the equipment OK, but on the first Bombing run, no bombs were dropped because the Bomb Aimer forgot to put the Master Switch on. I allowed this to happen in order to impress on the Bomb Aimer that, no matter how accurately he had lined up the target, no bombs would ever be dropped if the Master Switch had not been operated.

On coming in to land at Stornaway, Tom did a tight circuit with rate 3 turns, and on his final approach, realising he was a little too high, he side slipped the Whitley just as if he were flying a Tiger Moth, straightened up and made a perfect landing. I was standing behind the two pilots, and noticed that 'Wingco' had gone white. When the aircraft rolled to a stop, 'Wingco' said, "Tom – don't ever do that to me again!" With Irish eyes smiling, Tom said "OK, Sir!"

I flew several operational sorties with Tom's crew; it was always a pleasure to be flown in such a competent way.

In the Officers' Mess we lived like Lords. Our Station Commander was an aged Group Captain who I am sure would have been retired had it not been broadcast by Mr. Neville Chamberlain that a state of war existed, because he acted as if he did not know that there was a war on! The Station Catering Officer had been a chef at The Ritz Hotel in London, and we fed like fighting cocks! He was excellent at doing deals with the local Stornawegians, and at dinner, which was always a seven-course affair, Salmon was always available. At dinner we always had to wear our Best Blue Uniform, and it was always a very formal affair. Stornaway is noted for its Kippers – they were huge, and I have never tasted better. They were delicious, and always on the breakfast menu.

Our Group Captain had a table to himself, which could seat eight people and was sacrosanct. No one sat at that table uninvited – it was out of bounds.

On Saturdays he would invite our 'Wingco' and, of course, Helen, together with one or two officers whose faces fitted at that time, but everything was very formal which created a tense atmosphere, which nobody really enjoyed.

Reading the local newspaper I discovered there was a large hospital in Stornaway, and being confined to camp, I realised we were all lacking in female company. Therefore I contacted the Matron and asked her if she would allow any of her nurses to attend a dance in the Officers' Mess if I could arrange it. The Matron thought it was an excellent idea, and so I approached the President of the Mess Committee to see if I could have permission to organise a dance. He said he would have to get the Station Commander's permission, and he would let me know the result.

In a day or two, I was given the all clear, and so I got cracking. I told our Squadron Commander that I had permission to arrange a dance and asked if I could have his blessing, which was freely given, and I was on my way.

In co-operation with the Matron, a date was fixed, a Band ordered, and the Catering Officer detailed to provide food for the occasion. The former chef was chuffed because, he told me, when he was at The Ritz, he specialised in catering for Banquets, and so I left that side to him. Because of the numbers involved, I arranged a self help system from the Festive Board which was arranged on two full sized Billiards' Tables, with a Pig's Head as the centre piece, surrounded by salmon, trout etc, and it was a wonderful display. Our Chef surpassed himself. Where he got the food from, only he knew, and it would have been churlish to ask him. However, a good time was had by all, and some of the junior officers made complete 'pigs' of themselves!

We had a Flight Lieutenant Catholic Priest on the Station who was unable to attend our dance as he had pre-arranged to take 14 day's leave in Southern Ireland. However, our Wag Roberts turned up at the dance wearing the Priest's Dog Collar. Our Catholic Priest must have been very well known in Stornaway before our Squadron arrived as our Wag was surrounded by our lady guests from the hospital. Every now and again he would disappear with a nurse on his arm to such an extent he had to enlist help from some of his friends, but although they did their best to entertain, it was the Catholic Priest they really wanted!

Carriages were ordered for 0200 hours, but by the time I had organised the Batmen's supper from the Festive Board and made sure the Dining Room (where the dancing took place) was 'Ship shape and Bristol Fashion' for breakfast the next morning, it was 0330 hours before I got to bed. At 0630 hours my batman awoke me with a cup of tea, and I was down in the dining room at 0730 hours as usual.

There were not so many early risers as usual, and quite a number were suffering from hangovers, and were feeling very sorry for themselves which created a sombre atmosphere, when suddenly the Dining Room door burst open, and Wag Roberts, laughing like a Cheshire Cat, entered and marched sprightly across the room and sat at the Group Captain's table. That broke the tension because no one ever sat at 'Groupies' table without being invited, and even the 'Pissy types' who just wanted to die joined in the fun.

I had invited the local press to our dance as a PR job, and they sent along a photographer, and as a result several nurses reported what a good time they had, and the ban was lifted. All RAF personnel were once again welcomed into the Town. Our Wag took full advantage of this and met several of the nurses in town, properly dressed without the Priest's Dog Collar, and he had the greatest difficulty in trying to convince his female friends that he was not the Padré.......!

There was a pilot in our Squadron by the name of Flight Lieutenant Richards. He had attended Loughborough College where he had obtained a degree in Physical Education. A fine athlete who, when ordinary mess games such as Hick-cock-a-loram became boring, would introduce games of a more physical nature.

One night, he placed a four-seat sofa in the middle of the anteroom, and an armchair laid on its back touching one end of the sofa. He walked past the opposite end, turned, and ran towards the sofa, took a flying leap towards the far end of the sofa, placed his hands on the far end, did a neck roll, hit the edge of the armchair, causing it to rotate so that he finished sitting in the armchair. Very spectacular – and very difficult. 'Fingers' Hartley decided he'd have some of that! So, he tried a dozen times. Unfortunately his flying was not far enough, and each time he finished up in a crumpled heap at the far end of the sofa. Much to the delight of the onlookers. Fingers would not believe the trick was beyond him, and so he got the expert to show him again how to do it. How easy the expert made it look! Fingers just could not believe it.

Unfortunately, he never did get the hang of it, and his failure caused much amusement. However, he did get full marks for even trying.

Then, tired of being laughed at, he challenged his friends to try. All failed except for one pilot. That success was proof for Fingers that it was possible – so he started all over again – still without success. He then had a bright idea – everyone in the anteroom must try, starting with the 'Pissy Types'. There was one Officer named Storey, who, although he had been drinking, was completely sober, and he refused Fingers' challenge and was therefore immediately accused of being 'yellow', That had no effect, and so we sober types were challenged.

One of our number accepted and executed the manoeuvre with great aplomb. That caused such amazement that another challenge was made to Storey, who again refused downright to try. True to form, Fingers announced again the man was yellow.

When I was at Art School, we had a Sergeant Major who took our class twice a week for physical training, which included Box Horse work, Parallel Bars, Tumbling etc, and in all of which I became proficient. When it came to my turn to be challenged by Fingers I accepted, and to everyone's amazement, not least my own, I succeeded.

Fingers was beside himself. Once again he challenged Storey, saying if a bastard navigator can do it, why don't you try. Lo and behold, Storey took off his jacket, tried, and finished up sitting in the armchair! That did it! Fingers tried again and failed. He just kept on and on until Storey, a couple of others, and I, toddled off to bed.

We slept in a corrugated Nissan hut, and every night, when Fingers was not on operations, on his way to bed at about 0200 hours, he used to wake everyone up to say 'Goodnight'. This particular night, Storey, who was quite sober, kept saying "If Fingers wakes me on his way to bed and says I'm yellow, I'll kill him!"

Storey and six others shared the Nissan Hut where I slept. We had all retired, but Fingers, on his way to bed, with a piece of wood ratting against the corrugated sides of the hut and making a hell of a din, came into our hut, went straight to Storey's bed and told him he was yellow. Thereupon Storey, who had been waiting for this, jumped up and had Fingers by the throat, shaking the life out of him. It took several of us quite a while to separate the two with Fingers hurt, but still alive – just. I helped Fingers to his billet because he needed assistance to walk, but next night all had been forgotten, and everybody had to be wakened again for Fingers to say 'Goodnight'!

After patrolling for U Boats for about six months at Stornaway and not having seen any, the Squadron was posted to Holmsley South in the New Forest. There were still some of our crews operating in Whitley aircraft, mainly because our Squadron Commander was just too busy to train them on to Halifax aircraft.

A rumour went round that a qualified Instructor was going to join us to do that job.

One lovely, sunny morning, we were sitting enjoying the sunshine when a Halifax came into view. It did a rate 3 turn, lined up with the runway, and made a completely perfect landing.

All of our pilots were convinced this was our Instructor who had come to convert our remaining crew members. Several of us jumped into the Squadron Pick Up and dashed to our Airfield Control.

It must be remembered that our pilots never flew a Halifax with less than four crew – a Pilot, Navigator, Wireless Operator, and a Flight Engineer.

We opened the door of the Halifax, and nothing happened.

No crew got out.

We waited.

And then, after a while, a little girl, five feet nothing tall and dressed in a Pilot's Uniform, jumped out and said,

"Hi boys!"

One of our Pilots asked, "Where's the Pilot?"

"I'm the Pilot," responded the little girl.

"Where's the crew?" we asked.

"Crew?" She replied, "I don't have a crew, there's only me."

Our Pilots were flabbergasted!

One of them said "Jump in the Pick-up, we must buy you a drink".

She said, "I can't do that Sir, see that Tiger Moth in the circuit? That's come to pick me up – I've a Spitfire to deliver next!".

That was what was needed – there was no more talk about waiting for an Instructor – our Pilots got down to it, and in no time at all, all of our Squadron was fully operational with Halifax aircraft............

While RAF Station Holmsley South was being built in the New Forest, there was no permanent brick-built Officers' Mess, but a large house had been taken over which offered accommodation for both the public rooms and a few bedrooms. The rest of the Officers were housed in corrugated iron Nissen Huts in the Forest, which held 12 to 16 bed spaces according to how they had to cram us in!

These huts had a circular cast iron stove in the centre, which gave out excellent heat, and were kept going 24 hours a day. As the only officer in Jonah's crew, I shared a hut with two other crews. A certain amount of rivalry went on between the two crews, starting with arguments, and usually ending up with wrestling on the floor, and some non-combatants being turned out of bed for laughing too much at the antics.

As I was the lone ranger in this hut, I was never involved in these skirmishes, and I can only remember my bed being turned upside down, with me in it, for laughing too much on one occasion. It was usually not until the early hours before honour had been satisfied as to which crew was the better, which was OK, particularly in inclement weather when we were kept awake all night by the rain beating down on our cast iron roof. Even after it had stopped raining, we had the drips from the trees to contend with.

Living under these arduous communal sleeping conditions, and once again living out of suitcases, it was amazing how happy we were. Even our aristocratic CO had just got used to living under conditions far below those which he could normally expect as a Senior Wing Commander when he was posted, and a Wing Commander Wilfred Oulton took his place.

Our new CO had been commissioned in 1931. He was an experienced Flying Boat Pilot, and quickly got himself airborne in a Halifax to show everybody how he intended to carry on, falling into the category of a 'new broom sweeps clean.' He interviewed each one of his officers individually, and, when it came to my turn, he discovered I was the most Senior Navigator in the Squadron, and informed me he had passed a Specialist Navigation Course, and that was his supernumerary job was as a GD Officer. This was good news because it meant he was on our wavelength, and that he understood our problems.

It took him about a fortnight to settle into his new duties, after which he made his first operational flight as 2nd Pilot to Jonah's crew. He attended the briefing with us, which was quite routine, and with Jonah at the Controls, we set course for Bishops Rock, which was the datum point for all Patrols from which to start.

After about 2 hours Jonah handed over the control to our CO, and all went well. Dawn was just about to break, and I decided to check our wind speed and direction. I went down to the Bomb Aimer's position, and there, 5 miles dead ahead, was a U Boat. I immediately reported this on the intercom, and Wingco said, "OK, we will attack, I'll drop the Depth Charges". At this point our Captain took over on the intercom, and speaking at 300 words a minute, he reminded each member of the crew of the duties we had to perform.

I had previously set the distributor to drop a stick of 8 Depth Charges, and so, after switching 'ON' the Master Switch, I took up my position in the front gun turret.

By this time we were losing height fast, and when we were at a range of 600 yards, I opened fire. The U-Boat was still fully surfaced, but the look out crew must have been asleep because, although they were armed with a 37 MM cannon, they did not return my fire. By this time we were at a height of just 50 feet, and Wingco dropped his Depth Charges, but they overshot. We flew on for a bit, did a dogleg, and returned to where the U-Boat had been. However, it had by now submerged, and was most probably at a depth of 200 feet.

Although we photographed a large oil patch, we could only claim that the U-Boat had been damaged. We circled the area for about ten minutes, after which Wingco said, "OK, Gibby, give me a course to steer to continue our patrol."

At this point, our Captain, Jonah informed our CO that according to Coastal Command Procedure, we should continue to patrol the area until we were relieved in order to prevent the U-Boat from re-surfacing to carry out minor repairs or to recharge its batteries.

However, our Squadron Commander overruled our Captain, saying "Let's continue our Patrol – we might see another U-Boat." Lo and behold, an hour later with Wingco still at the controls, we saw another U-Boat and we went in to attack. I informed Wingco that the Master Switch was ON, and we commenced our dive from 2,000 feet, with the target 3,000 yards dead ahead.

This was a totally different proposition from our first attack for, at a range of 1500 yards, the U-Boat opened fire with its 37 MM Cannon. I only had a point 303 MM Browning Gun, which was the equivalent of a peashooter to Jerry's cannon, and so I had to wait until I was at 600 yards before I could open fire. It was at that time that U-Boats were not diving when spotted, but would remain on the surface and shoot it out with us, and they had army gunners firing their weapons.

While I was waiting to open fire, I saw a Tracer Shell heading straight towards us and enter the leading edge of our starboard wing. As soon as I opened fire, their cannon stopped firing because I had shot the three German gunners dead.

Our forward facing camera recorded the attack, and showed one gunner wearing a submarine 'frock' – a large roll top sweater which came down to the wearer's knees – and a leather helmet with large ear pieces. He did not need these any more however as he was dead. The other two gunners were slumped against the Conning Tower – again, dead.

Immediately after our attack, the U-Boat submerged.

Once again, our Depth Charges were overshot, but this time had done greater damage, evidenced by a much larger oil slick showing on the surface left by the U-Boat.

After the attack was over and we were continuing to circle the area, I spoke to our Wingco who was still at the controls, and told him that one of the Tracer Shells had hit us in the starboard wing. He replied, "Don't be bloody silly Gibson", to which I replied, "Sir, if you come down to the Bomb Aimer's position you will be able to see a hole in our starboard wing, two feet in diameter." This he did, and, when he saw the gaping hole in the leading edge of our starboard wing, he said, "Gibby, give Jonah a course back to base". "But", I said, "Sir, we are still airborne". "No matter Gibby, give Jonah a course for base." This I did, and we made an early, uneventful return to St. Eval for repairs before returning to the New Forest.

I will always remember watching that Tracer Shell leave the Cannon and head for our Halifax. It appeared to be travelling so slowly as it approached, and it was only as it struck our wing that I realised it had been travelling at 2,000 feet per second.

When the wing was stripped down for repairs it was found that the shell had entered our starboard wing, gone through our inner petrol tank, and lodged in the angled support of the petrol tank. It was our good fortune that we had made two attacks early on, when our petrol in the inner petrol tanks were still full, as if we had used some of the fuel in the starboard wing, the gases in the top part of the tank might have ignited and blown the wing off.

When this was being related to our Technical Wing Commander I said, "But, it didn't, and we were able to make it back to base". "But, Wingco", Tech added, "You were still lucky, especially as if the shell had struck 12 feet towards the fuselage, you still might have made base, but without a navigator!"

One occasion we were on the outward leg of an ante submarine patrol in the Bay of Biscay, and the Royal Navy had their 5th Mattapan Group operating off the coast of Spain. They were not observing W/T silence, and our Wireless Operator had tuned into their wavelength, and was listening to them nattering to one another. I decided to check my wind speed and direction.

We were flying over 3,000 feet and the normal practice was to look dead ahead to determine the wind direction by the sea wave lanes, but this time I looked dead underneath our aircraft, and as I did so, the sun shone on an orange coloured sail of a 'Q' type dinghy. I broadcast on the intercom that we had just flown over a dinghy and, fortunately, our Wireless Operator was using the Elsan, by the side of which was a flame float ready to be launched. This was done to mark the spot, because, at 3,000 feet, a dinghy looks no bigger than a small crumb of bread on the centre spot of a football pitch.

I entered in my log the Latitude and Longitude of my Dead Reckoning position while Jonah dropped down to 50 feet above sea level, did a dogleg, and flew back to our flame float. I switched on our camera, and as we approached the dinghy, I could see 5 men all shaking their fists at us, (which was recorded on our camera), but when we flew over them and they realised we were not going to open fire on them, the clenched fists turned into waving, which was also recorded.

The 'Q' Type Dinghy was similar to those which were provided for large crews, and I thought they were five U.S. Airmen in the dinghy. I suggested to Jonah that we fly to the Matapan Group and tell the Navy about the Dinghy with five bodies in it, and see what happens. That we did. On reaching the Matapan Group our Engineer fired the recognition signal of the day which was acknowledged, and our wireless operator sent a message by Aldis Lamp to the Navy about the Dinghy, and gave the Latitude and Longitude of its position.

That was acknowledged, and it was the most wonderful sight to see – five Royal Navy Sloops in brilliant sunshine, turn in line abreast, and start sailing towards the Dinghy.

We had dropped smoke floats every 20 miles as a guide towards the dinghy in case my estimated D.R. Position was inaccurate, and we carried on with our patrol. Later, we were told the five occupants in the dinghy turned out to be five German aviators who had been shot down in a long-range reconnaissance aircraft, a Condor 222, by an RAF Mosquito.

Of course, when the Royal Navy rescues anyone who is in peril on the sea, irrespective of their colour or creed, they get the star treatment.

The five aviators were so overwhelmed by the hospitality they received that they sang like canaries, and divulged the whole of the training programme for the Long Range Reconnaissance Aircraft.

As the war progressed, we had aircrew join our Squadron from several nations. We had two Canadian pilots and one American, and two navigators, one from Argentina, and the other from New Zealand.

On examining their Next of Kin Reports to find out what their preference was for organised games, I discovered the New Zealand Navigator's civilian job was as a Vicar. He was of a quiet disposition, and seemed to treat everybody as his friend, and when I spoke to him about his civilian job, he told me he had put that on one side for the duration of the war, and he did not want it broadcast.

Both Canadians were easy to get on with, and in both cases, they did their best to sell the advantages of being a Canadian, and said that the rest of us would be missing out if, after the war, if we did not emigrate to Canada.

One of the Canadians had been a Royal West Mounted Policeman. He had a team of eight Husky dogs, and it took him six months to patrol his beat. He would then be granted four week's holiday, and then start all over again. When he was not on 'ops', after dinner we would get him to tell us some of his experiences.

They sounded so romantic, and we were getting ready to pack our bags, until he reminded us that the temperature was minus 30 degrees centigrade!

The Argentinean was an extrovert; everybody's friend, and his nickname was Pampas. He was good at his job but the girls saw something in him which escaped us males. I took him to a dance in Newquay and the girls were all over him. In an 'Excuse Me' dance, he would be excused at least a dozen times. It was incredible! My regular dancing partner, who was a semi professional, didn't want to know me while Pampas was around, and so I had to settle for any number of the unattached girls who were not such good dancers.

All of our foreign types quickly settled into the British way of life except for the American. He was a member of the United States Air Force, but he got himself seconded to the RAF before the USA had officially declared war. He was the second pilot in Jonah's crew, and so I got to know him well.

At that time my pay, as a Senior Flight Lieutenant, was £31.00 per month after tax. However, our American 2nd Pilot, who was still paid by the United States Air Force, received £120.00 per month. It took me six months to get through to him that he did not have to buy drinks all round when he entered a bar. In an Officers' Mess, it is considered infra dig for officers to pay cash for drinks. Each officer has his own bar book, and any drinks ordered are recorded in that book, and for which the officer has to sign.

This system had two good points; firstly, when the officer comes to pay his mess bill, he can see how much he has spent on drinks during that month, and, secondly, the PMC is able to control the amount of alcohol an officer consumes if he thinks it is too high.

Our American officer, having dressed for dinner, would join his friends for an aperitif with over £100.00 in his tunic shirt breast pocket. This I considered vulgar, and as he, like me, was a member of Jonah's crew, I took it upon myself to explain to him it was not the right thing to do, and although it took some time for him to break this habit, I won in the end.

Our Squadron drinking place in Newquay was the Bristol Hotel. One night, a party of officers, of which I was one, decided to meet to celebrate at the Bristol, and on entering the establishment, I noted a crowd of American service men drinking at the bar. Our second pilot immediately excused himself, and went to join his compatriots, and I noticed within five minutes he had forsaken his English ways, and was flashing pound notes about and buying everyone a drink.......

Having had a look at Jonah's copy of the Pilots' notes on Halifax aircraft, I realised they had quite a lot to learn, and so when crews were hanging about in the crew room waiting to fly, particularly when the weather was too bad to operate, I used to organise quizzes. Tom Stoney had undergone a three-week Halifax engine course, and he could answer most problems. I would get each pilot to submit a question, and after the discussion, the pilot who had submitted the question had to produce what he thought was the correct answer. Sometimes, as a result, serious arguments would develop which caused much merriment among the rest of the aircrew present.

On one occasion, when the pilots had nearly come to blows, the questioner noticed the rest of us laughing at their antics, and he said,

"It's that bastard Gibson who started all this."

But harmony was soon restored when I replied with the pilots' definition,

"All navigators is bastards!"

There was one tricky question and Tom Stoney, who had not taken part in the discussion, was called upon to settle the matter, and he gave a completely lucid answer, which satisfied everyone. But the same question came up on another day, and Tom was once again called upon for the correct answer, and he gave a completely different answer.

I was present on both occasions, and I did not want to embarrass Tom, so I took him to one side and said, "How come? You gave a totally different answer last week to the same question?" Tom, with both Irish eyes smiling, said, "Yes, I know, its one of those questions when both answers are right!"

That to me was a typical piece of Irish blarney, and I left it at that!

Our Squadron Adjutant was a fat, jolly, sociable person with whom I became quite friendly, and I always knew where I could get a free cup of coffee, or join him in an afternoon cup of tea. He was a good administrator, but he was a lazy sod, and it was not long before, when paying him a visit, I would be helping him out doing routine office tasks.

He was the Inventory holder of the Officers' Mess, and on one of my visits he was bemoaning the fact that he had to check the Inventory, and he was not looking forward to doing it. So what did muggins do? Right. I volunteered to do that for him. It was while I was doing it that I realised what a cushy job the Adjutant had. There were only minor discrepancies to the Officers' Mess Inventory that I was able to put right, and so it only seemed natural that I should relieve the Adjutant of that particular responsibility.

It got to the stage that, when the Adjutant went on leave, I stood in for him.

We had a very good Sergeant in charge of the Orderly Room, and together, we were able to perform the Adjutant's duties without it interfering with my operational flying. On one occasion, while I was doing the Adjutant's job, some paper work came through marked for the Squadron Commander's eyes only, and with that was a copy of the Air Ministry Summary marked 'Secret'. So what does one do when thirsting for knowledge? Right for the second time! I read it from cover to cover before passing it on to the C.O.

It gave a summary of all the work had been carried out over the previous quarter by all the different Commands, and also included a section on World Affairs. That I found fascinating, and I was rather surprised to note that, after it had been lying in the CO's tray for several days, it was obvious he had not had time to read it.

Before locking it away in the secret filing cabinet, I made some notes regarding world news of a general nature, and I was giving a lecture in the crew room to the rest of the boys on current affairs, and in walked 'Wingco'. Of course I stopped, but Wingco said, "Carry on Gibson". After I had finished, there was a general discussion in which Wingco took part. Afterwards the CO button holed me and said, "Where did you get that information?" So, I waffled a bit, saying, "It was on the wireless and in The Times", but I got the impression he did not believe me, and so that was the end of current affairs!

On one occasion we were flying at 3,000 feet with five-eighths cloud cover on a routine ante-submarine patrol. It was at the time when Coastal Command had not made up its mind at what was the best height to fly. Jonah was at the controls, because he always took off and flew for the first two hours before handing over to the second pilot. He had just done that, and had come down to the bomb aimers' position look-out, when suddenly he rushed back past me, tore the second pilot out of his seat, and took over, announcing, "Action Stations, there are 8 JU88's at 1,500 feet below us".

Speaking at 200 words a minute, he rapidly told each one of us what to do while he opened the throttles and started to climb. Immediately I dropped out Depth Charges and passed our latitude and longitude to the first wireless operator for him to pass on to our Group Headquarters. I then took up my position in the Frazer Nash front gun turret.

The spare Wireless Operator was disposing of all of our surplus equipment, parachutes etc, and we were well on our way before the enemy spotted us. Jonah was taking evasive action, flying due West from one cloud to another, and I told him to continue to do that to take us further away from Brest, where I thought the JU88's had come from, and fly due North to take us towards St. Eval.

A Halifax aircraft, when divested of all its surplus equipment, is quite manoeuvrable, and by the time the JU88's started to attack, we were at 5,000 feet and still climbing. Our Flight Engineer was in the Astro Dome doing his Fighter Control bit, when the enemy commenced to attack us from both the port and starboard bows.

Here I came into my own for having trained Gunnery Leaders in my previous appointment, before I got on to an operational Squadron, I was able to put into practise what I knew an Air Gunner should do, and I loved firing from Gun Turrets.

Being attacked from the bows gave me the opportunity to open fire, but the enemy never closed within 400 yards with their attacks, and at that range, our Browning Guns would have to be very lucky to do any lethal damage.

With Jonah still taking evasive action and throwing our aircraft all over the sky, after one hour the JU88's broke off the engagement, and all we could honestly claim was that two of their aircraft broke away, diving to sea level, belching smoke.

Then, my job started, because for over an hour no one had been navigating. The only thing I knew for sure was, we were some 200 miles west of Brest, and, flying over the Atlantic Ocean. Therefore I drew a circle of 50 mile radius, and said to myself, we are somewhere in that circle. Jonah was flying due North, and so I told him I had some idea where we were, and to continue flying due North. Jonah replied, "Nice to hear your voice Gibby – carry on".

I worked out a course for St. Eval, and told Jonah to carry on flying due North for another ten minutes, and then turn East, and he said, "No, Gibby; let's keep flying due North for another ten minutes," "OK Jonah," I said. But, it wasn't OK with me. Jonah had never queried a course I had given him before, and I wasn't going to let him decide when to turn to base this time. Therefore, I rechecked all of my calculations, and when the second ten minutes was up, Jonah said, "What was that course you want me to fly Gibby?" I said, "Jonah, I've rechecked our position – let's fly another ten minutes due North and then turn 088 Magnetic." "OK", said Jonah. And that's what we did.

After we had been flying for over an hour towards St. Eval, I called up Jonah and said I thought it was safe to call up St. Eval for a Q.D.M. (a magnetic course to steer to under no wind conditions). So, Jonah gave instructions to the 1st Wireless Operator to call up St. Eval for a QDM and surprise surprise – to me!! The Magnetic course to reach St. Eval came back to us as 088 degrees – exactly to the degree to which we were flying. The rest of the crew thought I was marvellous, but I knew it was sheer luck and that the Lord was on our side.

We landed at St. Eval, took on some fuel, and took off again for Holmsley South.

One of my brother officers in 58 Squadron, Alec Hayward, was a close friend of mine. He was an excellent pilot, and I would have flown with him at any time. We used to go for walks together, and were on the same wavelength. While we were being attacked by the JU88's, I was thinking of my friend Alec. He was sitting on my shoulder, and I knew that we were going to be all right. When we finally landed at Holmsley South and taxied to our dispersal point, as usual our Corporal Armourer (who had never missed meeting an aircraft on its return from an 'Op') was there, and also my friend Alec.

I said, "Hello Alec, what are you doing here?"

He said, "You've had a bit of bother, haven't you?"

The cynics among you will call it 'Bullshit', but that's what happened to me.

Our survival was purely down to our Captain Warrant Officer Jones. He saw the enemy just minutes before they saw us, and by the time they started their attack we were well prepared. The news was spread abound the camp what a good navigator I was, but only I knew that all navigators need a bit of luck sometimes, and that was my day.

Several weeks later, an article appeared in the Air Ministry Summary stating that the JU88's had been fitted with long-range petrol tanks, and were operating in the Atlantic Ocean from an Operational Training Unit from Brest. I showed that article to Jonah, and he agreed with me that the JU88's which had attacked us were most probably from the O.T.U., and were still under training, and that was the reason why they never pressed home their attacks any closer than 400 yards.

Flying Officer Eric Hartley was another good friend of mine. He was always cheerful, full of confidence, and was a Captain of a good crew. On the times I flew with him as a screen navigator or Bombing Leader, I always had the happy feeling of a patrol well done.

We had a new station commander, a Group Captain from Bomber Command, who knew nothing about the work of Coastal Command, and so after a fortnight, when he asked our Squadron Commander if he could fly with one of 58 Squadron's crews, Wilf Oulton recommended Hartley's crew.

With the Group Captain acting as 2nd Pilot, when they were about 400 miles out in the Atlantic Ocean, Eric sighted a U-Boat, and immediately went into attack. The U-Boat opened fire with its 37 mm Cannon, and by the time Eric was dropping his stick of Depth Charges, the whole of the starboard side of his aircraft was on fire. He continued for a mile or two, during which time he warned his crew he was going to ditch and to take up crash landing positions, after which he landed in the sea.

The 'Q' type dinghy was released, and seven of Hartley's crew, including the Group Captain, got in to the dinghy.

The rear gunner got out of his turret and was in the water, but in the choppy sea conditions, the tail of the aircraft hit him on the head, and he disappeared, never to be seen again.

That left a total of seven aviators in the dinghy. Eric, being Captain of the aircraft, got everybody organised and reviewed the food position. It was discovered that half the food rations had been lost in the ditching. The Wireless Operator reported that he had sent the first Sighting Report that they were going into attack to 19 Group Headquarters, but they had had to crash land before he had received any acknowledgement of his signal.

The cloud base was 50 to 60 feet, and so it was decided to put out a sea anchor, and to wait in the area to see if search aircraft had been sent out to locate them. This they did, and for the next 48 hours aircraft could be heard in the vicinity, but due to the very low cloud base, no visual contact could be made. When no more aircraft could be heard, after a discussion among the crew, it was concluded that the search had been called off.

Eric rationed the food available to last 14 days. It was then discovered that one of his crew had still got his pyjamas on underneath his flying clothes. Those were duly converted into a sail, and so started an endeavour to get into the Destroyer stream of traffic from Gibraltar to the U.K.

Eric's main problem was they were short of water, and so he made the crew to immerse themselves fully in the Atlantic to try to combat dehydration. To add to their worries, the Atlantic rose to a full swell and turned their dinghy upside down.

They managed to right the dinghy and save their depleted rations, but in their state of exhaustion, that was an exercise they could have done without.

Water was being shipped in, and had to be baled out continually.

During the day the sunshine would dry their clothes, but the nights were hell.

As luck would have it, after 11 days of sailing eastwards, they were spotted by a Destroyer, which proceeded to circle them for 40 minutes until permission was given by the Admiralty to pick them up. They were so weak at this stage that they hardly knew what was happening until they were aboard the Destroyer, where they then received the Royal Navy's star treatment 'for those in peril on the sea.'

At the de-briefing, the Group Captain said Eric was doing such a fine job as Captain he never had to over rule him. As a result of the strict rationing and exposure, Hartley's crew were all suffering from sea boils, and they had all lost weight.

At 0230 hours one morning I was awoken to be told that my friend Eric had been picked up. That was it – I was so delighted at the news, because I had not expected to see Eric again, that there was no more sleep for me that night. I got up, went straight down to the Operations Room at St. Eval where the Intelligence Officer was able to give me full information.

At the subsequent Enquiry, Eric was criticised for being too stringent with the rations, but when I visited him in hospital, Eric said to me, "Bruce, how did I know that we were going to be picked up in the dinghy on the 11th day?"

Group Captain Mead was a good Station Commander, but on his first trip to find out how Coastal Command functioned, we had managed to ditch him.

It must be agreed, that is learning the hard way!

* * *

14

Fun - and ladies!!

The ladies at Ringwood were lacking in male company, and so they organised a dance, and our Station Commander was asked if he could help. A notice was put on the Notice Board in the Officers' Mess asking for volunteers. In no time at all, we had enough male officers who wished to attend to fill an Aircrew Coach!

When the day arrived, with the Group Captain in the van, off we set. When we arrived, there were only one or two ladies under 30 year's of age. The majority were middle aged, gentle ladies, aged 50 plus, who could converse better than they could dance.

The drinks were plentiful, and the food delicious. The most beautiful and attractive lady present was a Flight Officer WAAF, who came with us. The only thing wrong with her was she was already engaged to an Army Major job, and was strictly loyal, which we all respected. She was quite jolly going back to base in our Aircrew bus, and sitting next to her was a randy officer named Brown, who had obviously had too much to drink, and was as lecherous as a buck rabbit. He was definitely paying her too much attention and she kept pushing his arms away.

We had all had a good time, and were all talking at once, quite loudly, and the noise was considerable. Suddenly, by sheer coincidence, everyone stopped talking at the same time, and in the silence we heard our WAAF say, "Stop it!! If you think you're going to prang me tonight, you've had it!!"

Our Group Captain, who heard this remark and was sitting at the front of the coach, swung round and said, "Brown, stop mauling Flight Officer 'so and so', and come and sit here!!"

We all burst out laughing as Brown sheepishly changed seats with the Station Commander and we proceeded back to camp. A good time had certainly been had by all!

Whenever our Squadron Commander flew with Jonah's crew, it meant a lot more work for me because our 1st Wireless Operator was also the Squadron Radar Instructor, and he could tune in his apparatus and pick up and identify blips that lesser qualified operators failed to do.

After the first two hours, Jonah handed over to the Squadron Commander who was flying as Jonah's 2nd pilot, and every blip the radar operator reported to the Captain, Wilf Oulton insisted on not only inspecting every one of them, but photographing them as well. The blips however always turned out to be groups of Tunny Fisherman. As a result, on the CO's first trip with Jonah's crew, we flew 64 different courses, besides circling the ships, making Dead Reckoning navigation arduous.

After ten hours on patrol, Jonah (who had taken over the last leg), announced "Scillies dead ahead", which impressed our CO no end, and, after we landed, he congratulated me, which made me feel good.

After our photographs had been processed, in the middle of one group of Tunny Fisherman, was the Periscope of a U-Boat. That was reported to our Group Headquarters who notified Coastal Command, and for the next 14 days, leaflets were dropped over the fleet of Spanish Tunny Fisherman, ordering them to get out of the Bay of Biscay. As a result, the numbers of fisherman did decrease, but some chose to ignore our instruction. Therefore, Coastal Command ordered us to fire across their Bows. This had the desired effect, and within 48 hours, the Bay of Biscay was clear of Tunny Fisherman.

Our Squadron Commander had passed a Specialist Navigation Course, and understood the Dead Reckoning problem. This kept me on my toes whenever he flew on an 'ops' trip with Jonah's crew because there was simply no fooling him.

On one trip however, while he was in the 2nd Pilot's seat, he produced a Marine Sextant and started taking shots on the moon. I had my Mark 9 Bubble Sextant with me, and so I took shots on the Sun, and we navigated by Sun, Moon fixes for the whole of the patrol, much to his delight.

On another occasion, a new Black Box appeared in the Flight Deck area with a screen on the Navigation Table. The first thing I did on my next rest day was to find out what it was all about. I discovered it was a new 'Gee Navigation System', and, after a couple of hours reading, and then playing with my new toy in our aircraft at the disposal point, by the end of the morning, I was 'genned up'.

On our next Operational Trip I started to get Gee fixes, which supplemented my DR work, and proved quite accurate when near to one of the Gee stations, but not so accurate the further one went across the Atlantic. I had also discovered it was possible to home in to any point by pre-setting the Gee co-ordinates correctly.

As we approached Land's End from Bishops Rock, the cloud base started to get lower and lower, and so I suggested to Jonah that we do a Gee Homing to Holmsley South, to which he agreed. Therefore, I told him the safety height to fly, which was 1,500 feet above the highest point of land over which we would be flying, and I got my head stuck into reading the signals on my new toy. I gave Jonah the new compass course to steer, and started flying down one of the co-ordinate lines which passed through Holmsley South.

This new gadget also told me how far we were from base, and so when we were 50 miles away, I called up and told Jonah it was safe to start losing height, and asked the 1st Wireless Operator to get a QFE which would enable us to set the Altimeter correctly to give us the true height over our aerodrome.

At 20 miles from Base I asked Jonah what height he was flying, and the answer came back, "500 feet". I said, "When you break cloud base you should be able to see Holmsley South dead ahead."

At 10 miles, I called up Jonah and said, "Can you see the aerodrome?" Jonah said, "Drop down to the Bomb Aimer's position, Gibby, and have a look." I did that, and to my utter surprise, we were in brilliant sunshine, and there was our base, right in front of me, about 5 miles distant.

I asked Jonah, "How long have we been in visual contact with the ground?" He replied, "For the last 50 miles, but you were doing OK, and so I let you do your first Gee homing!"

"Bloody marvellous", said Wingco, who had witnessed what I had been doing from the 2nd Pilot's seat, "You'll have to teach the other navigators and pilots how to use Gee", was the CO's next remark.

The next day I got the Radar technicians to fix up a Gee unit in the Synthetic trainer whilst I got all genned up to start teaching the equipment. I was just about to start imparting my new knowledge when the door opened and the CO appeared. Being a Navigator as well as a Pilot, he wanted to know how to operate Gee.

One of the first things the RAF taught me was, if one really wanted to become top grade in any subject, one should teach someone else.

Pat Pollard was our Cypher Officer at Holmsley South, and she liked dancing. And so, quite a number of times, I took her as my partner to the local village dance, which was held every Tuesday evening. She was an up market girl who had been educated at Cheltenham Ladies College and Girton College, Cambridge, and although friendly disposed towards me, she warned me that we mustn't get too close because the gulf between us socially was too great, saying, "Bruce, it just wouldn't work!"

It was during her posting to Holmsley South that she resigned her commission, which was accepted, and that surprised me, as I did not know one could do that in wartime.

However, that was in 1942, and I hired a taxi and took her to the station and into retirement. I did not meet her again until 1946 when I was at the Air Ministry. The 'phone rang, and it was Pat. She invited me out to her Father's house at Cowley in Oxfordshire for lunch. I was working seven days a week at the Air Ministry, and so I was able to take a day off. Pat met me at Cowley Railway Station, and drove me to her home, which was a bloody great mansion with 20 bedrooms and acres of land.

Luncheon was prepared by the Housekeeper, and was thoroughly enjoyed by Pat, her sister, and me. I found out that her Father had a flat in town, was the Editor of a glossy Monthly Magazine , and during the war he had also been Editor of the sister magazine with no increase in salary. Pat was definitely County Class, and it was then I realised what she had meant when we used to go to dances together at Holmsley South, and she had said, "Bruce, we mustn't get too friendly as it just wouldn't work"!

The sisters invited me to stay the night, but I could not accept the offer as I had not come prepared, and also I had promised to call in at the office on my way home. I thoroughly enjoyed my day out in the country, walking in the grounds, where I noticed stables and horses grazing, and, back in the house where, in the gunroom, plenty of fishing tackle was about. Personally I have always been a soccer, tennis and squash player.

I know nothing about hunting, shooting and fishing and I had to give Pat full marks for her wisdom.

A defence of the aerodrome had been organised, and all those not operating were ordered to take part. The Leicester Regiment were to guard the aerodrome, and the rest of us were dropped off in various places, all of which were about 20 miles from base. Alec Haywood and I teamed up together, and were dropped in Bournemouth. We wandered around the shops for a while, but couldn't buy anything because we were only allowed to have 3d on us, the cost of a telephone call should we get lost or in case of an emergency.

We made good progress when we put our minds to it, and on passing through Christchurch, we came to Airspeed Oxford's place. At the briefing we had been told not to steal bicycles, motorcars etc, and that we had 12 hours to get back to Holmsley South without being captured.

Alec said, "Let's have a look around here".

It was lunchtime, and there was no one about as we passed Airspeed's office block. Out in the airfield we came to an aircraft. Alec tried the door, which opened first time, and sat in the Pilot's seat. I followed him and sat next to him in the 2nd Pilot's seat. Alec started switching things on, and suddenly the port engine burst into life, quickly followed by the starboard engine. Alec said, "Shut the door Bruce, we will go for a flip." I said, "Where to Alec?" "Holmsley South of course" was the reply, before I realised what Alec had in mind.

In no time at all he was using the correct call signs for Holmsley South, and was asking for permission to land. He made a perfect landing, taxied to Air Traffic Control where the Station Commander (as Chief Judge of the Defence Exercise) had his headquarters. Alec said, "Let's give the old man a fright!" Up the stairs we went, Alec leading, opening the door and straight to the Group Captain, saying, "Bang, bang, bang. You're all dead!" The Group Captain was flabbergasted. Red in the face, he asked, "Haywood, what the Hell are you doing here?" Alec replied, "Sir, we're on your defence exercise, and I have just killed you all with three hand grenades". Then 'Groupie' said, "How did you get in here?" "You just gave us permission to land, Sir" was the reply. "Oh! Did I? Where did you get that aircraft from?" "We borrowed it from Airspeed Oxford's placed in Christchurch". "Well, take it back to where you found it – and Flight Lieutenant Provost (who was the Head Station Policeman) – take your car to Christchurch, and bring these two fractious aircrew back, and put them in your Guard Room under Close Arrest. I'll deal with them later. I'll show them if I'm dead or not!"

It was only about five miles, and in no time at all we had put the aircraft back where we found it. The whole episode had lasted less than an hour, and there was still no one around to apologise to. So, we made our way to the entrance and the RAF Copper took us back to his Guard Room at Holmsley South to await the pleasure of meeting our 'Groupie'.

It was teatime before the Group Captain arrived and we were starving. We hadn't eaten since breakfast at 0700 hours, and Groupie knew that. His Defence Exercise had been a complete success, and by the time he saw us he had cooled down a bit, but was still furious, and he tore such a strip off us for disobeying orders that we were not allowed to steal Bicycles or motor cars, when Alec chimed in, saying, "But Sir, you did not mention borrowing an aircraft", at which Groupie saw the funny side and laughed, which broke the tension.

He finished up saying he had been in touch with our Squadron Commander, who told him we were both on 'Ops' the next day. Therefore we were ordered to get about our business, and to remember, he would be watching our conduct in the future, and also to make sure we never tried to take the piss out of him again! We both saluted smartly, and said, "Sir" and rushed back to our mess to get something to eat. Alec remarked, "That was a near one, Gibby, wasn't it" and of course, there was no answer to that.

However, that was not the end of the matter because we were summoned to the Squadron Commander's Office, where we were told how sad he was at our stupidity, how we had let the side down, and that it was only our good operational record that had saved us from much more serious consequences.

He made us both feel rotten. We both apologised, and that was the end of the matter, but we were frequently referred to by other Squadron Aircrews as 'Jail Birds'!!

When a group of Officers are left to their own devices, parties soon develop, and this is where Flight Lieutenant Montford would come into his own.

Monty would take part in every mess game, especially if pints of beer were involved.

There were times when the Station Commander and his wife would attend. The CO's wife was friendly disposed towards Monty, and would laugh uproariously at some of his antics. At one of these parties on a Friday night, which ran over into the small hours of Saturday, Monty somehow promised the CO's wife to join her on a shopping trip into Christchurch after the party. Of course Monty, being in his cups, forgot all about this, and when the lady appeared at the mess to pick him up, he was just having his breakfast, and still under the influence of drink.

But, he kept his promise, and off they went into Christchurch.

As they were walking around the shops, Monty was making funny remarks to all and sundry, much to the amusement of his lady companion, and it was not long before several children tagged on, and Monty kept them in fits of laughter.

He was smoking a cigarette, and, as they were passing a wet fish mongers, Monty picked up a Herring and put his cigarette in the fish's mouth. Then, by squashing the sides of the fish, which acted like a bellow, the kids were given a demonstration of a smoking Herring. It was hilarious – especially as the CO's wife then had to pay for the Herring!

As Holmsley South was a temporary RAF Aerodrome, it had no means of keeping aircrew physically fit. We had no gymnasium, squash courts etc, and we were delightfully surprised one day when 50 bicycles arrived, which we were encouraged to borrow.

That was something new, and Monty, on leaving a local pub (well tanked up), got on his bicycle, went straight across the road, and ended up in the ditch. Back in sick quarters, it was discovered he had broken a bone in his wrist, and he finished up with his arm, from the base of his hand to his elbow, in plaster. This meant he was off 'Ops', but it had its compensations because it meant more drinking time.

During those sessions arguments often arose, and Monty, if he was not doing too well, would dig his friends in the ribs in the hope it might impress his argument. Although those digs took place in fun, if one was at the receiving end, they would have cause to remember arguing with Monty the next day.

Those 'digs' became part of Monty's make up, and when in an argument he would say, "And if you don't believe it, I'll bonk you – you know me!" and that became Monty's catch phrase, 'I'll bonk you, you know me'!

On one occasion, Monty was engaged in an argument with some officers from another Squadron, and he swung his arm around, and hit one of his drinking pals in the face with his plastered arm, and laid his friend out. As I was the only sober one present, I organised a taxi, and took the injured man to sick quarters who, when revived, looked at me and said, "Who the hell are you?!"

The injured office could not remember what had happened, and so the Station MO gave him a jab, and he spent the night in sick quarters.

The next morning, Monty, full of contrition, visited his friend, but still there was no sign of recollection, and so all was forgiven.

However, in future when Monty started saying, "I'll bonk you – you know me", his friends made sure they were not within arm's length of him!

Every night, those of us who were not operating would go into Christchurch to the King's Head Hotel which was known as our local, and afterwards we would always finish up in a Greek Restaurant which was a few shops down the road where, despite food rationing, we could always have steak and chips.

One night, somehow or other, I was the only one left in the bar, and I was drinking my Coca Cola, chatting up Ann the barmaid. She was getting ready to close the bar when two of our Squadron Officers came into the bar and said, "Gibby, come and help us with Monty – he's had his meal and he won't pay for it; he won't let anyone else pay for it, we've a taxi waiting outside to take us back to camp, and he won't get in it!"

Monty was six foot two inches tall, and at seventeen stone, was one of our best forwards in the Station Rugby Football team.

I said, "What do you think I can do?" They said, "You're the Senior Officer present – you'll have to pull rank"

Ann, who knew Monty well, said, "Gibby, it's down to you"

I put on my peaked cap, and said, "Come along – let's see what we can do."

As I entered the restaurant I summed up the position in a second. There was Monty, swinging his arms about, acting like a blackguard, using dreadful airman's language. There were two Greek waiters cringing in a corner, and two of our officers were preventing the manager from calling the police. So – five foot seven, ten stone

Gibby, grabs hold of the lapels of Monty's tunic and says to six foot two, seventeen stone Monty,

"Monty, I've got a taxi waiting to take us back to Camp. You're going to get in that taxi, and if you don't, I'll bonk you – you know me!!"

Monty couldn't stop laughing; he said, "Gibby, you're lovely!"

He swung me round, picked me up in his arms, and carried me out to the taxi, and – laughing and joking about the cowardly waiters – within five minutes he was fast asleep.

It turned out the reason why Monty wouldn't pay for his Steak and Chips was because he said it was not Steak, but horseflesh. I found that out when Monty had sobered up, and I reasoned with him that he should have complained before he had eaten it.

To which he replied, "Up yours!"

And, of course, there's no answer to that! But, there was no supper for me that night!!

However I did manage to pull a fast one on Monty. It was after a guest night and Monty under the influence of drink was playing mess games, which no one in a sober frame of mind would take part in, when I challenged him to a £5.00 bet. I had already brought a gardener's wheelbarrow into the mess, and I bet Monty I could wheel a 17 stone load of my choosing in the wheelbarrow, down to the end of the mess, and that he could not wheel it back. "You're on", said Monty, "This is like taking candy from kids". I said "O.K. Monty, sit in the barrow". It took a second for my remark to sink in to Monty's fuddled brain, but then he said "You bastard Gibby!!, I can see why pilots say all navigators is bastards", amidst much laughter from Monty's drinking 'Oppos'.

One day, when our Adjutant was having a day off and I was doing his job for him, Wing Commander Wilfred Oulton came into the office and showed me an Air Ministry Order, which stated that, under the principle that as the careers of Pilots and Navigators were equal, it was permissible for Navigators to become Captains of Aircraft.

'Wingco' said, "Bruce, under the authority of this AMO, from now on you are a Captain of Aircraft."

"But Sir," I said, "Warrant Officer Jones is my Captain" "Not any more, you're the only officer in Jones' crew, and so you are Captain," was the reply.

I immediately told Jonah that I had been made Captain of Aircraft, that in future I would be responsible for crew training, but that when we were on an operational patrol, he would take on the role of Captain as normal. The only difference would be if anything went wrong with our crew – then I would 'carry the can'.

One of our pilots was named Flight Lieutenant Clutterbuck; right well named he was too! He would get involved in everything that was going; he would give answers to things that had nothing to do with him, and would enter into arguments without knowing anything about the subject under discussion. He was a proper Clutterbuck.

One afternoon I was acting Flight Commander. Most aircrew had finished work for the day and had gone to their billets, and I was about to follow when our Flight Sergeant Engineer asked me if I could find a pilot to do an air test on an aircraft which was needed for 'Ops' the next day. During my service career, I had always made it my policy to say, 'YES', and so I said, "Leave it to me Flight Sergeant, I'll see what I can do."

I rushed around to the crew room and, to my chagrin, the only pilot available was Clutterbuck, who was talking to some of his crew. Knowing how important it was, I said, "Clutterbuck, can you do an air test on 'A' for Apple for me? It's needed for 'Ops' tomorrow." He replied, "I'd love to Gibby, but I haven't got a navigator, but you'll do it with me, won't you?" This put me in a predicament. Under normal circumstances the last pilot I would have volunteered to fly with was Clutterbuck, but duty compelled me to say, "Of course".

Ten minutes later we were airborne. The take off was good, and so, while he and his engineer checked all of the things they had to do, I checked all of the navigation and Bomb Aimers' equipment etc, and 30 minutes later Clutterbuck made a perfect approach and landing, and taxied to dispersal where our Flight Sergeant was waiting for us with transport.

The look of relief on our Flight Sergeant's face when Clutterbuck reported, "'A' for Apple completely serviceable for 'Ops', Flight Sergeant" made our chore well worthwhile.

I went straight to the Flight Commander's Office to finish for the day, when who should come into the office but Clutterbuck. I said, "Thank you for doing the air test, it gives us another aircraft for 'Ops' tomorrow". "That's OK Gibby, any time" was the response. He then said, "Are you operating tomorrow?" I said, "No, Jonah's crew have got the day off tomorrow". "Well", he said, "I am due to operate tomorrow, but my navigator has gone sick; it would please the CO no end if you would volunteer to operate with me."

He had just done me a good turn, and normally he would be the last pilot I would have wanted to fly with, but my two faced Gemini part clicked in, when I said, "I would be delighted".

At the briefing the next day, Clutterbuck was really on form. He was asking questions, checking this, checking that, giving instructions to his crew, asking me if everything was OK, and so on.

At the aircraft, he did a thorough pre-flight check, and in no time at all I was giving him our first course to steer to Bishops Rock. Whilst on patrol for the next ten hours, apart from the usual communications to his crew, he flew a perfect anti submarine patrol until we were back at Bishops Rock, which he started to circle. After several circuits I asked, "Captain, what are we doing?" Clutterbuck said, "A fortnight ago a German Condor 222 shot my trailing aerial off, and so I was hoping to meet up with him again because no one does that to me with impunity!" I said, "Clutterbuck, don't be so bloody childish! Steer that course I gave you back to base, I've got a dance to go to tonight".

Back at base, we made a perfect approach and landing, and it was only then, when back on ground, that his antics started. On patrol he was the perfect Captain of aircraft. On the ground he was the biggest pain in the arse one would want to avoid.

Back in the mess my friend Alec came up to me and said, "Where have you been all day, we were supposed to have gone for a walk, remember?" I replied, "I'm sorry Alec, I clean forgot". I then remarked what an excellent trip I had just undertaken with Clutterbuck, and what a good crew he had. Alec said, "Bruce, Clutterbuck is one of our better pilots, and every one of his crew has volunteered to fly with him."

A few days later, when I was helping the Adjutant, I checked up and, true to form, Clutterbuck was a Gemini, and was a two faced bastard – just like me!! On the ground he was a bloody nuisance, but on operations he flew like an angel. Once again, I had been taught a lesson on how one's first thoughts can be so wrong.

The Wing Commander who became the Squadron Commander of 58 Squadron after Wilfred Oulton was a totally different type of officer. Whereas Wilf Oulton was a 'hands on' operational pilot, our new 'Wingco' never flew on 'Ops' during my last six months with the Squadron.

Also, although Pilots and Navigators were equal career-wise, it was apparent from his actions that he considered some aircrew were more important than others. He gave me the impression that he did not agree with my being a Captain of Aircraft by always dealing with Jonah as Captain of our crew. That was OK by me as Jonah and I had an understanding on this.

However, due to my seniority, as I was a qualified Bombing and Gunnery Leader, Navigation Officer, Stand-in Flight Commander, and Squadron Adjutant, he thought I was too big for my boots.

One day, when the whole Squadron was grounded because of bad weather, I was giving a lecture on current affairs in the crew room and he stumbled in, and for some unknown reason, he was furious. Although I had his permission to carry on, he did not join in the discussion period after my lecture, but left in a huff.

The next day we were preparing our aircraft for an 'Op', but our aircraft intercom system was unserviceable, and could not be fixed that day, and so 'Wingco' tried to talk Jonah into operating with written messages, which Jonah refused to do, and I agreed with him. This upset the 'old man' no end. We were due to go on leave the next day, and in his temper, he sent us on leave forthwith.

Whilst I was on leave with my parents in Seven Kings, I received a signal telling me to report back to Royal Air Force Station Haverford West. This I did, only to be told that Jonah's crew had been disbanded, and I was to be posted to the Air Ministry.

During my leave, the 'old man' had got his own back, had broken up Jonah's crew, and had got rid of me. There was nothing I could do about this as I had nearly completed two tours of duty, and it was 'fait accompli'.

I spent the first day at Haverford West getting clearance, which was a formality as I had not served on the Station, and, after saying my goodbyes to all my friends, but not my Squadron Commander, within 48 hours I was back at Seven Kings to serve as a Staff Officer at Air Ministry Kingsway.

My parents were delighted, especially my Nan, who gave me a big hug.

Wing Commander Wilfred Oulton, on being promoted to Group Captain, was awarded a DSO, which looked good alongside the DFC he had received while flying with Jonah's crew.

Jonah was also awarded a DFC, which was long overdue, for having sighted and attacked four U-Boats and successfully saved his aircraft from the attacks of seven JU88's.

He certainly was an experienced aviator.

* * *

15

1944 and beyond

On 1st January 1944, big decisions were made which were to hasten the demise of the Hitler regime.

General Dwight Eisenhower was confirmed as Supreme Commander of the Allied Armies, preparing to invade the Europe with the Contingent Operation 'Overlord'.

General Bernard Law Montgomery was appointed Commander of the British 21st Army Group, and was given overall charge of the Assault phase of the invasion, code named Neptune.

Flight Lieutenant Bruce Gibson was appointed as a Staff Officer under Air Chief Marshal Roderick Hill who was on the Air Council as Air Member for Training.

Why Hitler never capitulated on that day, only those 'Trick Cyclists' who have studied the workings of the mind of a Dictator know.

On 2nd January 1944, I reported for duty as an Air Ministry Staff Officer.

After booking in, I was told to report to a new Department which was being formed in Kingsway called the Department of Prevention of Accidents (DPA). There I met an established Civil Servant, named Priestley, who had been put into uniform as Squadron Leader. He was in charge of a sub branch of the DPA called PA2a. This sub branch was the administrative section, and Priestley was responsible for making the Department work because everything that happened in the Department started with the PA2a.

The Department was formed because it became too big for the Central Registry in Whitehall to handle, and so the breakaway commenced with the handing over of all of the existing files. Priestley organised the Sub Registry within PA2a to do this.

There were always at least 10,000 files in circulation, and PA2a had 38 Civil Servants to keep track of them all, and also to open a new file on every new accident.

The civilian staff consisted of a Staff Officer, equivalent in rank to a Squadron Leader; a Higher Clerical Officer, equivalent in rank to a Flight Lieutenant; and 36 Temporary Clerks, Grade III.

The Staff Officer did no actual work in the handling of the files, but he was responsible for overseeing the work of the Higher Clerical Officer, whose full time occupation was to make sure the Temporary Clerks arrived on time, and to ensure that they had coffee, tea, and lunch breaks!!

It was the 36 Temporary Clerks, Grade III, who did all of the work. Every accident to an aircraft had to be reported by signal on a form called Message 'A'. This gave all of the details of the accident, and the aircraft involved.

At the height of the 1,000 Bomber Raids, up to 10,000 new files a year had to be opened and circulated throughout the Air Ministry Branches in Kingsway, Whitehall, and the Ministry of Supply.

Each time a file was passed from one officer to another, it had to be passed through the Registry to be booked to the new department, so that it was possible to trace the file at any one time.

The system was fool proof. It only went wrong if the system was not used correctly. After a few weeks, Priestley seemed to disappear for hours on end, and when he did turn up, he only asked me if everything was OK, and off he went again.

After a few months of Priestley doing his disappearing act, I was promoted to Squadron Leader and found out I was in charge of PA2a. It was then I realised that the times when Priestley had been absent, he was just checking me out to make sure I could cope.

Early in 1944 Hitler started attacking London and the South of England with self-propelled VI bombs, which were nicknamed 'Doodlebugs', and later with V2 rockets. These were morale sapping weapons.

The VI bombs were worse than the V2's because there was no approach noise with the V2, and if one heard a V2 explode, that was OK because one knew that one hadn't been hit!!

But, the VI's could be heard from miles away and caused consternation and fear when the engine cut out, and they dived to earth, exploding upon landing just anywhere. That was classified as haphazard bombing. Those weapons caused many of my staff to evacuate from the towns to the country, thereby depleting the number of staff to do the work.

That meant those who did not run away had more work to do to keep pace with the daily routine.

Travelling from Seven Kings to Kingsway used to take me one and a half hours, but I always managed to be in my office by 0800 hours. My first job was to deal with the mail, which meant allocating new enclosures to existing accident files, or in the case of a new accident, to differentiate it from an ordinary accident to a Flying Battle Casualty.

In the case of the latter, if anyone had been killed, it was necessary to organise a Court of Enquiry. A Ledger was kept to record the movement of all files, making it possible to trace the whereabouts of any particular file should it be needed to answer a Parliamentary Question.

After a unit had sent the original message to PA2a, a more detailed report had to be sent with copies to the unit's Group and Command Headquarters. To ensure this action was taken, a Bring Forward System was kept which had to be dealt with daily to chase up the units who were dragging their feet.

If a Parliamentary Question was asked involving an aircraft accident, it was my personal responsibility to produce forthwith the file, whether it be in the Kingsway, Whitehall, or Ministry of Aircraft Production area. If the system worked properly, it was no problem, but if a file had been passed on without the movement being recorded in the Ledger it was a little more difficult.

In the three years that I was responsible for the DPA's registry, we never lost a file. The Department of Accident Prevention came within the Air Ministry for Training Branch, with Air Chief Marshal Sir Roderick Hill in charge. DPA had an Air Commodore as its Director, and as it was a new Directorate, the Head of Department got me to organise a Cocktail Party so that he could get to know socially the 70 officers in his Branch.

The Air Member attended as a guest, which resulted in me, for the rest of my stay at the Air Ministry, having to organise the social gatherings for Sir Roderick Hill, who had over 2,000 officers in his Training organisation.

One of those officers was Squadron Leader Ralph Reader who, before the war, had been the Producer of the Scouts Gang Shows for the BBC.

At one of these Social Gatherings that I was arranging for the Air Member, I invited Ralph Reader, in writing, to do a 20-minute spot to entertain the Air Chief Marshal's guests.

Ralph Reader replied, in writing, that he was far too busy to play about like that. Ralph of course was acting like a 'Big Shot' BBC Producer, and so I rang the gentleman up, and explained to him in words of one syllable, that there was only one rank higher in the Royal Air Force than an Air Chief Marshal, and when such an officer expressed a wish, it was equal to a COMMAND. He would, therefore, be well advised to put on a show.

Of course, I was able to say on the telephone what I would have been loath to put into writing, but it did the trick! As a result, the Air Chief Marshal and his guests thoroughly enjoyed Ralph's show, and all had a good time.

Being wartime, alcohol was difficult to come by, but one of my Flight Lieutenants was a cockney boy who had contacts. Suffice it to say, he provided adequate supplies, even including one hundred weight of ice!!

Sir Roderick Hill was the cleverest officer I ever worked for. Before the war he would take six month's unpaid leave to take an Engineering Degree. When war was declared, he had three Engineering Degrees!

I thought him exceptional as a pilot.

As I was responsible for the movement of all of the files in his Branch, he got to know me quite well, and on one occasion I was invited to his office for a coffee, during which time he informed me that he wanted me to be in charge of his Top Secret Files.

That meant during the next three weeks I was to be vetted.

Several weeks went by and I forgot all about it. I was summoned into the his presence, when the Air Chief Marshal told me that I had passed with flying colours. He presented me with the key to the safe containing all of the Top Secret Files, which I guarded thenceforth with my life.

The only other key was in the Air Chief Marshal's private safe. Any time I went off duty, the key had to be handed over to the Duty Officer, and in the event of a Top Secret File being needed during that time, the key was to be handed only to either one of two people: The Director of DPA, or a civilian equivalent in the Air Member's Branch, the latter being the Air Commodore in charge of Private Flying Accidents.

If a top-secret communication was received when I was off duty, either one of the above mentioned had to be informed, and he would decide what action to take.

Having proved myself to be completely free from any homosexual or heterosexual relationship, whereby I could be blackmailed, I was deemed to be completely dull and therefore safe to be entrusted as the Top Secret Registry Officer.

All of the Top Secret Files were sealed, and I knew them only by their Title and Number.

On three occasions, whilst I was in charge of the Registry, our Air Commodore received a Minute from the Prime Minister asking for one of the files. The Minutes were always written in red, starting with the command, ACTION THIS DAY. Followed by the word, PRAY, etc etc. To receive one of these minutes really did put the 'cat among the pigeons,' and all normal work in the Registry had to be stopped until the file had been found.

I became quite friendly with Flight Lieutenant Cyril Newman, who was the Head of the Section in our Directory that was responsible for coding every accident file. He had been a Navigator, but on medical grounds, had been transferred to the Administrative Branch of the RAF. He was a typical London man, and was as sharp as a whistle. He always had clothing coupons for sale, and, in periods of shortage, or when things were unobtainable, Cy Newman never went short of anything.

In this connection, if fresh fruit or vegetables were in short supply, my brother Cyril, who owned a stand in Covent Garden Market, would sell me the odd bag of vegetables or container of fruit, and Cy would barter these for more attractive goods which he could sell on.

Once a month, every staff officer, irrespective of rank up to Air Marshal, had to do a shift at Fire Watching, which was a 24-hour duty. But, once a quarter, it was a weekend duty.

One weekend, both Cy Newman and I were on Firewatch duty together, but Cy was also detailed to be the Duty Officer. I duly handed him the key to the Top Secret Registry, which scared the life out of him! He tried to persuade me to keep the key, but I insisted he do his Duty Officer job correctly, and to guard the key with his life.

Our Fire Guard duty started after duty hours on Friday, and lasted until 0900 hours on the next Monday.

On one particular Saturday evening, a Top Secret Signal was delivered to Cy Newman by a messenger. Cy immediately panicked, and came rushing up to me with the signal. I said, "Cy, I don't want it. You're the Duty Officer – open the envelope: read the message, and take the appropriate action." "Oh Bruce!!" he said, "Be a mate, open it for me!" "Give it to me you stupid sod!" I replied. Whereupon I read the contents, and, having decided it was a routine matter, I told Cy to lock the signal in the Top Secret Safe, ring the Under Secretary of State for our Department, and ask him if he agrees with your decision.

This Cy did, literally trembling with excitement.

This whole action worried Cy Newman so much he could talk about nothing else. He was so excited he could not go to the sleeping quarters provided for Duty Officers, and so in the end I said, "Cy, you can stay up all night if you want to, but I'm going to bed!" And off I went.

The next morning, was a Sunday, and at 0700 hours, I went to the ablutions to freshen up, and there was Cy, and it was obvious he had not slept a wink all night. After we had breakfasted together, I decided to play a trick on Cy. And so, I went to my office on the seventh floor and rang Cy's office on the floor below me. With a handkerchief over my mouth, I asked, "Is that Flight Lieutenant Newman?" and having received a reply in the affirmative, I continued, "Newman, this is the Under Secretary of State; I've changed my mind, I would like you to see that signal you spoke to me about. Could you bring it to me at St. John's Wood?" I gave Cy the address, and before I could say anything else, he slammed the 'phone down and was on his way to St. John's Wood.

I rushed to the lift, but Cy was already going down. I tore down seven flights of stairs, and just caught him going out of the front door. I called out, "Cy, where the hell do you think you're going?" He replied, "Don't stop me Bruce, I've got to go St. John's Wood". I answered, "You stupid sod, you haven't got to go anywhere, that was me on the phone to you just now!" "Oh Bruce", he said, "that's not fair!". "Fair or not" I replied, "Forget it, let's go and get another coffee".

For the rest of that Sunday I did routine work in my Registry, posting files through the ledgers so that we could be in the clear by Monday, and, although I saw Cy at meal times, and on and off during the day, this whole affair had upset him so badly he could not wait until 0900 hours on Monday before coming to my office to return to me the key to the Top Secret Safe, saying, "Bruce, don't ever do that to me again", and was gone.

We laughed together many times after that during nostalgic moments, but because of Cy's reaction at that time, I did not enjoy the practical joke I had played on him.

By picking Priestley's brains and experience I quickly learnt every aspect of aircraft accident and reporting, and at that time, when 1,000 Bomber raids were the norm, we were easily opening 10,000 new files a year, with another 10,000 files always in circulation.

After about six months, I had learnt everything about the Registry organisation that Priestley had laid on, to the extent that I kept an observant eye open with a view to improving the system. It did not take me long to realise that the Accident Reporting Form 765C was wrong. RAF accidents were being reported to our Branch from all over the world, and in many cases under very difficult circumstances. For example, Squadrons in the 2nd Tactical Air Force operating in Germany were frequently on the move and the Adjutants of these Squadrons were living in, and working from tents, and having to supply our Registry with seven copies of this form.

Having assisted the Adjutant of an operational Squadron on and off for two years, I knew the problem.

Therefore, I changed the shape of the Form 765C, and altered the questions from Civil Service jargon to RAF language. It was at that time that the Head of PA2 arrived. Until then we had acted quite successfully without such a person, but Wing Commander Harry Alsopp arrived to be in charge of PA2A, PA2B, and PA2C.

Harry had been in the RAF for over 20 years, the first 18 of which had been before the war, in the Administrative Branch, where he reached the rank of Warrant Officer. Administratively, Harry was a 'gen kiddy', and he knew how the air force worked.

Every day I accompanied Harry to lunch at the Aldwych Restaurant, where we had a large three-course meal for one shilling and three pence (6.5p!). It consisted of a large bowl of soup, a small portion for the main meal, and a good helping of dessert. For one shilling and three pence it was excellent value. And this was by the Government edict. Restaurants were not allowed to charge any more.

Harry quickly discovered that everything in the DPA started with the Registry. By opening a file on every new RAF aircraft accident, and keeping tabs on all of the files in circulation throughout

Kingsway, Whitehall and Kensington, if the system was operated correctly, it was possible to trace, within seconds, any one of the 20,000 files that were always in circulation at any one time.

Harry was a cagey old bird who worked on the principle, 'If it aint broke, don't fix it', and in his wisdom he took things very easy, but he was always available if a snag arose which needed his expertise.

He arrived just after Priestley had been posted and I had been promoted to Squadron Leader. He listened very carefully to the reasons I gave regarding my suggestion for a new type of Accident Reporting Form 765C. He digested my idea for several weeks, and then he presented it to the Head of our Directorate, who was an Air Commodore, and won his approval, which was good. A week's course was organised by the head of the Policy Department to show Adjutants how our Directorate worked, and it was my job to give the first two-hour lecture on the new accident reporting procedure.

I had 30 ladies working in the Registry, and I was always available to give a hand if any section was falling behind, mainly due to absentees after a night of heavy bombing. This gained me respect because it proved I knew how every section worked and that I could solve any problem that might develop. Also, women have their own problems, and are sometimes off colour, and fall behind with their work, but by giving a helping hand where necessary, the morale of our section was high. I took over a large room on the seventh floor of Alexandra House and designed 'Open Plan' working conditions with my desk at one end, so that we were all together.

Each year on 14th February, I always received at least a dozen Valentine's Cards, which I displayed on my desk for all to see amidst much banter.

One day, just after lunch, one of my ladies came to me in a dreadful state. Apparently before coming to work, she had put her horse out to graze, and we had experienced a sudden drop in temperature before her horse had been in its new environment for 24 hours, and could she dash home to look after it? Of course she could, and the next day I heard via the grape vine she was so grateful she could have kissed me.

Thank the Lord she didn't, because firstly, I am not the kissing type, and secondly, with 30 girls working in the Registry, I did not want to set a precedent!

The Welfare of the people I work with has always been a strong point of mine, and I was examining one of the forms from the Service, which required date of birth, next of kin etc, when I noticed one new lady employee had come from Manchester. And so, I sent for her, and was discussing the details she had registered when I said, "I notice you have come here from Manchester, how come?" I got more than I bargained for, because she told me she came to London to escape the clutches of her Polish boyfriend. She hoped he would not find her in London. She just wanted a good night's sleep.

Apparently, her boyfriend was so sexually active, every 25 minutes throughout the night he was at it – and so she just wanted a good night's sleep! She just had to leave.

I said, "I hope you have made the right move, because in London it's not sex that keeps you awake at night, but the bombing!" At this she laughed, and went about her business.

The Head of our Directorate was an Air Commodore who had been educated at Eton and Oxford University, and was a get-up-and-go type. His previous appointment had been as Liaison Officer to the American Air force, and when he left them, he came to us with an array of aircraft: a Flying Fortress, a Lighting, and a Dakota transport aircraft. These he kept at Hendon Aerodrome and were serviced by the RAF.

It was the Lighting aircraft that he kept for his own use, and the other two aircraft were freely available to any of his friends. They were in great demand! A thank you note was all the Air Commodore needed for a repeat performance.

After one trip he made to Germany, he presented our Air Chief Marshal with a Leica camera, the like of which were almost impossible to get in 1946. Sir Roderick Hill thanked our boss profusely, but asked if he could have the Customs Certificate giving the authority to bring the Leica into the UK. "Of course", said the Air Commodore, and he sought me out, and said,

"Gibson, I want you to make a liaison visit to Wing Commodore Deere at Buckeburg in Germany. Take this camera with you in your navigation bag, and when you leave Buckeburg, present this camera to Customs, and after paying the dues, make sure you get a receipt. I will ring Deere and tell him you're coming, and also make the necessary arrangements for a pilot and aircraft, so be ready to leave within the next two or three days!"

Wing Commodore Deere was waiting to meet and greet our aircraft, and I spent a couple of very pleasant hours in his company. Over lunch, Deere had to laugh at the embarrassing situation our Boss had put himself in, and recognised that an Air Chief Marshal could not accept an expensive Leica camera from Germany without a Customs receipt.

On another occasion, the Head of our Directorate took himself off on a six-week liaison trip to the Far East. He gave me a copy of his itinerary, and told me it was my job to keep him in touch with what was going on in his Directorate while he was away. This was a straightforward job of administration, and could be achieved by signalling to the aerodrome at which he was due to land.

This procedure was mainly to satisfy his ego because we had two very good Group Captains, and the Directorate functioned quite well without him. Of course, it was a sign of what a good organisation Priestley had set up, by proving how well the unit functioned when the Head Man was absent.

I had a Wolseley 16/50 motorcar in those days, and my Boss did not possess a car, and so it was arranged that I would meet him at Hendon Aerodrome, and take him home. I watched him land and drove to the dispersal point, and it was a good thing I had a big car because he had quite literally filled it with bolts of silks, and other valuable items (mainly bottles of liquors and spirits), and off we went to the Customs Office.

He told me to stop about twenty yards from Customs, where he disembarked, and with a large bunch of bananas and a bottle of sherry, he went into the Customs office. After about 20 minutes, the door opened, and the Head of Customs, his face wreathed in smiles and shaking my Air Commodore's hand profusely, wished him a safe journey home. As I drove out of Hendon Aerodrome I said, "Is that it, Sir?" "Yes Bruce", he said. "In times of shortages, it's not what you know but who you know what counts!"

The Air Chief Marshal had on his staff a Squadron Officer WAAF, who was one of the most charming ladies it was possible to meet. She used to keep the Head Man's diary up to 18 months ahead as there were certain dates he just had to keep, such as Remembrance Day at the Cenotaph, and Trooping the Colour, but her main job was the checking the English and grammar of all Air Ministry Orders sent out by the Air Member's Department.

She was a very 'homely' girl, with sensible, flat-heeled shoes, legs like a billiards table, and a face that would never make anyone look twice until she smiled. It portrayed the charm of her true character.

A spinster of just over 32 years of age, she was an excellent conversationalist and had a fund of stories to tell, and always when among her colleagues she would get around to saying "I am a very stupid virgin", but she was physically most unattractive, and her friends just did not want to know.

* * *

16

Air Raids and Dancing!

In 1944/45, the air raid warning signal would go off at frequent intervals, and the drill was for everyone in our Alexandra House office block to take shelter in the basement.

My office was on the seventh floor, and as I couldn't be bothered to go down seven floors, I used to go up one flight of stairs and onto the roof, and watch the V1's approaching from there.

It was quite dull until the Rocket Motor cut out, then it was very exciting because one wing would drop, and the missile would dive straight down to earth.

On one occasion I watched a V1 dive straight down into the basement of Bush House, which was about 50 yards from where I was standing.

Another time, when I was living with my parents at 10 Farrance Road, Chadwell Heath, a V2 fell into our garden and the house collapsed around us. It was in the early hours of the morning, and for some unknown reason, I did not hear the sound of the explosion.

I just heard the sound of the ceiling and walls caving in on us.

However, help was soon to hand, and we were taken to a rescue centre. Having satisfied myself that the rest of my family were being well cared for, I arrived at the Air Ministry a little late and dishevelled. In fact, well after my immediate boss, Harry Alsopp, which was most unusual.

After hearing of Hitler's failure to kill me, Harry told me to go home and sort things out, but it was at the time of the 1,000 Bomber Raids, and I knew there would be some Flying Battle casualties which would need my personal attention.

After convincing everyone that it took more than a V2 to stop a Gibson from performing his usual functions, I did avail myself of Harry's offer, and I went off home to see where my family had been re-housed, and where I was going to sleep that night.

The temporary accommodation the Council had provided for my family was superb.

It was a large, detached establishment and was owned by a Doctor who had thought it prudent to evacuate himself and his family to safer climes, because he worked on the premise that all buildings are replaceable, but human beings are not.

Brother Cyril, who lived not far away at Seven Kings and was a Councillor on Ilford Borough Council, was in close touch and able to use his knowledge to help our family get settled.

He lived at 28 Gartmore Road, Seven Kings, and next door to him at No 26 was a similar premises, which was for sale, and to cut a long story short, I bought the premises for £664.00, and we moved in to be neighbours of Cyril. His wife, Helen, was a wonderful neighbour. She was kind, thoughtful, and could not do enough to get us settled in after our traumatic experience.

However, life went on, with the constant bombing and all that went with it.

Next door at 24 Gartmore Road the owners had scarpered, and so the Ilford Borough Council had requisitioned the premises, and Mr. and Mrs. Fudge moved in. They had been living on the Isle of Dogs, but they had been forced to evacuate their home, as the whole area was a mass of flames due to enemy bombing.

The Fudge's had two children, a boy and a girl. Their son, Peter, was a gifted lad aged 7 at the time, and he had started to learn the bugle. How we suffered in silence because we noticed progress was being made! He joined the Salvation Army Brass Band, and moved on to a Cornet; before long he was playing the solos and writing his own music.

He gained a scholarship to Barking Abbey Grammar School where he excelled at Mathematics, and got a job with the Prudential

Insurance Company, and ultimately at the age of 25, he passed his final examination as an Actuary. Peter's immediate boss congratulated him on his success at passing his finals at the age of 25, saying, "I was 40 years of age before I passed, at my 3rd attempt".

No 26 Gartmore Road was a queer house – It was spooky. My parents did not notice this, but I did, and so did sister Betty. She used to have nightmares. There was always a coloured man standing at the foot of her bed. When she screamed, he would disappear through the wall into the Fudge's little girl's bedroom, and she would also see the coloured man as he disappeared.

I had the spare bedroom, and several times in the middle of the night, when I had to evacuate my bladder, there was a light of about one inch diameter shining over Betty's bedroom door. Many times, standing on a chair, I tried to find the source of the light, but it would always disappear. I was not pissed or anything, because I have always been of sober habits.

I repeat, the house was spooky!

One of the first things I discovered on rejoining my family in 1944 was that Betty, at 14 years of age, had had no proper schooling but through no fault of her own. Every time there was an air raid, the sirens would be sounded and she, together with all of the other pupils, would be sent home and the school closed. I discovered that Clarks College in Cranbrook Road never closed, and so it was agreed that Betty would be transferred there. Here Betty came into her own, and completed her basic education and at the same time she learnt Pitman's Shorthand and Typewriting.

When it came to Ballroom Dancing, I thought I was the cat's whiskers and I used to take both my sisters, Ellen and Betty, to the Grosvenor School of Dancing, where I met the Head Dance Instructor, Kay, who convinced me I was rubbish, and so I started taking private lessons.

Now, over 60 years later, I am still under her instruction in even the most basic tasks such as washing the dishes!

245

Kay got me to Gold Star Standard in the Imperial Society of Teachers of Dancing, and ultimately to professional competition standard where we used to compete with the top professionals.

Every night, after I had finished work at the Air Ministry, I would finish up at the Grosvenor where I would spend most of my time pushing beginners around, but at weekends we would go to private clubs where we would meet and dance with lots of other professional competition dancers.

It was a joy.

I had never done anything like ballroom dancing before that I enjoyed so much. Of course, Kay was a much better dancer than me. Her technical knowledge gained through teaching dancing was excellent. Her movement, with her long legs, was superb. Her best dance with her long legs was the Slow Fox Trot, and Victor Barrett, who was the best professional at this dance, could not out stride her.

His Feather Three Step was unbeatable, but when he danced with Kay, she made him look even better! Henry Jacques was one of the top judges. He had been a Squadron Leader in the Catering Corps of the Royal Air Force, and he became a good friend of ours. He had a studio in Kensington, just near Harrods, and each week we would go to him for professional coaching.

Victor Sylvester's wife was a top judge and teacher, and a good friend of Kays. We were mixing on a friendly basis with the best Ballroom Dancers in the world, and I was enjoying every minute of it. I loved the Latin American dances, and the rhythm of the Jive I found most exciting. Kay, in her studio, would get me to dance with all the best Dolly Birds. It was Heaven!! There was one very young girl named Violet who could spin like a top in the Jive, and sometimes, when Kay was busy giving private tuition, we two would go to the local Palais to Jive.

Violet was an attractive girl with legs that went right up to her armpits! As soon as the band commenced to play, we were always first on the floor, and I would get her spinning so that her skirts would fly out to such an extent that she would show her knickers, which was very daring in the 1950's, and everyone would clap.

246

On one occasion, a party of us from the Grosvenor went to a formal dance at the Ilford Palais, during which I noticed Violet was wearing a see through Gown with no Slip underneath. I had a word with the MC, and he put on a waltz, and by arrangement, after a bit, the MC switched all of the lights out, leaving just the spot light shining on the scintillating Ball in the centre of the dance floor.

I manoeuvred Violet so that everybody could see her gorgeous legs through her see through gown. After a while, the other dancers cottoned on and stopped dancing and began clapping, so that we were the only pair still dancing. Violet said, "What goes on Bruce?" I said, "Violet, everybody thinks you're gorgeous.............!"

Although the war was over, it was still compulsory for serving men to wear uniform, and at dances that Kay and I attended, in an 'excuse me' dance, it was amazing how many times I was excused.

The Imperial would hold an annual 'Tea Dance' at the Grosvenor Hotel in Park Lane. It was always a good social occasion with all of the top professionals attending. Wally Fryer and Violet Barnes were the World Champions at that time, and during the evening, Wally would always make a point of dancing a Slow Fox Trot with Kay. When the dance was over, he would bring Kay back to our table and say, "Thanks Ducks".

Wally was a typical cockney man, and a phrase such as that, coming from Wally, was praise indeed. After one of these dances I noticed that Kay was looking a little glum, and I said, "Kay, didn't you enjoy that?" "Oh yes," was the reply, "But I wish Wally wouldn't call me Ducks"!

I have always been interested in all indoor and outdoor games. If there is a ball involved, no matter what shape or size, you will find me taking part or expressing an opinion. However, the thing that struck me as odd with the professional dancing people was that, when they met, the only topic of conversation was dancing.

One year Kay and I took part in the Scottish Professional Dance Competition in Glasgow. We were having problems finding hotel accommodation until we met Major Eric Hancock and his partner,

Betty Wytch, and I was able to share Eric's room with him, and Kay was able to share with Betty.

Professional Dancing Competitions in those days were a complete farce! As soon as we knew who was entering, we all knew who was going to win, and could name the first six in the correct order. People like Kay and me were only needed to make up the competition for the senior professionals to beat.

This particular night, Wally Fryer was not competing, and so Eric Hancock was expecting to win, as he was to be reckoned to be second to Wally, and as long as Eric did not fall base over apex, he must win. However, a surprise Judge turned up, and he marked Eric down so that he came second. Several couples were staying at the same hotel as us, and on arriving back at the hotel after the competition, a drinking party soon developed, commiserating with Eric on coming second.

I went to bed just after midnight as the next day we were entering another competition in Aberdeen, and it had been agreed that Eric and Betty would join us on our drive north. The whole way, from Glasgow to Aberdeen, Eric, Betty and Kay talked dancing. On arriving at Aberdeen, once again, all of the hotels were fully booked, and so we did a repeat performance and shared rooms with Eric and Betty, and still they kept talking dancing.

The news had got around regarding Eric's displeasure at being marked second in Glasgow, and the general opinion was that decision would be rectified at Aberdeen.

I might have a homely sense of taste, but there is nothing wrong with my sense of smell. On our sight seeing tour of the 'Silver City by the Sea', wherever we went, I could smell kippers!

When we got back to the hotel, our dancing competitors were still at it, arguing about the dancing profession. Kay, being a Fellow of the Imperial and a qualified judge of competitive dancing, was in her element, and so I crept away and got stuck into a good book.

Via the grape vine, we heard that Charles Theabault, who had marked Eric down at Glasgow, was also on the panel of Judges for the Aberdeen competition, but everyone was convinced with the premise that 'lightening never strikes in the same place twice', and that the error of Glasgow would be rectified at the Aberdeen show, but low and behold, despite Eric and Betty putting on a superb show, they were still only placed in second position.

Back at the hotel Eric, who had been a Major in the Army, was using the language of a squaddy rather than that of an officer and gentleman in expressing his displeasure!

Just after midnight, I got Kay away, and we went our separate ways to bed. It was well after 0400 hours before Eric, still mumbling about injustice, got to bed. He was under the influence of drink and making a bit of noise, which awoke me, and I promised to call him at 0630 hours and get him on the train by 0800 hours back to Manchester.

This I did, and Betty, who was completely sober, thanked me for my help and said, "Eric will be OK, as he can sleep all of the way back to Manchester." I was serving at Kinloss at the time, and Kay and I had a lovely ride from Aberdeen coastwise via Elgin and Lossiemouth back to my camp.

Eric wrote to me, and thanked me for looking after him and getting him on the train to Manchester, and surprise, surprise, he and Betty had got into the same carriage as Charles Theabault, and that he had got no sleep at all as he and Charles had discussed the Dancing Profession all of the way back to Manchester!

* * *

17

Accidents will happen

In October 1946, I was posted to the Officers' Advanced Training School on the Directing Staff to teach officers (mainly aircrew), who, because of the war, had not had time to learn RAF Administration. I was delegated to Wing Commander Wight-Boycett's Syndicate together with two other Squadron Leaders.

The Head of the Unit was Air Commodore Andrew McKee who was a New Zealander. He was short in height, but he made up for this by being very broad shouldered. He was almost as broad as he was tall, and so his nickname was 'Square' McKee. The Directing Staff were split in two, with both Sections being controlled by a Group Caption. Section I taught Wing Commanders and Group Captains, and Section II taught Squadron Leaders and Flight Lieutenants.

Wight-Boycett was a disciplinarian. Before the war, he was a Special Detective at New Scotland Yard. He did not suffer fools gladly. He was very strict with his trainee officers, and accepted no nonsense. He commanded great respect from everyone as he had been a very successful Night Fighter Pilot, and had a DSO and DFC to prove it.

Quite a number of his instructors thought he was too strict, and during a tea break on one occasion, WB's attitude was being discussed. But, when it came to my turn to put my oar in, I said I thought they were exaggerating and that he was OK.

One of my friends said, "Gibby, how come you get on with WB so well?"

"Well, he thinks I am damn stupid and a complete nincompoop, and not worthy of his attention. He treats me as a father might, so its just like being at home. So, I accept it, and we get on like a house on

My maternal Grandmother, Emma Studd, who helped bring us up during World War I when my father was away with the Royal Flying Corps.

My parents, with my father in Royal Flying Corps uniform.

My younger sister Betty who is now 82 years old, whom I helped bring up.

Me after I retired.

My late wife Kay
and I dancing.

Another shot of Kay
and I dancing.

A photograph taken in 1941, when I was first commissioned as a Pilot Officer.

With Air Chief Marshall Sir Roderick Hill, taking the salute as a passing out parade.

Same parade, showing 300 Air Cadets.

A Brevet parade at Thorney Island in 1953.

Me, leading the RAF contingent at a Battle of Britain parade in Portsmouth, 1953.

My late wife with the silver trophy she won at the Imperial Society of Teachers of Dancing, as the 'Best Lady Dancer of the Year, 1950'.

A group of Officers and friends at a guest night I organised.

At a dinner dance.

fire. OK?" I replied.

But, there was more to it than that. Two of the subjects in the syllabus I knew more about than any other member of the Directing Staff, having spent nearly three years at the Air Ministry and having written the Air Ministry Order on Aircraft Accident Prevention, and, having learnt the correct way to present Service Papers there, I was considered the expert. And WB knew that. WB used to lecture on 'The Manual of Air Force Law and Kings Regulations', and with his previous pre war experience at Scotland Yard, he was excellent. The final period of each subject on the Course was used to examine students on that subject.

On one course, three students failed WB's subject on Air force Law. WB was livid. He ordered the whole course to be present, including the Directing Staff in his Syndicate, and he went 'spare'! He tore the whole gathering such a 'strip off', saying he accepted the three failures as a personal insult for failing a subject on which he was such an authority.

He worked himself up in to such a paddy that words failed him, and he stormed out of the room. The atmosphere in the room was electric. It was so tense, no one moved or said anything, and so I went up on the platform and said, "Gentlemen - you've made our Wing Commander cross!" which broke the tension amid much laughter. I then told the three officers to get swotting, and I would get WB to set a new paper on Air force Law, and get them a second chance. The other instructors in WB's syndicate warned me against this action saying that I was 'sticking my neck out', but I replied, "What have I got to lose?"

All of this happened during the first period after lunch, and so I waited for WB to cool down, and decided I would tackle the gallant Wing Commander at our tea break. However, WB did not turn up for tea, and so I went to his office and said, "Sir, I've got the squash court booked for 1730 hours, would you like to give me a game?" WB was still glum, and he looked at me as if I was something the cat had brought in, but said, "Gibson, I'd love to". "Right Sir," I said, "I'll see you on court at 1730 hours."

WB was a better squash player than me, and although I ran my arse off, and he finally beat me 3 games to 2, which took 50 minutes. After we had bathed, he joined me for a Shandy, during which time he said, "Gibby, thank you for that game, I needed that". And so, I broached the subject of the three failures and told him all three gentlemen had a very fine war record, and could he find a corner in his heart to set them a new paper, and give them a second chance?

Surprise, surprise, he agreed to do that, and needless to say, the three naughty officers passed with flying colours.

When the rest of the Directing Staff heard what I had achieved, with one voice they said, "Jammy Bastard!" "But", I replied, "WB can't frighten me, I'm too ignorant!"

My Supernumerary job was Office in charge of Farms. We had 300 sows, eight boars, the odd cow, and chickens, etc. We employed a civilian pig man, and misemployed as many service batmen as required. As soon as I was appointed, I did a 100% Inventory Check. I had nearly finished when I saw about 50 rabbits running around in various hutches. I said to the Head Man, "What about the rabbits?" "Rabbits!" he said, "We don't have Rabbits!" "What are they then, pussy cats?!" "Oh no!" said the Pigman, "A rabbit does not become a rabbit until it is old enough to breed, which is about 9 to 10 weeks of age. There's not one of these older than 8 week". "OK", I said, "That's your definition, mine is different. I am adding them to the Inventory forthwith."

What was happening was, the Pigman was using the bunnies as one of his perks, and just before they became rabbits (by his definition), he was giving them the chop and taking them home for the pot. As the Airmen's mess was providing the food for the bunnies I did not see why the Pigman should have sole rights of disposal of the pretty little creatures, and so from then on he had to share his perk with the Airmen's Mess.

I had heard via the Airmen's toilet that the Pigman thought I was a proper Bastard. Therefore, I kept a close watch on the activities of the Farm to make sure we did not make any more losses through perks by doing a spot check on two or three items on the Inventory weekly, instead of monthly. By doing this, I discovered we were raising more sows to the weight of 160 pounds (8 score) than the three Messes could consume, and for the first time I sent the surplus to the market for sale, and the proceeds went into the CO's Benevolent Fund.

According to the Pigman, I was a proper Bastard alright!

My other Supernumerary job on this unit was as President of the Mess Committee of the Officers' Mess. With 200 officers living there, running the Mess was like running a hotel. It was a job I loved, and as it was one of the subjects I had to teach, I was able to put into practise what I was telling the students.

The first job I did on taking over from my predecessor was to check the Inventory, and the second was to re-write the Officers' Mess Rules.

The Mess at Digby in Lincolnshire where I was stationed was a hutted camp, built by German Prisoners of World War I. It was quite serviceable, except for one section of about 3,000 square feet, the roof of which was porous and considered to be too expensive to repair. When it rained heavily, as only it can in Lincolnshire, the rain would seep through the irreparable roof, and buckets had to be placed strategically to catch the water. Officers had to go through this section to get from the Dining Room to the Ante Room, or vice versa, dodging the puddles where the rain had missed the buckets, but despite this, the cork lino floor covering was polished daily.

The whole mess was kept spotlessly clean by 47 German prisoners of war. They took their instructions from one of their number who had the rank of Warrant Officer, and he ruled his colleagues with a rod of iron, and woe betide any one of his prisoners who upset him. He would put them on fatigues, one of which was polishing the unusable floor.

RAF Digby, being out in the wilds of Lincolnshire, had a cinema where the programmes were changed every 48 hours, and so it was possible to see three full-length programmes every week. The first two rows were reserved for the prisoners, and if one of these gentlemen happened to upset their Warrant Officer, he would 'tear them a strip off' in German, and for the benefit of any RAF personnel present, he would finish his castigation with the punishment of 'no pictures for you for one week,' in English.

Every week we had a 36-hour break, starting at luncheon time on Saturday until 2359 hours on Sunday, and a 48-hour break once a month.

One Friday afternoon, I was a pillion rider on a motorcycle with Flight Lieutenant Dibber driving, and we were on our way to London. He was going to drop me off at Liverpool Street Station, from where I was going to proceed to Seven Kings by rail for a 48-hour break. I had arranged to meet Kay at the Grosvenor, but I had not told my parents of this arrangement.

Dibber, who was a pilot and a student on the course, was driving too fast for the road conditions. It was raining at the time and the roads were greasy, and, as we left the village of Epping on the A11, he started to pass a motorcar. There was a car coming in the opposite direction, and as soon as Dibber realised he was not going to make that manoeuvre, he braked hard, skidded, and we both ended up in a heap in the gutter. Dibber had the motorcycle handle bars to hang on to, and he stayed with the bike. However, I was thrown off and tried to dig up the tarmac road with my head, without success.

It was still pouring with rain and, lying by the side of the road, I was in no pain; in fact, I was quite comfortable and did not want to move. It was not long before an ambulance arrived, and took me to Epping General Hospital. I gave instructions to Dibber to contact Kay by telephone to let her know what had happened, and settled down to let the nurses do their stuff.

They put 18 stitches in my head, and patched me up with a broken right scapula, a damaged upper right arm and right wrist, and put me to bed. Kay contacted everyone, including brother-in-law Fred as he was the only one mobile, and it was not long before there was a gaggle of Gibsons around my bed, wanting to know how long I had got to live. The next day the RAF took over and collected me by ambulance to take me to RAF Ely Hospital, where I was put in the Orthopaedic Ward.

In the meantime, Kay 'phoned up Epping Hospital only to be told that the RAF had got me. The next thing that happened, Fred and Kay arrived at Digby, and as it was a Saturday, everyone was on a weekend break, but they were met by two of my friends, Wing Commander Tonge (Tongo), and Wing Commander Case ('Uncle'). While Uncle acted as host, Tongo found out where I was and, after giving Fred and Kay suitable refreshments, he gave Fred detailed instructions how to get to Ely from Digby, where they duly arrived.

It was a large ward, with ten beds on either side, and a Flight Officer Nursing Officer was in charge, who was most proficient. It was a happy ward because most of the patients were aircrew – mentally alert because it was only broken bones that were bothering them.

I had not been in the ward long before I had to go to the toilet to evacuate my bladder, and on my way back, the Ward Sister intercepted me. She said, "What the hell do you think you are doing?!" A look of amazement came over me, and I gave her my 'gormless' look and said, "Sister, I've been to have a pee". "Get back into that bed immediately, and don't dare get out of it unless I say so"!!

The rest of the ward were laughing their heads off at me 'being torn a strip off', and so I said, "Flight Officer Ward Sister, you are a Flight Officer, and I am a Squadron Leader, you are outranked." She replied, "I've got an Air Commodore in the next ward, and he obeys me. I can't be outranked in my own ward. Get back to bed forthwith!"

It was quite obvious from the uproarious laughter from the rest of the ward whose side they were on, and so I meekly got into bed, and covered my head with the bedclothes, but I could still hear the laughter of derision at my defeat!

At 0200 hours the next morning there was an awful kafuffle as a new patient was wheeled into the bed next to me. He had just been operated on, but before that could happen, he had to have his stomach pumped dry of alcohol. He was in a dreadful condition. He had borrowed his friend's Sports Car, without permission, and whilst driving with super confidence (the effect of the alcohol) he had wrapped it neatly around an Oak Tree. He was not expected to live. Everyone in the ward was wide awake, and so the officer in the bed opposite started a 'book', and was laying betting odds on what time our new patient was expected to die.

Business was brisk, and much money changed hands, but, after 48 hours, the 'book' was closed as the patient looked as if he was going to make it. After the next 72 hours the crisis was over, and he was on the mend when the rest of the ward ribbed him unmercifully for costing them so much money in lost bets, and I reminded him he would have done us all a favour if he had popped off! The only one in the ward who was laughing was the bookmaker.

Being an aircrew officer, the patient took our ribald criticisms in good part, and as his health improved, he was able to give as good as he got, knowing that he was accepted as one of us.

The only occupant of the ward next to us was the Air Commodore, and when he reached the stage in his treatment when he only needed physical therapy, he was moved into our ward, but part of his exercise was to polish the lino floor of the ward he had vacated with a heavy bumper until it shone like glass, and he forbade any one of us to walk on his floor. Had he not mentioned such a thing, we would have admired his floor from a distance, but to try and use his rank by threatening us was a challenge we could not ignore.

One of our fractious aircrew was kept mobile with the use of a wheelchair, and so, when the Air Com was resting after his exertions, our mobile conspirator would rush over the newly polished floor, leaving tyre marks wherever he went, and he then would disappear for an hour so that he had a perfect alibi when the Air Com discovered what had happened while he had been resting and our mobile friend was still absent.

The Air Com was furious, but he leant one quick lesson; it was easier to plead with us to help him keep his old ward 'shipshape and Bristol fashion' than to threaten us with dire consequences.

After a week, I had my 18 stitches removed from my head, and was officially allowed out of bed, but in the meantime my colleagues would always keep Sister engaged down the other end of the ward whilst I was on the toilet, and the nurses helping Sister never let on that I never needed a bedpan or bottle. I was so grateful at my newfound freedom that I tried to engage Sister in a romantic conversation, but looking me straight in the eye, she said, "Squadron Leader Gibson, have your bowels functioned in the last 24 hours?" That of course is the most perfect question from a member of the nursing staff to show where their priorities lie, and so I never tried that again.

The fractures to my Scapula, Upper Arm and Wrist, I just had to rest and let them mend themselves. With my arm in a sling, I was trussed up like a turkey waiting for the oven, wandering around trying to chat up other patients who were in a far worse condition than me. I was raring to get back to my unit and do some useful work.

However one day a Doctor approached me and said the Hospital had been granted six tickets for Newmarket Race Course, and would I like to take five other officers to the Meeting.

I had never been to a Race Meeting before, and so I accepted with alacrity and started to get organised. I got hold of the Transport Officer and he arranged for me to borrow an Aircrew Coach for the day, complete with driver, and so all I had to do was select five other 'bods' to join me.

My initial thought was to take walking wounded only, but when my friend 'Scotty', a pilot in a wheelchair heard this, he was completely crestfallen and said, "Gibby, that's not fair, I am the oldest inhabitant of this ward. I have a folding chair and, apart from a little help getting into and out of the coach, I promise I will be no trouble!"

For the next couple of days I couldn't wait for the Aircrew Coach to arrive, and we duly arrived at Newmarket Racecourse. I left my friends to get Scotty settled into his wheelchair while I went off to make arrangements for our entry to the Members' Stand. I met a Steward who was expecting our arrival, and, after that, all we had to do was follow him. We were shown how to display our Member's Badges, where the Tote and Parade Ring were, and he told us he would be in the enclosure should we want any further help.

Scotty, in his wheelchair, was perfectly self sufficient, and with his leg in plaster sticking straight out (he was having a bone graft from his lower leg to his upper arm), he said, "Just leave me in close proximity to the Tote and bugger off and enjoy yourselves!" This we did, although I kept my eye on him from a distance. I noticed that, apart from frequent visits to the Tote, he seemed OK.

In those days I knew nothing about the 'Sport of Kings', not even how to place a bet, but I found the colourful spectacle awe inspiring. When I was told that some of the horses parading the ring were worth hundreds of thousands of pounds, I was glad that I was in the RAF because at least in that environment I knew what I was doing!

All too quickly the meeting came to an end and, having thanked the Steward for his assistance, before long we were back in the aircrew coach and on our way back to Ely Hospital. Everyone was still excited, and we were all discussing our winnings. It seemed that each one of my friends had won, but I had finished up having lost a fiver. However, I noticed Scotty had gone all quiet which was unusual for him, and so I said "Did you enjoy that Scotty – did you win anything?" "Yes", he said, "I won £347.00" I said, "Come off it Scotty, don't give us that bullshit!" But Scotty said that after the first race, when he was trying to decide which horse to back, a gentleman came up to him and marked his card and said "Back that, but don't tell the others". Scotty then added that his new acquaintance marked his card for every other race, and he had won £347.00 as a result!

Apparently Scotty's friend was a professional backer, and seeing Scotty with his leg in plaster sticking straight out, had taken pity on him, hence this amazing result!

Back at the hospital I wrote a 'thank you' note to the Almoner on behalf of our party for a wonderful day out, and I made it my business to find the Doctor who had given me the tickets to the Members' Stand, when he told me the price of each ticket was £15.00. I was flabbergasted because in 1947, that was an awful lot of money!!

Later that evening in the ward, despite the rationing of Spirits, Scotty arrived with a bottle of Whisky, and everyone had a drink to his health, and a good time was had by all. As I was the only one who didn't like Whisky I was entrusted with the bottle to see fair play, and to make sure Sister didn't catch us out!

A walking wounded officer joined our ward, and he was wearing a knitted Balaclava over a plaster cast which came down to his shoulders. Whilst he was in Egypt, he had had an accident while swimming when a Speed Boat went right over him and broke his neck.

He had been in plaster for six months while at home on leave, and he had only come to Ely Hospital to have his Plaster Cast removed. When this was done, he was left with a beard six inches long, and his hair had grown down to his shoulders. His hair had gone virtually gangrenous, and it stunk to high heaven, and so after he had had a shampoo, he was ready for the Barbers.

My head had been shaved before being stitched up and needed a tidy up, and so I ordered a taxi, and off we went together to the hairdressers. I was wearing my Peak Cap, and my friend was wearing his Balaclava. I sat in the Barber's chair first, took off my cap displaying a large bald patch, and said to the Barber, "Please take it all off".

When it came to the turn of my friend, he pulled off his Balaclava and said, "Same as him; take it all off!" The Barber was nonplussed, but seeing my friend was a Squadron Leader Pilot, said, "What the hell have you been up to?", and he was laughing so much he had to sit down while he listened to the Pilot's descriptive details of the accident that had occurred while he was swimming.

As we were about to leave, the Barber refused payment, saying he had never had such a good laugh in all of his life, and he was still laughing as he opened the door for two Squadron Leaders to leave his establishment, both 'bald as a badger's arse.........'

I spent the second week in the ward as walking wounded. I still had my arm in a sling, and as my head was OK, there was nothing more they could do for me, and so they wanted to send me on three week's convalescence leave, but I was having none of that. If I just had to wait for my fractured scapula to heal itself, I would be better employed ensuring my 300 sows and 200 officers were fed properly, and in that order. And so, I went back to Digby.

I reported to my Group Captain, and when I told him I was as mentally fit as I ever would be and that I wanted to resume my normal duties, he was delighted. And so, off I went to check with my Officers' Mess Manager to let him know I was back, and for him to bring me up to date with what had been happening. I sought out Tongo and Uncle, and thanked them both for looking after Fred and Kay, and they both said it was a pleasure.

I then went off to the Farm, and surprise surprise, my Pigman was pleased to see me! During my absence, the standard of swill from the Messes had deteriorated, and tealeaves had not been segregated. A loose minute to the Messes stating my displeasure soon put that right, and within 24 hours, it was like I'd never been away!

In 1947 the privilege of walking out of camp was extended to the 47 German Prisoners of War, at the discretion of the German Warrant Officer, and only a few at a time. The local village girls thought it was wonderful, and it was noted that those prisoners who were granted that privilege never went without female company.

Every night at 2100 hours the Prisoners' Barrack Room had to be inspected by the Station Duty Officer for cleanliness and spot Inventory checks etc. Every German had to be standing by his bed, with the sheets and blankets folded according to the standard layout. At these inspections, any routine repairs to socks or boots etc could be dealt with.

It had been known that sometimes prisoners who had been allowed out of camp, and had failed to make the 2100-hour inspection, were not reported missing because their colleagues would cover for them by distracting the Inspecting Officer's attention, and so occupy the absent prisoner's bed space, thereby being counted twice.

This never happened to me because when I was Station Duty Officer, I always took two Sergeants with me, one to do any writing that might be necessary, and the other would be down the other end of the room that prevented any shenanigans.

As PMC of the Officers' Mess, the Warrant Officer reported to me daily to see if I had any complaints, or if there were any special duties I required. The only times I needed anything special was if I were organising a guest night or dance etc, otherwise, the WO kept the Mess and the surrounding gardens in immaculate condition, and his disciplinary control of his men was superb.

Despite the daily contact he had with me and the mutual respect with one another, at no time did he attempt any familiarity with me. There was always that distance of manager and servant.

Ultimately it came the time for the Germans to go back home. Some stayed and got jobs, which they found easy as they were excellent workers, but also some had made long-term attachments to their local girl friends, and they liked our way of life. This made it much more difficult for me to run the Mess, for although my 47 Germans were replaced with 64 English Batmen, the standard of cleanliness was not the same, and my Mess Manager was forever pointing out their short comings.

Annually, in common with other RAF Stations, Digby had an Open Day, and I was put in charge of security for the day. My first task was to liaise with the local civilian Police Inspector, when I discovered I could expect up to 5,000 visitors. I organised the odd Fighter, Bomber and Transport aircraft to be flown in to be on display, which kept the aircrews busy with visitors climbing all over them.

I provided a small refreshment tent with small eats and soft drinks at cost price, which was well supported, and portable toilets so that one could do what comes naturally in privacy instead of where one stood! I had signs put up everywhere, directing the public to the 'goodies' we had to offer, but the main attraction seemed to be our cinema where I had arranged short 'funnies' to be shown, much to the delight of the young at heart, me included.

That was about it. The Pig Farm was out of bounds, and I had the Pigman and all of his assistants on duty to ensure that.

On the actual day we had brilliant sunshine and all enjoyed a very relaxed day, but, above all, no airman went AWOL.

At the 'wash up' meeting afterwards, our Air Commodore who was Chairing the meeting paid particular attention to my security arrangements and said, "Well done Gibby – you can do the same again next year!", but it wasn't to be because our unit, The Officers' Advanced Training School, was moved to Hornchurch Aerodrome..........

* * *

18

Back to London - and a foody's paradise

W hat a difference going from rural Lincolnshire to urban cosmopolitan Greater London.

The Officers' mess at Hornchurch was only large enough to cater for the permanent staff of our unit, and so a second Mess had to be opened to accommodate the students. This was called Number Two Officers' mess, and once again I was made the PMC.

A large building was provided, and the Equipment Officer had orders to furnish it to Officers' Mess Standards. Everything went well except for the provision of wardrobes.

I was keeping in touch daily with the Equipment Officer and, according to him, wardrobes were unobtainable. I said to him, "But I know where there are thousands." "Do you? Clever clogs!" was the response. "Put me in touch with the unit where you think they are, and I'll do the rest."

At that time in 1947, the RAF was closing stations, and the furniture was being stored at a Maintenance Unit on the Great North Road, the C.O. of was a friend of mine. A quick 'phone call to my friend, who confirmed he could supply 100 wardrobes, was all that was required, and to cut a long story short, 100 wardrobes arrived at RAF Hornchurch within a week. The Equipment Officer was delighted, and said "Well done Gibby,"

"It's not what you know, its who you know that counts!" I glibly replied.

Then, students started to arrive, and we were back in business.

I had a civilian Mess Steward, and an Assistant Mess Steward, and enough service kitchen staff and batmen to run a 100 bedroom

Mess, but I was not happy with the Service Chef whose standard of cooking was a bit homely, and so I advertised and procured the services of a Chef who had come straight from the Ritz Hotel in London.

He was a Swiss gentleman who spoke French as his first language. He also spoke English, German and Italian because, he told me, he was born on the border of Switzerland, and it was common for people in that area to speak all four languages and which he had learnt from birth.

It was amazing how he could produce such incredible menus from the food supplied by the NAAFI, and on guest nights, with some added items that he had asked me to obtain, we fed like fighting cocks! I would have a weekly meeting with him and the Mess Steward to discuss the menus for the forthcoming week.

On one occasion I asked him why he had taken the job, because I could not afford to pay him anywhere near the salary he had been earning at The Ritz, and he said for many reasons. For the way I accepted him as a Swiss at the interview, I had made him feel at home. Also, he was fed up with being bombed, night and day, in the heart of London, but mainly, he had a house in Hornchurch from where he could commute daily, and he considered the job he was doing was a part of his war effort.

Every Thursday I organised a guest night which entailed a formal dinner, and which every officer had to attend. On these occasions, our Chef would excel himself, and it quickly became known throughout No. 1 Mess how well we ate in No. 2 Mess! This was partly due to my brother Cyril; he would let me know when certain fruits and vegetables had gone 'trumpy' (in short supply) in Covent Garden, and he would supply to me at wholesale price.

There was a time when onions went 'trumpy', and with a sack of onions, I was able to barter with the local traders and get anything the Mess wanted.

One day I had a telephone call from the Air Commodore's Adjutant, saying the Boss Man would like to be invited to one of our

Guest Nights. Of course, being Commandant of the Station, he did not have to be invited at all; he could have walked in at any time, but it was the nice way he had in his dealings with junior officers of letting them know his wishes.

The Air Commodore was living in married quarters with his wife, who was a Cordon Bleu Gold Medallist, and so I went to the local butcher, and although beef was still rationed, on the night that our Commodore came to dinner, everyone of the 146 officers attending had a steak for dinner, and which our Chef cooked to perfection.

The next day I received a hand written note from the Air Commodore, thanking me for an excellent Guest Night, but also he wanted to make sure everything our Chef produced to eat had come from legal sources! Subsequently there were many times when I would receive a 'phone call from Square McKee's Adjutant stating that he would like to dine with us, and on such occasions, our Chef would produce a menu fit for a King. On these formal occasions, I would be at the centre of the Head Table, complete with gavel to control the proceedings, and the Commandant would be to my right as Honoured Guest, completely relaxed and enjoying his repast, but the next day, as always, I would receive my 'thank you' note, reminding me to keep my food purchases within legal bounds.

These notes never worried me because anyone could have produced the same menus, providing they had the skills of my Swiss Chef.

The Commandant of the Officers' Advanced Training School was also Station Commander of RAF Hornchurch, and most days I would call on him in his Headquarters' Office, and if he were free, we would walk to Number One Mess, discussing the day-to-day happenings in my Mess. On one particular day, as I was approaching his office, the door opened, and the Station Warrant Officer marched an airman out who had been on a charge. I put my head round the door and said, "Sir!". Square looked up and said, "Come on in Gibby, I won't be a minute."

I went into the office and noticed that Square was making an entry on the Form 160, annotating 7 days confined to camp for the airman he had just punished. He then put on his peaked cap, and off we went to lunch. As we were passing the Warrant Officer's office, we heard the airman say, "If the old sod thinks I'm going to do 7 days confined to camp, he's got another think coming!" Square stopped in his tracks, he looked at me, and went straight into the Warrant Officer's office, up to the airman, and said "So, you're not going to do 7 days confined to camp son?", and the airman replied "No, Sir". Square replied, "But you will do 7 day's detention, won't you?" "Yes Sir" replied the airman. "Right son, you've got it!"

Square went back to his office and started to alter the punishment on the Form 160. I said, "Sir, you can't do that; if you give an airman detention, it affects his pay, and so you have to give him the option of a trial by Court Marshal!" Square said "I know that Gibby, but I offered it to him, and he took it, so he's got it – end of story!" And off we went to lunch.

The OATS syllabus was so arranged that the staff and students could have a week off at Christmas time. Everyone living in No. 2 Mess had gone off on their Christmas break, and I let all of the staff go their separate ways. I was the only one left sleeping in No. 2 Mess.

I was taking my meals in No. 1 Mess, and enjoying the company of all of my colleagues who were living in married quarters. As my family only living a 20-minute drive away at Seven Kings, I could visit them as often as I wished.

One day just before Christmas, Square came into the anteroom and, after wishing me the Compliments of the Season, said, "Gibby, 147lbs of meat has gone bad in the Sergeants' Mess. Do a Formal Enquiry for me and let me know what went wrong."

I started snooping around as if I were the Station Duty Officer. I visited the NAAFI and the Salvation Army recreation room with my ears wide open, listening to the airmen's gossip, until I eventually heard 200 lbs of meat had gone bad in the Sergeants' Mess. The next day, continuing my formal detective work, I discovered 250 lbs of meat had gone bad.

Come Christmas Day, 347 lbs of meat had gone bad.

On Boxing Day, Square came into the Mess and I informed him of my findings, that the amount of meat that had gone bad had risen by 200 lbs, and was now 347 lbs, and said "Instead of carrying out a Formal Enquiry, it would save a lot of time if we had a Summary of Evidence instead." To this Square agreed, with me as President, and he told me to select two other officers to assist, and get it put on the Station Routine Orders.

When everyone had returned from Christmas Leave, I got cracking. There was a Squadron Leader in my Syndicate on the Course whose ability to express himself in writing was excellent, and there was Flight Lieutenant Catering Officer in the other Syndicate, and so I got them to volunteer to assist me by posting on Station Duty Orders that we three were going to carry out a Summary of Evidence into the loss of 347 lbs of beef which had gone bad in the Sergeants' Mess over the Christmas period. I had done all of the preliminary work, and so we got started.

When doing a Summary of Evidence, we used to teach that the preliminary work should be carried out thoroughly to get some idea who might be responsible, and that person could then be the first witness. After they had given their evidence, if the panel of officers is still of the same mind, then that person should be invited to sit in to hear the remainder of the evidence from the other witnesses. They could then ask questions of any further witnesses if they so desired.

In this particular case, the evidence I had gathered over the Christmas period pointed to the Warrant Officer in charge of Catering as the one responsible for the meat going bad, and so I invited him to be the first witness. After he had given his evidence on oath, I advised him I considered he was to blame, and so I invited him to remain to hear the evidence of all the other witnesses, and said that he would be free to ask any questions of those witnesses if he so desired.

The Warrant Officer accepted my invitation to remain, and so we continued.

The next witness was the Sergeant butcher who had been on duty over the Christmas period. His evidence was that at the start of the Christmas break, the Airmen's Mess had a quantity of meat that they not could get into their refrigerator, and it was agreed to put that meat into the Sergeants' Mess Refrigerator until after Christmas. However, because the Sergeants' Mess Refrigerator was in constant use over Christmas, 347 lbs of meat had gone bad. This evidence was in total agreement with the Warrant officer's evidence. My Catering Officer, who was my specialist Officer, asked the Sergeant, "What did the meat look like?" The Sergeant replied, "It was a whole hind quarter".

I thanked the Sergeant for his evidence on oath, and told him to wait outside.

The next witness was the butcher from the Airmen's Mess who had put the meat in the Sergeants' Mess Refrigerator. Before the war, that airman had been trained by his father, who was a Master Butcher with his own business, and had joined the RAF as a qualified butcher. His evidence on oath was similar to the two previous witnesses, but when my Catering Officer asked the same question he had asked the Sergeant, he got a completely different answer. The airman replied, "He had ripped the meat up into pieces of 20 to 30 lbs each." The Catering Officer said to the airman, "But wasn't it a whole hind quarter?" and the airman replied, "No Sir, you would not be able to get a whole hind quarter into the Sergeants' Mess Refrigerator".

The Warrant Officer had no questions to ask,

At that point in the proceedings, I adjourned the Summary of Evidence for lunch. The Catering Store was next door to the Guard Room, and as I was passing the store with the Catering Officer on my way to lunch, I approached the store and tried the door, which was locked, but as I did that, I noticed one of the glass slats in the door was loose. I lifted the slat, put my hand inside the door, turned the lock, and entered the store. After a quick look around, I weighed a side of bacon, wrapped it in greaseproof paper, and took it to the Guard Room next door.

I said to the Sergeant in charge of the Guard Room, "Sergeant, here is 86 lbs of bacon. Please look after it for me until later on this afternoon. In the meantime, please give me a chit for 86 lbs of bacon", which the Sergeant did. And so, armed with this receipt, the Catering Officer and I continued on our way to the Officers' Mess for lunch.

After lunch we reassembled, and because of the discrepancy between the Sergeant and the Airman butcher's evidence in what the meat looked like, I invited both these airmen to remain to hear the rest of the evidence, and I told them they were free to ask questions if they so desired.

As no food can be issued without a requisition on a Form H 141, I asked the Warrant Officer to produce the Stock Control figure for meat made out from the H141's, and on examining that figure, I remarked that I doubted whether the figure shown was accurate. Therefore, I said to the Warrant Officer, I was going to adjourn this Summary of Evidence for one hour to allow him to do a snap check on the bacon stocks in the Stores, and to report back with the result.

On resuming one hour later, the Warrant Officer reported that the Bacon in the Stores was 26 lbs short of the recorded figure.

Before anyone could say anything, the Airman butcher volunteered the information that he issued the Officers' Mess 26 lbs of bacon on Christmas Eve, but had forgotten to make out the H141. I asked the Airman butcher if he was sure about that, because it was most irregular to issue stores without an H141. The Airman replied that he was positive. I said to the Warrant Officer, "Do you accept that evidence given on oath?", and he replied, "Yes, I do".

I said, "In that case, if I allow you to make out an H141 for 26 lbs of bacon, will that put your stocks right?" , and the Warrant Officer, Sergeant and Airman all agreed that it would.

I then said, "Right, before I allow you to do that," (remembering that H141's cannot be backdated) "on my way to the Officers' Mess for lunch, as I passed the Stores, I found it was easy to enter the Store by lifting up one of the glass slats, and by putting my hand inside, it was possible to reach the Yale lock and gain entry, which I did. I then weighed a side of bacon, which came to 86 lbs, which I then took to the Guard Room for safe keeping, and here is a receipt from the Sergeant in charge of the Guard Room to prove it. Therefore, if I allow you to raise an H141 for 26 lbs of bacon, that gives you a surplus of 86 lbs of bacon!"

Before I could say another word, the Airman butcher chimed in and said, "It's about time somebody started telling the truth!" I said, "I agree with that because my next witness was to be the Medical Officer, who had inspected the meat in the Sergeants' Mess on the day it had gone bad, and he had produced a Certificate to the effect that 147 lbs of meat had gone bad. He had shown me the Certificate during my preliminary investigations, and was going to produce this as evidence to prove it".

I discovered what had really happened from the Airman butcher.

In 1947, the Airmen's Mess was short of cooking materials, and the Airman had been ripping out surplus fat from meat at the request of the Airmen's Mess Chef, which he had been rendering down for cooking fat. These several, small quantities, over a period of time, had amounted to 200 lbs, but they had failed to raise the H141's for those several small amounts at the appropriate time, and that had made the meat stocks short.

When 147 lbs of meat had gone bad over the Christmas period, the Warrant Officer decided it was a good time to put his records straight. Therefore, I was able to complete the Summary of Evidence, and in doing so, included a separate report. During my enquiries, I had discovered the Warrant Officer had been on the Hornchurch Station for over eight years, and had become a bit set in his ways. If he had been on top of his job, the errors in the meat stock records would not have occurred. Also, as this misdemeanour was not worthy of a Courts Martial, the Commandant had the power to render whatever punishment he thought fit.

The next day, on our way to the Mess for lunch, the Air Commodore thanked me for the Summary of Evidence, and quoting Sir Walter Scott, said, "Oh what a tangled web we weave, when first we practise to deceive."

The final result was the Warrant Officer was reprimanded, and posted overseas.

CRDL Lloyd, 'Call me Peter', was the Group Captain in charge of our section. He was boiling with enthusiasm, and helpful to the extent of being interfering! When one went to do ordinary, routine jobs, one would find Peter had already done the job.

There was an occasion when that had got me into trouble!

A précis of any lecture that we were due to give was issued before the lecture, and these were revised every course. This was in the days of stencils, and each one had to be proof read before running off the copies. Every time I went to proof read my stencils, Peter had beaten me to it and had done the job for me. There was one subject where I was considered the expert, and on one occasion, Peter left the stencils for me to check. However, due to pressure of work, I did not get round to it.

It didn't worry me too much as I assumed Peter would have done the job for me, but on this occasion he hadn't, and the stencils were run off with two spelling errors, and that, for a teaching organisation, was simply not allowed.

When Peter spotted these errors, he 'tore me such a strip off' for failing to do my job properly which hurt me deeply. Throughout the whole of my Service career I had always been most conscientious, and yet there, for all to see, Gibson the expert had made a 'cock of it'. This happened late on a Friday afternoon, and I was still suffering from the effects from the Group Captain's remarks the next day.

Saturday was the commencement of a 48-hour pass, and all of the Staff and Students were away for the weekend. I had intended to go to Seven Kings in the afternoon, but in the morning I was working in my office, marking some examination papers. I thought I was the only one in the office block, but I could hear someone moving about upstairs, but that was none of my business, and so I ignored it.

My office was on the ground floor. It was a lovely sunny day, and I had my window open when, just before noon, the person I heard moving about upstairs came down, and, of course, it was the Group Captain (call me Peter) Lloyd. I was still looking glum and morose, and as he passed my window, he stopped dead in his tracks, put his head inside my window, and said "What the Hell are you looking so miserable? Pack up what you are doing, and come to the Mess with me and buy me a drink!"

I refrained from saying 'bollocks', but I shut my window and joined Peter, and as we walked back to the Mess, he was as charming as ever. In fact, he bought me a Coke while he had a shandy, which once again proved to me one of the basic principles of the RAF, 'Never bear malice.'

Because of my love of Ballroom Dancing, I regularly held dances in No. 2 Mess, so that when No. 1 Mess decided to hold a New Year's Eve Ball, I was asked to organise it.

I seconded my Swiss Chef to help, and was having a sampling session to decide which small eats to have, when Peter came into the Mess in search of me. When he found out what I was doing in the Mess kitchen, he joined me, during which he espied a pail full of oysters, and in between sampling the food he ate six dozen oysters. Now, I know oysters aren't everyone's first choice, and I still had enough left for the main function, but I had discovered a weakness in Peter's character because he was making a pig of himself to the extent that, by the time the sampling session was over, he couldn't remember why he had sought me out.

The actual function went off without a hitch, and everyone thoroughly enjoyed themselves. This was due in no small part to the waiter service I always provided. I always asked for volunteers from the Sergeants' Mess to act as waiters, and I was never short of an adequate supply. It was amazing how, after only a quick briefing from the Mess Steward regarding their duties, and the promise of a meal after the function, how skilful my volunteer waiters were. By the time I had supervised the fatigue party in clearing up the main debris after the Ball, it was 0330 hours, and I crept to bed.

Ultimately my Syndicate Leader, Wing Commander Wight-Boycott, got promoted to Group Captain and left to become Station

Commander at RAF Kemble.

His replacement was a Wing Commander Tom Pricket. Tom was charming and he had all of the social graces, with the most gorgeous wife who was admired by all of other wives in the married quarters, because at coffee mornings, although she would listen to the tittle-tattle prevalent on the patch, she was never known to repeat such stories.

Tom was basically lazy, and although he had a wide experience of RAF administration, it is one thing to practise it, but a whole new ball game when one comes to teach it.

I was one of three Squadron Leaders in his Syndicate, and one of his first jobs was to distribute among the rest of us the subjects WB used to teach and which he himself couldn't handle, such as Summary of Evidence, Courts-Martial, and Air Force Law. It was in these cases he exercised his charm and powers of delegation, for although he relieved me of the subject of Honours and Awards, and Court of Enquiry; I found I had gained Summary of Evidence and Courts-Martial!

And, when it came to his turn to lecture on Court of Enquiry, he asked me to sit in on his lecture to make sure he did not make a 'cock of it'.

Of course, I found this a pleasure, but when it came to his time to give the lecture, with me sitting at the back of the class, he introduced the lecture and what it was all about, but when he came to the nitty gritty details, he went on to say,

"The unit has the good fortune to have Bruce Gibson on the staff who has spent three years at the Air Ministry, and who had written the Air Ministry Order on Court of Enquiry, and as the expert, he will now take over, because Bruce can tell you more in 20 minutes on C of E's than I could in three hours".

And so, I found five feet seven inches Bruce Gibson feeling ten feet tall, and giving Tom's lecture for him, and liking it! But, that was not the end of the matter for the same thing happened every time Tom was scheduled to give his lecture on this subject.

There was another time when Tom exercised his charm. It

273

happened one Saturday lunch time and I was in No. 1 Mess, enjoying the company of my colleagues who were living in married quarters and who were having a quiet drink, when the Air Commodore joined us, and he went straight up to Tom and said, "Tom, I'm so glad you're here; I've got a Courts Martial to do and I want you to be President." "Sir", said Tom, chuckling affably, "You don't want me to be President, Bruce here is an expert on Courts Martial, it's one of his subjects. Bruce is your man"

Square turned to me and said, "Is that right Gibby, will you do the job for me?"

Once again, Tom's charm had worked and I found myself doing his work for him. This power of delegation stood Tom in good stead because he retired from the RAF as an Air Vice Marshal, and became a Vice President of an American Aircraft Manufacturing concern!

* * *

19

On to opportunities new..........

In 1948, the Officers' Advanced Training School moved from Hornchurch to Bircham, Newton Abbot.

About that time, an Air Ministry Order was published, stating that a new appointment was to be created, that of Senior Weapons Officer, and General Duties Officers were invited to apply.

It would involve a six-month course at the Empire Air Armament School at RAF Station, Manby, Lincolnshire. This was right up my street and as my stint at the OATS was drawing to its close, I made an application to join the course.

My application was strongly recommended by Air Commodore McKee (Square), and early in 1949, I found myself on my way to Manby. This was the third time I had been on a course at the Empire Air Armament School, and I knew quite a number of the Directing Staff. From my records they could also see I was a qualified Armament Instructor, and had held appointments as Gunner Leader as well as a Bombing Leader, whereas the remaining 24 students were pilots with no previous armament experience.

I therefore found this course a doddle, and was the only navigator on it. There were only two subjects on the course that I had not previously taught, and they were Toxicological Warfare, and Mathematics. However, I attended all of the lectures, and in some cases, I was able to help because no one knew more about Browning Guns than me – I could still strip a Browning Gun and put it back together again faster than anyone, and when it came to the operating of gun turrets, that was my specialist subject when I was teaching.

My colleagues on the course soon noticed I did not need to ask questions of the instructor, and they accepted me as the odd man out 'cos 'all navigators is Bastards', but I was not called upon to do the practical work of air firing and bomb aiming, and my services were often called upon to be the screen gunner, or bomb aimer for my colleagues.

One of the pilots on the course was a Squadron Leader Webster, a university educated Scotsman, who was a bachelor, and far above the intelligence of the average member of aircrew. Every night when the rest of us were doing our homework, 'Webby' would be off to Louth, soaking up the local brew, and enjoying the female population, and getting himself plastered! A group of us used to meet to have a drink before dinner, and 'Webby' would often join us, and borrow his taxi fare to take him into Louth.

One evening, there were eight of us enjoying our aperitif when we were joined by Webby, all dressed up in black bow tie and dinner jacket, and I said to him, "Where the Hell do you think you're going?" Webby replied, "I've got a very heavy date with the daughter of one of the biggest farmers in Lincolnshire; I've got a taxi coming for me at a quarter to eight; will you lend me £1.00 for the fare Gibby?"

Webby always paid back promptly any money he had borrowed, but on this occasion I said, "No". "What do you mean, No!!?" he replied. "Just that" I said, "It's homework time, no taxi fare!"

And for some unknown reason, each one of the remainder of us eight refused to lend Webby the £1.00. This caused quite a lot of laughter and banter, and so off we went to dine.

After our repast, the eight of us were back at the bar, and it was just past 7.00 pm, and Webby was getting frantic. But, still we refused to meet Webby's request.

He had one of the largest moustaches in the RAF, and I suddenly remembered what had happened to me in Blackpool, and I casually said "Webby, we won't lend you £1.00, but the eight of us will buy half of your moustache for £1.00, and then you won't have to pay us back. That's right fellas, isn't it?" My friends all agreed. "Oh no!!" said Webby, "Please say you're joking Gibby, and just lend me £1.00?" but we were all adamant, and the ribbing Webby was having to take was beginning to have its effect.

Webby said, "You're an arsehole Gibby". I said, "No I'm not, it's a straight forward business deal; half of your moustache for £1.00. Full stop"

It was getting near taxi time, when suddenly Webby said, "Alright! It's a deal!".

A pair of scissors was produced from the Bar and in no time at all, Webby was sans half his moustache. He quickly dashed to his room and returned clean-shaven. Webby, without his moustache, was a totally different personality. His mouth was 'ginormous', and when he laughed and opened his mouth, his face disappeared. It was one of the most amazing transformations of anyone's appearance one could imagine.

I gave Webby the £1.00, and said, "Here you are Webby, it's yours. Now you don't have to pay us back."

Webby said, "Thank you Gibby – it's true after all - all navigators is Bastards!"

All agreed it was one of the cheapest forms of merriment on record!

Among the 24 pilots on the course, we had Fighter Boys, Bomber and Transport Command pilots, and they all grabbed the opportunity to fly aircraft in which they did not usually operate.

Webby was a Bomber pilot, and could throw a Lancaster around the sky as if it were a Tiger Moth. On one air gunnery exercise, Webby chose to fly a Spitfire as the attacking aircraft on a Lancaster Bomber, and as I was already a qualified Gunnery Leader, my job was the screen gunner on the Lancaster where the six pilot gunners on board were to take it in turn to try and shoot the Spitfire down.

All the guns in the Spitfire and Lancaster had been fitted with cameras to record any hits that might be made. On this exercise, two Spitfires were to attack the Lancaster, which was to fly straight and level on the firing range, and in this case, one of the Spitfires was being flown by a Fighter Pilot, and the other by Webby.

The Fighter Pilot started the attacks from the Port or Starboard quarters, and then from behind (tail attacks). After each attack by the Fighter Boy, Webby tried to imitate.

Good show; everything went well. All of my six gunners completed their exercise, but the Fighter Boy had not finished. He climbed 2,000 feet above the Lancaster, did a roll off the top, and came screaming down in a dive on the Lancaster, just missing the nose by a few feet, and finally he finished up flying straight and level alongside the Lancaster, at about 400 feet on the Port bow.

Webby the Bomber Boy was not going to be beaten by the Fighter Boy, and so he performed the same manoeuvre, but on pulling out of the dive, Webby did not fly alongside us, but went straight back to base.

We trundled along, and by the time we had taxied to our dispersal point, we were surprised to see Webby being attended by sick quarters staff. I went over to investigate, and there was Webby, as green as a cabbage and looking extremely ill. Apparently, after he had done his 'roll off the top', when he went into his vertical dive, he was never more scared in his life, and he could not stop being sick, and so had to return to base.

After he had fully recovered the Fighter Boys ribbed him unmercifully, and told him to stick to the comfort of Bomber Aircraft, flying straight and level. Webby, being a Scot, was quite peeved because he had to pay an airman £5.00 to clean out his Spitfire!

As I was already a Category A1 Instructor in Armament subjects, when the 24 pilots were receiving instructions on to how to instruct in weapons, I was excused, and so I went to see the Station Adjutant who was a friend of mine from Chivers, where he went under the nickname of 'Stiffy'.

At Chivers he had been on the accountancy staff, and in 1936 he represented Great Britain in the Olympics at speed skating. The top three places, Gold, Silver and Bronze, were taken up by the Scandinavian countries, and Stiffy came 36th out of 50 contestants, and considering Stiffy could only practice at weekends at Hammersmith Ice Rink, which was sixty miles from where he lived, this was considered an excellent performance.

On one occasion, when I was having a coffee with Stiffy in his office, the Station Commander came in and Stiffy introduced me to the CO, and mentioned that I was an old buddy from Chivers, and stated what a good organiser I was. The Station Commander remembered this for, at the end of the Course, all of the 24 pilots were posted to appointments that had been created for them, but the 'Powers that Be' had overlooked the only Navigator Senior Weapons Officer in the RAF, and no appointment had been created for me. So – instead of skiving off into Louth, I went to see if I could help Stiffy.

At that time Mr. Churchill, the Prime Minister, was insisting that every Service establishment should have an organisation laid on for the defence of the aerodrome, and this was worrying Stiffy to death because it was his job. Because I was at a loose end, I volunteered to do this for him. Stiffy rushed in to the Station Commander's office, and later I was ushered in to be welcomed by the Commanding Officers who formally asked me if I would write the Operation Order for the Defence of Manby. "Sir, on the Senior Armament Officers' Course there is a Flight Lieutenant who is a member of the RAF Regiment. If I could have him seconded to assist me it would speed things up considerably, and I could start straight away."

That was arranged, and we got at it. Stiffy arranged for me to have the help of his secretary, and 14 days later I submitted 64 pages of Full Scap (as it was known in those days) for the Station Commander's perusal.

After a couple of rehearsals when amendments were made, the Station Commander gave it his stamp of approval. He then asked me to bring the Officers' Mess Rules up to date. That only took a day, and I was in the middle of bringing the Twenty Five Yards Range Safety Rules up to date, when my posting came through as Senior Weapons Officer at RAF Station Kinloss.

I had a few days to spare before reporting to my new posting, and so I was able to complete the Range safety rules, and after a 660 mile journey in my Wolseley, I found myself booking in at RAF Kinloss. Having got myself a room in the Mess, I spruced myself up and reported to the Station Commander.

I introduced myself as Squadron Leader Gibson, his new Senior Weapons Officer.

"Senior Weapons Officer!!" he said, "I don't want a Senior Weapons Officer – I've got a very good Bombing Leader, and an excellent Gunnery Leader; I repeat, I don't need a Senior Weapons Officer!"

I said, "That's OK by me Sir; I've just spent the last twelve hours on the road from Lincolnshire, may I have your permission to stay the night, and I will leave your Station first thing tomorrow and await a new Posting".

At that, the Group Captain's attitude changed completely and he said, "Steady on, let's not be too hasty, I've got plenty of work for a Squadron Leader to do. Where have you come from?"

I then explained to him that I had just completed the Senior Weapons Course, and that as I was the only Navigator on the Course, this appointment on his Station had been especially created for me. He then wanted to know my Service history, and when I mentioned I had been on the Directing Staff of the OATS, he became really interested and said, "I've got to get written an Operation Order for the Defence of this Station; could you do that for me?" I replied I used to lecture on how to write Operation Orders, and if I could use one of his typists and someone to show me around the Station, I could start straight away.

He detailed the Officer whose supernumerary job was to be in charge of the Fire Service, and who knew every nook and cranny of the Station, and so I began. I did not tell the Station Commander that I had just done the same thing for RAF Manby, and that I had a copy of that Operation Order with me, because he did not need to know. Suffice to say, in many cases I only had to delete Manby and insert Kinloss, and with a few additions to the Manby order which were peculiar to Kinloss, within 72 hours, I produced a 70 page full scap Operation Order on the Defence of RAF Kinloss.

To say that the CO was amazed at the speed at which I had produced this document was putting it mildly, and after a rehearsal had taken place when the necessary amendments were made, the job was complete.

Over a coffee in the CO's office to which I had been invited, there was no more mention that he did not want a Senior Weapons Officer, but he asked me what my supernumerary job was. I explained that, as I was usually the Senior Living In Officer, I was always PMC in charge of the Mess. At that the CO pressed a button on his desk, and in walked the Wing Commander Administration from the next office, and the CO said, "Terry, meet the new PMC". Terry said, "thank God for that!". Apparently Terry, who was living in married quarters, had been trying to get rid of the job for months, and so I took over, but not before I had done a 100% check of the Inventory, and of course, my next job was to bring the Officers' Mess rules up to date.

Kinloss was not a standard brick built Station, but a wooden hutted camp, and in checking the Inventory, I had the feeling I had been there before. I knew just where the Billiard's Room and the Library were without being shown: I had definitely been there before!

Also, I got on wonderfully well with all of the Scotsmen on the Station because with a name like Bruce Stuart Gibson, they thought I was one of them.

Next, the CO got me to rewrite the Sergeant's and Airmen's Mess Rules, and I realised he was giving me these jobs to stop me doing the work for which I had been posted. However, I was doing this administrative work whilst liaising with the Bombing Leader and the Gunner Leader; in fact the latter officer recognised me immediately because it was I who had trained him.

The acid test in this sort of training is the result in the air, and I was doing quite a bit of flying as the screen instructor, and I had to agree with the Station Commander that the Operations Training Unit on his Station did not need a Senior Weapons Officer.

I let my thoughts be known to the Commanding Officer when I suggested I draft a letter to 18 Group Headquarters, to the effect that my established post be cancelled. The CO was misemploying me to such an extent he did not want me to leave, but I reasoned with him that it was uneconomic for me to stay as I was not doing the job for which I was being paid. However, it was agreed to let the matter rest in abeyance whilst the CO decided what to do.

The Grapevine was very active, and word reached 18 Group Headquarters that the Senior Weapons Officer at Kinloss was surplus to requirements, and as 19 Group Headquarters was short of such an officer, a movement for me to Plymouth was in the offing.

While these rumours were being circulated, right out of the blue, Air Commodore McKee (Square) and Group Captain Lott (George) visited the Station, and after they had had a coffee with the Station Commander, they had lunch with me in the Mess. Afterwards I took them to my room for coffee, when I discovered the purpose of their visit.

I was told, confidentially, that they were in the process of forming a new unit to be called the RAF Flying College, and would I like to join them. I had already spent three happy postings under Square's Command, and so I told them I would be delighted. I was sworn to secrecy in case nothing came of the invitation, and after a very pleasant three hours in their company, off they went.

The rumours of my being posted to Plymouth increased, but my CO must have made the right noises in my favour, because the 18 Group man was posted to 19 Group, and I took his place at 18 Group HQ, which was at Pitreavie Castle, near Dunfermline.

Within 48 hours I got cleared from Kinloss, and was on my way south, through some of the most beautiful countryside to Inverkeithing, and from there on to 18 Group HQ at Pitreavie Castle. I reported to the Air Vice Marshal, and surprise surprise, I was made PMC of the Officers' Mess!

Every room in a Mess has a Form 22 on which is recorded the contents of the room. In doing my Inventory check, I found furniture had been moved from one room to another, and the move had not been recorded. After a day or two, I was able to put things right, and within a week the AVM received a copy of the new Mess rules. It was then that I had a stroke of luck. I was getting the Mess straight, the way I like it, when a new Squadron Officer WAAF was posted to us as head of WAAF staff, and she came into my office to make herself known to me. She was older than me, about fifty years of age, but oozing with charm.

She told me that before the war she had been secretary to Lloyd George, and knew how to meet and greet people, and although she was not a good WAAF (her words, not mine), she had a talent for flower decorating, and could she have my permission to do the floral decoration of the Mess.

We had about 40 acres of land, a large portion of which was covered with Rhododendrons, Azaleas, and every flowering shrub imaginable, and so the Head WAAF got cracking.

The AVM was a member of the Carnegie family and he lived out in a small estate in Fife in a grand style, but he regularly visited the Mess, and within a fortnight of becoming PMC, he congratulated me on the wonderful improvement I had made to the Mess, and especially the floral decorations.

I said "Sir, it's Squadron Officer Morgan you should be congratulating, it is her gift with flowers that has transformed the Mess."

"Gibson," he said, "You're PMC of the Mess; its your job to congratulate Morgan".

This of course I did on a regular basis over a cup of tea, listening to her political anecdotes when she was secretary to Lloyd George.

The time came when the AVM decided his Headquarters should have a Ball, as a Public Relations exercise to repay the hospitality that had been extended to us by all of the surrounding military establishments and friends we had in the area.

Here I came into my element. With an excellently decorated Mess, thanks to Morgan, a Band which made all of the right noises, a superb Festive Board, and enough drink to sink a battleship, all we needed were the guests, and these we had in a plenty.

We had Admirals from Rosyth Dockyard, Generals from Edinburgh, the odd Air Marshal friends of the AVM, not forgetting their wives and sweethearts. We had a Ball fit for a Monarch. But like all good things, it came to an end, and by 0230 hours all of our important guests had left except for a few unattached officers who were enjoying a night cap, and who quietly drifted away when they saw me getting the barmen organised to start cleaning up the place ready for breakfast, which was in five hours time.

As I went to close the bar, I espied three 'Pissy' officers, a Wing Commander, a Squadron Leader, and a Flight Officer WAAF getting steadily drunk.

I said to them, "I'm about to close the Bar, please order your last drinks".

The Wing Commander said, "Gibson, while I am drinking, the Bar stays open – you're outranked!"

I immediately thought of my time in Ely Hospital when the Ward Sister cut me down to size by saying she could not be outranked in her own ward, and so I said, "Sir, I am PMC of this Mess; I cannot be outranked in my own Mess; I will close the Bar at 0300 hours!"

At that I carried on doing my usual checks to see that no cigarette ends had been left smouldering in our Club armchairs, and at 0300 hours I returned to the Bar, and I said to the civilian barman, "Mr so-and-so, Close the Bar." The iron grating was being lowered, and then all hell was let loose. The WAAF Officer confronted me and let out such a tirade of abuse, I was flabbergasted. She criticised me for the dictatorial way I ran the Mess - and – as we were the only two living in members of the Mess, how I ignored her – she at one end of the ante room and me 40 feet away down at the other end. Of course, this was hilarious to her inebriated male companions, but I let her have her say, and when she took a deep breath, I then replied, "Flight Officer so-and-so, if I were you, I'd go to bed", and with that I left the room.

Ten minutes later, when I returned, all three had gone.

At 0700 hours on that Saturday morning, my batman woke me with my cup of tea and ran be a bath, and by 0730 hours I was enjoying my breakfast. Afterwards, I went to my office, and I was studying my diary to see what I had on for the next week, when there was a little tap on my door. I said, "Come in!" and in walked the Flight Officer WAAF who had made a fool of herself a few hours earlier.

I said, "Good Morning: what can I do for you?"

She was a plain, homely Scottish girl, with sensible flat-heeled shoes and wore no make up, and it was obvious she had a hangover. She looked dreadful. If she had come to my room in the middle of the night stark bollock naked with a condom in one hand and a bar of Cadbury's in the other, I would have chosen the chocolate!

"I've come to apologise for what happened last night", she said, "I was egged on by my two male companions, and I'm afraid I lost control of myself, and I've come to say I'm sorry for what I said". I replied, "If drinking to excess causes you to be put in the embarrassing position you find yourself in now, you might consider to mend your ways, and the next time you are thirsty, drink nothing stronger than Cocoa. Now, let me take you to the Mess and buy you a Bloody Mary."

That was the end of the matter, and I made it my business never to be alone with her in the Mess in the future.

Part of my job at 18 Group Headquarters was visiting the Armouries and Bombing Ranges in Scotland, and the wonderful scenery, and the friendliness of the Scots enthralled me, but alas, it all had to come to and end. I had not been at this posting long before the Air Vice Marshal sent for me to tell me he had a posting notice for me to the RAF Flying College at Manby, but as I had only been working for him for such a short while, he was going to get it cancelled.

I said, "That's OK by me Sir, because I am quite happy working for you."

But, within a fortnight, I was on my way to Manby. I reported to the Station Commander via his Adjutant, Stiffy, and I was warmly welcomed, for although I had been appointed to the Directing Staff and was also in charge of Plans and Progress of the RAF Flying College, he was glad to have me back on his Station,

When I reported to Square, I told him my old boss, the AVM, had tried to stop my posting. Square said, "But he could not do that, because on the establishment of the RAFFC, there was an appointment for a Senior Weapons Officer Navigator, which had been approved by the Air Ministry, and of course there was only one of them – and that is you."

Also, the Air Member for Personnel who had approved Square's Establishment was Godfather to one of Square's children. My old Boss had no chance of stopping my Posting!

My Plans and Progress Office was next door to the Commandant, and so I was only buzzing distance away. I had two Flight Lieutenants assisting me; one a pilot and the other a navigator, and they were in two separate offices near by. One of my jobs was to work from the Syllabus and plan the weekly flying and ground lecture programme, and keep a record of such events.

The 25 students on the course were all aircrew Squadron Leaders and Wing Commanders who had been specially selected and earmarked for higher things. Every Command had a representative on the Course. We had pilots from Bomber Command, Fighter, Coastal and Transport Commands, together with two Royal Naval Pilots, an American, a Canadian, a New Zealander, and one from Australia. The American was a very senior Test Pilot who had flown at Mach 2 (twice the speed of sound). This meant that with the 25 Directing Staff, it made a total of 50 senior aircrew officers, making a complete cross section of aircrew, all of whom had flown Military Aircraft on Operations.

Their job was to submit a Paper at the end of the year's course for The Bomber Aircraft requirements for the future. The students were split into three syndicates, each headed by a Wing Commander. Each syndicate was to produce a report at the end of the course, and it was my job to edit those reports and marry them into a single paper with correct headings and side headings, in conformance with the laid down procedure of writing service papers, before submitting them to the Air Ministry.

This was another reason why Square had chosen me, because one of my favourite subjects at the OATS was the Presentation of Service Papers. One of my Flight Lieutenants, Ken Ashley, was a pilot of exceptional ability who could write the Queen's English grammatically and with great clarity. It was necessary for all of the pilots to be able to fly every type of aircraft, and often Ken was called upon to convert pilots from one type of aircraft to another.

On one occasion, Ken was called upon to teach an Air Marshal how to fly a Jet Aircraft.

Ken was in the Control Tower, having sent his pupil on his first Jet solo, and as the AM was leaving the Control Tower, having completed his flight satisfactorily, Ken said, "Sir, your approach over the aerodrome threshold was a little fast wasn't it?" The Air Marshal was a little surprised at the question from a Flight Lieutenant, and he replied, "Son – all old pilots approach a little fast!" There was much laughter from the rest of the Control Room staff, because it was the equivalent in air force language of saying to Ken 'Up Yours!'

My navigator member of staff was meticulously careful at detail, and it was his job to interpret the weekly Flying and Lecture programme from the Syllabus. Between the three of us, we made a good team.

The 25 students were all good pilots or navigators, and in addition to being chosen from all of the various Commands, each was an expert in their particular role in the RAF.

We had every type of aircraft allocated to our unit. And every pilot had to be converted to every type at the beginning of the Course. This I found most interesting because Fighter Pilots, when flying aircraft with four engines, had to resist the temptation of doing aerobatics, while the heavy aircraft pilots, when flying Fighter Aircraft, tended to fly straight and level.

This conversion from one type of aircraft to another had its moments, and was brought home to me when I was acting as the Screen Bombing Leader. I was watching the Pilot and Navigator doing their pre-flight checks when the Wing Commander Pilot, who was a skilled Flying Boat Captain, suddenly said to his Navigator, "Joe, I thought we were going to do this exercise in a Lincoln?" and Joe replied, "Sir – this is a Lincoln!" I said, "Hold on Joe, I'm getting out of here – if the Pilot doesn't know which type of aircraft he's flying, I'm on my way out!" But Joe said, "Don't worry Gibby, that's how Percy is, but he's as good as gold; he could fly a Double Decker bus if it had wings!"

And so it proved, as Percy sat at the controls he exuded confidence, and a successful Bombing exercise was completed.

Lincolnshire weather can be very depressing when overcast, and there were times when Ken Ashley would order an aircraft, and we would get airborne and break cloud at about 20,000 feet into brilliant sunshine, and at 35,000 feet we would enjoy the peace and tranquillity of heaven on earth, and forget temporarily our daily problems.

Every Thursday night we had a Guest Night, and it was part of my job to arrange for a Guest Speaker to give a speech or lecture to the Staff and Students before dinner. It was amazing the high-ranking civilians or service officers who lined up to talk to us at the RAF Flying College.

As soon as the Commandant had decided who to invite, and, after he had verbally invited the chosen one, it was my duty to arrange travelling details, accommodation etc., before doing the meeting and greeting bit and ushering them into the warm hospitality of our Air Commodore Square.

The high light of the Course was the last month, when worldwide liaison flights by members of the staff and students were taken. Itineraries had to be made and a Press Conference had to be called before the Flights took place to gain maximum publicity.

One of our staff, a Wing Commander Russell Bell, had been awarded an MVO, and during the time the Press Reporters were being lavishly entertained, the Daily Mirror Rep asked me why Russell Bell had been made a Member of the Victorian Order. I replied "I don't know, but I will find out for you."

I told Bell that the Daily Mirror Rep had asked me to find out what he had done to get an MVO, and Bell told me to tell the Rep 'to mind his own bloody business!' I said to the officer, "That's not the answer he wants, you know!" The reply I got was, "that's his hard cheese!!"

I apologised profusely to the Reporter for failing to get the information he required, and he replied, "That's OK, I just thought I had a story"

The next day Bell came storming into my office and slammed a copy of The Daily Mirror on my desk, and said, "That Mirror Rep at the Press Conference yesterday – what did you tell him?" I replied, "That you did not wish to state why you had been awarded the MVO". "Right", he said "Well, read that!".

There on the front page of the Daily Mirror was an article about the end of the RAF College Course Worldwide liaison flights, which had been arranged by Wing Commander Russell Bell, Captain of the Queen's Flight, and for which the Monarch had presented him with an MVO.

At that time the Captain of the Queen's Flight was an Air Commodore Fielden, based at RAF Benson.

Russell Bell said, "Gibson, you've made me look a bloody fool – what are you going to do about it?" I said, "First, we must apologise to Air Commodore Fielden, and then contact the Mirror and get them to publish a correction. "Do that" said, Bell. And I replied, "But before I can do that, I will have to tell the Mirror why you were awarded an MVO, in order that they can publish a correction".

Apparently when the Duke of Gloucester had been Governor General of Australia, it was Russell Bell's job to fly him all over Australia for two years, and it was for this that he had been awarded the MVO.

I said, "Sir, I will get the record put straight, but it would have been a lot easier if you had given the correct story in the first place". Bell replied, "Get stuffed, Gibson" as he flounced out of my room.

I immediately telephoned RAF Benson, but I was unable to speak to the Captain of the Queen's Flight because he was airborne. But, I did speak to his Adjutant, who told me that the Air Commodore had seen the Mirror article, at which he had had a good laugh, and remarked, "So long as the Monarch knows I'm still in charge, there's no harm done!"

I told the Adjutant the cause of the Mirror article, and that his boss would be receiving a written apology forthwith. I next went and informed the Commandant, Square what had happened, and showed him the Mirror article and told him what action I had taken so far, and that the College should send a written apology.

At which, Square read the article, had a good laugh, and said, "Fielden is a buddy of mine; draught a letter and I will sign it". Square altered my draft with a few personal touches, and that ended an episode that simply need not have happened.

There was another occasion when I had a contra temps with Russell Bell when a Paper written by Ken Ashley was forwarded to the Air Ministry as if it had been written by him.

It had taken Ken over a year to gather all of the facts that were contained in the Paper, and Ken had called it 'Standard Power and Flap Settings'. The purpose of this Paper was to instruct Pilots how to land a Meteor Aircraft in zero visibility.

Every day, Ken would study the meteorological weather forecasts to find out where fog conditions existed, and if he were successful, he would immediately fly to that area to test his theory of blind landings. Papers of this nature from the College had to go through Russell Bell's Office before forwarding them on to the Air Ministry. Ken's Paper received the College's approval, but when Russell Bell forwarded it to the Air Ministry, he failed to mention that Ken was the author, and in so doing, it gave the impression that Bell was the author.

When Ken discovered what a 'shit's trick' Bell had pulled, he was furious, and went dashing into Bell's office, and in Billingsgate Fish Porters' language, told Bell exactly what he thought of him. I tried to step in and calm Ken down, but Ken had put his heart and soul into his Paper, and could not be consoled, and threatened to resign his commission forthwith.

I ultimately got through to Ken that now was not the time to make hasty decisions, and to sleep on it.

The next day, Ken still could not be placated, but I reasoned with him that, apart from being an excellent military pilot, he had no civilian qualifications, but that if he were to continue with his Service Career, his chances of reaching Air Rank were good. At that moment, one of Ken's friends telephoned him, with whom he used to perform stunt-flying acts with at RAF Open Days, and they were good buddies. Their animated conversation, with much laughter, was a joy to behold after what Ken had just gone through, and when Ken put the phone down, I said, "What was all that about?" Ken said, "That was one of my old 'Oppo's, Brian Trubshaw – he's just successfully completed the RAF Test Pilot's Course".

I jumped in immediately and said, "Ken, that's what you should do. Look up the AMO, and if you qualify, make an application and I'll strongly recommend it". By that time Ken had resorted to his glum position when he thought his RAF career had come to an end, but he said, "Let me think about it".

Ken arranged a liaison visit to the Royal Aeronautical Establishment at Farnborough, where he met his friend Brian Trubshaw, and on his return, he applied to become a Test Pilot, which was granted.

Ken was ultimately responsible for testing the Aircraft Britannia, which became the world's first large turboprop transport aircraft, for the Bristol Aircraft Company (BOAC)........

The Bomber Command Commander in Chief could not make one of our Thursday night Guest Nights, but he was keen to give our staff and students a talk about the work of his Command and its future. And so, it was arranged for him to give his talk in the afternoon. Therefore, for that evening lecture, it was arranged for an Atomic Scientist to give the evening talk.

The scientist turned out to be a Mr. Bill Penny, (a hugely respected British Physicist who was responsible for the development of British nuclear technology) and when I contacted him to make the travelling arrangements, and he discovered the Commander in Chief Bomber of Command was going to speak in the afternoon, he decided to come early and sit in on the Bomber Chief's lecture.

As agreed, I met Mr. Penny at Louth Railway Station and refreshed him in the Mess, prior to introducing him to Square, who then took over. The Bomber Chief, in giving his story, brilliantly portrayed the dash – the get up and go action that his aircrews would be taking – illustrated by much arm waving and the thrust of a Rapier as his pilots would be attacking their targets at nought feet, dropping Atomic Bombs left, right and centre. The rapport he acquired with his audience was infectious, and everyone was hanging on his words as they were carried away with the panache and swagger of the lecturer.

At tea and biscuits after the talk, the Commander in Chief was introduced to Bill Penny, and when he found out that Bill was the Atomic Energy's Expert, and that he was giving a lecture on Atomic Warfare before the Guest Night, the Commander in Chief decided he could stay after all to hear what Bill had to say.

Mr. Penny commenced his lecture by referring to the previous talk by the Commander in Chief Bomber Command, and how he thought it was most exciting, especially the bit where his Pilots were going to be dropping Atom Bombs at right, left and centre, at nought feet, but, he added, they weren't going to do it with his bomb! Such a remark made everybody sit up and take notice.

I had previously briefed Bill that it was usual to speak for forty minutes, and then have a thirty minute break period answering questions, and so for the next forty minutes, without mentioning a mathematical formulae, he kept us all enthralled so that when he asked if there were any questions, or did we want him to continue, Square spoke for all of us when he said "Please continue".

After another 40 minutes Mr. Penny said "I could go on like this for a long time", but it was then our Commandant took over, and interrupted saying that whilst everyone would love him to continue, due to the lateness of the hour, the body had to be fed as well as the mind, and he continued with his speech of thanks which was received with a standing ovation with the Commander in Chief Bomber Command joining in. It was then that everyone wanted to talk to Bill, and it was with great difficulty that I managed to escort Bill to his room in the Mess to prepare for dinner.

One anecdote regarding Bill Penny's atomic experiences that he related to me before his official talk was when the Americans were going to test an atomic device at a secluded island, he was sent as the U.K. Observer. The Government provided the wherewithal to get him there and back, and the Americans provided him with food and living accommodation, but no money had been provided for him to test the effects of the device.

The Americans had the most sophisticated, delicate instruments all around the Island to record the explosive blast of the device, and all Bill was able to procure were fifty, 50 gallon metal second-hand oil drums. He punctured holes in these and covered the holes with pieces of plastic of various thickness, the breaking strain of each he knew. He scattered these in various strategic parts of the Island, and then waited. When the atomic blast had subsided, Bill gathered his oil drums together and, although they were badly damaged, he was able to make his report.

The American's expensive, fragile equipment was blown to smithereens and could not be found. All was not lost however because Bill, with Government approval, was able to furnish the Americans with a copy of his report, which was the only true record of the experiment.

Probably the best Guest Night Speaker we had was a Dr. W. R. Matthews, who was the Dean of St. Pauls.

Six months before the due date, we received confirmation that the Dean would be pleased to talk to the Staff and Students of The RAF Flying College. Three months before the date, we had a letter from the Dean's secretary asking us we wanted the Dean to talk about. This put Square in a quandary because he naturally thought the Dean would be talking about religion. However, at this time, the 'Cold War' was at its height, and at Square's weekly meeting, it was decided to ask the Dean to speak on Communism.

When the day came, Ken Ashley, with me navigating, took off in an Anson from Manby and picked the Dean up at Hendon aerodrome, and brought him back to Manby in time for Square to take tea with the Dean before his lecture. The Dean's lecture on Communism was one of the finest I have ever heard, and the discussion, which followed as a result of questions asked, was superb. The dinner, which followed, went without a hitch, with no rough horseplay games that normally followed such occasions.

The next day Ken and I took the Dean back to Hendon, and the warm thanks we received for looking after him were way beyond what we deserved; we were only doing what the RAF expected of us, but the Dean was not the run of the usual cleric, he made us feel great!

One of the pilots on the course was a Wing Commander Binks who had no imagination, and therefore was fearless as he saw no danger!

Binks was renowned for literally playing with fire at after dinner Mess games. One guest night, the guest of honour was an Air Commodore who was a buddy of Binks, and this gentleman was relaxing after dinner with a brandy, standing in front of a roaring log fire with his legs wide apart, warming up his backside and enjoying the hospitality. Binks approached the Air Commodore with what appeared to be a glass of gin in his hand.

After they had greeted one another, Binks threw the contents of the glass through the Air Commodore's legs, into the fire. There was a huge Whoomf, and the whole of the back of the Air Commodore was on fire.

Binks, however, was always prepared in case of fire, and grabbed a fire extinguisher, which he had near to hand, and completely sprayed his victim with foam, and everyone else in the vicinity, especially those who had chosen to laugh. The only person free from foam was Binks, but he held the fire extinguisher in a threatening manner in case anyone wanted a second dose.

As the Air Commodore retired to make himself more comfortable, but completely unharmed, he said, "Binks – don't ever do that to me again", and left.

One of Binks favourite tricks was to cut the top off a plastic petrol capsule, light a cigarette lighter, and squirt the petrol from the capsule through the flame and produce a flame, three or four feet long. He could sidle up to his unsuspecting victim, and suddenly they would feel that their backside was hot, and Binks would have burnt the nap off of somebody's best blue pants.

He was quite mad, but by having no imagination, he was as brave as a lion.

When taking part in syndicate groups he would frighten the life out of mature battle hardened colleagues with the action he was prepared to take to defeat an enemy. It was a standing joke with everybody that they were glad they were on Binks' side.

At the end of World War II, it was decided to form a Squadron in Australia to bomb a target in the heart of Japan. It was to be a one-way sortie because we did not possess an aircraft with enough fuel to Bomb the unnamed target, and return to base. And so, the crews were to bomb their target, do a dogleg and bale out, and make their own way back if possible. Who did the Powers that Be choose to train and lead that Squadron on its suicide mission? You've guessed it – BINKS!

Fortunately for all concerned, the Japanese were defeated before Binks' Squadron had completed their training.

Before Binks' Squadron was disbanded, he found himself with a friend, nicely oiled, walking across Sydney Bridge.

Looking down at the fast flowing water, they struck a bet between themselves that, if they jumped from the centre of the Bridge, who would reach the side first.

Some other walkers over the Bridge were amazed to see two RAF Officers jump off the bridge. They quickly raised the alarm. However, both officers made the other side, and walked to the nearest Pub where they ordered whisky. Mine host noticed their plight, and took over, providing dry clothes, and a session developed with Binks the life and soul of the party!

When the time came for Binks and Co to return to base, both of them with a wet uniform in a carrier bag, they were amazed to see that searches still being made for two RAF Officers who had been seen to jump into the water.

The whole of the lectures, groundwork and administration to do with the Flying College took place in one large building called Tedder Block. It had been purposely designed and built for the Empire Air Armament School. It was a square building, with lecture rooms of various sizes and administrative offices, which was ideal for our purpose.

The corridors on all four sides were made of Teak, which were kept permanently polished by a team of cleaners to the highest RAF standards.

As Officer in Charge of Plans and Progress, my first job every morning was to inspect the cleanliness of Tedder Block and to ensure that any specialist items of equipment needed for that day's instruction were in place. The standards set by our Air Commodore were of the highest order, and were well known to me because this was the fourth time I had served Square, and I knew what he required.

Some of the things I had to do in this connection were pernickety, and although I was only carrying out Square's wishes, he would always help me out if, when all of the staff and students were together and I was rushing around (for remember, I was ordering Officers about who were senior to me), making sure everything was as Square wanted it. Square would laughingly say, "Come chaps; let's do what Gibby wants"

Every course that Air Commodore McKee had anything to do with had to be photographed, and it was my job to get all of the fifty staff and students in a suitable spot with a good backdrop, at a stated time. I would then arrange them in three rows with the front row sitting on chairs, the centre row standing, and the third row standing on forms, and not forgetting the seniority of the more important officers, all of whom all wanted to be in the front row near the Commandant, who would be in the centre spot.

Sounds easy, doesn't it. I can assure you – it aint!!

On one occasion when I was organising a group photograph, I knew Square always wanted to see the front row with the officers sitting, crossed legs to the centre. Therefore, once I had a everyone more or less in the right position, and checking with the civilian photographer that he was ready to shoot, starting from the right of the front row, I went along the row telling each officer how to cross his legs by touching each one saying, "left over right, left over right," etc., until I got to the Air Commodore who was in the Centre. I said to him, "You can do what you like with yours", and one wag among those being photographed said, "I should let them swing", because Square was only five feet tall, his feet did not touch the ground.

This caused much merriment and everybody was still laughing when I reached the end of the row and signalled for the photographer to shoot – we got one of the best group photographs ever!

* * *

20

Down Under

A t the end of the Course, it came to the time for the staff and students to go on their world wide flights to the four corners of the globe to spread the word about the Flying College, and also to give the pilots an opportunity to practise their navigation skills they had acquired on the course.

Obtaining approval from the various stations that we planned to visit was a routine administrative task, and the medical jabs were straightforward. Every officer had to carry a certificate stating which vaccinations and jabs he had been given, and these had to be issued by an approved organisation.

I arranged for all of the officers to be immunised at RAF Ely Hospital, but one of the students, a Wing Commander Andrew Humphries, made his own arrangements.

The flight to Australia only had one staff navigator, and I was able to wangle myself a trip as second navigator so that we could alternate the duties.

I navigated the first leg to Malta, and the staff navigator did the second leg to Habbaniya. Here the medical officer refused to recognise Andrew Humphries' medical certificate as, it was claimed, it had not been issued by an approved source, and as we left Habbaniya the last thing we saw was Andrew being led away to a Karachi Jail! He was put in a cell with seven Japanese able-bodied seamen, and it took him a fortnight to talk his way out. Being a man of initiative, he paid his own fare to Australia with Quantas Airways, and he caught up with us in Melbourne.

Before the rest of us reached Melbourne however, we had called into Ceylon where, on landing, I was presented with the best cup of tea I had ever tasted.

From Ceylon we flew across the Indian Ocean to Changi Aerodrome in Singapore. As we approached the half-way point, I switched on my H2S set, and there on the screen was displayed the largest thunder storm I had ever witnessed.

I called up the Captain and told him of the hazard we were flying into, and said we had three options; we could try and fly under it, or fly over it, or around it. My Captain's reply was, "I've got my four engines nicely synchronised, so give me a course to go around it." This I did, and it meant an extra six hundred miles to go round. As these weather conditions were different from those I had received at my pre-flight briefing, I sent an actual weather report to Changi airport so that they could brief other aviators.

This detour made us quite late reaching Changi, but after being debriefed, I went into the Met. Office to look at the current Met. Chart; I was amazed and furious to see that the Met. Chart showed no sign of the thunderstorm that I had gone to the trouble of reporting to them. So, I sought out the Met. Officer and said, "Did you get the Met. Report I sent you?"

"Yes", was the reply.

"Why the bloody hell isn't it on your chart?" I retorted angrily.

"I was waiting for confirmation from some other source" was the reply.

"Right Monkey – we are now two hours late due to having to fly around that thunder storm, and it took me over half an hour to code the message, so don't ever ask me to send you back a weather report again, so get lost!!!" I replied.

I was the Imprest Holder on our Flight, and so I had to go to Singapore to change some Sterling into Dollars. The Australian Air Force provided me with transport to go from Changi to Singapore, and Andrew Humphries together with another Wing Commander cadged a lift. I dropped them off at Raffles Hotel whilst I continued on my way to do my banking business. I picked them up one hour later to find them in a very happy state, and within minutes they on our way back to change were fast asleep.

It was a hot, sunny day, and having told our driver we wanted to be returned to the Officers' Mess, Changi, I promptly went to sleep too. The next thing I remember was waking up outside the Officers' Mess. I awoke my two Pissy companions, and having seen them staggering towards the Mess door, I then proceeded to complete my business at Changi SHQ. After 15 minutes a different driver took me to the Officers' Mess. As we approached the Mess, I saw my two Pissy friends still walking on the final stages to the Mess. I confronted them and said, "What the hell are you two up to?" Andrew said, "You bastard Gibson, you dropped us at the wrong Mess!"

Apparently Changi had two Messes, and my first driver had stopped at the wrong one while I was asleep. Had I been awake I might have noticed it. I tried to explain what had happened, but both my pilot friends agreed, 'All navigators is bastards!'

After a night stop in Changi, we went on to Perth, where for the next fortnight in Australia we received the most wonderful hospitality from the Australian Air Force. I found Australia the most wonderful continent, and from the first moment I landed at Perth, I felt at home. I could cope with the heat, and I found the people, in a brusque sort of way, very friendly and helpful.

In addition to being the Imprest Holder on our flight, if there was any administration or organisation that needed to be done, it was left to me. If any crew member needed anything, it was left to me to negotiate. In this regard I was most successful, and the Australians could not do enough to help me. It was most noticeable to our crew, and at one social gathering Andrew happened to mention this by saying, "How come, if any member of our crew wants anything, Bruce gets it?" The reply astonished our crew, including me, which was "It's because Bruce is one of us!" Because of my East London accent, the locals thought I was an Australian in RAF uniform!

At every place we went to, we were treated admirably, and the Australian Air Force arranged Guest Nights in our honour. I noticed that when impromptu speeches had to be made, it seemed natural for Andrew to reply on our behalf. At a Guest Night in Melbourne, everybody of local importance had been invited to attend, including the Lord Mayor of Melbourne. This gentleman was renowned for making long after dinner speeches, which went on for hours and sent everyone to sleep, and this information was common knowledge, and a rumour went round the RAF contingent that we were going to get a taste of what routinely happened to them. This rumour must have got back to the Mayor for, although we were prepared and had braced ourselves accordingly, when it came to the Mayor's turn to speak, he arose, took a deep breath, and said "Ladies and Gentlemen, on behalf of the Lady Mayoress and myself, thanks for a good nosh up", and sat down.

It lasted a mere ten seconds, and was rewarded by a standing ovation lasting one minute!

From Melbourne, our next stop was Sydney, where once again the Australian Air Force treated us royally.

During a weekend break, the whole crew decided to see a cricket Test Match, the Australians against the West Indies. The Australians had a man in their team named Miller who was a world-renowned all rounder. He was a medium fast bowler, an excellent fieldsman, and was known to be able to bat a bit as well.

The West Indies team had an excellent bowler names Gibbs, who was a left arm, slow spinner.

Miller went in to bat at third wicket to join one of the opening batsmen who, at that time, had scored fifty runs. Miller was on form and, before his partner had raised his score to sixty runs, Miller was on fifty. Then, the West Indies brought on Gibbs to bowl. The first four bowls of Gibbs first over, Miller tried to hit to the boundary as before, but each time Gibbs bowl beat the bat, and I remarked, "If Miller carries on like that, I bet he'll get himself out". An Australian sitting in front of us swung round and said to me," How much do you want to bet?" Before I could answer, Andrew, ever the diplomat, said, "My friend does not want to bet, he was using that term as a figure of speech". The Australian noticed we were in RAF uniform and replied, "Figure of speech bebuggered; if a Pommy Bastard uses the word 'bet', he must be prepared to put his money where his mouth is. Good day to you!"

Andrew said out of the corner of his mouth, "Gibby – so there!"

From Sydney we went to Brisbane, where en route we witnessed a forest fire. There was no wind, and the smoke went straight up to 15,000 feet and was so straight I was able to take running fixes on the smoke to check my ground speed.

From Brisbane, we went on to Woomera Rocket Range, which I found a most fascinating place. It was hot, and the sun shone all day, but it was a dry heat, and where a new town was developing.

It was there as the Senior Weapons Officer that I was able to tell the staff what weapons they would be testing in the future. There was a very clever Clerk of Works who was overseeing the development of Woomera, and who was an excellent gardener, and he was growing various plants from seed to discover which would grow best in that environment, and the results of his test he passed on to the new inhabitants for the benefit of all concerned.

I was keenly interested in his findings, and one thing he told me was that as the town grew, it had taken two years before they developed their own domestic fly. Until then, their flies stayed outdoors, but after two years they began to move indoors.

Although a lot of work to do while I was there, I felt quite invigorated in their heat. I could have lived there. On the station there was a compound in which Polish male immigrants lived in tents. Due to the high winds in the area, the Clerk of Works had built a wooden fence around the Compound to stop the tents being blown away.

They were all self employed. Most of them owned their own lorry and were contracted out to the Woomera station. True to their type, they were excellent workmen, and for the first two years of their stay they were classed as New Australians, until they had learnt the language; after that, if they had made the grade they were accepted and were free to travel as Australians.

The thing I noticed most about Australian Airmen was their love of gambling. Any spare moments they had, a school would be formed and one of their number put in charge, and they would gamble, mainly on the game called 'Two up', when three coins would be tossed in the air, and the winners would be those who called the right name of the majority of coins which fell either heads or tails. This type of gambling had no appeal to me, and I considered it a complete waste of time. However, the service driver provided for us at Woomera by the Australians had won over $1,000 Australian dollars, and he was going to use that money on a Round the World Holiday. He tried to talk our Captain into giving him a lift to the U.K. so that he could start from there, but our man said "No Dice".

On our next leg from Woomera to Darwin, it was Andrew Humphries' turn to navigate, with me holding his hand, and so, before the flight, I taught Andrew how to use a Mark IX Bubble Sextant. I always carried a Marine Sextant, and with Andrew taking shots on the Moon, I took shots on the Sun, and we navigated that leg with Sun, Moon fixes. They were not very good fixes, but as we were flying at 10,000 feet in brilliant sunshine, we could see that we were flying along the track we planned, and Andrew was able to see how Astro Navigation worked.

We had six pilots on board, and yet Andrew was the only one that actually did his stint of navigation. The others were quite happy to sit by the staff navigator and just watch what went on, and these were all of the officers who had been selected for higher promotion. Needless to say, Andrew was head and shoulders above his contemporaries, and ultimately he became Chief of the Air Staff as a Marshal of the RAF, and after that stint, Head of the Defence staff. He was one of the RAF College who reached his true potential.

Our visit to Woomera was the highlight of that trip for me; not only was I the negotiator for anything our crew members wanted, but I was among weapons specialists, and we spoke the same language.

At a cocktail party arranged in our honour, I was introduced to a sheep farmer who owned his own light aircraft, which was used mainly for his work so that he could visit his various farms. He told me that because Woomera was only three hundred miles north of Adelaide, fresh water supplies had been made available to Woomera from Adelaide, and he had been able to tap in to that supply line for his local farms.

He was a fascinating, down to earth Australian, and in seeking out information, I discovered that north of Woomera, due to the dryness of the terrain, he was only able to keep one sheep per acre. He also told me that when he was on some of his flying visits, he was away from home sometimes a week to a fortnight.

When I discovered the size of the area he covered, a quick bit of mental arithmetic told me he had over a million acres, which meant he had over a million sheep, and when I queried this with him he said, "Most probably, but I haven't counted them!"

A lovely statement coming from a typical male product of Australia, and as I have said, fascinating!

At Darwin, the heat was unbearable. The conditions were sultry and humid, and our clothes stuck to us from our perspiration. We only stayed one night, and that was under a muslin tent to protect us from mosquitos. After a quick briefing, we got airborne for Singapore, and so on back to the U.K.

When we got to Karachi, this time I made it my business to go through Customs with Andrew, because as the Administrative Officer, I was prepared to vouch for him should Customs query his vaccination certificate as they did when we were outward bound, but this time, there was no trouble.

The homeward journey was quite routine. No-one was air sick or tried to jump out to test his parachute; in fact, nothing happened at all until we got to Luga aerodrome, Malta, when we were told that King George VI had died that day, and that Queen Elizabeth II was flying home from a Safari holiday in Kenya.

This caused much sadness among the local inhabitants because they considered themselves special as the King had awarded Malta with the George Cross in recognition of their stoicism whilst being attacked by Germany during World War II.

While we were at Luga and our aircraft was being refuelled in the presence of a security guard we heard about a most unfortunate incident that had happened just a few weeks before. Apparently a Lancaster had landed there and while it was being refuelled, the crew had got out of the aircraft to stretch their legs when one of the crew decided to light a cigarette. That was the last thing he did on this earth. There was the most 'ginormous' explosion, and the aircraft, crew, etc, disappeared into eternity with no traces of them ever found.

The final leg from Luga to Manby was quite routine, but the landing was different because all of the wives and sweethearts of the crew were at the dispersal point to welcome their loved ones home. Kay was unable to meet me because Stuart, who had been born seven week's premature, was only seven months old, and as he was poorly, needed her undivided attention.

Therefore, I let all of our crew depart whilst I leisurely gathered my navigation equipment together, and who should come into the aircraft but my friend, Ken Ashley, and although I was the last off the aeroplane, with Ken's help I was the first to get home to the bosom of my family!

* * *

21

Moving swiftly on.

E very morning, Square would arrive in his office bang on time, and would send for me to discuss the day's programme. But one morning he came into my office and said, "Gibby – I've got to go to the Air Ministry to keep an appointment with the Air Chief Marshal in charge of Personnel. I'm afraid it's the end Gibby; I'll soon be growing sheep in New Zealand, but don't say a word to anyone until I get back."

There is little a Squadron Leader can say under those circumstances to an Air Commodore, but I said, "I hope not", and wished him well.

The first thing the next day, I was buzzed for by my Lord and Master, Square, and I entered his office as I did first thing every morning, and standing to attention with a Royal Nod, said "Good morning, Sir". After his usual reply, Square was full of the joys of spring.

"Gibby!" he said, "What do you think! I didn't get the sack yesterday; I got promotion to Air Vice Marshal, and I've been given the Command of 21 Group Headquarters in Swinderby in Lincolnshire!"

A few days after that a new Air Commodore arrived, and Square spent the day with him handing over before he departed to his new appointment.

The new Commandant was as different from Square as chalk and cheese. The Flying College was the fourth Station I had served under Square's Command, and he was like a father figure to me, but the new Commandant was quite formal while he was finding out what went on. He was a charming gentleman with only one eye, but he could see more with that one than most people could with four

306

eyes, and this he proved to me on more than one occasion when he played me at Squash!

About that time, Ken Ashley's posting came through for a Test Pilot's Course at the Royal Aeronautical Establishment at Farnborough in Hampshire, and so everyone was happy. Ken, because he was going to follow in the footsteps of his old 'Oppo' Brian Trubshaw, and Russell Bell, because it got him out of a difficult situation regarding Ken's paper on Standard Power and Flat Settings when it was brought home to him that he should not have forwarded Ken's paper under his own signature. And me - I was happy because it meant that Ken would stay in the Royal Air Force and reach his full potential.

I had just finished writing the Syllabus for No. 3 Course when my posting came through as Chief Ground Instructor to Number Three Navigation School at Thorney Island. This was quite sudden and unexpected.

There were a few jobs I had to do before handing over to my successor, and it was not until I was saying goodbye to Group Captain Lott, the Flying College Chief Instructor, that he reminded me to report to my new station properly dressed. It was not until then I found out that No 3 Navigation School was in 21 Group, and my new boss would be Square, and that he had promoted me to Wing Commander.

I arrived at Thorney Island to be welcomed with open arms because my predecessor had also been Wing Commander in charge of the Flying Wing, but Square had thought the ground instruction was worthy of its own Wing Commander, and the Thorny Island Station Commander had agreed.

At my first meeting with my new Station Commander, he wanted to know what my supernumerary job was, and when I told him that I was always the President of the Mess Committee, he said, "Wow!" and rang the buzzer for his Wing Commander Administration to come into the room.

When he entered, he said, "John, meet the new Chief Ground Instructor, Wing Commander Gibson, and, we've got a new PMC of the Mess!"

John said, "Thank God for that", shook my hand, and said, "When can you take over?"

And of course I said, "As soon as I've checked the Inventory".

Apparently he had been trying to get rid of the PMC's job for a long time, and I was the answer to his prayers.

My next call was to my office where I met my two Squadron Leaders, both Navigators, one of whom was in charge of the Ground Instruction, and the other in charge of Administration and Discipline. It was at that meeting that I learnt the 'nitty gritty' of what went on.

The Training Wing organisation consisted of 57 Flight Lieutenant Instructors teaching 300 students on a 6-month course. All of the Students were volunteers. They had either all passed their 'A' Levels and were going to University, or they were postgraduate students doing their National Service. They were all Officer Cadets under training, and so they were living in the Officers' Mess, learning Mess discipline.

On the successful completion of the Course they would attend a Brevet Parade and become Acting Pilot Officers. My first impression was that both my Squadron Leaders were very efficient, and that they were running a happy unit, and so for the first few weeks I left well alone, and kept a low profile.

Having included a Navigation Section in the Flying College Syllabus I had just written, I studied the Syllabus in front of me, and was astounded at the amount of information the Cadets were going to have pumped into them during their six-month course. I attended lectures and sat in and listened.

We had Varsity aircraft, which had been converted into flying classrooms with six student navigation stations, and above each one, was an Astrodome that gave ample room for air navigation training, and was known as the 'Flying Pig'.

I got myself airborne as soon as possible, and watched what sort of practical navigation they received from the Navigation Flying Instructor. It was good, and allowed me time to carry on my watching brief, and also to concentrate on finding somewhere for Kay (whom, I nearly forgot to mention, I marred on 27th July 1950!), and Stuart somewhere to live.

The reason for this was that the married quarter for the CGI was under construction as my predecessor had worn two hats, and was still living in the Flying Wing Commander's residence, and so, for the mean time, I was living in the Officers' Mess.

This building was of the Standard brick built structure with 146 bedrooms. It was in a very pleasant setting with a large forecourt and six steps leading up to the Entrance Hall, where the Mess Manager (a retired Major) was waiting to greet me. I noticed as I entered the Mess there were several children playing games on the forecourt, and several ladies, who were obviously the mothers of the children, standing about, and as it was a very hot day, some were sitting on the steps.

After the Major and I had exchanged the usual pleasantries I enquired of him, what were those people doing on the Mess Forecourt. I was informed they were waiting for the Bus. Apparently the local bus service used the Mess Forecourt as Termini to enable the bus driver to do a 'U' turn and go back to Emsworth.

The next day I did a local reconnaissance of the area and found an alternative suitable site where the Bus Driver could turn his bus around, and so I immediately telephoned the owner of the Bus Company and made an appointment for him to meet me. Over a coffee I explained that I did not want him to use our Officers' Mess forecourt as a Termini, and then took him to the new site that I had found for him. It was a few yards further on, and the Bus Owner accepted the new site with alacrity, and put the bus fares up one old penny!

Therefore, my first job on arrival was to get the forecourt, steps and hall 'Shipshape and Bristol fashion', and this gave notice to all concerned the new PMC intended to raise the Mess standards in the future.

Next, I did a 100% Inventory check and, with only a few adjustments needed which were within my powers as a Wing Commander, I brought it up to date. The Mess rules were 10 years out of date, but, within 72 hours, I was able to present the Station Commander with his own personal copy.

Next, I did my Man Manager bit, which was to interview the whole of the Mess staff. I had a Mess Manager, a Mess Steward, two Assistant Mess Stewards, and sixty-four Batmen, some of whom were civilians. Of the civilians, I found one had previously owned a Gardening Maintenance Business, and another had been a Master Painter and Decorator.

In my off duty hours, I was searching for living accommodation, but in the meantime Kay had taken Stuart off to her mother's house at Ilford, which went down very well with Grandma because she idolised Stuart, and his Grandfather thought it was a good idea too. However, after a while I realised I was not giving the house hunting the attention it deserved, and so I arranged for Kay and Stuart to stay in an hotel in Chichester, so that we could search the area together.

We ultimately found temporary accommodation in Havant, which suited, until my married quarter was completed.

Although this interrupts the history of my Service career, I suppose I should mention that Kay and I got married at Kensington Registry Office, with only Kay's parents and my mother as witnesses. We had a wedding breakfast at the Normandy Hotel, and then on to Rushington for a honeymoon at an RAF Officers' Holiday Home.

While we were there, by chance I met up with a former Station Commander of mine with whom I had served when I was at St. Eval, but who was now an Air Marshal. He was on holiday with his wife and two daughters, and surprise, surprise – he recognised me by name from my Flight Lieutenant days. Daily we would meet at meal times, and he had a fund of stories to tell his daughters which brought much childish laughter.

One of his stories was about a bus conductor who was about to be hanged for murder.

The culprit, with the noose around his neck, did not drop when the hangman pressed the switch because the platform on which the murderer was standing did not operate. The man was taken back to his cell while the electrical equipment was checked, but nothing could be found wrong with it. So, the same procedure was performed, but once again, when the switch was pressed, it refused to function. Once again, the equipment was thoroughly overhauled, but no fault could be found, and so they tried a third time, and once again when the electric button was pressed the platform refused to open, and therefore, because the equipment had failed three times, the murderer was set free.

When interviewed by the Press afterwards as to why the electrical equipment had failed to operate, the man said, "I guess it's just because I'm a bad conductor"

The girls' mother, Kay and I, laughed, but the little eight year old daughter said, "Daddy, I think you're silly!" which made me roar with laughter to hear a little girl tell an exalted Air Marshal in uniform, in front of junior officers, that he was silly, and that made my day!

When were first married, because of our mature years we had no time to lose, and I had just been posted to Manby. We could not wait for married quarters or a Hiring, and so we took some rooms with a Wheelwright and Undertaker, a Mr. Wright, in the local village of Alvingham.

Kay did not drive in those days, and Mrs. Wright would take Kay into Louth shopping. On one occasion, I went with them but I can't remember why because I had my Wolseley 16/50 at the time. The most amazing thing about Mrs. Wright's driving was, every time she approached a bend in the road or a corner, she sounded her hooter. I never found out the reason for this; whether it was to let people know we were coming or whether it was to warn other road users to give her plenty of room!

I warned Kay before we married that the policy would be 'Barefoot and pregnant', and it did not take Kay long to join the club.

After seven months of pregnancy, I noticed Kay's legs were swelling, and we contacted the Wing Commander Doctor at Manby who quickly took over, and whipped Kay into RAF Hospital Ely where she produced Stuart, who was seven weeks premature. The first thing I knew about it was when someone from Ely Hospital rang me to tell me I had a son. I have never been more delighted to this day.

By this time we had moved from the Wrights to a larger accommodation in Mablethorpe. I knew what Mablethorpe looked like from the air, due to the number of times I had flown over it on my approach to the Bombing Ranges off there, but I quickly found out it was not Kay's idea of the 'Garden of Eden' so as soon as I was offered a Hiring in Sutton on Sea, Kay could not move soon enough, and during our stay there, right on the east coast with the keen bracing Easterly winds, and quite often sea fog, as a family we were never more healthy.

Louth was the nearest town to Manby and was where we did our shopping, which was about five miles away. Some of our married airmen lived in Louth, and on one particular day, an airman walking from there to Manby arrived for duty half an hour late, and so he was put on a charge. When he came to explain the reason why he was late, he stated that he was walking to Manby and after a while he decided to light a cigarette. There was a wind blowing, and so he turned round to light up, and having done so, carried on walking and went straight back to Louth! This was one of the lighter moments of the C.O's day, and so the airman was let off with seven days Guard Duty, which effectively meant he was Confined to Camp for that period, but it would not show on the airman's record as a punishment, and so did not effect his good conduct pay.

It was at Manby we met the Thain's who now live opposite to us in Ripple. Wing Commander Thain, who was then a Squadron Leader on the Directing Staff of the RAF Flying College as a Staff Navigator, and it was his job to make sure the pilots on the course knew, in detail, the job of a navigator, both through lectures and practical work in the air. The Thains were living in married quarters at Manby, next door to the Ashleys.

Ken's wife, Noreen, was a Canadian he had met when he was on his pilot's training course in Canada. After Ken got his wings, they were posted back to the U.K.

Noreen was an attractive girl whose father was a member of the Canadian Diplomatic Corps, and before marrying Ken, had moved around in circles above that of the average RAF officer. On one occasion, Noreen told me, when Ken was courting her, he had told her his father owned three stores which ultimately would be his when he retired from the RAF. Noreen accepted this in good faith, thinking that an English store was similar to a Canadian store, or what we call a Supermarket.

Imagine her surprise when she first visited Ken's home to find his father owned three Pram come Toy Shops! But, she did not let it affect her marriage because she loved Ken dearly and the aviation friends she had been introduced to by Ken, but it did quite amuse her!

Knowing that Kay was happy in her new temporary accommodation allowed me to get settled into my new job properly.

The acid test for a student navigator is how well they do in the air, and so I spent at least three days every week watching what went on in the Flying Classroom. Each of the six stations in the Varsity aircraft were fitted out with all of the instruments a navigator needs, i.e., Compass, Altimeter, Airspeed Indicator etc, but only one student was actually navigating the aeroplane. However, if every student did the correct thing, all six logs at the end of the flight should be similar, and it was the job of the Flying Instructor to make sure this was so.

The Safety Height of 1500 feet above the highest point of land on any given track was impressed on each student's mind, and if they could remember that simple fact, their chances of living as long as Methuselah were increased tenfold!

It was a wonderful life, being able to pick and choose what work to do each day, and especially getting airborne, which my staff thought was fantastic, mainly because it was something my predecessor never did.

On my Armament Instructor's Course in 1939 I had received lessons in the art of Teaching, and over a period of time, in putting that knowledge into practise, I had gained the highest category of Teaching Instruction obtainable, and so I was able to help my Navigation Instructors in their classroom work, especially with my artistic ability combined with their blackboard work.

I thought some of my Instructors were a little harsh and expected too much, and I had to remind them we were pushing into our students in a matter of six months what they themselves had learnt over a period of ten years, and that if their students did not reach first time the standard required, that they should perhaps look at themselves because in many cases the students had achieved higher scholastic results than the Instructor had himself.

I introduced the practise that we had used at the Officer's Advanced Training School by issuing a précis with every classroom lecture, and this could also be used for homework revision.

Each student had to pass an examination on each subject at the end of the course. Some students did not do as well as I thought they should, and so I made it my business to find out why.

Firstly, I made every Instructor produce the examination question he was going to ask; together with the answer he expected to get to achieve top marks. In some cases, the problem was that the question itself was ambiguous. Therefore, I got the Squadron Leader in charge of Ground Training to get the Instructor to write the answer, and for him to write the question to fit that answer.

Result – no more ambiguous questions!

Some students suffered with examination nerves, and so I instigated a verbal question and answer period before each lecture as a revision of the previous lecture, and as progress was made in that subject, a written paper would be substituted in place of the oral session, and those written papers got more difficult as progress was made. Often, the penultimate revision paper covered the whole subject, and the nervous student had sat the final examination without realising it!

No more poor results because of nerves.

Historically, each new course of thirty students had been given an introductory talk by the Squadron Leader in charge of Administration and Discipline, but I decided that was my job. I explained it was a six-month course, and that the for first three months they would be confined to camp.

During those three months, they would be organised twenty four hours a day, either on ground navigation training or practical training in the air, homework, organised games, how to act like a Gentleman in an Officers' Mess etc. There were rules and regulations they would have to learn and obey, and as officer cadets, apply those rules and set a good example. The first rule they had to learn form the word go was that the WAAF quarters were strictly out of bounds!

If any cadet was caught in the WAAF quarters, the fine for the first offence was £10.00; second offence, £20.00; third offence, £50.00. I would then ask, "Are there any questions?"

On one course, one bright young lad asked, "Sir, how much for a season ticket?"

The general laughter it created was answer enough, but it reminded me of my elementary school days when anyone gave a good answer, and teacher would say, "That boy – go home ten minutes early".

I always reminded the cadets that they were all volunteers, and that they all possessed the academic capacity to become first class navigators, which meant a pass mark of 80% in ground and air subjects, and also 80% pass mark for officer qualities, and it was my job to create the environment to make that possible.

Each morning started with officer training. The whole of the 300 students had to be on parade, spic and span, at 0640 hours, for inspection. Squadron Leader Administrator would select by at random a cadet from each course to inspect the rest of his course. This was part of the officer training before breakfast.

Cadets were encouraged to correct any airman who was improperly dressed. As a result we had the smartest airmen on any camp. Most of the permanent officer staff were married and were either living in married quarters or a hiring. By doubling up the cadets in rooms, this enabled me to accommodate all 300 cadets in the Officers' Mess.

Each officer living in an Officers' Mess had to pay two monthly charges. Therefore including the permanent staff, I had 500 personnel, all subscribing for the privilege of being members of the Thorney Island Officers' Mess as opposed to only half that number in a normal station.

This meant as PMC, I had twice the income, and thus I was able to raise the standard of the Mess to the equivalent of a five star hotel. I made the cadets make their own beds, and keep their rooms tidy. This gave me batmen to spare.

I remembered that one of the civilian batmen, before the war, had his own Garden Maintenance Business, and he was only too keen to take on the responsibility of the grounds surrounding the Mess, and with the help of four volunteer batmen, in no time at all, our gardens were a picture.

My Mess Steward was above average, and he was able to train six volunteer Batmen to become very competent waiters. Part of the Cadets' training was to learn how to conduct themselves when they dined, and so every Thursday, I organised a Guest Night for half of the Students, and once a month there was an informal dance for them to 'let their hair down.'

Having been a PMC for many years, the thing I noticed most when visiting Royal Navy or Army Messes was their table decorations at their Guest Nights. The most luxurious Mess I ever visited was the Royal Marines Mess at Eastney Barracks. Their silver table decorations were superb.

This fact was known to King George VI, and on one occasion, when he visited Eastney Officers Mess as a guest, he presented the Mess with a pair of Silver Candelabra, and they were always displayed as the King's Candles. Therefore, I decided to purchase for the Mess Silver Candelabra.

After I thought I had saved enough money for my first purchase, I called on the Station Accountant Officer to enquire of the Officers' Mess cash balance. I immediately queried the figure he gave me because I knew we had more in the account than that which I had just been told, but, I was informed, the figure was right because the Air Ministry Central Fund had nicked £2,000 to start up new Officers' Messes, because they thought there was too much money in our account not being used.

I thought, 'Right Monkey', and from then on I never let our account build up, and I made sure I spent the money for the benefit of those officers who had subscribed it.

After two years as PMC from when I was posted, we had some of the finest silverware decorating our tables on Guest Nights that could be seen anywhere.

With so many officers using the Anteroom it got a bit scruffy, and so I approached the Clerk of Works with a view to redecorating. Alas, he told me, no refurbishing of the Anteroom was due for another two years, and so I decided to get the work done out of my own resources. I contacted the civilian batman on my staff who had been a Master Painter and Decorator, and asked him if he would care to undertake the work if I provided the wherewithal for him to do the work while he was employed on night duty. He jumped at the chance, and so, after agreeing a price, he started work.

He did a bit each night, and apart from the inconvenience of a part of the Anteroom being out of bounds, there were no complaints. The work was nearly completed when my Manager came into my office and said the local secretary of the Transport and General Workers Union wished to see me. A meeting was arranged, and, after he had refused my offer of a coffee, I asked the gentleman how I could help him. "Well", he said, "it has come to my notice that you are misemploying one of my members, and that if you do not stop, there might be a withdrawal of labour by my members".

"Not to my knowledge, but can you be more explicit?", I replied.

"You are misemploying a Batman, a member of my union, as a Painter and Decorator, and this must stop." was his response.

"Right," I said, "now I know what you are getting at! I am employing a Painter and Decorator, who is painting the Officers' Mess Anteroom, in his own time, at an agreed price, as a sub-contractor, and I don't think it is any of your business!"

"Oh!!" he said, "I did not know he was working as a sub-contractor; in which case my Union is not interested, and so if the offer of a coffee still stands, I'd be delighted to accept!"

I thought, saucy sod, but I said to my Manager who had stayed at my invitation to listen as a witness to what had just taken place, "Take this gentleman to the Staff Canteen and look after him".

And to the Union man, I said, "Good day to you".

No more trouble from the Union!

Each course of 30 Cadets appointed a different one of their number each day to march them from one lecture room to the next to give them a chance to practise giving drill orders, and they were also encouraged to form a group of three to maintain course discipline, but any punishment for minor offences had to be submitted to me to see fair play before any punishment was carried out. This was because it was found the type of punishment they wanted to impose on one of their own course members was out of all proportion to the supposed offence committed. They were far tougher on one another if one let the side down than the Queens Regulations or The Manual of Air Force Law would ever allow!

In most cases, where I considered the Course Leaders' punishment was too harsh, I would make the wrong doer confess to the rest of the Course the error of his ways and promise never to let the side down again. I normally made them do this during Physical Training instruction with the Drill Instructor present, when I would make them play the game of 'Whip the Gap', which was the same game that I had previously been taught at school. As outlined previously, the Drill Sergeant would walk around the circle of cadets who all had their eyes shut and hands behind their backs, and presented his choice of Cadet with the knotted handkerchief. The 'chosen one' would then very quietly get in position while the rest of the Cadets still had their eyes shut, whack the Cadet on his right with the knotted handkerchief, and then chase him around the circle while hitting him as many times as possible! This always caused much amusement for the rest of the Cadets who were not being hit!

By this means the Drill Sergeant was able to get one of the Cadets to dish out corporal punishment to any Cadet who might, in the Drill Sergeant's eyes, have committed a slight misdemeanour whilst playing this game. It was a very simple game, but the striker was always able to get at least one good hit before the receiver started to run. The Cadets loved it!

Another simple method of punishment I used was to make the culprit play me at Squash. I would get into the centre of the Court and make them run around the court until they were almost at the point of exhaustion, and once or twice during the game I would accidentally hit them with the ball. It did no lasting damage – it just used to sting for a bit, and was a means of dishing out corporal punishment with just a little hurt to their pride. It was well known to the Cadets what was going to happen, and was a standing joke, and I would hear them enquire of the culprit 'how many times did he hit you?"

After the morning inspection, the students went to breakfast, and from there on to their scheduled programme which started every day at 0800 hours. Organised games were part of the curriculum, and homework was set daily, which amounted to a set of questions on subjects which the cadet had already covered, and which also showed the section, and reference number where the answer could be found.

After dinner, I would casually wander around the Cadets' rooms, quite often to sort out arguments, or generally assist if necessary. I organised their lives, sleeping and waking, twenty-four hours a day, and at the end of the first three months, I sent them on a fortnight's leave.

Without fail most Cadets agreed they never knew three months could pass so quickly!

I kept a close watch on the progress they were making because my aim was to get a Cadet with a Distinguished Pass, which meant the achievement of 80% pass mark in each of the three disciplines, i.e. Ground Work, Air Work, and Officer Qualities. I got the impression my two Squadron Leaders were being a little harsh. Many were the times when Cadets passed easily on the Air and Groundwork, but failed on Officer Qualities, and in one case by 1%. I took them to task over this, and tried to reason with them, saying "How can a man be prevented by 1% from gaining a Distinguished Pass for Officer Qualities?" But, they were adamant that their system was fair, and they were not prepared to let me cheat and boost their final assessment.

In this connection, there was an occasion when they wanted to fail a Cadet because he had failed in his final Meteorology examination. I examined the Cadet's six month's course work for Ground subjects and Air Work, and he had made the grade quite easily, with the exception of that one subject. Next, I found from his records, he already had a degree in Mathematics, and so I sent for both my Squadron Leaders, and told them the last thing I was going to do was fail this Cadet.

I reasoned with them, this man had had a much better education than any of his instructors, including me, and that I was going to let him sit his Meteorology examination again, because to date we had spent over £10,000 on his Navigation education, and I was not going to let that money go to waste! But, before making my final decision, I told my Squadron Leader Disciplinarian to bring the Cadet to me so that I could have talk with him.

At the interview I had with this Cadet, I quickly put him at his ease, and discussed the Course generally with him, and how well he had done – with the exception of Meteorology, which he had failed abysmally. And so I asked him "How come?"

He apologised for failing the subject, but explained that he thought he knew it and, therefore, had not swotted it up. He was most contrite because he thought he had let the side down, but if I would give him a second chance, he assured me he would make the grade.

I said, "What you are suggesting is most unusual procedure, but I will arrange for this to happen, but if you do fail a second time and let me down, I will have your guts for garters!"

Needless to say, at the second attempt, he passed with flying colours. Therefore no more was said. I had made my point, and I hoped that some of the vast amount of income tax I was paying every month had not been entirely wasted!

At the end of every course, the cadets received their Navigator Brevets on a parade of all of the 300 Cadets, with the Station Band of five Bagpipes, two Kettle Drums, and a Big Base Drum, with the Station Commander presenting the Brevets.

This parade was performed before all of the proud parents and friends, and was followed by a Cocktail Party, after which the Cadets dispersed on leave to await their posting notices. The night before this Parade, the Brevet Course attended their last Guest Night at which everyone of that Course had their own bottle of wine. I used to add one shilling per week on each Cadet's Mess Bill (with their agreement) so that at the end of their Course, they were each entitled to their bottle of wine.

I had not been at Thorney long when we had a new Station Commander, and his first Passing Out Parade was under the above organisation. The 300 Cadets, in officer type uniform and doing Airman's drill with white Blancoed Belts and burnished, polished Bayonets in their rifles, looked magnificent. The Station Band was a bit corny, and I made a mental note to do something about that, but the Station Commander did a good job in the presentation of the Brevets.

At the Passing Out Guest Night, as the PMC, I was always Mr. President, and it was normal for me to give a speech to the Brevet Course, and their Senior Member would reply.

After the Port had been circulated, I rose to make my speech, but as this was the first time the Station Commander had attended such a function, I invited him to speak first. That was OK, but the next morning I was summoned to the presence of the Station Commander when, over coffee, he referred to the previous day's Parade, and when he found out we had one of those about every six weeks, he let me know in words of one syllable that he hoped I was not going to call upon him again to do that chore!

"Can't you get somebody else?" he concluded,

"Sir," I said, "I'm giving you first refusal: and if you don't want to do these Parades, have I your permission to make other arrangements?"

"Go ahead Gibson, if you can get someone else, do it!"

When I was at the Air Ministry on Sir Roderick Hill's staff organising his social gatherings, I had got to know many senior officers and I invited an Air Commodore to do this chore. "No problem Bruce, I will fly down in my Meteor. What did you say the date was?" was the reply. "Thank you sir" I said, "A letter will be in the post tonight with the time, date, and a brief of all the details, and if you want accommodation for the night, I can fix that too"

I informed the Group Captain of the arrangements I had been able to make, and he was generously pleased. It was agreed that the Station Commander would meet the Air Commodore in his Staff Car and escort him to the Parade Ground, and I said I would prepare an aide memoire for him with a copy of the brief I would be preparing for our honoured guest. The whole parade and cocktail party afterwards went off without a hitch, and the Air Commodore made an excellent speech to the Cadets which pleased our Station Commander because it relieved him of that chore, and allowed him to concentrate and be his usual charming host!

The next week I attended as a guest at the Royal Marines' Mess at Eastney Barracks. There I learnt that the Royal Marines Officer Ranks were senior to both the Army and Royal Air Force, and that a Major in the Marines was the equivalent of a Wing Commander in the Air Force, and that the officer detailed to look after me was the

Royal Marine Major Band Master.

From him I learnt quite a bit about the Royal Marines, and I was enthralled by the story he had to tell when I queried the opulence of the Mess, the dining room in particular, which had oil paintings of every Monarch from Charles I to the present day, all in golden frames, twelve inches wide. He told me the Mess had been built in Victorian times, and the civil servant handling the contract had a bet with a colleague that the politician who was due to sign never looked at what he was signing, and to win his bet, he was going to add a nought onto the cost of the building, which he did. Needless to say, he won his bet! Hence the magnificence of what one could see.

I told the Major about our Brevet Parades, and that a friend of mine, who was an Air Commodore, was going to do the honours at our next Parade, and would he like to join us, which he accepted with pleasure. This gave me time to invite Air Vice Marshal Andrew McKee Square to be our guest of honour at our subsequent parade.

The Royal Marines Band Major thought the drill by our 300 cadets was excellent, and this to our Station Bagpipe Band. I replied that it was kind of him to say so, and that it would be even better with the Royal Marines Band. He asked me to give him some dates, and he would see if anything could be arranged. It was ultimately agreed that The Royal Marines Band would play at the Brevet Parade where our Group Commander Air Vice Marshal Andrew McKee would officiate.

I always did my Public Relations bit and the local press would always attend, the result of which after this occasion, I never had to use the Bagpipe Band again! There were plenty of Service bands in our local area, always willing to play for our Cadets Brevet Parade.

My greatest capture for the officiating Officer was Air Chief Marshal Sir Roderick Hill, my old boss at the Air Ministry.

I telephoned and spoke to his Diary Secretary, Officer Pitts, and asked her if she thought Sir Roderick would dish out the Brevets at one of our Parades. She thought he would be delighted, and that she would speak to the great man and ring me back. That from my experience meant I was more than half way there, because if the Diary Secretary was in favour, she would find a place in Sir Roderick's diary to fit it in.

When the day arrived I had been suffering with Lumbago, and although it was a pain in the arse, it never stopped me working. It used to pull me on one side, and I used to walk around like a hairpin, but more of that later. My Station Commander was in his element looking after an Air Chief Marshal, whom I had served with pride and saw every day when I was at the Air Ministry. No one landed by air or visited officially on our Station without being met and escorted, but in this case, the Group Captain did his own chores and Sir Roderick loved every minute of it.

The pep talk given by the officiating officer was a dream because I knew, from experience, he liked navigators. He understood their work and, as he told the Cadets, Space Travel in the future was going to be a navigational problem, and there was no limit to what a young navigator starting out could achieve.

The whole parade, from start to finish, was a success, and the next morning my Group Captain spoke to me on the telephone to say so. During the actual parade we had an excellent crowd of parents, sweethearts and relatives of serving officers and men, with the Air Chief Marshal taking the Salute in the centre, the Station Commander on his right, and me standing like a hairpin on his left.

At Cocktails after the Parade was over, a Squadron Leader Medical Officer came up to me, and introduced himself at the new Station Doctor and asked "why are you standing like a hairpin; have you been in an aircraft accident?" "No", I told him, "it was due to flying in Halifax aircraft, which leaked like sieves – it isn't permanent, but sometimes it does hang around for several weeks" "Well", he said, "Come and see me tomorrow and I'll give you something for that". "Thanks very much Doc" I replied, and promptly forgot all about it, and went rushing around checking that the reception was functioning correctly.

A couple of days later, who should call on me but our new catchpenny apothecary. I said, "hello Doc, how nice to see you.

Come in and have a coffee"

I suddenly remembered that he had asked me to go and see him, and I'd forgotten all about it. I am not in the habit of telling lies, and so I kept mum. We had an enjoyable interlude, but just as the Doc was leaving, he said, "Thank you for the coffee – you did not come and see me, and so I've come to see you!". He gave me a bottle of tablets and said, "Take one of these tablets every four hours, right round the clock if you can. Don't miss out if you can help it. I'll see you around." And off he went.

I can wake up any time of the day or night, and so I started taking the Doc's pills religiously every four hours, and within 72 hours, I was standing ramrod straight. Therefore, I just had to go and see our new Medical Officer. When I entered his room I said, "Doc, what do you think?"

"Have you been taking the pills?" he said.

"Yes", I said, "Look at me! What are they?"

"You'll never guess", he said, "– they're Aspirin!"

So, nowadays, I take one Aspirin a day but if I feel the slightest twinge I step up the dose, and remain pain free!

One day the Wing Commander Administrator rang me up and said the NAAFI Manager wanted some help, and had I got any students who could assist? I looked on the daily programme, and saw that one course was just about to start a free period. I sent for the Head Man of that Course and told him to report, with his Course Members, to the NAAFI Manager who was in need of some help, and to report back to me after the job was completed, and off he went.

One hour later he was back to report, "Fatigue completed – Sir!" I was confused. I did not believe what I had been told. The NAAFI was across the other side of the Station, which took 15 minutes for 30 cadets to cross, and 15 minutes back, and so I rang the NAAFI Manager and asked him if my Cadets had completed his task. "Yes", came the reply. Apparently they had each been given a sack to fill with potatoes, which had just been freshly dug, and the manager had been presented with 30 full sacks, and so he was happy, and thanked me for helping him out. I said to the Head Cadet, "Well done - carry on", but I could not carry on. I kept thinking of 30 sacks of potatoes in 30 minutes. It bugged me! However, time went by and, about three weeks later, I had another call from Wing Commander Admin. who said, "Gibby, do you remember some of your students picking up some potatoes for the NAAFI Manager a few weeks ago?"

"Of course John", I replied.

"Well", Wingco said, "The NAAFI Manager has just telephoned and told me those sacks were full of earth, with only a thin layer of potatoes on top!"

We both had a good laugh, especially when I told him that this particular Fatigue had worried me for a couple of days, but that I would be able to sleep alright tonight, and I finished by saying, "You can't win them all John!"

I heard via the grapevine that a certain course had pulled a fast one over the old man, but I took no action – I let it ride, but when it came to that particular Course's Passing Out Guest Night, in my speech I wished them well, and I reminded them that now they were Acting Pilot Officers, they would be called upon to make decisions, and some you win, and some you lose, and from my experience as an aged Wing Commander, I had learnt it was not possible to win them all. This statement brought laughter, but when their appointed Head Man said in reply how much they had enjoyed the Course, the excellent living conditions in the Mess, and the food – the potatoes in particular – this brought uproar, and a good time was had by all! Honour had been served.

Our new Group Captain was an excellent Station Commander; the only thing wrong with him was that he didn't like Navigators, which was HARD LUCK, because with the Officer Cadet Students, he had about 360 of us on his Station! He knew no more about navigation than the average pilot, but he was a superb Administrator, and a good Helmsman. It was because he liked sailing that he wangled himself the Posting to Thorny Island which had a good sailing club, with 50 small ketches on Chichester Creek, and of which he appointed himself as Commodore.

Right from a child I had always been interested in games. Before I was two year's old, I can remember playing mothers and fathers; in fact I was quite grown up before I discovered the same game had grown up connotations. However, I took over the responsibility of arranging the Cadets' Organised Games. Rugby Union, Soccer and Hockey were the three best games for mass distribution, because with referees and linesmen, they got rid of most of the bodies, and they taught the value of teamwork.

Individual games were permitted, such as Squash, Tennis, and at Thorney Island, Sailing; but it was those students I checked most thoroughly because I found they were the ones who tended to skive off, and were laughing their heads off at their colleagues sweating their guts out on a Rugby Field.

On the first afternoon that I took over, I had just finished my game of Squash and I was on my way to bathe, when I found two cadets asleep on their beds. They had stated they were going to play each other at Squash, but I knew that wasn't possible because that was my game, and I knew the Courts were booked solid until 2130 hours. However they did play Squash that day because I booked the Court for 2200 hours and ordered them to be there, and I played both them, and made them run from Arsehole to Breakfast time They never skived at Squash again.

In examining the Cadets' forms for their preferences for organised games, two saucy sods had put down 'walking'. That was easy to organise. I just handed them over to our Drill Instructor and told him that walking was their organised game, and would he amuse them for the next hour or two; I have always suspected there was a sadistic nature in Drill Sergeants. If I had given our Drill Sergeant 14 day's extra leave he could not have been more pleased! "They like walking do they Sir?" He said. "You can have them for as long as you like for the next four Wednesday afternoons" was my response. He was so pleased that if I had been that way inclined he would have kissed me!

I used to play Squash every day, and sometimes twice a day, but on Wednesdays I used to have an early light lunch and get my game over with, and then I would go around visiting all of the other games that were taking place. The rugby and other team players couldn't stop laughing. They had finished their game, and were looking forward to a hot bath when – strolling by the Parade Ground – they saw the two 'would be walkers' in full kit, doing Arms Drill with the Drill Sergeant who was in his element!

There is an American saying, 'when you've got them by the balls; their hearts and minds soon change'.

First thing the next morning I was presented with 2 new Organised Games forms from the 2 'would be walkers', stating their preference was for a team game. I told my Adjutant I would deal with the new request as soon as possible, but in the meantime to tell the 2 cadets to carry on with their first choice with cooperation from the Drill sergeant for the next three weeks. There was a permanent message on the Grapevine after that to all new cadets starting the course, "Whatever you do, don't put down 'walking' as your Organised Game".

That message worked because for the next two years while I was CGI at Thorney, no one ever tried to pull a fast one on me again!

In all of my experience of being in charge of organised games, there were only two genuine cases of the officers stating walking as their preference. The first was a Squadron Leader Navigator who was on a Bombing raid over Germany, when the aircraft he was navigating was completely enveloped in flames. They were at 10,000 feet and his parachute was on fire. Rather than be burnt alive in a crashed aircraft, he jumped without a parachute and landed feet first in two feet of snow which broke his fall, but in so doing damaged both of his ankles, and he could no longer run.

The second case was of a Squadron Leader who went to London for an investiture to get a DFC. He booked in at an hotel in Shaftsbury Avenue, met up with other officers on a similar jaunt, and got sloshed. He went to bed on the third floor of his hotel, and in the middle of the night got up to go to the toilet.

It was very hot weather and the French Windows in his room had been left open. He was in a strange room, but at 0430 hours he saw the light from the windows and walked towards them on to the balcony, hit the protective rail, and landed feet first in Shaftsbury Avenue and sat down.

The policeman on his beat stated that he saw the officer fall over the balcony rail, and do a complete somersault before landing on his feet and sitting down. As a result the officer was now one and three quarters of an inch shorter than he used to be, and could no longer take part in team games. The Doctor was doing his rounds one day while the officer's parents were visiting him.

The Doctor said to the parents, "Your son must consider himself very lucky, because if he had not been drunk when he fell, the consequences might have been far more serious."

The parents were flabbergasted, and the mother said, "But our son doesn't drink!"

For each Course of 30 Cadets I allocated a Flight Lieutenant Instructor to be responsible for their overall training. I noticed on one particular Course the examination marks for Ground Training subjects left much to be desired, and so I started to sit in on those particular Instructor's lectures.

Afterwards I sent for my two Squadron Leaders and pointed out the low standard the Cadets had achieved, and said I was going to have the Flight Lieutenant Instructor involved posted because of his lack of ability to teach.

My Squadron Leader Admin immediately jumped to his defence saying, "But Sir, he's a good navigator, and my Navigating Training Squadron Leader said his Course Ground marks might not be good, and the Course Air Work is average, but the Course Officer Quality marks are above average; we can't afford to lose a man like that!"

"But", I said, "he can't teach". Then the Admin man chimed in "He's Captain of the Station Rugby Team – they'd be lost without him". "OK," I said, "next time the Station Rugby team plays, I'll make a point of attending."

This I did, and I was amazed at the Jekyll and Hyde Instructor I had, because on the Rugby pitch he was indeed King. He not only played by example, but he galvanised the whole team into action, and was the most superb Captain.

That did it – the Station Rugby Team could not afford to lose a man of that quality, and so I relieved him of his Course Commander duties, and employed him full time as an Airborne Navigation Instructor, where he was able to oversee the airborne navigating work, and everybody was happy.

In the meantime work went on, and another Wednesday had arrived with organised games, and having played my game and inspected all of the others, I suddenly thought I would visit the Sailing Club. I decided to see how my Cadet, who had claimed to be a Helmsman, and his crewman were getting on. All of the boats were out on Chichester Creek, but my Cadet, whose name was also Gibson, and his crewman were working on the most clapped out sailing vessel one could imagine. They had pulled it out of the water, baled the water out, and were studying the wreck to decide what was to be done.

In the summer evenings quite a bit of sailing went on, and I heard via the Grapevine that most evenings my two students were kept busy working on their boat. Such keenness pleased me no end, and so I kept my ear to the ground and let them get on with it. I was therefore most surprised when the Group Captain telephoned me and invited me to his office for a coffee. There were several other officers present, and I made a mental note that they were all members of the Sailing Club, and sailing was the main topic of conversation.

After a few minutes of socialising, the Commodore said, "By the way Gibson, I want to talk to you about Helmsman Gibson".

I was immediately on the defensive and said, "What's he been up to?"

I learned that my two students had made a wonderful repair job

330

of the Ketch they had been allocated, and most of it at their own expense, I was told that once a month, the Sailing Club held races on Chichester Creek, and that the Station Commander usually won, but since my two students had started to race, he was being beaten into second place.

He didn't mind being beaten by a better Helmsman, but when his name was Gibson, he found it a little hard to take! At this we both laughed, but he added, "your Cadet is a superb Helmsman, and I thought you would like to know".

This I thought was extremely generous of him.

The weekly dances I ran for the students were very popular, especially as I had a working relationship with the Matron of the local hospital, and I was able to bring Aircrew busloads of nurses into camp to meet the demand.

On one occasion, when the nurses were returning to their quarters, one of my students was in the act of following his partner when the Matron's arm barred his way with the words, "I don't think you're on my staff Sir!" By which time the Aircrew Bus had left, and the Cadet had to walk back to Thorney Island.

On New Year's Eve, I ran a dance for the staff, wives, and girlfriends to see the New Year in. This was quite a formal affair, and guests from other stations were invited. Gatecrashers were not allowed, and everyone attending had to be announced to the Station Commander and his wife who did their meeting and greeting bit. A group of officers and their wives were enjoying their glass of wine just inside the entrance hall when a Squadron Leader entered with a beautiful young girl, and one of the Flight Lieutenants said, "Cor! Couldn't I do her a bit of good!" The man's wife, who was one of the group, looked round and said, "Hark at old once a fortnight talking!" That is the advantage of wives over husbands – they know everything!!

Our Group Captain was in his element, and was talking to a small group of Pilots from our Flying Wing, one of whom was a highly decorated, dashing Fighter Boy. The dance was only just really getting going when the Squadron Leader's wife, who was getting under the influence of drink, pushed through the Group and, looking straight up into her husband's face, said in a loud voice, "Pat – take me home and make love to me". Everybody roared with laughter, but Pat, with a perfectly straight face said to the Group Captain, "Sir, have I your permission to stand down?" The Group Captain who was thoroughly enjoying the joke said, "Pat, how could I refuse?!"

On nights such as these, by the time I had got rid of everybody and supervised the Batmen in clearing up ready for Breakfast in a few hours time, it was quite late, and so I would spend the night in my room in the Mess.

One night, I had not been asleep long when suddenly I was wide-awake. I got up – put on a dressing gown, and at a brisk walk went rushing downstairs and through the entrance hall, which disturbed the civilian night batman who came rushing after me, saying "Can I help you Sir?"

I went straight into the Anteroom, and over to a large Club Sofa, and there I found a smouldering cushion about to burst into a blaze caused by a burning cigarette end. I said to the Batman, "You can put that out for a start." And, after a thorough search of the room, the Batman said, "How did you know that was burning?" I said, "Just because I'm asleep upstairs, don't think I don't know what's going on down here", and went back to bed.

Within 24 hours via the Grapevine the story doing the rounds was, the Old Bastard was psychic!

Within 48 hours I was summoned to Coffee in the Group Captain's office where I joined a group of colleagues who were already imbibing, and after the usual pleasantries, the Group Captain said, "I hear we have a psychic Navigator in the Mess." Amidst much laughter I replied, "So long as the Old Bastard doesn't start teaching your Cadets Navigation with a Crystal Ball, I don't think you will have anything to worry about!" which caused more merriment, and that little episode closed with one of the pilots present saying, "All Navigators is bastards!"

I did not always have it my own way because, at one staff Guest Night, after we had dined, I was standing with my Pink Tonic Water which everybody thought was Pink Gin, talking to some friends, when a Group Captain (who was the guest of someone) came up to me and said, "I believe you're Wing Commander Gibson?" I replied, "Sir", and gave him the Royal Nod. He said, "I believe you play Squash" I replied, "I've been known to". He said, "We must have a game sometime". In my stupidity I used the cliché, "Any time".

The Group Captain looked at his watch and said, "It's ten to eleven – I'll see you on the court at eleven!"

"Sir, you won't", I said.

"Gibson," he said, "you're outranked. I'm going to change," and he left the room.

I said to my friends, who were laughing at my displeasure, "Now what do I do?!" All in one voice they said, "You will go and get changed."

So that's what I did. The first five games I won nine nil, and I thought, what a waste of time.

"Right" said Groupie, "Now let us have another rubber of three".

Of course during the first five games had sobered him up, and when we started the next game he really set about me, and although they were closely fought games, he really made me run and won all three games.

After the game my partner had a bath, and went to bed. I had a bath, and although I was completely knackered, being PMC I had to go and supervise the clearing up after the Guest Night.

The next day I checked up on my opponent and discovered that he was the Captain of the RAF Squash Team! However it taught me a lesson, to make sure I knew whom I was talking to before using the cliché, 'any time'!

Clearing up after guest nights often presented problems for my Bar Staff, but I made it my duty to see fair play.

Student guest nights always finished up with songs around a

piano, and a certain amount of horseplay, with beer being poured over the songsters, and of course the piano got thirsty and had to have a drink also!

As Mess members pay for their refreshments by signing for their purchases in their own personal account book, with the time recorded when the goods were bought, it was easy to trace the persons who had been present during the Mess games, and so I would charge those Cadets involved extra for the drinks, and that extra money I used to give to the Batmen who had to clear up the mess made by the roisterers.

* * *

22

It's a Cadet's life

We had a large Concert Grand Piano in the Anteroom that was very heavy, and it took six men to move it. It was placed in a corner of the room with a notice on it, stating 'On no account must this Piano be moved'.

Of course, a heavy object which was difficult to move and with a notice on it stating that it was not be moved was asking for trouble where frisky young Cadets were concerned, and after a party, the Piano was always to be found without legs, top and keyboard, down the opposite end of the Anteroom from its allocated place.

Also this movement would always take place after I had gone to bed, and I thought the party was over. This naughty act on the part of the Cadets was to show 'the Old Gaffer' if they wanted to move the piano, they would move it.

I had a fixed price for the movement and dismantlement of the piano, and all those Cadets who were present in the Anteroom at a certain hour were charged a proportion of that price, and that money went towards the wine on the Cadets' final Guest Night.

I always provided an excellent display of newspapers, periodicals, and magazines in the Anteroom. Among the latter there was always a copy of The Illustrated London News, The Tatler, and The Sketch. In the centre page of The Sketch there was always a double page spread, in colour, of a beautiful, scantily dressed, young lady, by an artist named Wright.

It was a monthly magazine, and every Thursday when it was delivered, I would make it my business to be in my Mess Office so that I could look at Wright's creation. One Thursday, to my surprise, when I looked there was no illustration by Wright. I was peeved to say the least, but the same thing happened the following month; no picture by Wright, but on looking more closely, I could see the centre double page spread had been removed; someone was nicking Wright's illustration!

The next month, I waited for the newspapers to be delivered, and I was the first person to witness that The Sketch had its picture of Wright's gorgeous girl. I stayed in the Anteroom for the next ten minutes, reading the newspapers and watching to see who came in to nick Wright's picture.

After ten minutes, I decided I had work to do, and I could not waste any more time playing detective, but before going back to my office, I decided to check The Sketch, and lo and behold, Wright's picture had gone. No one to my knowledge had entered the Anteroom in those ten minutes in mid morning, but someone was having a game with me.

I had expressed verbally my displeasure and what I would do the culprit if I caught him, but after a couple of months, the nicking stopped just as suddenly as it had started. Somehow, someone had put one over on me!

From the 300 Cadets we were able to produce quite a good Rugby team. One of my Instructors, who was the Captain of the Station Rugby Team, had knocked them into shape, and one Wednesday afternoon they flew to play the Station Team at RAF Halton. After the game, they had just got airborne to return to Thorney Island, when a snowstorm developed.

Although there were 15 navigators on board, no one had bothered to navigate. They had all left it to the Sergeant Pilot, and on his homeward track, instead of climbing to the safety height of 1500 feet above the highest point of land, he tried to stay in contact with the ground so that he could see where he was going.

Unfortunately, he flew into high ground, and tragically all but one cadet was killed.

The cadet who survived was thrown clear, and suffered a broken thigh.

As soon as I heard of this tragedy I reported directly to the

Station Commander

I reminded him that when I was at the Air Ministry, I had written the Air Ministry Order dealing with the Reporting of Aircraft Accidents, and I volunteered to do all of the paperwork relating to this accident that my cadets had been involved in, if he so desired. My offer was accepted, and I got cracking.

The thing that struck me most odd was, that only 16 aviators had left Thorney Island to go to Halton; 15 rugby players, and the Sergeant pilot, and yet 17 bodies had been found – 16 dead, and one in hospital.

Having sent off the first report to the Air Ministry (Message 'A') I took a copy to the Station Commander but told him we had a problem. We had an extra body to identify, and I would do my best to find out who it was. I immediately contacted Halton, and they informed me the dead were a Sergeant pilot, a Flight Lieutenant Navigator, and 14 cadets, with a further cadet in hospital. And so, it was a case of 'thinking hats on' – who was the deceased Flight Lieutenant Navigator?

By this time it was nearly 2200 hours, and the whole Station knew of the tragedy, including those in married quarters and both of my Squadron Leaders, who had just joined me. The three of us put our heads together, and came up with the conclusion that the man we were looking for was one of our Instructors, who had been due back from leave the following day. He was a single man, a keen rugby player, and had spent his holiday with his mother in London. We surmised he had made his own way from Barking in Essex to Halton to watch the Rugby, and after the game, had joined the Rugby team in their aircraft to return to Thorney Island.

I reported our suppositions to our Station Commander, and I told him I thought it was one of our Instructors, a Flight Lieutenant Claire, who we were looking for, and suggested that I contact the dead man's mother to try and confirm our thoughts.

Therefore, at 2300 hours I rang Claire's mother and asked her if David had left to return from leave. "Oh yes!!" she said, "He had left to go to Halton to watch the Rugby, and he was going to return from there."

I rang Halton, and they confirmed they had evidence among the items that had been found that the dead Flight Lieutenant was Claire. After a discussion with the Station Commander, it was agreed that I should telephone Mrs. Claire and break the sad news to her. At 0230 hours, I rang Mrs. Claire, and told her that there had been an aircraft accident and that with great sadness, her son David was one of the victims.

I was quite surprised how calmly she took this information, and she thanked me for letting her know. I said I would be writing to her in the near future, at which she thanked me once again, and rang off.

In the case of death due to a flying accident, a Court of Inquiry has to be held, and the findings rendered on a special form. Once this had taken place, we were free to bury the casualties, and this we did at a mass grave at RAF Halton. The funeral service, with full military honours, was conducted by the Chaplain in Chief of the RAF with over 200 relatives and friends present, who were most impressed with the solemnity of the occasion.

I was in charge of the RAF Funeral party which, being a Gemini, I was able to do without being affected by the sadness of the occasion. Fourteen days later, a memorial service was held at our Church at Thorney Island, which was conducted by Bishop Bell of Chichester Cathedral, and so many people attended that we had to relay the Service to the many mourners outside the church.

At refreshments afterwards in the Officers' Mess, I made it a point to have a word with Mrs. Claire, and I was once again amazed at how relaxed and jolly she was; she was acting as if she was at a cocktail party, and far too bright for such an occasion.

Three month's later, when Mrs. Claire realised she was not going to see her son David on leave any more, it hit her for six, and she had a nervous breakdown.

As an officer, the worst job I ever had to do was telling the next of kin of a casualty. I always took the Padré along with me; not only did they look the part, but they knew the right words to use, which is never easy. But, it is a job that has to be undertaken.

The Cadets who we had to train came from all walks of life, and as long as they were able to cope with the intensive training we were giving them, they ultimately became Acting Pilot Officers. Therefore, they had to be taught what was expected of them as officers and gentlemen, and how to conduct themselves in an Officers' Mess.

The customs of the Service are legion, and are not learnt overnight. They must remember they are officers, twenty-four hours a day, and even in minor matters apart from Service affairs, such as the gentlemanly conduct of gallantry, and chivalry towards the opposite sex should not be overlooked. One of the most important customs is to always tell the truth, because the life of a comrade might depend on it.

In my case, I had the advantage of having been a civilian at our Volunteer Reserve Centre, where Air Vice Marshal Sir Tom Webb-Bowen had operated our centre as an Officers' Mess.

I noticed that with some cadets, table etiquette was a problem. On one occasion I noticed that a cadet had eight slices of bread in front of him, which he commenced to butter. I called the cadet to one side, and asked him if he was going to eat all eight slices. He looked at me as if I had taken leave of my senses, but replied, "Yes, Sir". I said, "You can have eighty slices of bread if you are hungry, but in an Officers' Mess, you only take one at a time!" His colleagues laughed at that remark, but the culprit looked at me as if I had gone bonkers!

I checked on the Course progress of that particular cadet, and he was doing well on ground subjects, and also in the air, and so I decided to keep an eye on him in the Mess to make sure he did not let himself down.

Every year at Thorney Island, 600 Cadets from the RAF Training Corps spent 14 days holiday there, gaining Air force experience. This they did under canvas, and I was given the job to organise a Class 'B' Camp to enable this to happen.

Having got all of the tents erected, I wanted to test the organisation regarding outdoor cooking facilities, swill collection, toilets, ablutions etc, and so I arranged for the first fortnight to have 600 boys from approved schools as guinea pigs. With 600 boys, you get a complete cross section of society, but coming from approved schools, in the past they had all been naughty, but worse still, they had been found out.

I was in my element. I had been a little sod myself when younger, and I only differed from them in that I was never caught, and so I knew how to handle them.

At my welcoming address to the boys, I explained there were routine rules to abide by, but in particular, the WAAF Quarters was strictly out of bounds, and made a point of explaining the fining system that would apply should there be any offenders who were caught.

Having recorded all of their details; next of kin etc, I got all of them airborne. The air trip took less than half an hour, but there were no complaints. In fact, some showed such interest that if they had been academically qualified, they could have been considered for aircrew.

We kept them busy all day with lectures, physical training, organised games etc, and after their evening meal, they were allowed out of camp until 2200 hours. On one occasion when I was the Station Duty Officer, at about 2100 hours I received a telephone call from the Emsworth police saying, "Please come and pick up your boys – they are threatening to smash the place up!" I rang the Military Transport and ordered 3 aircrew coaches. I then grabbed 6 Cadets and gave them a quick briefing that we were going to round up our wayward Air Training Cadets with the lure that we were going to take them for a ride, and off we went.

When we got to Emsworth there seemed to be more police than airmen, but of course the youths we were looking for were in the local hostelries, and working with the cooperation of the police, in no time at all I had 3 coach loads of trainee cadets who were in the happy stages of inebriation.

I sat in the leading coach and, with 2 of my Cadets in each coach to see fair play, and after a short trip around Havant, by 2200 hours I had them all back in their tents. I don't know what the Police were worrying about because, with the help of my Cadets, they were no trouble at all. The following morning I had a word with my 600 truculent boys, and told them we wanted them to enjoy their stay with us, but in so doing, they were not to go 'over the top'. For any boy who did step out of line, there would be no more flying for him. I had no further trouble from then on!

We did not have to stay long at Havant before our married quarter was ready for us to move in. Kay was then fully employed, not only looking after Stuart, but everything had to be cleaned, because one just can't start using things straight after the builders have left it, can one?

I was entitled to a House Help, and I was able to get the wife of one of my civilian Batmen, a Mrs. Allen, to fill that capacity. She had a grown up family, and she thought Stuart was marvellous and she spoilt him rotten.

Every week the Station Commander's wife held a coffee morning to get to know the wives of Officers who were on the Station. The first time Kay went, she took Stuart, and that was that. Every week Kay had to attend the CO's wife's coffee morning, so long as she took Stuart. The Group Captain's family were getting grown up, the youngest boy being ten, and so Stuart took his place. Stuart started playing with his toys, and after the first coffee morning, he came home with a Dinky Toy. I had never seen a Dinky toy before, and I thought they were cute, and so that was the start of Stuart's collection. I used to buy him a Dinky toy every week, and it was not long before we had every Dinky car and lorry that was ever made. And so, we then started on Corgi toys.

Stuart got into the bad habit of taking the tyres off the motorcars, and putting them into lorries as goods to deliver, and every night it took me over an hour to put the tyres back on to the motorcars.

One day I was in the toyshop looking for something to buy when I spotted boxes of toy motorcar tyres. They were the answer to my prayer! I bought several boxes, filled up the lorries, and never had to put another Dinky toy car tyre on again.

Having acquired every Dinky and Corgi toy that had been made, we set about collecting 'Push and Go' toys, but specialising in Red Double Decker London Buses. When we got to 86, I thought we had enough, and we used to play Bus Stations.

As my mother had 7 children, any toy that any of us were given we had to share and, in fact, we never felt we owned anything personally, because it became second nature to us to share. We therefore encouraged Stuart to have lots of friends, some of whom virtually lived in our house, playing with Stuart's toys, but it taught him to share.

Every week, the local Council dustmen called to take away our rubbish, and they became Stuart's special friends. On the day they were due, he would go part way to meet them, pushing the dolls' pram that had been given to him by the CO's wife, and which was usually full of toys, and in his childish way, he would meet and greet his dustmen friends.

The postman and milkman also got their share of attention, but they were not special like the dustmen.

At this growing up stage, Stuart was difficult to feed. He would not open his mouth to be fed, especially at breakfast. One morning we were having our usual problem, when suddenly the alarm clock started ringing, at which Stuart opened his mouth, and we were able to shovel some food down him. I switched the alarm clock off, re-wound it, and re-set it – and every time the alarm went off, Stuart would eat. And so, that became our ritual; with the alarm clock making a din we ate, no alarm clock, his mouth remained closed shut tight.

On one occasion when Pat, Kay's sister, was visiting us from America, and when she saw our antics with the alarm clock at Stuart's feeding time at Breakfast, she just couldn't stop laughing.

It was always Kay's aim to have Stuart ready for bed by 1800 hours, and this was not easy, but in this connection I could help because I could please myself what working hours I kept, and so after Kay had got Stuart ready for bed, I would give him a 'Flying Angel' and walk around, singing, 'Over the mountains, over the sea – that's where my heart is longing to be – please let the light that shines on me – shine on the one I love. Bombedy, bombedy, bomb – over the mountains' etc, until he was asleep, and I developed a knack of swinging him round into my arms without waking him up, and was able to put him into his cot, which then left me free to get some work done.

Little did we know that even before he was 2 years old and not able to construct sentences properly, through playing with his Dinky and Corgi motor cars, he knew the name of every car on the road. When we were out driving in the car, with Stuart on Kay's knee, I would say, "Look at that Morris", and Stuart would say, "Austin", and he would be right! Now, he drives all over Europe and thinks nothing of it.

When I used to put Stuart on my shoulders and do 'Flying Angel', he used to call this 'Tojo', and many was the time that when I was around, he would hold up his arms in the air in the most appealing fashion, and say 'Tojo', and we would start all over again, "over the mountains etc".

One of Stuart's friends lived in the married quarter next door to us, and he was the Padré's son, Peter. He was older, bigger and twice as heavy as Stuart, but he too insisted on having a 'Tojo', and the Padre and I used to walk around together with our sons in this fashion. However, the Padré's thoughts on the resulting fatigue that this imposed on him were not be found in the Book of Common Prayer!

With 300 Officer Cadets plus 200 permanent staff, we had 500 Officers in the Mess. We were running a 24 hour day flying programme, which meant we were providing 2,000 meals a day to young, fit, hungry officers, which is quite a lot of grub!

Each officer was entitled to one and one eighth ounces of bacon a day, which amounts to quite a lot of bacon, but I had the feeling that our full rationed amount delivered to us by the NAAFI was not being consumed in our Mess, and so I had to put my detective hat on once more, and started to investigate.

During this process I discovered many valuable items were disappearing from officers' rooms, such as portable radios, cameras, fountain pens etc, and so I put a notice on the Board to remind everyone that the most serious offence in the Services was 'stealing from a comrade', and if I caught the culprit, they would be in serious trouble. As a result, the petty thieving stopped, but I still had the feeling that food rations were disappearing from the Mess, and so I got in touch with the Special Investigating Branch at Air Ministry.

A Wing Commander from that Branch visited me, and he agreed, I needed help, and he would provide it.

About a fortnight later, I saw a mature airman working in the Mess. I stopped him, and said, "Who are you?" He replied, "I'm a Batman". I said, "No you're not – I've got 64 Batmen, and I know every one of them by name. Come into my office".

When we got there I said, "Now, cut out the bullshit, who are you?" He told me he was a Squadron Leader from the Air Ministry Special Investigation Branch, and that he and five Flight Lieutenants, dressed as airmen, would be working in the Mess, and investigating the food loss I had reported. My Mess Manager had been told, and it had been agreed the fewer personnel who knew about the investigation the better, and that I should not be told. "OK", I said, "That's better; tell your colleagues to report to me before they start work, and I'll sort out my Mess Manager later".

And so, six so-called Batmen were employed as Waiters, and quite good they were at it too. After about six weeks, their Wing Commander called on me, and in making an interim report, he told me he had suspicions as to how my bacon was disappearing, but he was not quite sure, but that he might know in a week or two's time. I weeded out of him what his suspicions were, saying that I might be able to help.

Apparently the investigators thought the bacon was disappearing on Thursdays, which was the day of our weekly Cadets' Guest Night. Every Thursday the fishmonger would deliver 150 two ounce fillets of Plaice, and it was thought that he was taking out the bacon in his fish trays, and one of my staff was meeting up later with the fishmonger, and they were splitting the swag between them.

That put me in a real dilemma because, if they were right, it would be one of my senior members involved, and the last thing I wanted was to lose any one of them. After much soul searching, I called a meeting of my Mess Manager, my Mess Steward, and his two assistants and I told them of my suspicions regarding my bacon loss. I also told them that the six mature waiters were actually members of the Air Ministry Special Investigation Branch, and that they were to give them all the help they could because I was determined to stop the stealing of the Officers' Mess Bacon, and if I found the culprit, he would be in for the high jump.

Sadly to say, the pilfering stopped forthwith, and the senior policemen reported they were wrong about the fishmonger, and was I sure I was losing any of my food supplies. I replied I was not sure, it was only a suspicion that I had, and we agreed to leave it at that; but, nevertheless, I had achieved my aim – the pilfering stopped, and I kept all my senior members of my Mess staff.

Headquarters 21 Group RAF Swinderby were responsible for all of the UK Navigation Training Schools, and the Air Vice Marshal in charge was my old boss, Andrew McKee.

My Group Captain informed me that there was to be a meeting of all the heads of the UK Navigation Schools, where progress was to be reported and any suggestions for the improvement in training, if any, were to be submitted, and that we two were to attend.

My appointment at Thorney Island was the fifth time I had served under Andrew McKee, and having been Secretary to hundreds of meetings with him in the Chair, I knew how he loved meetings, and I knew therefore what to expect.

My Group Captain's knowledge of Navigation was typical of most pilots – he knew all of the basic rules, but the rest he left to the

Navigator. He was however a superb Administrator, and to his credit, while we were turning out 30 new navigators every five or six weeks, he let me get on with it.

A few days before the meeting I gave my Station Commander a complete run through our training syllabus, and showed him all over my section so that he knew what went on, and he made a couple of extra visits to refresh his memory, where he was able to talk to my two Squadron Leaders until he was quite happy. He was so confident he knew just what went on in his Navigation School that he decided to do all of the talking at the meeting, and I was only to speak if he asked for my assistance. That was OK by me, all I had to do was navigate to Swinderby and enjoy Square's hospitality after the meeting, which I knew would be laid on for us.

It came the day, and Thorney Island was completely covered in sea fog, but I was greatly relieved to see one of the senior pilots of Flying Wing was going to fly us up north to Swinderby. We took off on instruments, and at 25 feet we were above the ground mist, with church steeples and high buildings sticking up through it. It was an amazing sight.

As we flew inland northwards, the fog disappeared and we were in brilliant sunshine, and I noticed my Group Captain had taken over, and was piloting from the second pilot's seat. He completed the rest of the trip, and we landed without any hitches, and in no time at all we were sitting around a large conference table, being greeted by Square as the first item on the Agenda.

When we came to the item on the Agenda when each school had to report, I was amazed how much information my Group Captain had picked up in the last fortnight, and also how well he presented it, but above all, I admired his memory. However, I knew from previous experience the last item on Square's agenda would be when he asked every member individually if they had anything to add.

When it came to my turn, Square said to me, "Nice to see you here Gibby – are you alright?" I said, "Sir, I've never felt better, but my Group Captain has presented our case well, and I have nothing to add". Square replied, "Well, that's a turn up for the book, Gibby;

at a meeting with nothing to say!", and he moved on.

After an excellent meal and drinks afterwards, Square circulated among us and wanted to know how Kay and Stuart were, and was genuinely pleased to see me.

Back at Thorney Island the next day, at 0900 hours my telephone rang, and it was the Group Captain, who wanted to see me in his office. On arrival I was greeted most cordially, and I was told how pleased he was as a result of the previous day's meeting, but he said "What's all this Gibby lark?" "Well," I said, "He (the AVM) always calls me Gibby unless I've upset him, when he calls me 'Gibson'".

This astounded my boss, who said, "What do you mean, he always calls you Gibby?" I replied, "Well Sir, this is the fifth time I have served under the Air Vice Marshal. In fact, it was he who got me promoted to Wing Commander to do my job here for him."

This really perplexed my Group Captain who said, "Why the bloody hell didn't you tell me?" I said, "Sir, the occasion never arose. We haven't got that sort of relationship."

From this I followed with the many happy years I had spent working under 'Square'; how I had been his PMC in various messes for years, and how he loved the guest nights at Hornchurch with steak for dinner. How I was able to get him petrol coupons to keep his car running; how he flew up to Kinloss to invite me to join the staff that he was getting together to form the Flying College, and as I had spent most of my time with him as a bachelor, he was like a father figure to me. In fact, I have in writing his permission for me to marry!

From that moment on, I knew that as soon as my two-year tour of duty was up at Thorney, I would be on my way. He was simply not going to have someone on his Station who knew his boss as intimately as I did. We had nothing in common. He liked to drink a lot, and that is something I have never done. While he was drinking in the Mess, I would be helping Kay with her chores.

Stuart, in his early years, used to suffer from Croup, and in no time at all, he would have a temperature of 103 degrees, and then it was a case of 'all hands on deck'. On one occasion I was washing nappies, and Kay was helping and was totally shattered, but I made her laugh by saying, "I reckon I'm the only Wing Commander in the RAF washing nappies at midnight!"

But, that was how it was, but most nights, my day finished in the mess to make sure the Bar closed on time, and to deal with any truculent drinkers who planned to drink all night. If I had a £1.00 for every junior officer I had ordered to bed, I would have a nice little nest egg now!

It came to the time of the Monarch's Coronation. And, at a special Mess Meeting, I was given permission to organise a Coronation Ball. I was in my element. We had Admirals and Generals from Portsmouth; Air Marshals from the Air Ministry, Group Captains galore, and all of our staff. We had a good band, an excellent festive board, and enough drink to float Nelson's Victory, which at that time was in dry dock!

In the Dining Room, where the dancing was to take place, we had a Minstrels' Gallery, and it was here the Station Commander had his table together with a special drink supply, and during the course of the evening, everyone was invited to drink with the Group Captain, and on this occasion he excelled himself with his hospitality. During the course of the evening, he got rid of 120 bottles of Champagne.

The lady owner of the Garden Centre at Chichester undertook the floral decorations of the Mess, and she did a magnificent job. The Entrance Hall, where the Group Captain and his wife did the meeting and greeting bit to everyone attending, was decorated from floor to ceiling with flowers, and it was a truly wonderful spectacle.

Of course, at Officers' Mess functions, all drinks are free, and as soon as my guests started to arrive, my job was done, but I could not relax in case of any unseen calamity, such as ordering junior officers to bed for over indulging, just because the drinks were free! They always made complete pigs of themselves.

At 2100 hours, I found one bachelor Squadron Leader legless. With help, I got him to my office where I tried to make him comfortable, and in no time at all, he started to go to sleep, and so I left him to return to the Ball. After a bit, everything was going smoothly, and so I returned to my office, only to see a pair of shoes disappearing out of my office fanlight in to the quadrangle below, which was about a nine-foot drop. I telephoned the sick quarters for an ambulance, and they arrived pronto just as I reached the quadrangle.

There was my pissy officer, sitting up, unhurt, saying, "What's happened – where the bloody hell am I?" I said, "You're pissed, so shut up, and that's an order!"

That was the end of the Coronation Ball for him. The medical staff took over, and the drunken sod spent the night sedated in sick quarters.

On my return, the chef was performing at the Festive Board, and the Sergeant Waiters were doing fine.

At these functions I always put up a notice in the Sergeants' Mess asking for volunteers to act as waiters or barmen, with the promise of a good meal after the function ended, and as much as they wanted to drink.

I was never short of volunteers, and they did a fine job. Our Wing Commander Admin was a wonderfully sociable character, who really could drink. He could drink all night, but still be as sober as I was who drank nothing stronger than cocoa.

With him and our Station Commander both doing their stuff, our Coronation Ball was talked about for many months after the event, and from the bread and butter thank you letters received by our Group Captain, it would appear that our guests also enjoyed themselves, especially the ladies who all wore glorious long, colourful evening gowns, which combined with the floral decorations, it was quite a spectacle.

The Squadron Leader pilot who spent the night in sick quarters came to see me the next morning to thank me for looking after him, saying "I am sorry, but I cannot remember a thing!" I told him to save that old toffee for his drinking friends, because it wouldn't wash with me. However, we parted the best of friends, with the typical pilot's remark, "All Navigators is bastards!"

I had not been PMC of the Thorney Island Mess for long when an AMO came out, stating that Messes were free to make their own purchases of food, instead of having to get everything from NAAFI. This was pennies from heaven, and with all our major suppliers, i.e. Milkman, Butcher, Fishmonger and Grocer, I was able to negotiate substantial discounts, which meant more money to spend on the improvements to the Mess.

As I have mentioned, during my two-year tour of duty I raised the Mess standard to that of a five star hotel. We were running a 24-hour day flying programme, and supplying 2,000 meals a day. I was able to have a Batman on all night manning the entrance hall, and he was able to supply liquid refreshment to crews when they landed in the middle of the night. By the time I was made the Chief Ground Instructor of Thorney Island, I had personally been instructing armament, administration and navigation subjects for over seven years, and possessed the highest lecturing category to prove it, and therefore I was able to help my instructors to raise their teaching methods to such a standard I was able to achieve my aim of getting one of my Cadets to the Distinction level pass. To achieve this, he had obtained over 80% for each of the three disciplines; Ground Work, Air Work, and Officer Qualities. This was truly an amazing feat, and as a reward, I got him a Permanent Commission.

At the Guest Night for the course which was leaving after the Brevet Parade, I always gave a farewell speech congratulating them on successfully becoming fully fledged RAF Navigators which entitled them to wear the Brevet they had just earned, and to impress upon them the importance of their role at getting an aircraft from 'A' to 'B' successfully. That their job started before the flight commenced at the briefing, and did not finish until after the aircraft had landed at its planned destination, and they were back in the operation room, and, they had been debriefed. That there was never a time when a navigator, when in flight, had nothing to do. Even after he has felt he had solved the triangle of velocities on that flight, it was his job to check that that was so, by which time the wind might have changed, and so it was his job to recheck that the ETA he had given to his Captain of Aircraft was true. I reminded them that, after fifteen years of navigating aircraft even short distances, I still found it the most satisfying job to do, and I hoped they would enjoy the experience likewise.

The 30 students on their final Guest Night, each with his own bottle of wine, were always jolly occasions, and happiness reigned supreme.

I regretted having to leave Thorney Island, but on the dot, after my two year stint was up, I was posted as Station Commander of RAF Station Alviston, which was a good posting, and proved my Group Captain, although pleased to see me go, had done me proud.

* * *

23

Some Interesting Activities........

M y only regret at leaving Thorney Island was that I never learnt to sail. There was a reason for this. Firstly, the Station Commander, who was at Thorney Island when I arrived, was a very keen golfer, something I would never be, mainly because at that age I could not merely walk after a ball, I would have had to run; something which is not allowed on a Golf Course! And secondly, because many of the officers on the Station had taken up golf in order to speak to the same language as their boss.

However, I let it be known that the next Spring I would learn to sail – and what happened? Our new Group Captain arrived to take up his appointment in a massive Motor Launch, and let it be known that he was a qualified Helmsman, and that he would automatically become the new Commodore of Thorney Island Sailing Club, and as things turned out, I did not want to spend my spare time socially in his company, and so that put the kibosh on my learning how to sail!

On entering the gates of my new Station at Derby, the first thing I noticed was **SPEED LIMIT 5 M P H**. Now, all motorists know, from a Provisional Learner to a Formula 1 Driver, 'there ain't no such speed' and so that was the first thing I did on taking over was to raise the speed limit to 20 MPH, to enable motorists to conform to the rule!

The next thing I learnt was that my predecessor had been a bachelor, and that my married quarters was being occupied by one of my officers, and it would be a few weeks before the occupant would be moving into the Hiring which had been procured for him. At the time I thought 'that's nice, when I 'phone Kay tonight, that will make her feel very happy', but there was nothing I could do about it, and Kay would just have to soldier on at Thorney, and the same thing will happen to my successor; he'll just have to wait until Kay leaves.

That night I attended a Guest Night for the departing CO which gave me a chance to meet my officers informally, and the next day I interviewed each one individually, and from then on, we were in business.

My Adjutant was the brightest one of the bunch, and I got him to drive me round my station to all the nooks and crannies in my staff car with my Flag flying. It was a good feeling to be a Station Commander

Next I split up the Station into four Sections geographically, and put an officer in charge of each one. I instructed each one of them to carry out an inspection of his area, and to give me a report in writing within 72 hours of any damages or maintenance that needed attention. Acting on those reports, and with the cooperation of the Clerk of Works, my Station started to look as if somebody cared.

I used to inspect a quarter of the Station every week, which meant the whole place had been inspected once a month. As the reports came in from each section, I was able to double check on my weekly inspections, and in no time at all, with the help again of a cooperative Clerk of Works, I had the Station up to Air Officer Commander Inspection standards.

At my next weekly meeting with my Section Commanders, I congratulated them on getting our Station on the top line so quickly, but I told them that was how it had got to be kept in the future, and that any damage I found on my inspections which had not been reported by them, and which I considered was not due to fair wear and tear, they would have to pay for by F664b action! It is amazing the effect the mention of the Form 664b has, which means an individual has to pay for the loss or damage out of his own pocket. I never had to exercise that threat

I discovered Marching Bands were very popular in the Derbyshire area, and I granted permission for one particular Club to practise on part of my Station, marching and counter marching. Each member of the band played an instrument, and the percussion section consisted of a Big Base Drum, 2 Kettle Drums, Cymbals, and a Triangle. They practised three times a week for two hours to the same tune, but as time went by, it was obvious that progress was thankfully being made.

As RAF Alveston was on the outskirts of the town of Derby, we had two large Barrage Balloon Hangars on the Station. One of these had been commandeered to keep Stores Equipment, and the other had been turned into a Badminton Court, and for that it was ideal. It had the necessary length and width, but above all, it had the height. There was a Badminton Club on the Station, and the standard was good.

Each Mess had the usual indoor games; Billiards, Table Tennis etc, but we also had a 25 yard Indoor Rifle Range. All of these activities were well supported, and the last chap they wanted to poke his nose in was me!! And so, I left them to it, and before Kay and Stuart arrived, I was back to my bachelor days living in the Mess, which I found most comfortable.

I had no chores to do, no washing nappies etc, and with a Mess Manager and several Batmen to do my bidding, no wife could compete! But, it wasn't to last. On my nightly telephone calls to Kay I discovered that although she loved our married quarter at Thorney Island, she had to leave because Stuart was fretting for me. That was it! If Stuart wants it, Stuart has it. That's how it was, and that's how it has been all of his life!

I moved them both into a local Pub until I could get them into the Navigation Hotel in Derby. There they stayed until I could arrange Hiring Accommodation in a very pleasant house in a small village just outside Derby, and so we became a family again

This was new country to explore, and Kay took Stuart out for long walks every day, and as ever, she was fully employed. I used to commute to work. I loved what I was doing, and the days just flew by. Kay was happy because Stuart was happy, and every night on my return from work I got a wonderful welcome, especially from Stuart who immediately demanded a 'Tojo'.

During one of my weekly inspections of the Station I noticed the Clerk of Works had purloined one of my hard standings, and was using it as a rubbish tip, but on closer inspection, I found some valuable metal, copper, lead, and an old aircraft engine, but I decided it was an eyesore and it had to go.

I tackled the Clerk of Works, but he said he had nowhere else to dump his builders' waste, and it was impossible for him to move it. I said, "OK – if you can't move it, I will!".

"If you think you can move it, Sir," he said, "go ahead!".

I immediately got in touch with the local scrap metal merchant who, upon inspection, said he would not only clear the hard standing completely of all of the rubbish, but that he would give me £50.00 for the scrap metal within the rubbish. Within a week, the hard standing was cleared, and I was able to start a CO's Benevolent Fund with a deposit of £50.00.

Alveston was a hutted camp, and just inside the main gate, opposite the Guard Room, was a large wooden building which was not being used because it was not weather proof, and the Service Policemen who were in charge of the Guard Room complained it was being used surreptitiously by airmen with the local lady of their choice! In cases such as this it is better for an officer not to know, but when untoward occurrences are brought to his attention, he must do something about it.

On approaching the Clerk of Works, I discovered it was an uneconomical proposition to repair the building, and that he had been relieved of that responsibility, and that it had been dedicated to an encroachment.

"Right" I said, "In that case, I want it removed".

As it was an encroachment, I was told, it was out of his hands, and I would have to see his boss at Group Headquarters. I made an appointment for the Group Engineer to visit Alveston, but he only confirmed what my Clerk of Works had told me, and that he was not prepared to waste public money in removing the encroachment.

"In that case" I said, "Have you any objection if I get it removed?"

"Wing Commander Gibson", he said, "If you think you can get the encroachment removed, you have my Blessing to do so!".

"Can I have that in writing?"

"You don't need it in writing; the encroachment is of no value," was the reply.

During lunch with the Engineer, he told me I would be doing him a favour if I could achieve my aim. I couldn't wait to contact my scrap metal merchant.

When I told him I had a large, portable office building to dispose of, he said he would have a look at it. At the inspection that followed, I told my buyer I wanted the building taken away, and the concrete slab left clean and tidy. I was not very hopeful as I watched my man make a detailed inspection of the building, and my heart sank when he said, "It's not worth much". At that moment I did not expect anything, but I said, "How much will you give me for it?" He said, "My best offer is £250.00" I grabbed his hand and said, "Done!"

Within 72 hours, I had a clean concrete slab, and £250.00 in greenbacks in my hand, which I gave to my accountant to put in the CO's Benevolent Fund. I couldn't stop laughing, but a Station Commander walking round smiling is news, and this quickly filtered back to Group Headquarters in York

Within a few days the Group Accountant Officer was speaking to me on the telephone saying that he intended to pay a liaison visit to my Accountant Officer, and could I find the time to see him to have a chat. I agreed to meet him informally in the Mess at noon for refreshments, and then on to Luncheon.

Apparently he had been at Group HQ for sometime, and knew my Station well, and over lunch he congratulated me on having cleaned up the entrance, and asked me what had happened to the building that I had cleared away. When I told him that I had sold it for £250.00, he came back at me, quick as a flash, and asked, "What have you done with the money?" I told him it was in the CO's Benevolent Fund. His reply was, "But you didn't use to have a Benevolent Fund?" "Yes, I know", I said, "but we have now". "Bloody marvellous", he said. But that really did confirm to me the real reason for his visit; however I was quite happy when my Accountant Officer informed me that our CO's Benevolent Fund was now official, having been audited by the Group Accountant Officer.

This account came in very handy because my Warrant Officer, in charge of the Guard Room, came to see me to explain he had an airman posted on compassionate grounds on to his staff so that the airman could be near his family address to save the break up of the airman's marriage. I got the local Branch of the Sailors, Soldiers and Air force Families Association to investigate the case, and they convinced me it was genuine, and so my Benevolent Fund was able to put to the use for which it was intended.

After a while, my married quarters became available, and we took up residence. This was next door to one of my Flight Lieutenants, a John Meredith, who had a most attractive wife and four daughters. The youngest one, Barbara, was just a little older than Stuart, and at that age he did not have anything against girls, and so they became immediate friends, and would spend all day together.

As Alveston was a hutted camp, there were wooden receptacles full of sand dotted around. One day, on approaching the Officers' Mess at lunchtime, I noticed one of the sandpits was half empty, and the sand was strewn all across the road. That was quickly put right by a couple of batmen with shovels, and I thought that was the end of the matter.

A couple of days later, I had cause to go to the Mess at coffee break time, and as I approached, I saw Stuart and his four girl friends in one of the sandpits, throwing sand all over the roadway.

"Stop that", I shouted, and suddenly ten little legs were running towards my married quarter. I noticed a batman in close proximity and who had witnessed the event laughing his head off, and I said to him, "Why didn't you stop those children emptying that bin?"

He replied, "Sir, I told them many times to stop, but they took no notice of me."

"Right", I said, "Get yourself a shovel and put that sand back, and I can assure you that won't happen again!"

I had a word with John about what his girls and Stuart had been up to, and he said he would speak to his tribe, and I said I would deal with Stuart. However, we did have to laugh at how they had ignored an airman when he told them to stop, but they were off like a shot when I spoke to them, and that was the end of that little escapade.

On Saturday mornings while Kay was preparing our lunch, I used to take Stuart for a ride out into the country. However, one Saturday, Stuart and the Meredith girls were playing with some other children on the patch, and after getting permission from their parents, I ended up with thirteen children in my car, and off we went.

I was quite amused at the game they were playing, counting lamp posts or something, and when we went under Electric Power Cables, Stuart used to squeal, claiming he could feel a tingle from the Power Cables – much to the amusement of the other kids.

We had not been going long when I found I was driving down the High Street of Ashby De La Zouch. At that point, Stuart espied Woolworths and immediately said, "Ice Cream".

In 1954, there was not much traffic and no yellow lines, and so I did a quick 'U' turn and parked outside Woolworths. I locked the car doors to make sure I did not lose any of my charges, went inside the shop, and ordered 13 Ice Cream Cornets. While they were being prepared, I ordered 13 bottles of coke. The shop assistant was very apologetic, and said that they could only have the coke if they were consumed on the premises. I said, "You know that I've got 13 children out there?" The lady said, "If they stand in that corner, they can have their cornet and coke there." I was in battle dress uniform, and I was like Pied Piper shepherding 13 children into Woolworths to have refreshments.

It would not be possible to do that in this year of our Lord 2010, but we did it then, and the kids loved it!

On an RAF Station with married quarters where men and women live and work together in harmony, stories will always abound via the grape vine, most of which die a natural death. But there was one airman bully who was working in the Officers' Mess that I think is worthy of note.

He was huge, and he was making a nuisance of himself, and the rest of the airmen were dead scared of him. I knew if it came to my notice officially, I would have to do something about it. I used to pay frequent visits to all three Messes unannounced, mainly at meal times to check the menu and presentation of food.

One day as I entered the kitchen of the Officers' Mess, there was this bullying gentleman with his hands around another airman's neck, trying – and nearly succeeding – to separate his head from his body. There were several other airmen present, including a Corporal, and all were too scared to do anything about it. But, I knew what I had to do and said, "Corporal, put that man on a charge".

As soon as the bully heard my voice, he dropped his prey, and laughingly said to me, "I was only having a game". When this disgusting hulk of humanity stood before me in my office on a charge of Common Assault, I observed a very belligerent individual, ready to take on the world.

There was no shortage of witnesses who were quite happy to say their piece because the whole camp knew that I had witnessed the assault. And then it was my turn. I told the accused I did not intend to have, on my Station, any airmen of a quarrelsome nature, who adopted offensive attitudes to smaller or weaker airmen, and that all unprovoked aggression must cease forthwith. I continued that I found him guilty of the charge, and that the punishment I was about to award him gave him the right to elect trial by Courts-Marshal, after which, if found guilty, it could mean a spell in Aldershot's Glass House.

At that, he broke down completely, and in his helpless frustration, he burst into tears, crying like a baby, and said, "Please don't Court Marshal me; I'll take your punishment." I remanded the case for one hour to allow the accused to compose himself, but on his return, I awarded him the lesser punishment, which was confinement to camp.

He had already imposed on himself the greater punishment, the loss of his self esteem by breaking down in front of me and his contemporaries.

Within 24 hours, the whole camp knew what had happened. In fact, the rest of the airmen were no longer afraid of him, and, were making his life Hell to such an extent I had to have him posted to another Station where he could make a fresh start.

If I had actually hit him as a punishment, he probably would not have felt it, and he might have carried on as before. But he could not take words, and I shattered his self-esteem.

The famous words of Philip Sydney made many moons ago came to mind,

"Our greatest enemies are those who ruin the good opinion we have of ourselves."

At Alveston I made it a practice to always be in my office by 0800 hours. This particular day was no exception, other than the fact that my next-door neighbour, John Meredith, accompanied me on my walk from our married quarters to work.

That was a little unusual because John did not normally get to his office before 0900 hours, but I always have been an early riser. It is amazing how much work can be done before that horrible contraption, the telephone, starts ringing!

Just before 0900 hours I had a query that I wished to speak to John about, and so I dialled his number – but no answer. I redialled, but again – still no answer. I knew John was in his office, and so I put the phone down on my desk and walked along to his office. I opened the door, and there was John sitting there and the phone still ringing!

"John" I said, "have you given up answering the telephone?" He jumped up and said, "Was that you ringing Sir?"

He was full of apologies, but said he was so busy and had wanted to finish what he was doing before 0900 hours.

"That's OK John, what I wanted you for can wait, but I was

worried because I knew you were in your office, and I could not fathom out why my call to you was not answered!" I replied.

Then I noticed John's desk was covered with copies of the Sporting Life and racing handbooks, and John had been scribbling away, and I asked, "What's all this John?"

"Oh!! It's the big race meeting at Ascot today, Sir, and I'm trying to work out what to bet!"

"I didn't know you were in the gambling business John".

"It's a long story – I'll tell you about it in 5 minutes", he replied.

It was not long before John came to my office and told me that, before the war, he was the professional racing tipster of one of the top Racing Newspapers, and that now on big race days, to keep his hand in, he would invest to make a little petty cash.

He mentioned that he never bet on Handicap Races or 'over the sticks', as that was gambling. When he invested, if he had done his work properly, he won 90% of the time, but it was a painstaking business studying the Form, ground and weather conditions; who was the trainer, and was his horse going to try to win, etc.

"John", I said, "I know nothing of the Sport of Kings. I thought the only people who made money out of racing were the bookies!"

And we left it at that!

Rolls Royce of Derby had their own Air Training Corps, and by a long-standing mutual agreement, they always used our Parade Ground for drill practise, and annually, the Chairman of Rolls Royce, Lord Hives, gave a prize for the Cadet of the Year.

He was a wonderful Chairman; he had started off as an apprentice in the factory, and graduated through every department, ultimately reaching head of the Board Room. There were times, the story goes, when he would don overalls and go into the workshops and demonstrate to an apprentice the correct way to do a certain task, without the lad knowing who it was that had helped him.

On the evening before the Cadet of the Year Parade, we had a Cocktail Party which Lord Hives attended with Lady Hives.

He arrived in a Chauffeur driven Rolls Royce with a Footman in attendance, and the colour of the car was a very deep plum – almost black.

On the day of the Parade, which was the next day, he arrived with the same staff, but in a Bentley, but once again the colour was the same deep plum. I mentioned this to Lord Hives at drinks after the Parade when I asked, "Why the same colour?"

"Gibson", he said, "Each car has 30 coats of paint, and deep plum is the longest serving colour we use; with luck, it will last the life of the car"

As Alveston was a hutted camp, it needed quite a lot of maintenance, but being in close proximity to the Rolls Royce factory, artisan workers – painters, plumbers, electricians etc – were very hard to find, and the Clerk of Works was permitted to negotiate contracts plus 200% over the national standard rate. I thought this was exorbitant, and it gave me much to think about!

One day, my Adjutant told me there was an Irish navvy in his office, wanting to see me. I asked, "What about?"

"It's something to do with laying a gas pipe through your Station, Sir"

"Oh, is it?", I said. "Wheel him in and let's see what he has to say."

The Irish navvy who stood before me took me back to my Aldergrove days. He was courteous to the extent of being obsequious towards me for granting him permission to see me so that he could submit his plan to come through my camp to lay his Gas Main. If he had been an Englishman, I would have told him to cut out the 'bullshit', and get down to business, but the natural Irish charm and blarney came through to the extent that one never knew whether it was genuine, or if one's leg was being pulled!

However, the gist of his conversation was that he was laying a gas main from Leicester to Derby, and that within a fortnight he would be ready to come though my Station on his way to Derby. He produced maps showing where he had come from, and a complete layout of my camp, showing where he intended to lay his pipe.

362

On closer examination I noticed that his pipe was going within six inches of the office in which we were talking. When I pointed this out to my new found 'brother' (his description, not mine!), he said, "That doesn't matter; this building will be coming down!"

"Thank you very much," I said, "Please wait while I check what you have said".

"On St. Patrick's honour, why would I tell a lie?" He said.

"It's not a case of that, I just have to get my facts right" I told him.

I rang for my Adjutant, and told him to join us and to look after our guest while I made some calls. It was while I was 'phoning my Clerk of Works that three coffees arrived, and so I knew my Adjutant was doing his stuff, but – alas – my Clerk of Works thought I was playing games! And so, my next call was to his Superior at Group Headquarters, but he too was in complete ignorance.

I stressed the urgency, and that I had the Head Navvy in my office waiting for a decision, and that his group of Navvies hoped to start coming through my Station in fourteen days time, and that time was of the essence, and could he please help me.

I was told that he could not promise anything, but he would do his best.

The next two hours just flew past whilst I listened, enthralled, at the exploits and experiences of my Irish friend. The Gas Pipe he was laying was three feet in diameter, and had to be ten feet underground. He had started in Leicester, 26 miles away, and had only another 4 miles to go to Derby. That the line he was taking was that of the proposed new arterial road, and that my camp was to be abolished. He had had his problems digging ten feet holes down main, metalled roads, but nothing he could not handle.

He had experienced greater difficulties digging a main through water logged ground, or building an electrical pylon up a mountain, but it was all in a day's work!

His next job, after reaching Derby, was to be in Cumbria where he would have to form a new gang because some of his present gang did not fancy a winter up north, but because his work was of a transient nature, and his gang had to live in caravans, the wages were very attractive. Hence, he was able to pick and choose whom he employed.

During the six months I had served in Ireland, I came to love the Irish and my new acquaintance was one of the most loveable kind – I could have listened to him forever.

However, someone had 'pulled their finger out', and suddenly I had a call from the Air Ministry telling me that I would shortly be receiving a signal giving me permission to allow the Pipe laying gentleman to start work.

Sure enough, when I received the final details in writing, the plan showing where the gas pipe was going was similar to that shown me by the Irishman, with the added details showing the new arterial road that was to be built where my SHQ was.

I therefore knew my Station was doomed.

The next day, caravans started to arrive, and were driven to the area I had allocated to them, and which was in close proximity to water and electricity supplies. And it only remained for me to issue instructions in case of fire, for which I was thanked, but the Irishman told me that his gang had lived in caravans for years, and had never had a fire, and that in three month's time they hoped to be finished in Derby, for which they would be paid a bonus, and so they would not waste time going through my camp.

In no time, my entire perimeter fence was taken down, and earth-moving equipment started to arrive, and the digging commenced.

Each section fitted in to each other, and was about 20 feet long. Several sections were laid each day, and they all had to be sealed together by means of welding from inside and out. This was highly skilled and dangerous work. Each welded seal had to be checked for leakage by air pressure for a period of 24 hours, after which, if no leakage was detected, a £12.00 bonus was paid for each successful seal.

Also, when several sections had been sealed together, they had to be checked for alignment. To do this, a light was placed at the beginning and end of each section to be checked, and a Theodolite was used to check the level.

Part of my camp, 10 feet down, was water logged, and the ground over 3 sections, each 60 feet long, had to be reopened, and these sections had to be concreted into position. To have to reopen such a large section of ground was, to me, heart breaking, but the Irishman thought nothing of it. It was a nuisance – yes – but it was all in a day's work. It wouldn't worry him if he had to dig up the whole bloody 27 miles back to Leicester, so long as he got paid!

Going past my office was a bit tricky because he had to disturb the foundations, but he overcame the problem, and there was no resulting subsidence.

The whole operation went smoothly, and apart from the noise and the knowledge that RAF Alveston was doomed, I had no worries.

Most of the gang were bachelors, and those few who were married had their wives with them, and they had led the nomadic life for years, and it suited them.

* * *

24

On the move - again........

In 1950, the princely sum of £31.00 per month was being deducted from my pay for Income Tax, which in those days was a lot of money.

After searching around I found another Station, which could accommodate the units on my Station. Therefore I wrote a paper suggesting that they be moved, and Alveston closed as planned. That was agreed upon; the move took place, and I was posted as Wing Commander Organisation at 61 Group Headquarters at RAF Kenley.

What annoyed me most was that the maintenance contracts for Alveston were still in existence, and the last job I saw being done was the painting of my office, which was never to be used again!

Kenley suited me fine because I had been warned that in 2 year's time, on my 43rd birthday, I was due for retirement unless I wished to transfer to some other Branch, such as Air Traffic Control, Equipment, or Mercantile Marine, but I decided if I were too old to fly, I would retire.

Kay and Stuart were getting quite used to these upheavals when they moved into married quarters near the aerodrome. On arrival at Kenley I presented myself to my new Air Vice Marshal, the Air Officer Commanding the Group, and at the end of the interview, I left with the supernumerary job of President of the Officers' Mess Committee.

I found in my new job I was responsible for 2,000 Hirings, which were all around London; 3 hospitals, the paper work for building 99 married quarters at Ruislip, and a disembarkation unit at Surrey Docks.

The authorisation of the Centrifuge Unit at RAE Farnborough,

366

which had cost £2,000,000 to build, had been completed by my predecessor, but when it came to me to get my AVM to approve a further £2,000,000 to furnish the building, I suggested that this project be handled by Air Ministry, which was approved.

I found I had some capable officers in my section, and so my first job was to check the Officers' Mess inventory, and bring the rules up to date. I also discovered that the Group was responsible for the organising requirements of 3 NATO Headquarters at Naples, Paris, and Oslo. I had been briefed that each year, the AOC paid an official visit to a few of his Stations, and it was my job to accompany him and write out his reports.

I looked up the records and produced a list of Stations that were due for one of his inspections, and sent the file to my boss, asking him to make the final choice. The file came back with the Stations to be inspected ticked, with a minute particularly stating he would like to inspect the unit at the West India Docks, and would I inform the Superintendent of the London Docks, and invite him to join us at The Prospect of Whitby Public House for luncheon.

I could not fathom why the AOC wanted to pay an official visit to a unit with only two Flight Lieutenants and 60 airmen. However, I made the arrangements and fixed a date convenient to the Superintendent, and went and saw my boss to tell him of the arrangements, and suggested he might like to talk to the Super before the official meeting.

That was done, and I informed The Prospect of Whitby the number of our Party, and that we would be arriving at 1300 hours precisely. I contacted the Superintendent's Personal Assistant (who was my opposite number), and it was over a telephone conversation with him I found out the true reason for our visit to the Docks.

When the day arrived the AOC's official car, gleaming and chauffeur driven by a Sergeant, with a Provost Sergeant as footman, and the official Flag flying, with the AOC and me in the back, we were due to arrive at the West India Docks by 1000 hours, and travelling from Kenley to London during the rush hour presented no problem because, on arriving at London Bridge with the traffic solid, as if by magic, a motor cyclist policeman arrived and, seeing our flag flying, he escorted us around all of the stationary traffic and into the clear, so that we arrived at our destination bang on time.

The 60 airmen were ready on Parade, awaiting the AOC to take the General Salute, after which he duly inspected them, and on to coffee, where a general discussion took place regarding the work of the unit. There were no sleeping quarters to inspect because everyone was billeted out, and so, because the inspection had finished early, we proceeded to walk to The Prospect of Whitby for lunch, arriving just before noon.

The Prospect of Whitby is an up market Pub of historical value, and it is said that everyone should visit at least once. In my case once is enough because I prefer five star hotels! But, be that as it may. I had told the Superintendent we would meet him at 1230 hours, and so we had some time to kill.

We were sitting by the Thames in brilliant sunshine with our aperitifs when, out of the blue, a huge motor launch arrived, and out stepped the Superintendent, complete with silk top hat and morning frock coat, and he was cordially welcomed by our Air Vice Marshal. I had been in touch with the Super's PA, and so I knew what his Boss's favourite drink was, enabling me to brief the Pub Manager, and also let him know that the Tab would rest with me, and to give the AOC and his party 'the treatment'.

With The Prospect of Whitby living up to its reputation, we had an excellent lunch, after which the Superintendent took over. We embarked on to his Launch, and we went down river to the Royal Group of Docks. Here we were shown huge warehouses stacked full of goods, waiting for their owners to collect.

The AOC was enjoying every moment of his warehouse tour until we came to one warehouse, full of cocooned machinery. We were told that each one of those machines would automate the dock work and would do away with 10 Dockers, and because of that, they had never been unpacked, and had been there for over three years, and that there was no sign that the union bosses were going to change their minds.

And so, the Union Bosses won their case, the machines stayed cocooned, and the work went to the Netherlands. Hooray for competent negotiators!

Following that we were escorted to the underground cellars. I had never seen such an amazing sight. There were literally miles of tunnels with huge barrels of Sherry and Spirits. Each barrel was about 6 feet long, and about 4 feet in diameter, and there were hordes of workers in attendance. The Superintendent knew his way around, and every now and then would stop, and the Wine Steward, with a long, glass pipette tube, would take a sample of the contents of the barrel from the centre of the cask, enough to fill 2 or 3 Schooner Sherry glasses for the Super's guests to taste.

My AOC was in his element. I tried one glass, and it was potent. The AOC and I were offered samples from several other casks, which my boss accepted, but I wasn't going to start that lark. One of us had to keep sober, and it had to be me because it was my job to write the report of our visit, but I knew immediately why my Boss wanted to visit his Disembarkation Unit at the docks because he was enthralled.

In between the Casks, hanging from the roof were years and years of cobwebs, and which I was told were disturbed as little as possible so as not to alter the atmosphere and general environment of the Casks' contents. When the owners of the contents of the casks wished to make a substantial withdrawal, it had to be in the presence of an official from Customs and Excise. The sampling session took up most of the afternoon, but we managed to leave before the exit rush hour out of London.

My AOC thoroughly enjoyed his visit because he could hold his drink, and laying back in his chauffeur driving limousine, he adopted a very contented attitude, and it was not long before he was fast asleep.

I had not been at Kenley long when a new Senior Administrator Officer was posted to our Group, and to my surprise and delight, it turned out to be my old friend from the Air Ministry, Group Captain

Andersen, with whom I had shared many happy memories. He was the only officer I ever met who had been in Fighter Command for the whole of World War II, first as a Fighter Pilot, then on to Group, and then Command Headquarters, but always with Fighters.

Fighter Command had an American fighter Aircraft, a Mustang, which was bigger than a Spitfire, and cost about £31,000, whereas a Spitfire cost only about £12,000.

Structural alterations were made to allow two pilots to fly the aeroplane in tandem. The conversion was made to enable General Eisenhower to be flown over France to note the progress of the second front. Group Captain Andersen was always the pilot.

One day, like all good fighter pilots, he was 'shooting a line' in the Mess, when one of the Party, a Flight Officer WAAF, said that she was 'not very impressed'. Andy challenged her to occupy the rear seat of the Mustang on a flight over France. That invitation was accepted, and the Fighter Sweep took place at a very low level, and far from scaring the Flight Officer, she said, "that was OK, when can we do it again?"

She ultimately became Andy's wife.

My Branch of Organisation at Kenley fell within the realms of the Senior Administrator Officer, Andy, and so we were always working closely together. Officers had to submit annually a Form 1369, which was a record of their service, with spaces for their Senior Officers to complete an assessment of the Officer's ability. These forms ultimately ended up in the Air Ministry's Personnel Department to assist them with the Officer's next posting.

It was my job to check those forms to ensure they had been completed correctly, before passing them on to Andy for the Group's assessment, prior to onward transmission to Command Headquarters etc.

On one occasion when I was examining one of those forms, which had been made out by a Wing Commander, I noticed he had completed many courses of instruction, including the Staff College Course, and in the results column, he had put 'Failed'. I telephoned the gentleman concerned, and told him that no one wanted to know the Courses that he had failed; that Section was purely for Courses that he had taken and PASSED, to assist Personnel for his next Posting.

I added that I would be sending him a replacement Form for him to fill out correctly. His reply astounded me because he said; "Don't bother Bruce, because I will fill it out in exactly the same way as I am too old to start telling lies." I tried to reason with him but I failed. As an Officer of integrity, he would not change his mind. I knew this officer quite well, and I knew that he had a Bachelor of Arts Degree, and so I took the form in to Andy, and explained the position.

He said, "OK Bruce, leave it to me".

I do not know what Andy said to this officer, but in the course of time, a new F1369 came in to my possession from that officer, sans Staff College Course entry, which I forwarded without comment.

It always amazed me during my career that I met many officers who had received a much better education than I, but when it came to common sense, I could solve problems that they did not even know how to start. They were dim!

All aviators in the RAF are members of the General Duties Branch, and are given flying pay, whether they fly or not, as sometimes aircrew other than pilots, find it difficult to get airborne when they are on a ground job. But not when pilots like Andy are around. They will always find some way of borrowing an aircraft to keep in flying practise. That suited me fine, because he always knew I was available when he wanted a navigator.

One evening we were returning to Kenley when fog started to form. We were in a Tiger Moth, with no navigational aids, and so we flew lower and lower in order to stay in contact with the ground, and with me map reading, we were able to make Kenley at roof top height and land straight in, without doing a circuit of the aerodrome, with no official complaint. If we had hit a church steeple or pranged the aircraft, they would have thrown the book at us, but because we made it, the only remarks we got were, "Good show"!

Our next AOC's visits were to the three NATO Headquarters.

We started off with Oslo, then Naples, and ended up with Paris. Our Party consisted of the AOC, our Group Captain in charge of Administration, a Squadron Leader Pilot, a Flight Lieutenant Navigator, and me. We spent one night and two days at each headquarters, and our job was mainly one of liaison, getting to meet the Officers who needed the help of our headquarters.

I cannot remember anything of note about Oslo, but we had a good time in Naples with its free and easy way of going on. I was most impressed with Pompeii and the wonderful propagation qualities of the volcanic gasses from when Mount Vesuvius erupted.

We finished up in Paris, with a guided tour by our Group Captain who knew Paris well as he had spent a two-year tour at Versailles. On our last night in Paris, we went off to the Moulin Rouge for dinner. Of course I had heard of the wonderful floorshow produced by that establishment, and I kept on saying, "Bring on the dancing girls". I was the only one on soft drinks, and completely sober.

We had a good meal, and I still persisted in "Bring on the Dancing Girls!" much to everybody's amusement. After which, I slowly opened my eyes, and woke up.

The restaurant was in semi darkness, and waiters and waitresses were clearing up, and I asked, "What time is it?" My good friend, the Group Captain, said, "Bruce, it's half past two in the morning; we have all been waiting for you to wake up – these people are waiting to close up shop!"

It was then I realised I had been asleep for nearly three hours. Someone, to shut me up about the Dancing Girls, had spiked my Coca Cola, and I had missed the floorshow completely. My friends, including the AOC, were highly amused at my look of astonishment, and so I kept my mouth shut. I was feeling very unsteady on my legs, and so I was helped back to our hotel, which sobered me up nicely, and by 0300 hours I was in bed where I literally passed out and slept like a newborn babe!

But I never did see the Dancing Girls!

We approximated one AOC's inspection per month during the Spring and Summer. My staff did most of the routine work of my branch, and quite often my signature was just required for letters, which left me time to do my supernumerary work.

On arrival at the larger stations of 61 Group, over 1500 airmen would be lined up in Wing Parade Formation, ready for the AOC to take the General Salute. Every Station we visited was in a magnificent state of preparedness. The Station Commanders never knew which section the AOC was going to inspect. It might be the Engineering Wing, or the Flying Wing, or even the Airmen's Sleeping Quarters, and so the whole Station had to be in tip top condition, and in this connection the AOC was never let down.

I was always pleasantly surprised at the high standard of Drill, especially after my stint at the Officers' Advanced Training School where I was always in charge of drill. If there is anything Senior Officers are not much good at, it is drill. The more intelligent the person, the worse they are at drill. Some suffered from a complete lack of co-ordination between arms and legs. Instead of stepping off with the left foot and swinging the right arm, they would step off with the left foot and left arm – something that ordinary people find very difficult to do. Fortunately, less than 1% of people are affected in this way! But, be that as it may, after the AOC's inspection we were normally in the Mess Anteroom by noon where we would have aperitifs, followed by an informal luncheon with the officers and their wives present.

On our return back to base, the AOC would discuss with me points of interest he had noted, which helped me considerably in writing his report. As we were returning from one inspection, the AOC told me he intended to go to Epsom to see the Derby, and would I make arrangements for a party of officers to join him. I immediately put a notice on the Mess Notice Board stating that a visit to the Derby was being planned, and would any interested officers append their names so that the necessary arrangements could be put in hand.

For the next 14 days, I looked at this notice daily, and not a soul had intimated their intention to attend. Then one day our AOC popped into the Mess: saw my notice, and immediately put his name on the list plus five guests. This entry acted like Magic! As soon as members of the Mess saw the AOC was going to the Derby, everybody wanted to go, and within 48 hours, I had 40 names, and I ultimately finished up with 72 names, which meant 2 coach loads.

I went into a huddle with my Mess Manager to decide what food to take for a picnic lunch. On the day, our Mess Chef had roast turkey and chicken, various cold meats, rolls and bread etc, in fact, a repast fit for a King. Fortnum and Mason could not have done better.

The Mess Manager was in charge with Batman Waiters to do his bidding, and to keep his eye on the bottles of Champagne, wine and other liquid refreshments. I hired picnic tables with large sunshades, all of which had to be delivered by separate transport.

When the actual day arrived, it was brilliant sunshine, and that was forecast for the rest of the day. I had to attend on my own, as Stuart was unwell, and Kay would not leave him under such circumstances. That suited me really, because when I am organising things, I like to supervise and be on hand should problems develop which need to be solved, and on this day I didn't want any pissy Batmen serving!

The coaches arrived early, and the Mess Manager seemed to have everything under control, when I suddenly realised I did not know which horses to bet on. And so, I rang my old friend John Meredith, the former professional tipster, and asked him what he was backing. "Nothing", he said, "That's OK for you John", I said, "but I can't go to the Derby and not back anything!" "Hold on a minute", he said, "and I'll go through the paper."

John gave me a horse to back in each of the six races.

He said, "Only have a small bet – no more than £20.00". "£20.00!!"

I said in astonishment, "That to me is a small fortune to waste!!"

He then added; if I won anything in the first five races, I was to put all my winnings on the horse he had tipped for the last race, because that was the best horse running at that meeting.

So, armed with John's tips, off we went.

We arrived at Epsom quite early, and were able to get a good position for our coaches on rising ground, with a good view of the course. Our Batmen had plenty of time to get the tables and chairs and everything set up, while we wandered around, enjoying the sideshows, before returning for a 'slap up' English Picnic Lunch, which everyone enjoyed.

We were not far from a string of Bookmakers, and it was a most thrilling and colourful spectacle, watching the Tic Tac men waving their arms about, not to mention some very beautiful ladies in lovely summer dresses.

It came to the time for the first race, and I went and placed a bet on the horse John had given me, but at the same time I backed a horse of my own choice, simply because I liked its name. John's horse won, and on my return to the party everyone could tell from my expression that I had backed the winner. When challenged by one of the ladies, I had to admit I had won, but I did not tell her the horse of my choice had lost.

In no time at all, everyone knew that I had won some money, and that I was the only member of our party to have done so. All of the ladies wanted to know what I was going to back in the second race.

I said, "It's no good asking me, because I don't know what I'm doing. It's just beginners luck, but I'm going to back it".

And I gave them the name of John's horse, and I told them I was going to back it each way.

Lo and behold, John's horse came in second. However, once again I had backed a horse of my own choosing, and lost, which taught me a lesson, because that was the last time I did that.

The joy and laughter of the ladies in our party after they collected their winnings made my day.......

The third race was the Derby, and although I tried to convince my friends that I really didn't know what I was doing, they said that to have backed the winners in the first two races was good enough for them – so what are we going to back in the Derby?!

I had no resistance left, and so I just gave them the name of John's horse.

Having placed our bets, and sitting in our elevated position, I was enthralled by the colourful, wonderful scene, and as the horses came around Tattenham Corner, they were all bunched together, but when they were about three furlongs from the finish, it was as if someone had put a squib up the backside of one of the horses, because, suddenly, it was ten lengths in front, and won the race in a canter! Of course, it was the horse that John had given me, and so once again, I had to go and collect my winnings.

It did not matter what I said after that. I just broadcast to our party what I was going to back in the fourth race, and then the fifth, and both horses won. When John had given me the names of the horses to back, he had said, 'If you win anything on the first five races, put all of your winnings on the horse in the last race. Because, it is the only horse worth backing at the meeting.' When the ladies came to ask me the name of the horse in the last race, I said, "To round off our afternoon, we ought to go home Rejoicing", which was the name of the horse John had given me.

Suffice to say, it won by a distance, but unfortunately I did not put all of my previous winnings on the horse, because I chickened out!

The AOC was delighted with the happiness of our party, and later he found out from his wife the reason. The next day I received a short note from the AOC, thanking me for organising such a happy party, finishing with the words, "Bruce, I did not know you were such a gambling man".

Perhaps I should have told my lady friends that the horses we were backing were John's choice, not mine, but this I failed to do, and so my AOC had got the wrong impression of me, but it was too late by then to do anything about it, so I let it rest..........

I was reading a newspaper one morning before starting work when I spotted an article where the IRA had broken into an armoury on one army camp, and stolen all of the weapons.

As soon as Group Captain Anderson, my immediate boss, arrived in his office, I showed him the article, and together we had a good laugh. After laughing and joking about the poor bloody infantry men with no arms to fight with I said,

"Come to think of it, the same thing could happen to any one of our armoury's – we wouldn't be laughing then would we Sir?"

"What do you mean Bruce?"

I said, "Give me a lorry and six men, and I could clean out any one of our armouries out in ten minutes, Sir".

"You bloody crook Bruce, I never thought you had it in you!"

"No Sir, I'm not a crook, but what the IRA did, I could do too, to any one of our armouries on our hutted Stations."

"OK" said Andy, "take your rogue hat off, and put on your Organisation hat, and tell me what you suggest."

"Well Sir, it's ten years since World War II ended, and our Stations do not need to have their Hutted Armouries stacked full or Ordnance, and so I suggest we bring all of the arms, and store them in our brick built Armoury here at Kenley, and I could make it burglar proof and properly guarded until such time Stations need to be armed again. In any case, I think that if that circumstance arose, we would have some previous warning, and so we would not be caught out by the IRA."

"Right – Gibby, put those thoughts in writing, and I will think about it."

The next day Andy said, "How's your Security Mind working?"

"I'm making progress," I said, "but I'm making arrangements to make a liaison visit to one of our Stations to study the problem on the spot."

"Leave that to me", said Andy, "And I'll come with you, and we can fly down in a Tiger Moth, and get some flying hours in."

In the presence of the Station Commander we were visiting, I demonstrated to Andy how, with a heavy lorry and a couple of railway sleepers, I could push over a wooden Armoury, and, with six men, I could strip it and be away with any ordnance of my choice within ten minutes.

"Let me have those suggestions in writing ASAP, and I'll take it from there"

Andy had previously briefed the Station Commander (who was his buddy) the reason for our visit, who then said, "Andy, if you have finished, please accompany me to the Mess for Luncheon."

In the company of two old Fighter boys, our liaison visit turned into a social occasion, which was thoroughly enjoyable.

Back at Kenley, Andy submitted my suggestions to our AOC and I was instructed to get estimates for making the Kenley Armoury burglarproof. Ultimately the work was put in hand, which took longer than expected because the system was so efficient that even with a low ground mist at dawn, the burglar alarm would go off, and all hell was let loose with the Guard Room at Action Stations until the Alarm signal was switched off.

After that problem had been put right, the real fun started!

My suggestion had been accepted that after duty hours at 1800 hours, the Kenley Armoury was to be locked, with a Corporal and two airmen inside, and they were to remain inside until they were relieved at 0800 hours the next morning. That on no account was the Armoury to be opened. If someone did try to gain admittance, they were to be challenged by a PASSWORD, which only myself together with the Corporal and two airmen inside the Armoury knew. That Password I would change daily. Anyone trying to gain admittance without the Password was to be refused.

The Station Commander published on Daily Routine Orders that, after duty hours, the Station Armoury was out of bounds until 0800 hours the following day, and I waited to test my organisation.

We had a Polish Flight Lieutenant Officer on the Station. He was an Administrative Officer, a bit staid, and generally difficult to get to know socially. Quite different from the Polish Officers I had taught gunnery to in the past who used to steal our girlfriends, and that with a very limited knowledge of the English Language! They were considered one of us and fitted in socially. This particular Polish Officer however always adopted a frigid attitude towards me as if I did not like him, which was not true – I just never even thought about him.

One day he was Station Duty Officer, and that evening I was having a tonic water at the bar, when he sidled up to me and said, "Sir, I've just been in your Armoury" "Don't be so bloody silly" I said, "You don't know the Password!" "You don't have to know the Password" was the reply. "What do you mean?" I said. "I went up to the Armoury, knocked on the door, and the Corporal said, 'Who's there?' and then I replied, 'the Station Duty Officer', and the Corporal opened the door and let me in."

I was nonplussed. I said, "I don't believe it!!! You're trying to get me going!!!" He said, "Sir, you know how to prove me wrong."

I grabbed my hat and went dashing down to the Armoury, and bashed on the door, and the Corporal said, "Who's there?" I replied, "I'm Wing Commander Org. - open the bloody door!"

The result? The Corporal opened the door and let me in!

I went bananas.

Didn't he understand that the Armoury, when once closed after duty hours, was not be opened to anybody unless they gave the Password, and the only people who knew the Password today was Myself, Himself, and his two airmen. So, why did he open the door to the Polish officer – and me – without challenging either of us for the Password?

He said, "I recognised the Station Duty Officer, and you, and so I thought it was OK to let you both in."

I said, "Well, you know now that it wasn't; don't you?!"

He replied, "Yes Sir, it won't happen again!"

The next day, the first thing I did was to relate to my boss, Andy, what had happened the previous night in the Armoury, and concluded by saying that I had torn the Corporal such a strip off that I thought he had got the message, and that it would not happen again.

That night, I was in the bar having a quiet drink with my Mess Manager, and who should come into the bar but Group Captain Anderson, who was living in married quarters. I jumped up and said, "Good Evening, Sir, may I buy you a drink?" "That's very kind of you Bruce, I'd like a half of Bitter."

It was so unusual for Andy to come into the Bar at night. I was saying how nice it was to see him. Andy seemed in a very light mood, and after a while, he said, "Bruce," (laughing all over his face) "I've just been in your Armoury." I said, "Sir, you're joking – you don't know the Password!"

Andy, still smiling, said, "you don't have to know the Password".

I'd heard that phrase the previous night from the Station Duty Officer, and I was immediately on my guard.

Andy continued, "I went to the Armoury – knocked on the door, and when challenged, I said to the Corporal, 'I'm Group Captain Anderson; I want to see if you're comfortable locked up in there.' And, the Corporal opened the door and let me in, but he won't do it again Bruce. I've spoken to him like a Dutch Uncle; he's got the message this time!"

Andy was a very sociable character, and we were joined by other officers in the Mess so that I was able to drift away, because I was in a quandary – what was I going to do? Tearing a strip off the man had not had the desired affect, but I had to go and see the Corporal and see what he had to say.

And so, I went along to the Armoury – knocked on the door, and the Corporal said, "Who's there?" I said, "It's me, Wing Commander Gibson."

If I had been a female I would have passed out, because the Corporal opened the door and let me in! I took him into the Armoury Office and sat him down, and sitting opposite him I said, "So you've done it again Corporal" "Done what, Sir?" "Oh, give me strength – you've let me in to the Armoury without asking me for a Password!"

The Corporal failed to get the point.

He said, "But I know you Sir, and I know you are responsible for this system, and you decide what the Password should be, and so I did not think it was necessary to ask you for it".

I said, "If Jesus Christ Himself wanted to come into the Armoury, if he did not now the Password, he should be refused permission to enter. Is that clear Corporal?"

"Oh, Gawd, sorry Sir!" was the answer.

As I left I said, "Don't let it happen again, Goodnight."

I went back to the Bar, and as I entered, there was Andy, thoroughly enjoying himself, and he said, "What's wrong Bruce, why are you looking so glum?"

I said, "Sir, I've just been in the Armoury, and I was let in without the Password, I don't know what to do!"

"Well, don't worry about it tonight; let me buy you a Coke; we'll sort it out in the morning".

We did sort it out in the morning, but it meant up-grading the importance of the duty, and instead of a Corporal and two airmen on a weekly roster, we had to have a Flight Sergeant and two airmen on a twenty-four hour roster. That solved the problem. The Flight Sergeant, when on night duty, would say PASSWORD to anyone trying to gain entry to the Armoury, and if that was not forthcoming, entry was politely refused.

The Group Captain was refused permission twice during the next week when he tried it on, and so it was agreed to bring all of the ordnance from our Stations into our Kenley Armoury, until such times as they might be needed in the future.

We discovered that Corporals lacked the experience and authority to demand from Senior personnel whether or not they knew the Password. I can laugh about it now, but at the time it was very worrying!

At Kenley, Stuart was growing up and so we decided to buy a dog so that he would get used to animals.

John Meredith's mother-in-law had a Great Dane which was too big for her, and so we bought that. Kay knew all about Great Danes from a previous friend who had one, and so Panda very quickly became one of the family. Panda was a bitch, and before Stuart could walk properly, she used to stand by the side of Stuart, and he would grab two handfuls of her skin, and pull himself up. Panda would walk one step, followed by Stuart, and so on. Panda taught Stuart how to walk!

Stuart and Panda became great pals, and there were times when Panda was so happy, she would wag her tail and knock Stuart over. The childish laughter, giggles and chuckles that followed were a joy to behold.

We decided to breed from Panda, and we did our homework and chose a champion pedigree Great Dane with which to mate her. In due course of time we prepared our coal shed at our Kenley married quarters to be the delivery room, and Yours Truly was chosen as the midwife.

We made the room quite warm and comfortable, and I sat up the whole of one night whilst Panda did the work, producing eight puppies.

Then the fun really started!

The aim with Great Danes pups is to get them to eat 3 lbs of meat and 1 pint of milk per day, as quickly as possible. Because they grew so quickly, they each had to have a daily ration of Casio Glycerine Phosphide to help their bone structure, and prevent Rickets.

At the end of 3 months, each puppy was eating its fair share of 3 lbs of meat and 1 pint of milk daily, and were becoming big dogs! Panda accidentally hurt one of her puppies which affected its brain, and the Vet advised us to have it put to sleep because it would not be safe to have a fully grown Great Dane with something wrong with it's brain.

However, Panda successfully reared the remaining 7 puppies, and at the end of 3 months, I was cutting up 21 lbs of meat daily, which took one and a half hours!

Then came the task of finding suitable homes for the puppies. People came and saw them and chose the one they wanted, and thought all they had to do was pay for it and go. But Kay had other ideas. Where did they come from? What sort of accommodation would they have for the puppy which would grow to the size of a small donkey? How would they exercise it? Had they any children? Did the children like animals? Was it a town or country abode? Did they know of a good Vet? Did they know how much it cost to keep a Great Dane? Did they know that Danes were very intelligent, loveable creatures who needed a lot of tender, loving care?

If the prospective owners got through the first two hours of that sort of interrogation, Kay would then stall and suggest they go home and think about it, and let her know in a week's time whether they still wanted to go ahead or not.

In the meantime, Kay would go to the address of the intending purchaser and study the area and the environment, and if it was not up to the standard required for her puppies, she would not let them go. In this way, only the genuine buyers who lived in suitable accommodation were allowed to have one of our puppies. However, it didn't finish there because several weeks later Kay would find some excuse to be in the area of one of her puppies (because, you see, they were her responsibility), and she would call and ask to see the puppy to see if it was happy, and were the new owners content with their purchase.

One visit Kay used to make on a regular basis was to visit a couple who bought a puppy and who lived at Wraysbury, and which sometimes got flooded when the River Thames overflowed. But all was well, because those people had a boat, and would evacuate to another property they owned on dry land.

The new owners remarked to Kay, when the water was rising and preparations were being made to move, the first one in the boat was the Great Dane. "Quite right too" remarked Kay, because cats and dogs are more important than people; you never have to question their love or loyalty.

When it came to my time to retire from the RAF, we still had Panda and four puppies. One of the puppies Kay had got really attached to, and that one she could not bring herself to sell, and so we finished up with Panda and one of her daughters, Brenda.

During the war, Kenley was one of the main Stations which housed fighter aircraft, Spitfires and Hurricanes, and was bombed heavily to stop the aeroplanes from operating. Quite a lot of damage was done, and replacement buildings in the form of Nissen Huts were built, and the war carried on from there.

Those Nissen Huts were semi circular in design, made of corrugated iron, and were built as temporary living accommodation, but after the war fell into disuse. One of those Nissen Huts was commandeered by a Squatter who moved in with his family. It was on the perimeter of the Station, and in close proximity with the main road. That fact was communicated to Command Headquarters who could not be bothered with evicting our squatter by the legal process, and so it was agreed to charge our trespasser rent.

That was no problem to our Squatter, but he demanded a rent book, which was duly given him and his weekly rent recorded.

That became my problem, because our occupier was no longer a Squatter that we could have evicted, but a legal Tenant with a rent book to prove it. He had not only paid his rent, but he had maintained the building, and had the best kept grounds and garden on the Station. If we had not been so clever as to charge our Squatter rent, we could have had him evicted. But, we had boobed, and he remained our tenant, and there was nothing I could do about it, which one might call HARD LUCK!!

We had a Pilot Officer in the Mess who was very good at making model aircraft. One he made was very special. It was a Glider with a 6-foot wingspan. One beautiful summer evening, with lots of thermal up currents, he came to the perimeter of the aerodrome with his model aircraft. I was out walking the dogs, and I had the opportunity to examine the workmanship of the model with all of its surfaces functioning properly.

Standing dead into the wind, he launched his super model Glider, and it just climbed, dead into wind, at about 50 feet a minute, until it reached over 1,000 feet, and still climbing, it disappeared over the far boundary of the aerodrome, and he never did see it again.

As a result, he learnt two quick lessons. One, that he was capable of making a perfectly balanced aircraft which would fly; and two, the perfect weather conditions for a glider, and when not to launch such a model if one wants to see it again!

In 1955, Stuart was coming up to 4 years of age, and it was Kay's intention to have him in bed each night at 1800 hours, but Stuart was having such a wonderful time with his toys and Panda, he had other ideas. Push and Go toy buses were at the time very popular, and Stuart had 86 of them. Not all of them worked, and those which had broken down were parked in the maintenance section of the garage, while those which were serviceable were spread out all over the floor of the playroom, and it was my job each night to park them in the garage to make it all 'ship shape and Bristol fashion' to meet his mother's demands of tidiness.

When it was bedtime, a certain amount of difficulty arose in trying to get Stuart's pyjamas on. Initially we solved that problem by me giving him a 'Tojo', and singing 'Over the mountains etc' until I felt his head fall on top of my head, when I knew he was asleep, and I had a knack swinging him round so that he finished up in my arms, but still fast asleep, when I was able to put him in his cot.

Another ruse we had was taking him out for a ride in the Wolseley at bedtime to the bus station at Purley, which was not far from Kenley. As the buses came into the Garage after a day's work, they all went through a Shower and were washed clean.

That to a four-year-old boy was truly magic, and we used to sit in the car, just outside the garage door, watching the buses be showered until he started to feel tired, and Kay and I could then put him to bed.

* * *

25

And on to pastures news...............

Because I was approaching the ripe old age of 43, I was considered too old to continue flying in the RAF as a Navigator and, unless I chose to re-muster as an Accountant, Equipment Officer, Air Traffic Control or even Mercantile Marine Branch, I would have to retire on my 43rd birthday.

For many years I had made a lot of money for Officers' Messes, and so I decided to retire, and try and make some for myself.

Group Captain Andersen, my boss, knew I had delegated most of my work, and so he was most kind to me. For the last six months, I was able to take whatever time it took to get myself organised for civilian life. The last formal function I put on at Kenley was the 1956 New Year's Eve Ball. The very last function of all was my own farewell Guest Night, which the AOC did me the honour of attending.

For weeks I had been studying Dalton's Weekly with a view to buying a business. Because of my love of dancing at which, with Kay's help, I had acquired a basic knowledge, I started to look seriously at Ballrooms. I thought with a Ballroom I could run a show like my friend, Albert White, in Belfast; or I could run dinner dances, Masonic Ladies Nights, or Rotarian meetings, but Kay had other ideas.

Every place we looked at, Kay had 20 reasons why it should not be bought. I ultimately found out the real reason – she did not like the dancing people! She did not mind dancing with Wally Fryer, the World Champion, at the Imperial Society's Annual Tea Dance, but she didn't want to talk to him, or to most of the other professionals. The actual number of top dancers she really liked, you could count on one hand. So that put the kibosh on my Ballrooms!

Next, my mother told me that lease of the Restaurant at Seven Ways, Ilford, which was owned and run by Ilford Borough Council, was coming on to the market and was open for bids. Brother Cyril was an Alderman on the Council, and I asked his advice about what was a reasonable rent to offer to secure a lease, and Brother Cyril, looking down his nose at me in his most sanctimonious voice, said, "Don't ask me to get involved in your nefarious business deals". So, I told him, "Get stuffed!"

By now I had wasted a lot of time looking for something I could be interested in. During my advertising days at Chivers I had found out quite a lot about the newspaper business, and so back I went to Dalton's Weekly. In that publication every week, there were literally 100's of Newsagents, Confectioners and Tobacconists for sale. Kay's first remark was, "If you think it's such a good idea, why are there so many shops for sale?"

A good question, but I knew the answer.

Having been a paperboy for nearly 9 years, I knew it was the hours, from early morning until late at night and for seven days a week – that's what made the owners want to sell. But, I was looking for a large shop with a manager to run it, and they were not so easy to find.

My local newsagent had a large business, and so I spoke to him, and told him what I was thinking of doing. He was most interested and volunteered to help me find a shop. I contacted many Business Transfer Agents who sent me details of shops they had for sale.

The location of the shop was most important, but the preliminary details would only state 'On the Surrey/Hants border', or, 'in Kent, near the sea'.

Such locations were far too nebulous, but the final address would only be given after the Agent had made an appointment for the prospective purchaser to view the business.

I discussed details of various shops with my newsagent friend, and we spent many hours over the pros and cons, keeping an open mind as to which one we would inspect. I had met a policeman friend of Fred's from Shooters Hill Police Station, who had gone back to his old job, which was as a Legal Executive to a firm of solicitors, and I was able to get valuable advice from that quarter.

One of the first shops I looked at was in Ramsgate. It was a very smart shop with a black, marble shop front, and well fitted out inside. Before the owner would let me see the accounts, he insisted on a 10% deposit to show good faith. My legal friend had warned me about paying deposits, telling me never to give a deposit without stating the magic words, 'Subject to Contract'. Apparently if one does not do that, and then does not complete the purchase, it is not always easy to get the deposit back. I thought, 'RIGHT, MONKEY!', and so I got Stan, my legal expert, to pay the deposit for me, and he paid it to the Vendor's solicitor so that there would be no trouble.

One day, as I was on my way to Ramsgate to investigate the area, I popped into Manston aerodrome and went to the meteorological section. I was in uniform, and I told the Met. Man what I planned to do, and he shook me to the tits by just uttering one word, 'SNOW!!!'. He said if the UK gets snow, 95% of the time Kent gets if first and is cut off. Hence – roads blocked, no newspaper supplies. That was good enough for me, and so that was the end of Ramsgate.

The newsagent, knowing I was a dim Wing Commander, tried to make me go ahead, but I just left it to Stan, and he got my deposit back. Some of the shops were in dreadful areas that I knew Kay would not consider bringing Stuart up in, let alone the Great Danes, and I became quite an expert at making my escapes.

I became very interested in a shop that came up for sale in Maidenhead. It was a good business in the High Street, with living accommodation above the shop occupied by a competent manager and his wife. I paid many visits to Maidenhead and the surrounding area, and Kay agreed that we would be very happy to live in Medmenham, which was close by.

I was just about to pay a deposit (subject to contract), when the manager told me that after the business was sold, he and his wife would be leaving to buy their own business.

That set me thinking.

Why was he trying to sell the Maidenhead business for his owner and not buy it himself?

Firstly, he said, the business was too big for him which he could not afford; and secondly, many of the customers were celebrities who only settled their newspaper account every six months; and thirdly, a newspaper shop should be at the centre of all its customers. At the Maidenhead shop however, they were all in one direction.

Therefore, I reluctantly let the Maidenhead shop go because of the determination of the manager and his wife to leave. I then found the perfect Newsagents business in the City of London. It had a monopoly position, and, it was serving all of the large businesses in the area. The Bank of England, for example, was having 24 copies of The Times, 18 copies of the Financial Times, 18 copies of the Daily Telegraph, and 6 copies of each of the other National dailies, Monday through til Saturday. Many of the other large companies in the area had multiples of papers delivered, and although they took extended credit, they were a more reliable business risk than serving some celebrity who might do a moonlight flit.

But, there was a snag.

The owner had made his money out of the business, and had retired to Jersey in the Channel Islands, and he wanted to sell because he thought his manager was fiddling him. It was to be a cash sale, and the business would go to the highest bidder by a certain date.

The Business Transfer Agent was keen to sell, but he had failed so far because it was not the usual type of Newsagents, and the closing date was getting near. The accounts were available, and I paid several visits examining them and getting friendly with one of the Agent's lady assistants who told me, 24 hours before the closing date for the bids, that there had been no offers. Therefore I took the bull by the horns, and delivered to the Agency, by hand, a sealed bid for £5,000.00 – which in 1956 was a lot of money.

I did not get the business however as the Agent cheated on me. They were the sole purveyors of the business, and when they saw the ridiculously low figure I was going to get the business for, they got a nominee to put in a bid £50.00 higher than my bid, and did me out of it.

I found out 6 month's later that they sold the business for an enhanced profit. But, I had learnt a valuable lesson. Business Transfer Agents in the 1950's were a dodgy lot, and if one puts in a bid - £50.00 over a rounded sum can win. So that was one agent I refused to do any more business with, but I carried on looking to find a business in an area where we could bring Stuart up in the way we had planned.

One day however, in the post came the details of a business from Lincoln Business Transfer Agency which, albeit the best of a bad lot, did sound good. And so, I took it to Joe, my local newsagent, and he agreed it was worth a visit.

I contacted the Lincoln Agency, who gave me the address so that I could visit the area before making a formal appointment to view the business. The next weekend, during the winter of 1955, we found ourselves sitting in our car outside a shop in Cove, Hampshire, and feeling very glum. The weather was miserable. It had been raining, but it was still overcast, dank, damp, in fact not the best time to view an area. There were not many people about, and those who were had nothing to look happy about, and Kay and I had to agree – which is not often – we had chosen the wrong day to visit. It was mid-morning on a Sunday, and the shop was closed.

It was described as a village shop, but it was not my idea of a village as it was continuous with Farnborough, and it was difficult to tell where Farnborough finished and Cove began. The shop itself looked OK. It was the middle one of three, with a butcher's on one side, and a General Grocery on the other, and all were shut. Farnborough Aerodrome I knew quite well because I had handled the paperwork as Wing Commander Organisation at Kenley for the building of the Centrifuge for the RAF Medical Offices to test weightlessness of Astronauts, and I had visited that establishment many times when the sun was shining.

I reported back to the Agents our first thoughts about the area, but they convinced me the business was what I was looking for, and that I should investigate further. An appointment was made to view the business, and Joe agreed to go with me, to hold my hand when meeting the owner of the business for the first time.

Joe and I arrived at 67 Cove Road, Farnborough, Hants, on a nice sunny afternoon, with all of the shops open. And plenty of people about. So that was a good start.

The owner of the shop was a Bill Munday, and I gave him the impression that Joe was going to be my manager of any business that I bought on my retirement, and so Joe got stuck in, asking the right sort of questions. It was not the usual type of newsagents shop because it was big enough to have its own direct supplies from the newspapers' owners, and these were delivered daily to Farnborough Railway Station, and were then picked up by Bill at 4.00 am. every morning, and taken back to the shop before setting up 15 newspaper rounds.

That impressed Joe completely, and so long as I was prepared to do the work, it was a good buy.

Stan Gibbons, Fred's old policemen friend, agreed to handle the legal transaction for me, and so I sent him a cheque to forward on to Bill Munday's Agent as the deposit, subject to contract. That then entitled me to have copies of 3 years' tax accounts, which I sent on to my Accountant to verify the figures produced by Bill. I also sent copies to my Bank Manager with whom I had banked for 15 years, who agreed it was an excellent business, but did I know how much work I was taking on? "Yes", I told him, "I am buying a 21 year renewable lease". To be honest, the freehold was available for £6,000 but I could not afford that at the time. Kay's parents knew what I was planning to do, and Kay's dad thought I was making a big mistake buying leasehold. Leaseholds were out – Freeholds were in.

It was getting near the date for my retirement, and although the legal process for the purchase of the shop at Cove had been going on for months, there was no sign of a completion date, and there was no chance of my moving from RAF married quarters straight into the living accommodation above the shop. The rules were for married officers to vacate their married quarters on the day of their retirement, and as Wing Commander Organisation, I had applied them most strictly – so, what was good the Goose was good for the Gander, and so I had to vacate my married quarters. But, where was I to go with a wife, son, and 4 Great Danes?

Fortunately the Station Commander of Kenley was a friend of mine, and he gave me permission to park a caravan on the perimeter of the aerodrome. Therefore, I bought a Berkeley Governor General Caravan, which was 36 feet long, could sleep six, and had all mod cons such as shower etc. That was ideal for the dogs because they had the whole of the aerodrome to exercise in, and Stuart was quite happy, and so everything was OK.

The transfer of the Cove Road shop was due to the thoroughness of my legal man Stan. In doing his searches, he discovered there was a road-widening scheme in the offing, and because that could reduce the shop's 17-foot forecourt, that to Stan was a major snag, and he asked me to give the matter serious thought as to whether I should proceed.

RAF Officers, as far as the business world is concerned, lead a charmed life, sheltered from any business worries, and so I had to take Stan's advice and investigate the hiccup. I went to the Planning Division at Farnborough Town Offices, and discovered the road widening scheme which was worrying Stan had been muted in 1932, and as it was then 1956, I chose to ignore the objection, and gave Stan written instructions to settle forthwith. But Stan wasn't finished even then; because the 21-year lease I was buying (which was renewable) was a fully insuring and repairing lease which included the roof and outside brickwork, and Stan thought was asking too much.

The freehold was owned by Bill Munday's father, and at the final meeting when contracts were to be exchanged; Stan raised that point and said he wasn't happy. Now, those negotiations had been going on for six months, and the frustration got to Bill's father who exploded, and said, "I had that shop built, and I know how well it has been constructed, so that clause can be struck out!"

After the clause had been deleted, Stan was happy. Contracts were exchanged, and a date agreed for me to take over. Part of the final agreement was that Bill Munday would stay with me for one month to ensure a smooth transfer.

While I had been concentrating on buying Bill Munday's shop, Kay had been busy disposing of the remainder of the Great Dane pups, so that when the time came for us to move, we only had Panda and one of her puppies left, which we decided to keep.

We had very little furniture of our own, as we had always lived in fully furnished accommodation, and so our move to 67 Cove Road went without a hitch, and we settled in above the shop quite quickly.

We had looked at many businesses, paying particular attention to the living accommodation, and in this respect we were lucky because Cove Road was excellent. It was centrally heated from a boiler in the downstairs kitchen, and at the age of 4, was the 17th place that Stuart had lived in. After we had lived at Cove for six months, Stuart said, "When are we going to move?" He thought everybody moved every six months!

My first day at work at my new venture started at 4.00 am when the newspapers had to be collected at Farnborough Railway Station. We had a 10 cwt van to do this, which we completely filled, and then came the chore of collating 20 newspaper rounds. This was done by Bill, his wife Margaret, and 3 part-time men who did this job for 'pin money', before they went to their full time jobs.

Every round was annotated in a book of its own, but Bill and Margaret knew the rounds off by heart, and only had to refer to them when adding periodicals or magazines to the papers. Bill was quick, but Margaret was quicker, and they both made it look easy. Margaret could get two rounds up together while a part time worker managed just one. The periodicals used to be delivered the day before they were due to be delivered, and so they were already marked up and waiting to be inserted in the appropriate newspaper so that they were delivered together.

By 6.30 am the first of the paperboys started to arrive and as the Mundays knew who it might be, and so those rounds were always got up first so that the deliverer could get away pronto. The deadline was always considered to be 7.15 am. This meant if by then there were still any paper round, which hadn't been collected by the regular deliverers, alternative arrangements had to be made. There were always two or three boys who could be relied upon to do a second round because the aim was to have all deliveries made by 8.00 am.

To begin with I started to help Bill; after a while I started to get some rounds up on my own because I knew Bill and Margaret would be leaving at the end of the month, and then it would all be down to me. These rounds were collated behind a partition at the back of the shop which opened at 6.00 pm. A civil servant used to do that chore until 8.00 am, seven days a week, before going on to work at RAF Farnborough. He was relieved by regular Counter Staff who manned the shop until 7.00 pm, six days a week, because the Mundays closed at 10.00 am on Sundays.

After Margaret had got her rounds together, she left to prepare Bill some breakfast, and he remained in the shop to make sure all deliveries were complete. The Mundays were so well organised they made the work look easy. It was only after they had left and I was on my own that I discovered the difficulties I had to overcome.

After breakfast, Bill would spend the rest of the day with me so that I got to know 'the customer is always right', and how to deal with public generally, which was far more difficult than just giving orders to get things done in the RAF! The shop was so busy, time just flew by, and it was 7.00 pm and closing time before I realised it. The shop was not large; it had counters on three sides with a scale for weighing out confectionery, and one for tobacco and snuff. I had no trouble in remembering the price of everything because, in those days, I had a photographic memory, and Mr. Griffiths at Holbrook Road School had taught me numeracy, and so adding up together mentally the value of purchases and the giving of change was no trouble at all.

At my last appointment in the RAF it was my job to assess the damage done to married quarters or hirings, and any losses or damage had to be paid for by the vacating tenant. I was most meticulous when I retired that I left completely clean, and without even accidentally being in possession of a minor item, such as a pencil.

To my amazement, on my first day helping Bill Munday, he threw me a knife to cut a bundle of newspapers, and having cut them, I said, "Bill, where did you get that knife?" He said, "I did my National Service in the RAF as a Policeman, and when I left, I nicked it!" I said, "Well, stuff me!" And I told Bill the trouble I had gone to in order to leave the RAF clean. The knife that Bill had given me was an Air Sea rescue knife from a 'Q' type dinghy!

The representatives of the various suppliers called every five weeks, and Bill took great pleasure in introducing me as the new owner. Each firm took up my references, and the accounts were transferred to my name, although I still kept the name 'Mundays' on the Fascia Board, and continued to trade under that name.

I noticed while I was serving the public, Bill was marking up the magazines and periodicals to be delivered the next day, and I made a mental note that this was a chore I would have to do when Bill had left. Also, alterations to the rounds by cancellations or additions to the rounds that Bill did, and papers which had to be stopped for holiday periods was also his chore. And this was all very time consuming, and very difficult to get right. That was mainly due to lady customers giving ambiguous instructions. They said one thing, but meant another, but then it was ever thus!

It took me several weeks to solve that problem. I did it by getting a full scap ledger and dating each page. Then, dividing each page with a line down the middle. The left hand half of the page was marked OFF, and the right hand side, ON.

When customers wanted me to make a holiday cancellation, the way to get it right was to ask WHAT IS THE LAST DAY YOU WANT DELIVERIES?! And the entry was made on the dated page in the OFF column.

The next question was, WHAT IS THE FIRST DAY YOU WANT THE PAPERS BACK ON? That entry was made on that date page in the ON column. It solved the problem, but it was not always easy to extract dates from some lady customers. They would say, 'Friday', but they really meant 'Friday week'.

Because we received our supplies direct from all of the National Daily Newspapers, representatives would call to induce me to increase the daily supply of their particular paper. They were quite happy that I had bought Bill's business, but on being introduced to one of the Sunday newspapers reps, I was told that I could not buy the Sunday Newspaper Agency because it was vested in Bill Munday, and Bill could not sell it without the prior permission of the Sunday Circulation Managers.

What Bill should have done was to tell the Circulations Managers of his intention to sell and get their agreement, and he hadn't done that.

I was to learn later that because Bill used to shut up shop after he had got his papers away on Sundays, the Circulation Managers decided to teach him a lesson, and I lost the Sunday Agency, which meant I lost the wholesale profit from not having the Agency, and another wholesaler was given the job to deliver my papers on a Sunday instead of my having to collect them from Farnborough Railway Station.

When I told that to Stan, he was in his element, and he went to town, and ultimately got a reduction in the price that I had originally paid Bill Munday for his business.

After my first month was up, Bill left and became a Director of a local Wholesale Business, the owner of which was a friend of mine, and so I was able to keep in touch with Bill.

I took over my new venture at the beginning of July, and so by the beginning of August I was on my own. Fortunately, the school holidays had started, and I had no problem getting some of the senior boys to do a second or even third paper round, but when the holidays came to an end, I had to do any rounds that were left over – truly learning the hard way. My aim was to get every delivery made by 8.00 am, and sometimes I was left with 2, and sometimes 3 rounds to do, and this made it impossible to achieve my 8.00 am deadline.

And so, I started a recruitment drive.

That was very successful, and I recruited some girls, and ended up with 3 surplus deliverers, and if by 7.15 am there were rounds left to be delivered, I would take the surplus deliverers in my car and split the round up between us, and in a matter of minutes, the round would be done.

As a newsagent I found many human beings did not reach their best until 10.00 am. Before that, if they had the wrong paper delivered, the scene they created was out of all proportion to the sin committed!

The paper boys and girls quickly learnt their rounds off by heart, and although all papers were numbered, the deliverers sometimes did not look at the number, and so if one of their customers had gone on holiday, despite the fact they had been informed of that, if the deliverer persisted in leaving a paper at that holiday address, everybody got the wrong paper after that address. Of course, those errors had to be put right, but sometimes before that could happen the shop assistant had to show much tact and diplomacy in handling upset customers on the telephone.

Some difficult situations arose which were caused by naughty paperboys. In one case, a customer button holed me and accused my paperboy of damaging his rose bushes, and I agreed to investigate. Apparently the rose bushes were in a strip of garden in between two semi-detached houses, and my paperboy, instead of going round to the entrance to each house, was stepping over the rose bushes, and in so doing was damaging them. That particular boy was a very intelligent Grammar School boy, and when I spoke to him about damaging the rose bushes, he denied all knowledge of the fact, but nevertheless I told him not to step over the rose bushes, but to go round to the next entrance.

All seemed to go well for a few days, but once again, the same irate gentleman told me my paperboy was still damaging his rose bushes, and as a result he wanted to cancel his newspaper order. I accepted his cancellation, and apologised for the damage, and said I would have another word with my paperboy. That I did, and I told my boy that as the man had cancelled, I had rewritten the round so that instead of going down one side of the road and up the other, in future he would have to zig zag, and so now there was no need to go anywhere near the rose bushes.

A few days later, another male customer came to me and said that he was sorry, but he would have to cancel his newspaper order because my paperboy was damaging his new next-door neighbour's rose bushes. Once again I apologised, and said I thought I had solved the problem, but apparently not. But, I added I would investigate.

The next morning, having got all of the rounds away, I got in my car and drove round to investigate the rose bush problem. I got to the road concerned, and parked in close proximity to the rose address, and waited. Ere long, my paper boy hove into view and was zig zagging down the road, and when he got to the rose bush address, although he had no need to go anywhere near that particular house, he deliberately crossed over and jumped over the rose bushes.

I immediately got out of my car, and called to Kenneth; "Get in this car!"

My paperboy was astounded when he saw me, but then started to laugh. He laughed so much that I had to join in, but then I said to him, "Kenneth, why did you do it?" He said, "Just because the old sod cancelled his papers doesn't mean I can't jump over his roses." I said, "Kenneth, you are just starting your gap year and are going on to Cambridge – promise me you will not do that again?" He replied, "OK, Wing Commander, I give you my word".

And that was the end of that little episode.

But in my RAF days I never knew that things like that happened. Kenneth's elder brother John, who had also been one of my paperboys, got himself a job with Lloyds Bank as a cashier. One day, while I was paying in the day's takings, I asked him how he was getting on. He said, "This is an easy job – any time you want to knock the bank over, come to me. I'll give you all the money and we will go 50/50 afterwards." I said, "You make it sound a lot easier than delivering newspapers to 2,000 houses every day; I'll think about it". And that was the end of that!

The first thing I did after Bill left was to change the opening hours. I arranged for the shop to be opened at 6.00 am, and close at 7.00 pm, seven days a week. By doing that we opened one hour earlier, and closed 30 minutes later, with no break for lunch. As a result our takings increased so much I decided to have a shop refit.

The shop parlour behind the shop we did not use as such, and so by taking down the partition, we doubled the size of the shop, and when completed with modern shop fittings, we were able to have a much larger display area. As a result, after five months, our takings had increased by £300 per week. When I bought the lease of the shop I could not at that time afford to buy the Freehold, which was owned by Bill's dad, and so I approached Mr. Munday Senior and said I would like to buy the freehold.

"OK", he said, "its £7,000."

"No", I said, "It's £6,000" "That was six month's ago; look at how the trade has improved, its £7,000 now."

I had seen an advertisement in The Daily Telegraph that mortgages were available and I applied, and two Jewish gentlemen called and said they would lend me £4,500 if I found the rest. Because of the increase in the price of the freehold, which I thought was unfair, I was loath to proceed.

After a few weeks my two Jewish gentlemen called again, and asked what was happening. I told them the price had gone up to £7,000, and that I was loath to proceed. They said, "If it's worth £6,000, it's worth £7,000 – go ahead". But, I didn't know what they meant, but I know now because that shop's freehold is now worth half a million pounds.

My sister Jess and her husband Fred had been with me on this venture from the very beginning, and after 6 months they decided to join me to help me run the shop.

Within a mile of the shop, Wimpeys had built an estate, and so

Kay and I moved to 40 West Heath Road, so that Jess and Fred could live over the shop. That was a very big upheaval for Jess because their children, Clive and Heather, were still at school, and they had lived at 84 Dunblane Road, Eltham for a very long time. But, they coped, and we all worked in harmony together.

The newspaper industry was going through a very difficult period with strikes etc., but somehow the newspapers got though, although not always on time. This of course upset quite a number of people, but here Fred came into his own and was able to placate most of the disgruntled customers, but there were two types who were quite unreasonable. One type were those who had the Methodist Recorder and the other were the Angling Times customers. They were paying to have their papers delivered, and we were failing to do so. For the first two hours on those days when their publication didn't turn up, the telephone never stopped ringing.

The Daily Telegraph had more staff trouble than most, and they would often turn up after all of the rounds had been delivered, and so it was down to Fred and myself to personally deliver that newspaper. On one Friday morning, I was just about to deliver my last Daily Telegraph. It was about 10.30 am. and I was just about to push the paper through the letterbox when the door opened, and the lady said, "Good morning Wing Commander" (she knew I had recently retired from the RAF because her husband was a scientist at the RAF Farnborough, and he knew me from my Air Force days). "It is kind of you to go to all this trouble over a silly newspaper, come in and have a coffee."

She lived in a very large house with a lot of land, and I remarked what a lovely house it was, just for something to say. She told me she and her husband had lived in it since 1931, after they first got married. She went on to say that an architect had owned the land, and it was agreed that he would design the house and supervise its construction. They had one or two arguments over the design, but in all cases the architect had his way. Eventually the building was finished, and she and her husband moved in.

400

Then came the punch line - "Do you know Mr. Gibson, to this day we have never received an invoice!"

"What a lovely story" I said, "thank you for the coffee, please excuse my dashing off, but I have a very busy shop to run!"

I joined the Aldershot Branch of the National Federation of Newsagents, and soon became its Branch Secretary. We used to meet once a month, and it gave me an insight as to how other newsagents operated.

Apart from News/Confectionery/Tobacco, which was the main stay of our business, we sold stationery, greeting cards, chemists' sundries such as aspirins etc, but one of the members sold tea and sugar, and sold 1 cwt of sugar a week.

Once a year I would go to London to the AGM of the Federation to represent the Aldershot branch. At one of those meetings our attention was drawn to an ancient member of the Federation. I recognised the name Taylor immediately, particularly because he was still living at his shop in Upton Park. During the lunch break I made myself known to him as the paperboy who, every summer, had helped him out when his paperboy went on holiday. I did not recognise him or him me, but he remembered the occasions, which had happened 40 years previous, and once again he thanked me, and stated how glad he was to see that I had become a newsagent.

In the late 1950's it was not possible to open a new newsagent shop within half a mile of an existing one. Any new applicant was inspected by a representative of the Newspaper Proprietors Association, and if in the Aldershot area, by me. If a new applicant met the distance requirement, but did not intend to deliver newspapers, he once again was turned down. But today, all of that has changed; anyone can sell newspapers, and on much better terms than off yore.

I discovered, before I bought the Cove shop, from the Planning Department, that Cove was going to be an expanding area. And true to their forecast my business continued to grow.

It was a full time job on Fridays and Saturdays when Customers came in to pay their paper bill, and I made it a practise to always do that chore. At the monthly meetings of our Federation I found that the method I had inherited from the Mundays was out of date, and in some cases led to arguments, and so I changed to the Huggler system, whereby when a customer paid, they received a dated slip, for each week that they had owed, as proof of payment. Therefore, if there were any weekly dated slips in the account book, that was how many weeks the customer owed. If there were no dated slips, it meant the customer had paid. A wonderful system – no more arguments!

Staffing problems had to be overcome because Bill had two sisters serving in the shop, both of whom soon left after I was left on my own.

One of the best assistants I had was a Mrs. Miles. She was in her mid 70's, and whilst not as quick as my younger assistants, she was thorough and honest. She had lived in the Cove area all of her working life and knew all of my customers, some since birth. She taught me how to become a good newsagent.

John, one of my better paperboys, lived only a few doors away from my shop, and he could always be relied upon to do a second round.

On one occasion, John's stepfather Arthur was chatting me up, and after a bit, Mrs. Miles sidled up to me and said, "Good morning Arthur", and it was noticeable that Arthur, having made a suitable reply, abruptly ended our conversation, and left.

I said to Mrs. Miles, "How come?"

"Mr. Gibson", she said, "I've known John's father since the day he was born – he is a nice man, but don't ever lend him any money!"

Newsagents in my day only sold newspapers because they brought customers into the shop daily to buy counter news, and weekly to pay their paper bills, and it was at those times they bought their other purchases such as confectionary, stationery etc. Those customers who paid monthly rarely bought anything else. One of those customers, a farmer, ran up a bill of over £14.00, which was then, and still is, a lot of money. Small businesses cannot afford to give unlimited credit, and so I sent him a Statement. A few days after that the farmer came into the shop and, abruptly, asked me to make his Statement up to date so that he could pay. I did that, and the farmer wrote out a cheque. "Now, I wish to cancel" he said, "Very good Sir," I said. And the farmer waited while I did that. As he was about to leave I said, "By the way, you seem upset – is there anything the matter?" "Yes", he said, "An old lady in our local was saying that you intended to prosecute me for non-payment of my newspapers." "Well", I said, "You can take it from me, I have never sued anybody for unpaid newspapers yet, and I have never said that I am going to adopt that method."

The attitude of the farmer changed completely and he said, "In that case, you can put the papers back on again."

"Oh no Sir," I said, "I am making the apology for what the old lady said. I don't however want to deliver newspapers to you any more. I cannot afford to give unlimited credit – I am in this business to make money. Good day to you."

"Well, stuff me!" said the farmer, and he left my shop quite embarrassed.

Mrs. Miles, who had heard this contra temps, made eye contact with me, but nothing was said because – let's face it – she had done me a favour, and that was the end of the matter!

As our business grew, and our paper rounds expanded to 20 rounds, a certain amount of difficulty arose trying to get people to mark up the rounds. It was in that connection I missed Bill and Margaret Munday the most. Bill was quick, but Margaret could mark up 3 rounds to Bill's 2. I was getting faster with practise, and my sister Jess would appear at about 5.00 am and she would read the round book to me so that I was able to get up 7 rounds, while the other 3 markers got up 13 rounds between them. In trying to be quick, errors did occur, and 'sack cloth and ashes' had to be worn by the staff in apologising for the customer receiving a Daily Herald instead of a Mail etc.

To hear customers complaining, one would think the world was coming to an end!

One of our first customers every morning was a Mr. Whitehouse, the local road sweeper, who would appear just before 6.00 am. Every day he would buy a Daily Mirror and 10 Wild Woodbines, which cost one shilling and five and a half pence. I used to serve him because it was before 6.00 am, when my assistant would arrive to start work. One morning, after about six months, Mr. Whitehouse placed his usual order, and then after a lot of fumbling about, he said, "I'm sorry Mr. Gibson, I've come without any money. Can I have these on a slate?"

That was OK, but Mr. Whitehouse did not come in to my shop again. I used to see him from time to time, sweeping the roads, and he always tried to avoid eye contact, but I always made it my business to wish him the time of day.

This went on for six months, and then, lo and behold, who was my first customer one morning but Mr. Whitehouse. He had his usual order of 10 Woodbines, and nothing was said. Then, after a few months, Mr. Whitehouse once again had no money, and could he have them on the slate? I produced the 10 Woodbines, and said, "Mr. Whitehouse, the last time you did this to me, I didn't see you in my shop for over six months. I value your custom and I cannot afford to lose it for long periods, and so have these 10 Woodbines on me, and now you don't owe me anything".

That solved the problem because the first customer every day was Mr. Whitehouse, and he never asked for credit again.

In 1957 cigarette smokers were offered a smart wooden cabinet with an attractive clock on top on loan, provided they smoke 200 plus cigarettes a week. The supplier of those cabinets had a team of canvassers going around, door-to-door, enticing households to have a cabinet on loan. For each placement the supplier charged £15.00, plus £30.00 for the cabinet. I decided to speculate on this idea, and another local newsagent, a Mr. Sweet, approached me and said he was going to do the same thing, and so we decided to make a joint venture of it, and do it together.

Mr. Sweet's shop was one that I had previously tried to buy when it came on the market, but Mr. Sweet had beaten me to it. I mentioned this fact to Mr. Sweet, and so we further agreed that if our joint venture with the cabinets worked out, we would join our shops together so that we could expand more quickly.

About that time our house at Camberley was nearing completion, and our cigarette rounds were getting bigger, and so it was agreed that Kay's brother Bill should join us and be in charge of that side of our business. It all worked out because brother-in-law Bill bought the house that we were vacating at 40 West Heath Road as we moved to Camberley.

The number of our newspaper rounds was increasing also, and getting farther afield.

Two miles away from Cove, a new estate of 1,000 houses was nearing completion, and which had a parade of six shops. I secured the Lease of one of those shops to be a Newsagent, Confectioner and Tobacconist, and when it opened, I transferred six rounds from the Cove Shop, and by so doing the shop made a profit from day one.

One of my lady assistants agreed to be the new Manageress, and as her husband was about to leave the Blues and Royal Regiment, I agreed to employ him as a Trainee Manager. He was 6 feet 4 inches tall, and broad with it. He did not walk; he glided, as taught by the Army. He had a commanding presence and was an apt pupil.

Although the transfer of paper rounds eased the pressure at Cove, it was not long before we had in excess of 20 rounds again, and so I sought the means to transfer some more rounds. I did that by taking on another shop, opposite 67 Cove Road, and it was here that we decided to get all of the paper rounds made up, in the new shop, and to do this we built purpose made counters.

Here, brother-in-law Bill came into his own, being a former 'chippy', and he and Mr. Sweet set about building the new counters at the back of the new shop. Bill was quite a quick carpenter, and Mr. Sweet thought himself a dab hand at DIY, and it was quite funny watching those two silly sods trying to go faster than the other.

About that time I became a Rotarian, at the instigation of one of my customers, and I quite enjoyed the weekly luncheon meetings, and I made some good friends. It was not long before I was appointed Secretary of the Overseas Committee, and I was soon writing to other Rotarian Branches on behalf of the Farnborough Branch worldwide.

Besides the increasing number of paper rounds the Cove shop had to handle, it had three Army camps to supply. They were at Morval, the Guillement Barracks, and the Minley Staff College. Special boys had to be employed to do those chores because evening papers as well as morning papers had to be delivered, and in the evenings, paper back books and periodicals had to be taken and sold to the 'squaddies'.

Jess, Fred and I had some laughs at the main choice of periodical titles that were enjoyed by the soldiers because they were the comics of Beano and Dandy!

The Staff College at Minley Manor was a different kettle of fish. As it was two miles from the shop, and they had so many papers, magazines and periodicals, it amounted to half the boy's round, but of course he got rid of them in one drop, but he still had to get there. Fortunately however the boy lived in close proximity to the college, and that helped. The snag with that account was that in addition to the morning delivery, they also needed just nine evening papers delivered each evening. That chore used to fall to either Fred or me.

Most times when I did that evening delivery, I would take Stuart with some of his friends for the ride. Half way down Minley Road there was a humped back bridge, and with the boys egging me on, I would hit the hump back bridge so fast the car went airborne, and my passengers left their seats and hit the roof. The hilarity that followed from the boys was well worth the risk of ruining my car suspension. Needless to say, I never hit the bridge fast enough for the boys.

That delivery, from start to finish, would take thirty minutes each week day evening, and although it was a big account overall with the morning papers, due to the evening delivery, we were not making any money out of the account.

However, because the Major in charge of the Mess was quite charming, and I knew the need for officers to have a regular supply of newspapers, I persevered with the arrangement. In the course of time though, the officer in charge of the Mess changed, and a stroppy Major took over who started complaining about the service I was giving.

This was out of my control because the newspaper proprietors were also having trouble, and sometimes my deliveries of papers would arrive late at Farnborough Railway Station, or were even being delivered to my shop by road. I explained this to the new Major, but he continued to complain and he would telephone the shop, and be so rude that he upset my sister Jess, who took these calls, and so I was not going to have that.

I wrote to the Major, and told him that I was discontinuing to supply the Mess from the end of the month, and would he please make alternative arrangements.

As a result of that letter, a member of our Newsagents' Federation called on me and, over a coffee, he told me that Minley Manor had approached him, asking if he would deliver newspapers daily, but because he knew I had previously been supplying the College, he wanted to know why I was discontinuing. I explained that this was for two reasons. First, I was not making any money out of the account; and secondly, he was upsetting my staff with his abusive 'phone calls, and I was not going to stand for that. If however he wished to work for nothing and take on the account, and be abused for the privilege, he had my blessing!

A few days later, a civilian batman from Minley Manor called on me and asked if I would continue to supply Minley Manor, either he or someone else would pick up the papers daily on their way to work. That suited me fine, and for the first time I started to make money on that venture.

Mr. Sweet had a large shop on the main Farnborough Road with a large passing trade, and by joining forces with him, we had a much larger cash flow which thus enabled us to expand quicker. Our cigarette cabinet rounds were expanding, and we went in for large vending machines, which we placed at various, strategic places, and at the army barracks. The RAF at Farnborough also asked me to install cigarette vending machines, and I installed several at different sites within that vast establishment. After a while however, I had to take them out again because although they were supposed to be fool proof, there was some clever devil who had made a coin which emptied all of the machines, even though I had placed them in close proximity to the Sergeant Commissionaire, who swore he never saw it happen!

From our Cove shop we used to sell over 1,000 (50 quires) of the Radio Times every week, and arrived with us on a Friday, and we used to deliver them on a Saturday. When however, Radio Times changed their delivery date to a Wednesday, I altered all of the round books and delivered them to our customers on Thursday.

The first week that happened, an irate lady customer came into our shop, threw her copy of the Radio Times onto the counter and said, "Mr. Gibson; I've had the Radio Times delivered from this shop for over 20 years on a Saturday. You have chosen to deliver it to me today – Thursday. I don't want it delivered on Thursdays; I want it delivered on a Saturday."

I said, "Very good Madam. I'll alter the round book so that you get it on a Saturday, but you can take this week's copy today, can't you?"

"No, I can't Mr. Gibson. I pay 3d a week for delivery; deliver it to me on Saturday. Good day."

There is none so queer as folk!

60% of our customers had a local paper delivered on a Friday. It was a large broadsheet paper and quite heavy. Friday was also the day that most weekly periodicals had to be delivered, and inserting them into the daily newspapers considerably slowed down the getting up of rounds. Therefore, to ensure deliveries were made on time, I arranged with the printers of the local newspapers to collect my supplies as they came off the press.

On a good week, with no printing snags, my supplies were ready to collect at midnight, and so at 11.30pm on a Friday I would appear at the Printers, and prepared to wait. On one Friday, I arrived to find the machine minders sitting around, drinking coffee, because the machine had broken down, and so I joined them. When midnight came, they all went home, and another shift of machine minders took over, and more coffee was consumed by the new shift. After a while the maintenance engineers reported that the fault had been corrected, and everything was ready to roll, but nobody moved.

Half an hour later I said, "Can we start printing?" And I was amazed to be told they were waiting for 'Fred' to turn up to complete their shift before they could start work. It was at least another half an hour before Fred turned up, full of apologies, that he had been delayed in some other part of the building. Fred was welcomed with open arms, and the presses commenced to roll, but Fred stayed with me, drinking coffee. After a while I said to Fred, "What's your job, Fred?" He replied, "Oh! I have to sweep up and keep the place clean, but there's nothing for me to do yet!"

Seven machines minders, on double time, were not allowed to start work until the eighth member of the shift arrived, despite the fact there was nothing for the eighth member to do until the other seven had started to make a mess!

Fred said, "It's Union Rules; there is nothing we can do about it". Well!!!!!

After that all I could do was collect my local papers, I returned to the shop, and started marking them up to save time later.

Regularly my sister Jess would turn up and together we would get all of the local papers marked up before 4.00 am when the national dailies had to be collected from Farnborough Railway Station. There were several Porters employed at the station to handle the early morning traffic, but there was only one, a Mr. Morgan, who had any intelligence. He really knew how the railway system worked, and when he retired on a pension of ten shillings a week, a local firm were quick to give him employment, at the age of 65, at the rate of four times his weekly railway wage.

409

Mr. Morgan was a great help to me in collecting my papers, and was also a good customer of mine, and I was greatly saddened when he died at the age of 70 because, at his funeral, apart from his wife I was the only other mourner…

Our business continued to grow, and Fred Sweet and I were in the process of looking at a near by shop with a view to purchase, but Jess and her husband Fred beat us to it, and became newsagents in their own right. 'You win some, you lose some, but you cannot win them all'!

That left the living accommodation at 67 Cove Street vacant.

My mother, who was living on her own at Seven Kings, had been having the odd accident and had started to fall over. So, I decided to move her over the shop where she would see me every day, and Jess was close at hand. She did not like the idea of losing her independence but when once she settled in, she loved it, and although the shop was out of bounds to her, in that connection I failed miserably as I could not keep her out of it!!

Frequently when I was out on business, on my return I would find her in the shop, chatting up the staff and customers, and on some occasions, trying to serve. She absolutely loved it, but when I confronted her, she would look at me truculently and say, "So!!" and because I didn't want to make a scene in the shop, I would say, "Mother, would you please make me a coffee", or any other excuse to get her out of the shop!

One of the most successful ways of achieving my aim was, as I had cause to visit one or two of our other shops on a daily basis, I would take her with me for the ride. That did two things; one, it kept her out of the shop, and two, she loved the motorcar ride to such an extent she was in her second childhood.

Just inside the Cove Road shop I had a low table, no more than one foot high, on which I displayed about 100 different types of sweets for children, the dearest of which was one penny per sweet. The kids loved that self help service, and a blind eye was taken if a very young infant popped a sweet into their mouth without paying.

That upset my mother, but I insisted to my mother that she was not to remonstrate with my customers because, I told her, the young ones may only buy a penny sweet from me today, but in no time at all they could all be buying 20 cigarettes.

The kids' counter, as I called it, fascinated my mother, and any time I was not around she would be at that counter serving the kids. She did that quite well, but even there I had to keep an eye on her. On one occasion, the following incident occurred.

Little boy: "I want one of those, and one of those" – pointing to two different sweets.

Mother: "Did you say please may I have? Here's your four pence change from sixpence – did you say thank you?!!"

I got one of the staff to tell her that she was wanted on the telephone, and when she went into the living room to answer the phone I said, "Gotcher! Mother, it's not your job to teach my customers manners; if their parents haven't done it, hard luck, so don't do it again!"

Her reply was, "I'm not going to let them talk to me like that!

"Right" I said, "Keep out of the shop, and it won't happen!"

On another occasion, I was doing the Relief Manager's job on a Sunday morning during the summer. At that time of year, due to holidays and normal alterations to the round books for the following week, and in between serving, that would take all day. Also on Sundays, it was the only day in the week that we closed for one hour for lunch. On the Sunday in question, we were not busy, and I had sent the two shop assistants home early for lunch. That gave my mother the chance to come into the shop to tell me my lunch was ready.

Just before 1.00 pm, I was working on the rounds books at the back of the shop behind the partition, when I heard the door open, and a man ask my mother for half a pound of butter. I heard my mother apologise and say she was sorry but we did not sell butter. I was amazed to hear the man say, "But I know you do!" As I started to enter the shop, my mother came up to me and said, "We don't sell butter, do we?" At which I took over.

411

The gentleman customer was over six feet tall, and was wearing policeman's trousers, a blue shirt and black tie with a navy blue blazer with brass buttons, and was accompanied by a much smaller man. I repeated what my mother had said, and as it was 1.00pm. My mother opened the door to let the gentlemen out. Then I had second thoughts, because I knew where butter could be procured on a Sunday morning, but when I reached my would be customer, I heard him say to his friend, "It's the last time that I go into that bloody shop!"

So, I left it at that, and went back and had the lunch that my mother had prepared for me.

The next day a lady came into the shop and said that she wanted to cancel her newspapers. I said, "Very good Madam, when is the first day you don't want your papers delivered?" She replied, quite curtly, "Tomorrow"

It was at that point that I realised something was wrong, and so I said, "You seem quite upset, is there anything wrong?" "Yes" she said, "Yesterday my husband came to this shop for some butter, and an old lady called him an April Fool!"

"I'm awfully sorry about that, but not to my knowledge. I do however know the old lady you refer to well, leave it me and I will investigate." And the customer left.

I went rushing into the kitchen and said, "Mother, do you remember the gentleman who came into the shop yesterday for some butter?" "Yes" she said, "Well, his wife has just come into the shop and cancelled her papers. She seemed upset and so I asked her if there was anything wrong, and she said an old lady had called her husband an April Fool. I'm not worried about her cancellation because as one door shuts, another one opens, but did you call him an April Fool?"

"No" she said, "I didn't call him an April Fool.

I said, "Level with me mother - what did you say to him?

She said, "As he went out of the shop I said, 'it's not April the First you know!'"

"That's it mother – you called him an April Fool – now I'll have to go and apologise"

I got in the car and went straight round to 8 Stuart Close where the lady lived, and got there just as the lady was opening her door.

I said, "I've come to apologise for what my mother said; I've had a word with her and I can promise you she won't say anything like that again!"

"That's very kind of you Mr. Gibson, in that case, you can put the papers back on again."

The cancellation did not worry me because since Mr. Sweet and I became partners, we owned all of the paper shops in the area, and so she would have had to get her papers form one of our shops anyway!

* * *

26

Its all in the news

Two of our biggest customers were the two army barracks, Morval and Guillemont. We had to deliver to the married quarters in the morning, and at night the same delivery boy took evening papers together with paperback books and periodicals to sell to the Squaddies. They were difficult customers to serve because of the problem of the sudden movement of troops. The numbers to cater for could vary plus or minus 500 without any warning.

Sam, the Morval paperboy, was a mature lad, articulate, numerate, and quite capable of serving soldiers.

One day the weather was bad, but Sam turned up as usual to do his Morval barracks paper round, but later in the day, officers in the married quarters were ringing to say that their newspapers had not been delivered. There were so many complaints that I got up a duplicate round and delivered them myself. In the evening, Sam turned up to sell his comics etc to the Morval barrack soldiers, and so I asked him what happened to his morning paper round.

"Nothing", Sam said, "I did my round as usual".

I could see I was not going to get any sense out of Sam, and as he was irreplaceable at short notice to get someone to do his evening selling job, I let the matter rest.

A few weeks later, the Major at Morval barracks rang me up and asked me to call on him at his office as he had something to show me. I duly kept the appointment, and the Major took me to a ditch, and there was a bundle of newspapers blowing about in the ditch. I gathered the bundle of papers up and took them back to the shop. I showed it to Fred, and there was the complete round that should have been delivered to the Morval married quarters.

Fred was completely nonplussed, but we both agreed that Sam was such a good salesman and we could not afford to lose his services – and so we left it at that.

Sam had taken a calculated risk, as he knew ultimately I would find out what had actually happened, and it had worked!

Another of our newspaper delivery boys, John, was a machine tool apprentice at the RAE Farnborough. He was intelligent albeit a bit precocious – in fact he came under the classification of 'Wide Boy'. He progressed from a delivery boy to a 'Marker Up' of newspaper rounds, and in the evenings he would serve in the shop.

After he had finished his apprenticeship, he did not take up full time employment offered to him by the RAE, but instead rented a tiny kiosk type shop a few doors away from our shop, and started to sell market trader goods very cheaply. I kept my tabs on him because he was selling stuff so cheaply that it could only have fallen off the back of a lorry. I tried to find out who his suppliers were, but the nearest I could get was a location – Hounsditch in East London.

I warned John about the risk of selling stolen goods, but he didn't want to know.

The main problem for any thriving business is storage space, and I had converted the garage behind the Cove Road shop into a warehouse for cigarettes and tobacco, and I always had over a million cigarettes in store. One day I was working in the warehouse and John came round to see me. When he saw the levels of stock I had, his eyes nearly popped out of his head!

"What an Aladdin's cave", he said, "have you got it burglar alarmed?"

"Of course" was my answer.

"Pity" was John's reply, "Because I could have got the boys to break that window, and in twenty minutes we could empty this store; you could claim on your insurance, and I could then sell you the stuff back later at half price!"

I ended that conversation by saying, "John, you're joking!

Anyway, what can I do for you?"

I told my mother what had occurred because I could see how his mind was working. Forever after, whenever John was serving in the evenings, my mother kept in close proximity, keeping a beady, watchful eye on him.

One evening, it was getting near to 7.00 pm and closing time, and there was only John serving with Mum, of course, in close attention, when he said, "Mrs. Gibson, shall we have a fish and chip supper?" My mum thought that was a great idea, and so he said, "You go and get the fish and chips, and I'll close up."

However, my mum wasn't having any of that, and she said, "No John; here's the money for whatever we want – you go, and I'll close up." John said, "Blimey!! Mrs. Gibson, with you around, I can't even pinch a box of matches!"

Sad to say, John went from bad to worse and ended up doing three years in jail. He was a bright lad, and if he had been patient, he could have made himself a fortune, but he couldn't wait – and he paid the price.

With the building developments still taking place in the area, our Cove Road shop had grown to 33 newspaper rounds. Of the 33 newspaper deliverers, 3 were girls, and to my surprise, they were far more reliable than the boys! In inclement weather, some mothers did not want their sons to get up and do their round because they did not want their boy to get wet! They called their girls, but not their boys. The girls never let me down.

To speed up getting the rounds together I had a 'caller' who would read the round book to me, and by that method, I was able to get 15 rounds up, leaving the remaining 18 rounds to the other 5 markers to do between them. On Sundays, the odd marker would not turn up, and so I put a stop to any skiving by doing all 33 rounds myself.

One of my customers was a policeman, working in plain clothes as a detective. I got to know him quite well because he used to smoke Tortoiseshell cigarettes, made by Churchman, and he was the only one to smoke that brand. I always had 200 on show, and another 200 in store as a back up.

One day, he came into the shop and asked to speak to me in private. I took him into the front parlour, which I used as an office, and he told me minor offences were taking place in his domain, and he thought it might be one of my paperboys. Immediately my hackles were up, and I said, "Not on your Nelly; I can vouch for all of my paper boys and girls". However, my copper friend continued and said items were being stolen, such as tools, screwdrivers, garden tools etc. Those items were going missing while the houses were empty with the occupants on holiday. In such cases, the culprits had a habit of leaving their trademark behind.

I asked him what he meant by that.

He told me, often when housebreaking or burglaries were taking place, the culprit was so highly strung or nervous that they would wet themselves, and the smell of urine would persist, but the specific cases that he was currently investigating, whoever was committing the crime, was messing in the bath.

Naturally, I was shocked, but I was sure that it was none of my boys or girls, but I assured him that I would keep it in mind.

One Sunday, the papers arrived two hours late. I was on my own and I had the usual 33 rounds to get up. So, it was a case of 'eyeballs out', and I went at it hammer and tongs. But, alas, the delivery boys and girls started to arrive before I had got their rounds up. In no time at all I had 15 boys and girls waiting for their round. Of course, true to form, the boys started to show off in front of the girls. Much laughter from the dirty stories being told was distracting me because I was tending to listen instead of concentrating on the business I had on hand. Every now and then I would shout "SHUT UP", but the quiet only lasted a few seconds, and then the boys were at it again.

At one story, I heard one of the boys say, "Oh!! I'd love to shit in her bath". I swung round and noted who had made the remark, but the boys were so full of their own merriment that they did not notice me, and so I continued, and in due course I got all of the rounds on their way.

417

Now, what was I going to do about the bath messing culprit? I knew something about his background; he was an only boy of a broken marriage and whose parents were in the process of getting a divorce. His father had a good executive job at the RAE, but he was a bully at home, who would throw his weight around. There was no physical violence, but much verbal abuse. The boy used to call in to the shop on his way to school to buy a bag of crisps, and so I made it my business to talk to him.

One morning I trapped him, and asked him to call and see me on his way home from school. I discovered he was 15 years of age, and was getting ready to leave school. He had no idea what he wanted to do, and he came under the classification of 'easily led'. And so, I suggested that he join the Royal Air Force and learn a trade. I was completely surprised when he did not say no, and so I went to town, singing the praises of the RAF, how I had joined as an airman and retired as a Wing Commander, and that if he wished, I could arrange for him to see an RAF Careers Officer to discuss the matter further.

That was agreed, and my next job was to get the detective off the trail of the culprit who was messing up people's baths.

The next time the detective came to buy his Tortoiseshell cigarettes, I told him I thought I knew the person he was looking for, and I explained the boy's circumstances, and that I was going to get him to join the RAF. The detective was quite sensible, and said the Bathroom Case was of a very low priority, and if I could sort out the naughty person, that was fine by him.

The boy was perfectly fit and of average mental ability. He passed the RAF joining test and started to learn a trade at RAF Halton. His mates knew that it was me who had got him into the RAF, and a few weeks later, one of my papergirls told me she would like to join the RAF after she had passed her 'A' levels, and could I help her? Using one of my friends I had made when I was at the Air Ministry, I contacted a Group Officer, and to cut a long story short, my paper girl got herself a Commission in the RAF – on her own ability – and so that was her career settled for life.

I was able to help another one of my paperboys because he

wanted to get into the printing trade. That was at the time when the Printing Unions were all powerful, as I knew to my cost.

When I was starting out as a Commercial Artist and was living at Seven Kings, our next-door neighbour was the Father of a Printing Chapel, and he arranged for me to see the head of the Lithographic Department who needed someone. I attended an interview and got the job, and was told to report to the Secretary of their Union to get a Union Card. I duly presented myself but was told that I could not have a Union Card unless I had a job. I told the Secretary that I had a job. But the Secretary said that I couldn't have job without a Union Card!!!

I said to myself, 'Right monkey', and I never tried to work as a Union Employee again!

But being the biggest customer of the local paper, the Farnborough Chronicle, I knew the Managing Director well – he was a Rotarian and I used to meet him socially every week, and, working on Bobby Sharpe's premise of 'It's not what you know but who you know', I was able to get my paperboy a 7-year apprenticeship. The lad was so grateful he came to work for me from 5.00 am to 7.00 am every morning, marking up my paper rounds.

After he qualified as a Printing Machine Minder he stayed on, working five days a week with the local paper, and at weekends, he got himself a Machine Minder's job with one of the big Sunday newspapers. He came to see me on his way home from his first stint in London, and I asked him how he was getting on. He was not very happy because, although he was a qualified Machine Minder, he was not allowed to touch any of the machines. All he had to do was sweep up, make tea, and generally keep the place tidy. That was the pecking order, and he had to do that for six months before he was permitted to do the job for which he was paid.

About this time, my partner, Mr. Sweet, was not feeling too well. He owned a petrol station in London, which his mother operated for him. Every Tuesday he would visit her and at the same time keep an appointment with his General Practitioner, whom he had known for donkey's years. Despite weekly visits and many tests, his Doctor could find nothing wrong with him.

His main job in our partnership was to keep the accounts, and do the daily banking etc. This he was able to do, but it was obvious he was not well, and this went on for over a year.

One Tuesday, when he returned from London, he looked dreadful, and I asked him if he had seen his Doctor. "Yes", he replied, "And he still cannot find anything wrong with me." I said, "Doctor Bellamy is a customer of ours, and a Rotarian friend of mine; why don't you let me arrange an appointment for you with him and get a second opinion?"

To my amazement, Fred Sweet said, "Will you do that?" He kept his appointment, and the next day Dr. Bellamy had him in hospital where cancer of the Bowel was diagnosed. From then on he went down hill fast. Kay took over the accounts and I did the donkeywork of collecting the takings from the shops daily, and doing the banking, and after several months working like that, Fred Sweet suggested he sell his share of our partnership.

At that time I was working 120 hours a week, which was making me a little short tempered and difficult to live with, and so I approached a friend of mine, Eddy Miller, and explained the position to him and asked if he would like to buy Fred Sweet's share of our business.

After many visits from his home in Beckenham in Kent, Eddy bought Fred's shares, and, I am sorry to say, within 6 months Fred was dead.

It was through Kay that I had got to know Eddy because she taught him how to dance, and he became a good friend of hers. For about a year, Eddy travelled from Beckenham, but after a while he bought 2 acres of land at Compton, near Farnham, Surrey, where he had a super house built to his own design.

One of our customers was an architect, and he mentioned he had watched my business grow over the last few years, and did I know of any land that could be developed in our area. I told him that

Farnborough was a developing area, and that I knew all of the local landowners.

He invited me to his office in Victoria, London, where I met another architect from my friend's partnership. It was agreed that if I found the land, the three of us would form a partnership, and they would do the rest, such as obtaining planning permission etc. That was no problem, and I made arrangements with the owner of 10 acres of land, which was ripe for development.

That particular deal got to an advanced stage, and I was paying regular visits to the architects in Victoria with other parcels of land when, on one of my visits, I was told that the other partners in the Architect's business were objecting to what my partners were doing in our new venture, and that they would have to pull me out. That was a pity because what I was doing did not interfere with my running a newspaper business, and on one of my visits to Victoria, I had met a Jewish gentleman who was a financier, and who always had £750,000 in cash available to finance deals, and he had friends who – between them – could raise two or three million pounds within 48 hours.

However, news got around that we were not going to proceed with our first development, but within weeks, some super four-bedroom houses started to be built, and although the architect on this project was nothing to do with the two architects with whom I was associated, I had the feeling that the new developer had been tipped off.

Just a few doors away from 67 Cove Road was Tower Hill Garage, where I used to buy my petrol. On several occasions I went to fill up, and after two or three gallons the pump would cut off because it was out of petrol. One day when this happened, the owner of the petrol station had been speaking to a gentleman, and from the gist of what I had overheard, he was the Shell Petrol Representative, and while the owner went to get my change, I said to the Rep, "Why don't you give him some petrol?"

The Rep said, "He can have as much as his tanks can hold, so long as he pays for it."

I said, "That's a pity, because Cove does need a petrol station."

"Find yourself a site and Shell will build you a Petrol Station" was the reply.

Opposite 67 Cove Road was a piece of wasteland, and I had found out, in my previous failed development venture, that Calethorpes Estates owned it. I went along to Calethorpes Offices, just the other side of Fleet, and discovered that they were vast land owners, and that they would investigate my enquiry as to the possibility of a sale, and they would let me know the result.

The Senior Partner of the largest Estate Agency in Farnborough was a Rotarian friend of mine, and he agreed to act for me if the land was for sale. A few weeks later, Calethorpes came back to me and said that the land was for sale, and that it would be auctioned in the near future.

I contacted my architect friend, and a local builder, and they both felt, separately, the front portion of land that I was interested in was worth £3,500 to £4,000. My estate agency friend contacted me and told me he couldn't act for me in the purchaser of the land as he had been appointed the Auctioneer.

The land had been split into two lots; the front bit, which was large enough for a petrol station, was Lot 1, and the rear portion, which had been designated for house building, was Lot 2. As the estate agent was no longer able to act for me, I decided to go it alone. I had never bought anything from an auction before, and so I approached the sale filled with trepidation, and prepared to splash out up to £4,000.

The Auctioneer opened the sale with Lot 1, and before I could even start to bid, Lot 1 had been sold for over £7,000, and Lot 2 went for £26,000. I was flabbergasted – I had always looked on the land as an eyesore and of no value, and so I decided to stick to being a newsagent!

One evening at about 8.00 pm, I was on my way home to Camberley and I saw one of my customers all 'dolled up to the nines', and I stopped and offered her a lift, which she gratefully accepted.

The next day, Mrs. Miles said, "Mr. Gibson, you gave a lift to Mrs. So and So, didn't you?" I replied, "Yes, I gave her a lift to Farnborough Railway Station." Mrs. Miles continued, "If you don't want to get yourself a bad name, don't ever do that again. She goes to London every night; she has 500 yards of The Strand as her pitch – she's on the game!" I said, "Thanks for telling me, but how was I to know?" "Well Mr. Gibson, everyone else knows; she lives in one of the prefabs behind your shop, and it is not furnished on her husband's pay!"

So, once again, I had to thank Mrs. Miles for keeping me on the straight and narrow with her local knowledge!

A Mrs. Bishop was the wife of a mobile policeman, and he was so dedicated to his job that he never let up for one second. It did not matter who it was, he showed no discrimination – he would even have booked his own grandmother. They lived in a Council house, with houses both side of a long, oval, grass covered island. There was only one entrance/exit to the Island Estate, and it had a one-way traffic system.

His next-door neighbour was a motor mechanic, and at the time, temporarily unemployed. While he was searching for employment he bought himself a 'clapped out' old van. He stripped the engine right down, and thoroughly overhauled it. One day, Mr. Bishop arrived home having just finished his 6.00 am to 2.00 pm shift, and he saw his next door neighbour driving his van off the road and into his garage. Having greeted one another, Mr. Bishop asked, "is it OK now?" His neighbour replied, "I've just tested it around the island, and it's fine now".

That happened five days before Quarter Day, and the neighbour was about to start a new job, and so he decided to keep the van. Consequently he taxed the vehicle from the first day of the new Quarter. That was a basic error, because Mr. Bishop then issued a summons on his neighbour for driving a vehicle on the Highway without a road tax licence.

All of the neighbours thought that this was a 'Shit's trick', but Mr. Bishop saw nothing wrong with it all!

67 Cove Road had a 17-foot forecourt, and I used to display advertising material on it. I had a square box on each of the four sides; on which were displayed Imperial sized posters, advertising women's magazines. These were changed on a regular basis by a Bill Poster, and were placed one on top of the other until they became quite thick. After a while, it became quite heavy, and so at nighttime I would lay the box on its side, and put it in the shop porch.

One day, Mr. Bishop asked to see me just before he started his 2.00 pm shift. He reported that as he went off duty just after 10.00 pm the previous night, he had caught two Squaddies sitting on my advertising box in my shop doorway, and they were amusing themselves by stripping the posters off my box, and would I make a statement as to the damage and the cost thereof.

I replied that there was no damage done, and therefore there was no cost; in fact, the Squaddies had done me a favour by tearing of off the several layers of posters.

Mr. Bishop persisted that the soldiers should be summonsed for the damage they had done.

I reiterated that it was not worth police time to prosecute, but I suggested that he leave it to me, and I would speak to the soldiers' Commanding Officer and let him deal with the matter.

The soldiers who were based at the three Army Camps that I served were some of my best customers, and the last thing I was going to do was upset them. However, I called on the Major in charge of the naughty soldiers, and explained the situation regarding the odd man out policeman, and it was agreed that the Major would deal with the matter.

I informed Mr. Bishop what action I had taken, and that was the end of that storm in a teacup!

At that time, I owned a white Ford Consul motorcar. It was one of the first major developments in car manufacture that Ford had made since the war, and any time I stopped, a crowd would gather round to admire my car.

I was driving down Cove Road one day, when suddenly an announcement from a loud hailer nearby nearly split my ear drums with the message, "Will the driver of the white Consul reduce speed to 30 mph!"

I slowed down immediately because I recognised Mr. Bishop's voice.

No further police action was taken, but Mr. Bishop followed me all the way into Aldershot to make sure I did not break any more speed limits!

Mr. Bishop's main fault was that he lacked common sense, which was very hard on his wife because some of her neighbours gave her a very hard time. However, he did not last long at Farnborough, and everyone breathed a sign of relied when he was posted to the Bournemouth area.

The shop that Fred Sweet had brought to our partnership was located at Pinehurst corner, on the main Farnborough Road. It was a fine, large shop and had a very large passing trade. Harry Skipp was the Manager, and he was also the husband of Kay's sister, Joyce. Prior to becoming the Manager, Harry had been employed as a troubleshooter with David Greig's chain of shops for 30 years, and he knew more about running a shop than any of us. All we did was keep his shop well stocked, and he did the rest.

Joyce had not been very well, and another of her sisters, Winifred, who had been a Ward Sister as Whipps Cross Hospital, was staying at Pinehurst Corner and nursing Joyce. Edgar, Winifred's husband, was a scientist at Beechams, and he came to see Joyce to wish her well. When it came the time for him to leave, Edgar said goodbye to each of us in turn, and came last of all to Winifred, and he was shaking her hand and obviously a bit nonplussed, when Winifred said, "you don't have to shake my hand; I'm your wife!" Edgar replied, "I know you are my wife, but I can't remember your name!"

Edgar was one of Beecham's Senior Scientists and was responsible for the work of many other scientists, but this was one of those days when he just was not on our Planet!!

The head of the Engineering Department on Farnborough Council was an acquaintance of mine who I had met at various Rotarian and Masonic meetings, and at one of these dos, he invited me to have coffee with him at his office.

The coffee was good, and I was enjoying the company, when I noticed a large, framed, coloured picture of a roundabout. My friend noticed that I was admiring the picture, and I said, "That's the Frimley Road roundabout, isn't it?" My engineer friend said, "Yes – that's my pride and joy, and I'm going to build another, even bigger, just here" and he pointed to a spot on a large wall map. I looked and said, "You can't do that – that's where my Pinehurst Corner shop is." "Oh! Is it?" my friend, said, "Well, that whole row of shops and the cinema will all be coming down."

Bobby Sharp's words sprang to mind again; 'its not what you know, it's who you know that counts.'

I thanked my host for the coffee, and told him I'd enjoyed our little chat, and immediately went back to work, and told Eddy Miller of the Engineer's plans for the future, and we both decided to put Pinehurst Corner up for sale in the near future.

My new partner, Eddy Miller, was a cool customer. He owned a half share in a sand pit with his sister-in-law, which he decided to sell so that he could concentrate on shops. He never lost his temper, was adept at figures, and quickly learnt the retail trade. In disposing of his share in the sand business, there were some debts to collect, and he was having difficulty with one client in getting his money. So, one day he called on that firm, and asked to see the Managing Director. Many excuses were made as to why that wasn't possible; one being that he was in a meeting and he could not be disturbed. Eddy was prepared for such tactics; he took a chair, made himself comfortable, and told the receptionist he had plenty of time and he would wait.

He had a large briefcase out of which he took the Times newspaper and started to read. Come lunch time and he produced from his brief case a flask of coffee and a plastic box of sandwiches, and started to have lunch. He invited the receptionist to join him over a coffee, or would she prefer tea as he had tea with him also.

Eddy never did get to see the Managing Director, but when it was realised that Eddy was not going to leave empty handed, a cheque soon arrived, to Eddy's entire satisfaction, but he was still in no hurry to leave, and so he finished his lunch in his own time before thanking the receptionist profusely for her help.

Eddy was a good partner, and soon got the hang of running a small chain of shops. I did all of the donkeywork, and we continued to expand.

He bought a wealth of business experience, which was invaluable. There was a shop in Waterlooville, which came on to the market, and we went to see what it was all about. When once the Vendor was convinced that we were genuine buyers, he opened up to all of the fiddles that he was up to.

As we were investigating the accounts, Eddy was amazed at the tax-free items to such an extent that he said, "Where do you keep all this spare cash?"

At the time, we were in the bedroom, standing by the side of a dressing table, and the vendor opened several drawers, each one of which was stuffed with £5 notes. I was so embarrassed I blushed all over, and I had to leave the room, supposedly examining the state of the interior decoration. As we were on our way home, with Eddy driving, I said, "Fancy asking the man where he kept all of his spare cash!" Eddy said, "I just didn't believe him; in any case, I never ask a question I would not be prepared to answer myself"

I still blush when I think of that episode in my life!

I used to do all the buying, and we had a parlour behind the shop at 67 where I would meet the various representatives of all of our suppliers. It was comfortably furnished with a large coffee table, on which were various brands of cigarettes, ashtrays, cigarette lighters, etc. Stuart was about 10 years old at the time, and one day he came into the parlour and was nosing around. He saw all of these packets of cigarettes, and he said, "Dad, why don't you smoke?"

I said, "Because it's a filthy habit which I have never started, but above all, I don't like it."

Stuart said, "Can I have a cigarette?"

I said, "Of course son; have one of these", and I offered him a Capstan Full Strength.

He put one in his mouth, and I flicked a cigarette lighter for him. He took one puff, and immediately spat it out. I said, "Now you know why I don't smoke!"

That, to my knowledge, was the first and last time Stuart tried to smoke.

I would take Stuart to Yateley Manor Prep School on the mornings that Kay couldn't make it, but every afternoon I would pick him up and take him home for tea. One day, I picked him up, but instead of going home, I took him back to our shop at Queensmead. This was a shop in a brand new development of 100 shops, and was in between Pinehurst Corner and our shop at 64 Victoria Road. The developers had experienced great difficulty in letting those shops, but I knew that if there were 100 shops to be built, one would have to be a newsagent, and so I knew it had to be me.

Much adverse publicity was being circulated, that Farnborough did not need 100 new shops, but I kept my eye on the ball, and the first shop to be signed up for a 21-year lease, at a rent of £400.00 per week, was me. The shop was in the middle of the parade, and just before we opened, the Post Office approached me and said, ultimately, when the parade was fully let, they would be having a Crown Post Office in one of the shops, but in the meantime would I agree to be a Sub Post Master and have the Post Office in my shop?

I couldn't stop laughing. That enabled me to change the interior of the shop slightly, and besides it being the usual Newsagents/Confectioners/Tobacconist, I had a 32 foot run of Hallmark Greeting Cards, a specialist Stationery and Gift section, with all of the top suppliers; Royal Dalton, Stuart Crystal, etc, and because of the Post office, when we opened, we made a profit from day one.

However, on this particular day I took Stuart straight to the Queensmead shop from school because the Commercial Stationery section needed tidying up, and our lady manageress had not had time to do it. After about two hours we left it 'ship shape and Bristol fashion', and I took Stuart home for tea.

About a week later, I had need to check something in the Post office, and so having collected Stuart from school, we went straight to Queensmead. My business did not take too long, and we were just about to leave when Stuart heard a customer ask for some A4 Square Cut Folders, and he heard our manageress apologise and say we did not have any.

"Yes we have" said 10 year old Stuart, and he took our manageress to the exact spot where, a week previously, he had straightened that particular cupboard.

I was hoping for Stuart to ultimately take over our shops, but alas that was not to be. Anything with wheels with an internal combustion engine attached, that was his preference, and so it has turned out to be.

We bought the shop at Farnborough Road, which had formerly been the Post Office, and we used it as a storage depot, and it was from here that we did all of the buying for our shops.

At this time my sister, Betty, who had just returned from a long stay in Italy, joined us, and worked from that location until she sorted out what she wanted to do next.

While she was with us I helped her to make her mind up about taking driving lessons, as this would give her a much wider scope for future employment.

* * *

27

Cabbages and Kings

At this stage, 1965, Kay had taken over doing the accounts completely from Eddy as his health was deteriorating. On one occasion I went to visit him in his super house at Compton. When I arrived, Eddy was watching television with the volume turned right down, and after a while he said, "What do you think of it?"

I said, "Think of what?"

"The colour television", he said.

And it was then that I noticed the colour, but before Eddy had drawn my attention to it, the colour was so faint I had not noticed it.

I was doing all of the donkey work, working about 120 hours a week, and Eddy did not think that was fair, and so we decided to sell the business and split the freehold shops between us, and so, that's what we did.

After a short break, brother Cyril, who had a Stand in the Jubilee section of Covent Garden Market, wanted to expand his business by procuring the Stand next to his, and as I had liquid capital available, it was decided that I buy that Stand which was then owned by a Limited Company called C J Smith Ltd, and Cyril would teach me the Wholesale greengrocery business.

While the legal proceedings were taking place for the transfer, I used to go to the market to get the feel of my new environment. The business I was buying not only doubled the size of Cyril's business, but also had a Stand in the Central Arcade of Covent Garden, which was a superb position being next door to T J Pouparts, the largest firm in the market, and opposite Monro's, the second largest firm.

In the interim period before I officially owned C J Smiths, Cyril introduced me to a salesman named Bob Geedon who, he said, would be available to show me the ropes. Bob was obviously a good salesman, but he created no doubt in my mind as to whether I was making the right move. He knew all of the buyers, and treated them all very familiarly.

On one occasion, a buyer had walked past Cyril's Stand before Bob had noticed it. Bob shouted, "Johnny – you can't walk past my f****** stand without buying anything!" Johnny seemed quite pleased to be so accosted, and returned in an affable mood, and was not allowed to leave until Bob had sold him 50 bags of carrots. The vocabulary used by both sides with many expletives was so different from that used during my Air Force career it made me laugh, and realise what a sheltered life I had lived.

After all of the formalities had been concluded, I arrived at Covent Garden at 4.00 am where Cyril greeted me with, "Here's your Salesman and Porter – off you go to the centre Stand."

Bob, my salesman, and Michael, my porter, (who was one of Cyril's porters who had volunteered to work with me) had obviously been briefed by Cyril, and so off we went to my new centre Stand, and that was all the help I got from brother Cyril. He chucked me in at the deep end! However, on arriving at my Stand, I found it full of packages of fruit, which Cyril's night porter had stored for me, and so our first job was to make a display to show buyers what we had to sell. A wire framework called 'Jiggers', which was padlocked for security, enclosed the Stand but it was possible for passers by to see what was inside the stand.

The whole of the Centre Stand was open to the public, and they had right of way as they went about their business. My Stand was about 15 feet wide, and about 40 feet deep. It had a portable desk, about 2 feet square, at which the salesman stood to do the paperwork. So then we only needed customers. The size of my Stand was tiny in comparison to what Bob my salesman had been used to, and by 8.00 am, Bob had sold out. Michael, my porter, had the job of delivering the goods to the customers' lorries while Bob, having finished his work, went home.

Unfortunately this arrangement didn't work for long because Bob became unwell, and it was found he had cancer, and that his working days were over.

The salesman supplied by Cyril in place of Bob could clear the Stand every day, but it took him longer. At 8.00 am every morning my salesman went to breakfast, and I would take over the selling. Michael knew many of the buyers by their Christian name, and he would call them over, and I welcomed my would be customers by saying, "How do you do, it's most kind of you to stop to see my produce", and all I got in return were strange looks, as if I were speaking a foreign language. However, I continued to meet new people, some of whom just came to see the new, naïve owner of C J Smiths.

I discovered it was usual practise that all porters salesmen were given a 'Cotchell' each Saturday. This amounted to a week's supply of fruit and vegetables. I used to take Michael over to Cyril's Stand and give him a sack of cabbages, carrots or a crate of cauliflower, or whatever Michael wanted.

I never took a Cotchell home; it was something I could never be bothered with, but a sack of cabbages or a crate of 24 cauliflowers was far too much for two people, and so Michael used to share the rest between Pouparts and Munro's porters, and they in turn would give him grapefruit or oranges or some other imported fruit which I did not sell on my Stand. Therefore, although they all thought I was stupid, I was in good standing with all of the porters and salesmen in the Centre Arcade, and I could do no wrong.

In the Royal Air Force and other services, one is always taught to tell the truth, because the life of a comrade might depend on it, but that maxim never worked in the market.

There was no fixed price for goods; when the customer asked the price of anything the salesman always gave the top market price, and the customer would make a bid, and an argument would ensue. For example, the salesman would be trying to sell crates of superb cauliflower, and the customer was refusing to pay that sort of money for crates of manure!

It was a way of life I could never get used to. I realised why Cyril was so successful in the Market because he was the biggest self-confessed liar born!

One of my farmers who sent to me every day some of the finest tomatoes in the market, and I was doing the selling at that time because my salesman was at breakfast, and I had quoted the top price to a Turkish Cypriot customer, who started to use the most foul language because I wouldn't budge on the price, and before he knew what time of day it was, he was surrounded by half a dozen porters telling my customer to 'F*** off; you don't use language like that to Bruce' and he was sent on his way.

When my salesman returned from breakfast, Michael would go and get sandwiches for breakfast for the two of us, and quite often Sid, a porter friend of Michaels, and who worked for another company would accompany us. I used to enjoy breakfast when Sid joined us because he was a Fulham supporter, and we would have good, friendly arguments about football. Michael was a big, strong man, and worked quite quickly, and there were times when he was free, he would help Sid with some of his turns.

One morning I was on my own. My salesman was at breakfast and Michael was out doing a turn, when Sid came by with a sack truck, on which were 30 x 40 lb boxes of apples. When he reached my Stand, he said, "Can I drop the handles Bruce? I've got to go down the road for a minute", and off he went. He was not gone long, and when he returned he said, "Tell Michael I've gone down Bedford Road", and off he went again. He hadn't been gone long when Michael returned, and so I gave him Sid's message, and off Michael went to help Sid.

Later when we three were having breakfast I heard Sid and Michael having a quiet, private conversation, and I heard Sid say, "We made a score here, and a score there", which rather perplexed me, and so after Sid had gone back to work, I said,

"Michael – what was all that about – a score here and a score there – what was Sid talking about?"

"Oh!!" Said Michael, "It was those apples you looked after for him – they were all nicked!"

One day early in December, after the market had finished for the day, I had 100 boxes of Golden Delicious Apples delivered to my Stand to be sold the next day. Mr. Hughes was my immediate next-door neighbour and whose Stand was 6 times larger than mine, and part of which went behind my Stand, and he had 300 boxes of Golden Delicious Apples from the same sender as mine, which the porters had stacked there.

The next day as I was approaching my Stand at 4.00 am, I noticed a lot more activity going on than usual which I ignored, and I was just unlocking my Stand when a voice shouted, "Stop doing that!" I looked around, and there stood a civilian gentleman, accompanied by 3 uniformed policemen, and he said, "Who the hell are you?" I said, "I'm Bruce Gibson, and this is my Stand, and who the hell are you?" He said, "I'm Sergeant Detective Wheelbarrow, and I'll talk to you later, and until then you are not to open your Stand until I say so".

At that moment Michael arrived, and I told him I was not allowed to open up. I said, "Be a good chap, and try and find out what's going on?"

Ten minutes later, Michael returned and reported there had been a break in on Mr. Hughes stand, and they had stolen his 300 boxes of Golden Delicious Apples. To achieve this, at least five men must have been involved, because to get to Mr. Hughes' apples, they had to lift them over my Stand, which was quite an arduous task, before taking them away, but the problem that the Detective was trying to solve was why they hadn't stolen any of my apples of the same brand. I said to Michael, "how come they didn't take any of my apples?" He replied, "Don't be stupid Bruce; Mr. Hughes is a bastard to us porters, and the boys know you look after us with our cotchells – they'll never nick anything of yours."

It took me over an hour to convince the Detective I was not involved in that piece of skulduggery, but once again, the Porters questioned by the police vouched for my integrity, which once again proved there is loyalty among thieves!

Word soon got around what a stupid soft touch I was, and that from 4.00 am to 6.00 am until my salesman arrived, I was on my own selling. Michael warned me that he had heard via the grapevine that the Barrow Boys were planning to pull a fast one on me, and to watch out. True to Michael's word, I noticed quite a number of new young faces making stupid bids for my produce, but I had been warned, and so there was no deal.

Every morning a Masonic acquaintance of mine, Joe, who was one of the biggest buyers in the market, used to pass the time of day with me, and while I could seldom sell to him, he would pass on any advice if he could see I was doing something wrong.

At one time I was receiving daily 30 lb boxes of Cox's Orange Pippin Apples. They were well packed, of superb quality, and for which I could hang out for the top price. That was the sort of gear Joe was interested in, and although he was not an early buyer, he would take all I had left when he came without querying the price. Barrow boys had been asking the price of my delicious apples, but I was always too pricey for them, but this did not deter them, and they would enquire every day.

One morning, at 4.00 am, a Barrow boy enquired the price, and to my amazement, bought 10 boxes of my delicious apples and asked if he could borrow Michael's sack truck because he was in a hurry to get away, despite the fact that I charged him porterage for Michael to deliver. The same thing happened several times, and by the time Joe arrived, I only had 10 boxes left which had been sold and were waiting to be picked up.

Joe said, "Didn't you have your usual delivery of Cox's today?" I was delighted to say, "Yes Joe, but I've cleared the Stand!"

"What price did you get Bruce?" He asked.

"The same as yesterday Joe!!"

"Oh!!" Said Joe, "that's why you've sold out!"

I said, "why Joe?"

"Well", said Joe, "until yesterday, those Cox's were in 30 lb boxes but those ten boxes over there are 40 lb boxes – you will have to put it down to inexperience – you won't make that error again will you?!"

My first Barrow boy had spotted my error, and he had told all his mates, and they cleared me out before I realised it, and were laughing their heads of at my stupidity!

One of the biggest buyers in the market was a man nicknamed 'The Godfather'. He was always to be seen in the market at around 4.00 am, with his two henchmen who were always two paces behind him. They never spoke or conducted any business, but they were the holders of the Godfather's ready cash, because the headman did not have a bank account. He could not read or write, but his mental arithmetic ability was second to none. He did not need a calculator, although at that time they hadn't come on the scene, but if he bought one hundred crates of cauliflowers at one shilling and nine pence per crate, he knew to the penny how much he had spent. He had several lorries and he used to supply hospitals and hotels, and he also used to buy in bulk to supply Barrow Boys their gear at the right price.

He always made a complete circuit of the market early on to see what the market had to sell and at what price, but I was told that was his alibi. If any large scale of villainy was taking place he was in the clear as everyone in the market could vouchsafe for him. He would stop at my Stand every morning and say, "Good morning Bruce", look to see what I had to sell, and move on, never bothering to ask the price of anything because he knew I was far too pricey for him.

One morning he turned up at my Stand when I was on my own as my salesman was at breakfast, and Michael was out doing a delivery.

He said, "Good morning Bruce," and to one of his bodyguards he said, "Give Bruce the money", at which the henchman produced three bundles of £5.00 notes. He said to me, "Count the money Bruce."

Having done the banking for my shops for years, there was nothing I liked better than counting notes. There was quite a little crowd round my desk. There was the Godfather and his two bodyguards, and I noticed a Greek Cypriot customer of mine, Johnny, watching, and so I got cracking. Each bundle contained £1,000 in £5.00 notes. The Godfather said, "Thank you Bruce; give Johnny the money", and off he went, and my Greek customer started putting the money in his pouch.

I said, "What goes on Johnny?"

"He's just lent me £3,000, and you're the witness."

I was flabbergasted. I said, "He's just lent you £3,000 – at what interest?"

Johnny said, "At no interest; I just want to buy the shop next door to me to expand, and if he wants the money back, I'll have 48 hours to produce the money, and if I don't, I'll have my throat cut; that's the interest."

I said, "Johnny, don't get me involved in your business affairs."

Johnny said, "It's OK Bruce; we both agreed you should be the witness. I have the money in Cyprus, but it will take me two or three weeks to get it"

I was still nonplussed when Michael returned, and I told him what had happened in his absence, and he said, "Well, that's how it is Bruce; they both know you're stupidly honest, and there are not many honest men they can trust in the market!"

Once again I was on my own when George, a regular customer of mine who had a shop in Kensington, and only bought the best gear, brought two 12 lb trays of black grapes back to me and said, "Look at this load of rubbish you sold me yesterday." I said, "I'm sorry George; put the trays down and take two more."

When Michael returned he said, "What are those two trays of grapes doing here?" I related that George had brought them back, and I had exchanged them. Michael went spare!! "Wait until I see that bastard George – he didn't get those grapes from us – we don't sell that marque!" "Oh!!! Michael," I said, "I'm sorry, but don't go upsetting my customers for just two trays of grapes." Just after that Sid came by with 32 trays of grapes on his trolley. Michael said,

"Drop the handles Sid" and proceeded to take two trays of grapes from off Sid's trolley and replace them with the two that George had returned. "Off you go Sid," "Michael," I said, "What the hell are you doing? You can't do that" He replied, "It's done Bruce; anyone with 32 trays of grapes wont' mind having a couple of duff ones".

It was one of the ways Michael went out of his way to look after me – he thought I was so stupid that I shouldn't be let out in the market on my own.

One Friday as we were packing up, Michael said, "Do you mind if I don't come to work tomorrow? My sister is getting married." I said, "That's fine Michael, I can get Cyril to let me have one of his porters. By the way, would you like to borrow my car?"

Michael said," You're joking! The Bentley?!"

"Yes", I said, "You can borrow my Bentley, and I can use your old banger".

It was another reason why Michael thought I was so stupid, but he was a better driver than me, and so I had no fears on that score.

Quite often after that, when I went to Lincoln Inn Fields to pick up my car, Michael's wife would be just finishing washing it. Michael had got his wife looking after me too!

One of the biggest buyers in the market heard of the stupid, retired Wing Commander, and he made it his business to make my acquaintance.

On our first meeting, we both found we were on the Square, and were senior Masons. We often breakfasted together, and there were times when, if I were stuck, he would buy the rest of my produce and clear my stand. Again Bobby Sharpe's name came to mind; 'It's not what you know, its who you know which counts'.

In my Air Force days, I had bought a very expensive gold watch that I used for navigation purposes because it was accurate to the second. It was too good to wear in the market, especially as there were some shady characters around, but one day on my return home to Camberley I found my watch missing. The next day I had a job to do for Cyril in the Borough Market which made me later than usual arriving at Covent Garden.

I parked my car as usual in Lincoln Inn Fields and, as I was passing Bow Street Police Station at about 6.00 am on my way to Cyril's stand in the jubilee market, I popped into the Police Station to report the loss of my watch in the hope that it had been found by some honest person and handed in to the police.

At about 6.15 am I was met by a very irate brother Cyril whose greeting to me was, "Where the hell have you been?" I said, "I've been to the Borough Market for you – remember?" "I don't mean that," said Cyril, "Where have you just come from?" I said, "I've just come from the Police Station". "What the hell for?" Said Cyril. "I went to report the loss of my watch". "You bloody fool Bruce," said Cyril, who did not usually swear. "Can you see any Porters around?" I said, "What's that got to do with it?" "Someone saw you go into the Police Station, and all the Porters are down in the basement emptying their lockers of all the stuff they have nicked; go down to the basement and tell them what you've been up to."

At the entrance to the basement there was a porter who barred my way, and so I said to him, "Tell the brothers I lost my watch yesterday, and I've just been to the Bow Street Runners to report my loss, and say I'm sorry if I have caused unnecessary consternation".

As the Porters started to drift back to work, Cyril said, "You stupid sod Bruce; you'll never learn – don't ever do anything like that again!"

On the Stand immediately next to me was a man who used to be in my class at Holbrook Road School, and who was now Head Porter of T J Pouparts. He was still living in Plaistow, and we used to have the occasional meeting and talk about old times. He was good to know because he was in the 'Cotchell' squad to everybody's benefit.

I had three Tottenham Hotspurs season tickets, and some of the other porters supported other London clubs, and if their teams were playing Tottenham I was always able to get them tickets, which was greatly appreciated. One of the porters had a second job as a scene shifter in a West End Theatre, and many were the times I would be presented with complimentary tickets for some excellent shows.

At one of our Breakfast soirées, Michael's friend Sid related that their Salesman had left, and the job had been given to their Cashier (who had occasionally done selling in the absence of the Salesman), and on his first day as Salesman he had sold out of a day's supply of lettuces by 4.30 am, and was feeling very chuffed with himself – until his Governor arrived when it was pointed out to him the boys had cleared him out because, for the first time the sender had packed his lettuces in packages of 24 instead of the usual 18, and the Salesman had sold them at the 18 price. Of course everybody had a good laugh at his error. I said to Sid, "Don't laugh too much – it can easily happen as it has happened to me!"

I quickly went round and commiserated with the new Salesman and told him I had made the same mistake, and to take comfort in the fact that he would never make the same mistake again. The Salesman thanked me, but could not console himself for his stupidity because, he said, my error had been due to inexperience, whereas he had been a Cashier for over 20 years, and he should have known better.

One Saturday morning I had cleared my Stand quite early, and so after Breakfast I went round to see how Cyril was getting on. It was getting near 10.00 am and the market was more or less finished, but Cyril had 100 crates of cauliflowers, packed in crates of 24's, which nobody wanted. My Godfather acquaintance was hovering around, and several times Cyril tried to attract his attention, but the old villain was not interested, and did not want to know at the price that Cyril was asking.

Ultimately all of the buyers had gone, except for the old rascal, and as he once again walked past Cyril's Stand, Cyril said, "100 crates of cauliflowers?" and not breaking his step, the old man just held up one finger.

I said, "Cyril, he's offering you £1; why don't you take it?"

Cyril replied, "You bloody fool; he's not offering £1, he's offering one shilling! The crates cost two shillings without the contents, but I'll have to take it, otherwise they will be rotten by Monday, and I'll have to pay the road sweeper £5 to take them away."

I said, "But that's unfair".

Cyril said, "Unfair bebuggered, that's how the market works – you'll never learn – you should have stayed in the Royal Air Force!"

I said, "Maybe you're right – at least I knew what I was doing there!"

One weekend when shopping, I noticed that a shop in Camberley High Street had become vacant. I drew Cyril's attention to this, and reminded him how, when I was 18 years old, I trebled the takings of the greengrocery shop in Addiscombe that I managed for him, and as I did not like working in the Covent Garden environment, would he agree to my opening a chain of retail shops, and a van delivery service selling to all retail outlets whose owners were too lazy to get up early and go to the market themselves? Cyril agreed to that, and so I took on a lease on a warehouse in Aldershot to use as a store and as a base from which to work, and we bought a 5-ton lorry, second-hand from Sainsburys, and employed an experienced Van Salesman. We were in business!

We also took a lease on the shop in Camberley High Street, which we started to fit out. One of Cyril's big buyers was a man named Roy Beeke. His parents owned a greengrocery shop, and so he had been born in to the trade. Cyril introduced him to me, and it was agreed that Roy would advise and help me to get the Camberley shop fitted out. That was how I met Albert, who was a carpenter come greengrocer, and who was a friend of Roys. He and Roy got cracking, and in no time at all the High Street shop was ready for business, and to start with, on Roy's recommendation, Albert was to be temporary Manager until the shop got going.

Our shop in the High Street was just a few doors away from the biggest and best greengrocer in Camberley, but I knew that we would be getting our produce direct from the farmer, via Covent Garden, and that we would be able to be very competitive price-wise.

Within a few months, we had five lorry driver/salesmen working from Aldershot, and we had got the Camberley shop taking £1,000 per week. To supply the Aldershot depot, we bought a 7 ton lorry which I used to drive to Covent Garden every morning, even though we had a driver, Ian, to do this.

We used to park the lorry near to where I lived, and in those days I loved driving heavy lorries. And so, every morning, I would drive it to Bagshot, pick up our driver, and drive to market while Ian, our driver, finished his night's sleep. I used to 'phone over the previous night to Cyril what our requirements were for the shop and lorries, and Ian would collect all of our gear and load the lorry. Once the lorry was loaded, I would drive it back to Aldershot – while Ian finished his sleep – in time for the lorry salesmen to start loading their lorries prior to doing their rounds.

By this time, our shop and rounds were getting so busy that it was agreed Roy Beeke would join us full time. This worked a treat because Roy knew all about running the retail shops, and he relieved Cyril from doing our buying, and we got better – and cheaper – gear as a result.

Ian was a big strong man, and he would help the lorry salesmen to load their lorries, and in this connection he was a show off! The salesmen were not quick enough for Ian, and he would cajole them with phrases such as, 'Come on you lazy lot of bastards; get a move on!' All to no avail, because the salesmen only ever went at their own pace.

One Saturday morning, Ian went to Covent Garden on his own to pick up our gear because Cyril had decided to visit the Warehouse to check our paperwork, and I had to be there.......

Everything went to plan, and Ian arrived back at the warehouse, and was helping to load the lorries and barracking the salesmen as usual, and I went to the loading bay to tell Ian to 'lay off' as it was annoying Cyril, when Ian said, "By the way Bruce, somebody backed in to me at the market, and you can see the damage from here."

Ian's lorry was parked about 15 yards away, and a dent could be seen which was about the size of a wash hand basin in the near side wing, and the head lamp was broken.

I said, "That's a nuisance Ian – that will take the vehicle off the road for a week." He replied, "I'm sorry Bruce, but you know what it's like in the market."

Nothing more was said, and I ultimately sent Ian off to deliver the goods needed by the Camberley shop. At about 10.00 am, Cyril was working in the office and I was straightening things up in the warehouse, when a mobile policeman drove up and parked his motorcycle. There was nothing unusual about that, except that he normally arrived at about coffee time.

A very sombre policeman approached me, and who did not return my greeting, but in a formal way, said, "Did you go to market this morning Mr. Gibson?" I said, "No, why do you ask?" "Are you sure, Mr. Gibson?" "Oh yes!!" I replied, "my brother Cyril came to check my paper work, and so I had to be here."

I could see that I had not convinced the policeman and so I said, "You look a bit glum – what is all this about?"

"Well," he said, "I have reason to believe you did go to the market this morning, and that the vehicle you were in was involved in an accident at Egham, and a cyclist was knocked down by your lorry and killed."

The penny dropped immediately – Ian's dent in his lorry.

I said, "I can assure you I did not go to market this morning, but Ian went on his own. He is out at the moment, but he will be back in about 30 minutes, and you can interview him then. In the meantime, come in to the office and have a coffee until his return."

I went into the office, and told Cyril to make a coffee, and to keep the Policeman interested until I returned. Off I shot to intercept Ian, and stopped at the first roundabout that I knew Ian must come to on his return. It was not long before I was able to wave Ian down to stop.

I got into his cab and said, "Ian, I know you told me about an accident you had in the market this morning – well, forget about that because there is a policeman back at the warehouse, waiting to interview you, because he has reason to believe that you were involved in an accident at Egham where a cyclist was killed. Cyril is entertaining the policeman, who does not know that I've come to see you here. So, forget what you told me, and give me 10 minutes so that you can start to collect your thoughts – but whatever you say in a statement to the policeman, let it be the truth, because if it goes to court, the legal people will be making rings around you if you tell them any lies. And so I repeat, whatever you say, let it be the truth."

And off I dashed back to have a coffee. 15 minutes later, I heard Ian's lorry arrive, and I said to the constable "Here's Ian – come and meet him." I said to Ian, "This police constable thinks you had an accident on your way back from market this morning; go into the office and talk to him." I told Cyril to make himself scarce, and I sat in on the interview to give Ian some moral support, and also to see fair play.

The gist of Ian's statement was that he drove to Covent Garden, loaded his lorry, and returned to Aldershot. He was adamant that he knew nothing about an accident at Egham, and no mention was made of the dent in the wing of Ian's lorry.

The policeman, having taken Ian's statement, left, and Ian completely broke down and cried like a baby. This was the tough guy who used to throw his weight around.

A strong, hot mug of tea worked its magic, but he was unfit to drive, and so he had to wait until I could drive him home. He did not turn up for work for the next fortnight. That didn't worry me – it meant a bit more work for me to do, but that was all.

One day however, when I was on my way back to Aldershot, I drove to Ian's house and ordered him to drive me back to the warehouse. This he did, and from then on he carried on as usual, rushing about and showing how strong he was.

I introduced Ian to a good litigation solicitor because I knew that he would have to attend the Inquest due to be held on the dead cyclist.

A fortnight before the Inquest, Ian once again went to pieces, and was unable to work.

On the day, I took Ian and his wife in my motorcar to Kingston Crown Court, where the truth of what happened was divulged.

On the day of the accident, Ian had loaded his lorry and was driving back to Aldershot. He knew the road well; the weather was overcast and the road damp.

As he was driving out of Egham, the combination of overhanging trees and a badly lit portion of road meant that at 7.40 am, visibility was very poor, and Ian's lorry struck a local female cyclist who was on her way to work, which resulted in her death. Ian must have felt the impact because he swerved to the right, and in doing so, struck a Rover car going in the opposite direction, and tore the side out of the Rover.

The forensic scientist, a young lady of 24 years, stated that Ian's lorry was being driven with dipped headlights, and the lady cyclist was cycling along a very dark portion of the road. She had no lights on her bike as the batteries in both her front and rear lights were dead. The chipped paint and broken glass from Ian's lorry that was left at the scene of the accident appeared to match Ian's lorry perfectly.

Ian was not called to give evidence, neither was he cross-examined on the statement which he had given to the policeman.

The Coroner, in summing up on the basis of the forensic evidence, stated that the lady cyclist had died as a result of a road accident, with no apportion of blame to Ian. The relatives of the lady cyclist were in court, and the teenage daughter was in great distress, creating a most traumatic atmosphere.

As I drove Ian and his wife home, Ian's conscience got the better of him, and he cried all of the way home.

I, being a Gemini - or a two faced Bastard, as my colleagues in the Air force used to describe me – was able to cope with the emotional side, and carry on as usual.

I dropped Ian and his wife off at their home, and Ian's wife thanked me for my support because Ian was unable to talk, but in parting I said, "Ian, do snap out it; I will call for you tomorrow at 4.00 am. Be there!!"

In the late 1960's there was full employment, and workers could move from one job to another with no regard to any inconvenience that this would cause the employer. A few months after the accident, one Friday while I was giving Ian his wages, he said, "I won't be in on Monday Bruce, I'm starting a new job at Crittals in Camberley making concrete pipes."

I said, "You can't start a new job on Monday Ian; you've got to give me a week's notice." "Come off it Bruce" was the reply, "get up to date – if that's the way you want to play it, I'll be in next Friday with a sick note from my Doctor, but I'll be making concrete pipes on Monday."

And that's what Ian did. It didn't worry me because I always drove the lorry to the market and back, and I got my porter to load the lorry for me, and he did it better than Ian. Back at Aldershot, my salesmen loaded their own lorries, which took a little longer, but without the aggravation from Ian.

Several months passed, and I had just got rid of the lorries on their rounds and was just having a coffee before going to the Camberley shop, when in walked Ian. I was quite pleased to see him, and over a coffee, he casually said, "Are you still going to market on your own Bruce?" "Of course Ian, why do you ask?" was my reply. "Well" said Ian, "If the job is still open, I'd like to come back."

My first reaction was total astonishment!

"But you were going to make so much more money Ian – how come?"

"Well" said Ian, "I am making more money, but it is much harder work lifting several hundred weight sacks of cement, and at the end of the day I am absolutely knackered!"

I said, "You should have thought of that before you did the dirty on me. But, you can have your job back – on one condition."

"What's that?" he asked.

"As long as you give Crittal Pipes one week's notice!" was my reply.

So, we were back in the old routine, which lasted for a few more months.

One day, I was helping Ian move stuff around in the warehouse when he said, "You used to be a Wing Commander, didn't you

Bruce?" "Yes, why do you ask?" "Well" he said, "There's a job going at Heathrow Airport for a baggage handler, and if you would give me a reference signed as Wing Commander, I reckon I could get it".

Apparently the money was better; the only snag was that it was a five-day working week out of seven days, which meant Ian would sometimes have to work over the weekend. Ian got the job however, and did very well. After a while he was made in charge of a shift and was sent to Manchester Airport.

Every day I would let Cyril know what my requirements were to keep the warehouse stocked, and he would pass my order on to Roy Beeke who did the buying. On one occasion, everything arrived except the potatoes, and I tore Roy a mild strip off in the market for that failure.

A couple of days later, when I had just got rid of the lorries and I was on my own, 15 tons of potatoes arrived. Of course I was delighted, and so, after a coffee, the driver and I started to stack the 56 lb sacks of potatoes 8 high. The driver was most helpful by putting each sack on my shoulder because he was only allowed to bring the sacks to the tail board of his lorry, and by 12 noon, I had them all stacked – all 'ship shape and Bristol fashion', and the driver went on his way.

I was just enjoying my sandwiches for lunch, when lo and behold, another 15 tons of potatoes arrived. When I bawled Roy out, he thought he had forgotten to order my potatoes, and so he ordered another 15 tons from a different supplier. From having no potatoes, I now had 30 tons!

With the help of the new driver, once he had shared my sandwiches with me and had a short break, I was able to do a repeat performance, and by 3.00 pm I was completely knackered – but I had finished!

The second shop we opened was in North Street, Guildford, and once again Roy Beeke and Albert fitted the shop out, and we were in business.

Having staffed it out, I took over the responsibility of controlling the shop, which I did as soon as I got the lorries away at Aldershot. Roy Beeke recommended his brother Terry to put up the shows for our products, but Albert, who was temporarily in charge when I was not there, said, "Bruce, there is no one better at arranging fruit and vegetables than Terry – but don't let him get near the tills!"

Our shop was in a good secondary position, with an open front and plenty of passing trade, and in no time at all, we were doing £1,000 per week trade. Roy taught me that the key to selling fruit and vegetables was to get the price ticket right. For example, if the price ticket says 'Peaches 9d each', you might sell 2 or 3, but if it says '9d each or 6 for 4 shillings', most times the customer buys six at a time.

Roy would buy 100 trays of peaches with 36 in a tray, and Terry would make a mass display. As people walked passed out shop they could smell the peaches, and it would stop them in their tracks, and we would sell out of peaches every day.

Everything was priced, with well-written, clear tickets, which I taught the staff how to write, and together with Terry's displays, our shop looked a treat. With goods at the right price, we always had a queue waiting to be served.

This was another trick that Roy taught me. Women will always join a queue out of curiosity. It must never get too long because women are impatient, but a short queue they cannot resist. Before the days of now when customers select their own produce, it was a greengrocer's trick to serve the odd bruised apple or pear, but I would have none of that, and behind the shop in the storeroom I would sort out our produce so that we only sold sound gear.

We had a lady customer who had 13 children, and 2 or 3 times a week, and for a nominal sum of 1d per pound, she would buy all of our bruised goods. Normally I would work on my own in the storeroom, but if I needed help, I always had two lady staff to help me – never one on her own to prevent the charge of rape or assault.

One day I was busy putting stuff away in our cold store, when the lady with 13 children came into the store. I greeted her by saying "How nice to see you". I immediately picked up the box of bruised fruit, and went back into the shop, and there was Terry waiting, with an evil leer on his face, and said to the two of us, "Well, that didn't hurt, did it?!" Much to the hilarity of the staff who were in on Terry's ploy at my embarrassment.

One section of our shop was for the display of superb gear – grapes, cherries, strawberries, etc – and to the customers who were interested in the sort of gear, price was no object.

We had one young lady customer, a Miss Ashton, who was a real high stepper, and she was always beautifully turned out, and she would leave her Porsche motorcar outside our shop. Terry, who had never had anything other than a greengrocer's van or an old Banger, was enthralled with this posh girl and her car, and he used to chat her up and make her laugh, which was always good for business.

Terry had a wonderful sense of humour, and he got to know many of the regular passers by to whom he always gave a greeting.

We had three tills which were always in operation, and one day I was serving Miss Ashton when she said to me, "Mr. Gibson, Terry has invited me out on a date in London – what shall I do?"

I said, "Terry is a married man, but his wife has left him. But, I can guarantee you'll have an excellent time because he is good company – but, don't go on your own – take a friend with you and make it a foursome because there's safety in numbers."

This she did, and she made it her business to report to me afterwards. She said, "My friend and I have never had such a good time; we did a West End show with dinner afterwards, and we never stopped laughing!"

Terry and his friend had a fund of stories, and there was never a dull moment. To her it was fabulous meeting people who were so unlike her normal friends who normally had nothing to say.

I said, "By the way, what did Terry's friend say he did for a living?"

She replied, "His friend was charming, and when I asked him

what he did for a living, he said he was a burglar!!!"

This answer caused much laughter, but I looked my customer straight in the face and said, "Miss Ashton, be careful, because he probably is a burglar!"

"Oh no!!" she said, "They have asked us to do a repeat performance next week."

"Miss Ashton" I said, "With people like Terry there is no such thing as a free lunch; you've had your fun – but you would be wise to keep out of Terry's way for a bit."

One day, I arrived at North Street a bit later than usual, and as I was admiring Terry's display I noticed that a price ticket on the grapefruit was wrong, but before I could do anything about it, an artisan gentleman was walking passed our shop with his wife, who was walking two paces behind him.

"Look Ted – Grapefruit 8d each, or 3 for 2 shillings – how much do you save?", she said.

Without breaking his stride, her husband responded, "Nothing, you stupid cow", and carried on walking.

Roy produced another man to act as Manager who was familiar with Terry's foibles, and so that relieved me a bit so that I could work at the Camberley shop. One Saturday when I was serving in the Camberley shop, Cyril arrived and decided to help.

There is however a wealth of difference between selling wholesale in Covent Garden and retail in Camberley High Street.

Cyril was serving a lady with 1lb of tomatoes, and was just putting them in a bag when the lady said, "I don't want that one".

Cyril adopted his superior, snotty, attitude as he looked at the customer as if she were a bit of dirt and said, "You don't want that one Madam? – well I suggest you get your tomatoes some place else!" and with that he tipped the tomatoes out of the bag, back into the display, and walked off.

I finished serving my customer and went charging into the back room where Cyril was having a coffee, and I tore him such a strip off.

"You've lost me a customer" I said, "That's not the way to talk to customers – you're not in Covent Garden now. Don't you realise the customer is always right? Even if they are not, you still have to give them the impression that they are, and that their wish is your command!"

Cyril was not used to being spoken to like that, and he said, "To use one of your Air force expressions – 'Bullshit'. I'm not having people speak to me like that."

"Right," I said, "You don't know how to serve retail customers, so keep out of the shop and it won't happen again."

The next time I met Cyril in the market all was forgiven because he was delighted with the progress I was making on the retail side. We had just opened out third shop, which had been opened by Roy Beeke and who was going to in charge.

When we were young boys, we used to see a boy who was younger than us who lived in the local greengrocer's shop. His parents were always busy in the shop, and the lad had to fare for himself. We noticed that the boy always had holes in his trousers, and Cyril nicknamed him 'Bumholes'. And that's how he was always referred to – 'Bumholes'.

50 years had passed by, and one day in the market Cyril pointed out to me a gentleman and said, "Do you know who that gentleman is?" "No" I said. Cyril said, "You'll never guess, but that's 'Bumholes'!"

As far as Cyril was concerned, he would never be remembered as anything else!

* * *

28

Better the devil you know........

The argument that Cyril and I had at the Camberley shop was the beginning of the end of our business relationship. He didn't like selling retail, and I did not like selling wholesale in the Covent Garden environment. And so, I closed the Aldershot depot and sold the five lorries, and with the help of Roy Beeke, we sold the three shops.

They were all thriving businesses. Camberley was taking £1,200 per week, Guildford was taking £1,400 per week, and Brixton, £1,100 per week – all showing excellent profits. While I was looking around for my next venture I returned to my Stand at Covent Garden.

We sold the Guildford shop to a gentleman, Joe Cliff, and some weeks later he called at my Stand and I could see that he was not happy, and so I said, "Joe, what's wrong?"

He replied, "Bruce, those figures you gave me when I bought the shop were not right." (And this was despite the fact that I had stayed with him for a month during the handover period).

I said, "What makes you say that Joe?"

"Because I'm down to £600.00 per week in takings," he replied.

"Joe" I said, "You saw what the business was doing during the handover period; I'm in between jobs at the moment, but from Monday I'll come and see what you are doing wrong, and help you build the business back up again."

During the first few days I diagnosed what Joe's problem was. He was not buying correctly. For example, he was buying 3 trays of peaches which would take him 2 days to sell, whereas Roy would buy 100 trays, and with the mass display put up by Terry, and with the right price ticket, we would clear them in a day. It was a case of impulse buying – not only could the customers see the wonderful display, but they could also smell them, and it worked. Joe just did not know how to buy.

His previous job had been selling grain to farmers, and he knew nothing about greengrocery. What it amounted to was that Joe was a gentleman, and the salesmen in the market were taking advantage of that fact and were ripping him off, and making him pay top price. Whereas, when Roy Beeke had been doing the buying for himself and us, it was the other way round. It did not matter what the market price was at the point in time when Roy bought the produce, he did not settle up until the end of the working day, when he would only pay the rock bottom price for the day. Because he was such a big buyer, there was nothing the salesmen could do about it if they wanted to keep his trade.

There was a Masonic friend of mine who was a buyer for other County Markets, and I had discovered Joe was on the Square, and so I introduced him to my buyer friend, and the arrangement was that he would buy for Joe at a cost of 3d per package.

To build a business from scratch is much easier than trying to rebuild a run down business, but over the next few months, and through good buying combined with Terry's displays, I got Joe up to £1,000 per week.

On one day in the market, as there was a glut of strawberries, and the price had fallen.

Roy knew I was helping Joe, and he rang Joe and it was agreed that Roy would bring to Guildford a load of strawberries to sell. Roy arrived late morning with 500 trays of 12 lbs of strawberries, at 3d per pound. The queue started to build before we were ready to sell, but once we started selling, and with Terry giving the spiel, Joe was taking money faster than he had ever done before.

Terry had created a mass display of the strawberries on a 12-foot long table top with a set of scales, and he was in his element, with Joe taking the money. He had the coins in a box, with the notes in a mug, and within 3 hours, the strawberries were sold out. Women were buying 10 lbs at a time for jam making, and Joe was delighted.

However, he made one error. It was lunchtime and he went to the toilet. On his return, the coins were still in the box, but the mug with the notes was empty, and there was no Terry.

Joe asked me, "Have you got the notes Bruce?" I was serving in the shop at the time, and said, "What do you mean Joe?"

He replied, "The mug's empty, and the notes have gone."

"Where's Terry" I said.

"I don't know, but he's not here".

"Joe" I said, "I warned you about Terry; I bet that's where your notes are."

Terry returned from his lunch break, and he swore on his mother's grave that the notes were still in the mug when he went for lunch, and no one could prove otherwise.

Joe complained to Roy, but there was nothing that Roy was prepared to do about it, and so by mutual consent, Terry left Joe's employ.

Joe used to 'phone his requirements over to his buyer every day, and so all he had to do was drive his 5 ton lorry to market and pick his gear up. Once I had got Joe into a routine, and with his trade increasing and he was starting to feel confident about being left on his own, I started to investigate a Newsagent, Confectioner and Tobacconist in Hove, West Sussex. It was a good shop that was run by a Yorkshire man and his wife, and they convinced me that the figures that the owner had given me were genuine. Also, if I wanted them, they would both like to stay, and that seemed like a good arrangement.

It was a double fronted shop with a basement and 3 floors of living accommodation, and on the top floor there was a bedroom that I could use, and there was a café around the corner where I could eat. The business had several advantages, but the main one was that it sold counter newspapers only. There were no deliveries, and also the Vendor owned the Freehold.

After the usual haggling over the price, I told the owner I would only buy his business if he sold me the Freehold. I estimated the value of the bricks and mortar was worth about £12,000. "That's OK," said the Vendor, "The price is £14,000."

I remembered how I had lost out in buying the Cove Road shop, and so I said, "Done!" and we shook hands on it

Stan Gibbons, my Legal Eagle, pulled his finger out and within weeks I was living over the Hove shop Monday through to Friday, and loving every minute of it. I had the shop refitted, and by adding a few items that I knew were good little earners, within 6 months I had doubled the takings.

Through my previous contacts I was able to buy cigars direct from Havana, which showed me a profit of 22%. Therefore I was able to undercut all of my local competitors and corner the market for cigar sales for Brighton and Hove. One band that I used to buy came in square boxes of 50, and had no band name on them. They were in fact large Havana cigars and which at my price of £1.00 each were a bargain. The local Bookmaker used to buy 7 a day. He only smoked 3 a day himself, as each one would last well over an hour to smoke, and the others he would give away to his regular but misguided gamblers.

Another gentleman who became my friend owned an antique shop in Brighton, and each evening on his way home from work he would call in the shop, and would buy 3 cigars for his own consumption, and half a pound of loose sweets for his young wife.

With other regular customers, I was selling several boxes of 50 cigars per week. Suddenly, I could not get any more boxes of 50 cigars. I contacted the Rep, and he told me to sell a banded named cigar, which I always held in stock, and which the Rep guaranteed was the same as those in the boxes of 50 – the only difference being that they were packed in boxes of 25, and that they were banded.

However, while some customers took the banded cigars and were quite happy, my bookmaker customer and the Antique Dealer did not agree and changed to another band completely. But, they kept on asking me to get the old band in boxes of 50.

The next time the Rep came I explained my difficulty, but he said, "The Havana company are not packing them in boxes of 50 any more, but I'll tell you what you can do….."

We were down in the basement cigarette storeroom where I did the buying, and he saw an empty box, which used to hold 50 cigars. He took a box of 25 cigars, and proceeded to cut off the advertising band, and put them in the empty box, which held 50. He then said, "I guarantee you they are the same make as those you are used to. Don't tell anyone else, but this is what you will have to do."

True to the Rep's word, the bookmaker and Antique Dealer were as happy as sand boys at being able to acquire the old band.

As I was not at the shop on weekends, I had to confide in my Manager, George, how to acquire boxes of 50 cigars, but I swore him to secrecy. When it came to Christmas time, my Antique Dealer friend asked me if I could get a box of 25 cigars, similar to those he usually had as he wanted to give it to one of his customers as a Christmas present. Of course, I could not let him know the cigars he regularly bought came out of a box of 25, and so I said, "Give me a couple of days and I will see what I can do." Friday night came, and I produced a box of 25 cigars. My friend was delighted! He bought his usual 3 cigars, and sweets for his wife, and off he went, a happy little bunny!

The following Monday my friend came into the shop and said, "Do you think you can get me another box of 25 cigars because I started to smoke those others that you gave me on Friday over the weekend, and I liked them better than those I usually have; if anything, they are a little bigger!"

The next time George and I were down in the basement, cutting the bands off the banded boxes of 25 and putting them in boxes of 50, I said to him, "I don't know why we are doing this!" and he replied, "You know Bruce, the customer is always right!"

Among the laughter that followed, I said, "Silly sods, some of them!"

Our new business continued to grow, and at one time I did not have time to eat, and was existing on 5 pints of milk a day, and only eating properly at weekends. My brother-in-law, Edgar Searle, the Senior

456

Scientist at Beechams, told me that was fine as long as I did not get ill, but if I did then my immune system would not be able to cope and I might become seriously ill.

So that straightened me out on that score, and I started to eat properly. I was having a proper breakfast at the café one day when I noticed a good-looking young man reading the Telegraph. At the time I thought nothing of it, but then I noticed he was there every morning, and he was still there when I left.

This perplexed me, until I saw one of my customers talking to him. I collared my customer the next time he came into the shop, and I asked him who the young man was that he had been speaking to in the café. I was told that he and his brother had a building business in Gloucestershire, and the bank had foreclosed on them, and put them out of business. He had just come back from Paris, and right now he had nothing to do. I thought, 'right monkey', and so the next time I went to the café for breakfast I said, "Do you mind if I join you?" and that was the start of a beautiful friendship.

After a few sentences of polite conversation, I asked him what he did for a living, and he said, "I'm in the building trade, but right now I've got nothing on." He told me his name was Kent, and I said, "Meet Bruce Gibson", and we shook hands. I said, "I've got a safe in my basement that I would like bricked up – could you do that for me?"

After breakfast I took Ken – as I had decided to call him – down to my shop basement where I had three storerooms. One for cigarettes and tobacco, the second for confectionary, and the third was a stationery store, which was where I wanted my safe bricked up.

Ken cast an expert eye on the wooden floor, jumped up and down a bit, and said, "This floor won't take a bricked up safe; we could do it if we took up the floor and had a concrete base." "Right!!" I cleared the Stationery store, and Ken took up the floor, and he ordered the ready mix concrete that we then had tipped down into the basement via the cellar flap, and I commenced to take a barrow load at a time to where Ken wanted it. All was going well until I got such a bollocking off Ken for not going fast enough, because the cement was going ORF! So, I got stuck in until we were finished, by which time I was knackered.

We allowed 48 hours for the concrete to harden, and then Ken bricked up the safe. Excellent – but true to all good builders who are always looking for the next job, Ken said, "The plaster on these walls is damaged and needs replacing." I said, "Can you do that Ken?"

I mixed the plaster, which for me was bloody hard work, and Ken plastered the walls, after which he said, "What colour do you want the walls painted?" When Ken was finished I had a brand, spanking new Stationery Store with a bricked up safe, which was a treat. While he was doing that work, he noticed the basement toilet needed attention, and so he fixed that, and so within a fortnight I found Ken could lay concrete floors, do brick work, plastering, painting, and also plumbing – and we had formed a good working relationship.

The next job I got Ken to do was the upstairs kitchen. We had a door from the kitchen which led to a flat roof, and which adjoined the Cinema next door. I noticed in hot weather the cinema people would open their door which led to my flat roof, and sometimes Cinema Patrons would walk out onto my flat roof to get some fresh air. That was fine, but for the best part of the day the kitchen was not being used, and there was nothing to stop people breaking into the kitchen. I said to Ken, "I would like some iron bars put through the window frames to prevent a break in." "A good idea" said Ken, "but these frames won't take iron bars - however I can make you some new frames which will do the job."

To do that, Ken worked on the flat roof and when he had finished, our kitchen was as strong as a battleship!

A shop immediately opposite mine in Western Road in Hove closed down. At the time Western Road was the main road from Hove to Brighton, and was so busy with traffic going through at 30 mph, my customers were finding it difficult to cross over the road. Therefore, I took a lease on the other shop, and Ken started to fit it out. It had a partition half way down the shop, and this was the first thing that

Ken ripped out.

The walls were covered in dark brown, tongue and groove panelling, and when he started to move them, a mass of huge bugs were disturbed – and so we had to call the Council to fumigate the premises.

That's when things started for Ken.

He bought a vehicle to take the rubbish and ballast away, and people saw what he was capable to doing. He fitted out the shop, and put a new shop front in. When we opened the shop, it did not affect the main shop opposite; all of the trade was additional.

People then wanted to hire Ken's mini truck. Ken's reply was always, "Only with the driver", and as a result he got into the moving business.

With the help of his girlfriend Sheila who went on to become his wife, and by dint of hard work and entrepreneurial skills, they became a respected, successful business partnership.

On one occasion when he was still building up his business, he had a load of furniture to be delivered to a firm in Worthing, but no driver. Ken knew I loved driving heavy lorries and so he asked me to help him out, which of course I did.

It was the last time I drove a lorry, and Ken insisted paying me because, he said, "I would have to pay any other driver!" and as a result, I earned £10.00.

We staffed the new shop with part time staff, with the Manager of the main shop, George, in charge. After initially stocking the shop, George kept it fully stocked daily from the storerooms opposite. George and his wife Mary were the best partnership to run a business that I had ever had. They were hard working, honest, and with Mary as the boss woman, we all did what Mary decided was right, and a more harmonious working relationship never existed.

I kept my eye on Ken as he started out on his new venture, but with Sheila helping him, they went from strength to strength, and I quickly realised they did not need me any more.

In the front of the main shop we had a section where customers could advertise things they had for sale. It was very low key; it was mainly to provide a service to our customers.

One day, the local police detective asked to see me, and he pointed a postcard out to me that he said I would be well advised to have removed. I looked at the postcard, and it said, "White Mini for sale, good bodywork", and it gave a telephone number.

I said, "What's objectionable about that?"

He replied, "Come off it Mr. Gibson – she's at it!" "At it?" I said, "At what?" "You're pulling my leg, Mr. Gibson; every male in Brighton knows that telephone number – she's a prostitute!"

"Good Lord!" I said, "How on earth was I supposed to know that?!"

"Well, one way to query it would be to look to see how long the customer has booked the advertisement."

"Right" I said, "We'll do that". I looked on the back of the postcard, and it had been booked for 6 months.

"If you were selling a motor car, you would expect to sell it in 6 days, not 6 months. To display a postcard like that leaves you open to be charged with living on the immoral earnings of a prostitute".

"Don't make me laugh," I said, "At six pence a week, I'd not get fat on that."

I tore up the postcard, and just as the detective was about to leave he said,

"I've just noticed you've got another postcard here." It said, 'Wicker chairs repaired – good cane work."

"Well" I said, "What's wrong with that?"

"She's inviting people for flagellation, and once again the telephone number is the clue," was the reply.

I removed the second postcard, and thanked the policeman for his help, and apologised for my lack of knowledge of prostitutes' phone numbers.

A few weeks later the detective called again and said, "You've got another postcard you should remove; it's a practical joke that someone is playing on a very respectable member of our society, and the lady's husband is complaining."

The postcard read, 'Full body massage service offered, 24/7, ring any time.' Apparently the lady was pushing 60 and her telephone had not stopped ringing!

One of my regular customers was a Canadian drug addict. He never surfaced before midday, and he always had a string of young girls with him, and whom he had got addicted. They were all living off the state, and getting their drugs by prescription. But it was quite pitiful to see these young, gaunt, skinny girls, with needle pricks up their arms, existing at the behest of their Canadian Master.

On two occasions he passed out in my shop. The first time I rang for an ambulance, but the police who had been informed arrived first. He was known to them and they searched his pockets, and they discovered he had used a fortnight's supply of drugs in 48 hours. The girls with him were just like zombies, quite incapable of helping their Master, and when the ambulance took him to hospital, the police had to escort the girls back to where they were living in squalor.

The police told me that he had got the girls hooked so that he could pinch some of their prescription to satisfy his own cravings.

One day when I was serving an elderly lady, and I was 'chatting her up', and discovered that she was 94 years of age. I flattered her by saying she did not look her age. She told me she was a widow, and although Brighton and Hove were busy places, sometimes she felt quite lonely. I said I would visit her one evening, and promptly forgot all about it. A few days later she was back in the shop, and she made it her business to see me.

I said, "Hello Mrs. James; how nice to see you." The reply I got was, "You promised to come and see me – Well!! You haven't been yet!" I said, "I'm so sorry, but I just have not had the time." "Are you doing anything next Monday?" she asked. "I don't think so." "Well, shall we say 7 o'clock? I live at 64 York Road." And off she went.

I'd never had a date with a 94 year old girlfriend before, and so I did not know what to expect, but I was greeted with an excellent glass of Port which took me back to my Air force days, and I discovered her name was Winifred James, and she was the widow of a General Practitioner, and had been a Matron in a large hospital. She had a fund of stories to tell, and it was one of those sessions that was most unusual for me where I did all of the listening.

I managed to get away at 9.00 pm, having enjoyed the hospitality of a remarkable old lady.

A few days later she sought me out to tell me how much she had enjoyed my visit, and she would expect me again the following Monday at 7.00 pm. I duly arrived, at 7.05 pm, to be greeted with "You're late – I'd given up on you!" I said, "I've got a busy shop to run, and I was unable to get away."

Port was produced, followed by a four-course meal of soup, main course, pudding, and cheese and biscuits with coffee. Naturally I insisted on helping her with the washing up, when I thanked her for an excellent meal, and said that I enjoyed visiting her, but I did not expect her to feed me.

She knew about Kay and Stuart, and that I lived at Camberley, and worked in the shop from Monday to Friday, and during general conversation I mentioned that the following Saturday afternoon I was going to a Masonic meeting in Brighton.

"Right!!" She said, "You can come and visit me on Friday evening." I said, "I will do that on one condition – that you do not go to the trouble of cooking for me!"

What started out with my visiting her one night a week finished up with my attending four nights a week, and I had difficulty getting away by 10.30 pm! This was not the first time a throw away line had landed me with commitments I did not originally intend to make. Winnie lived in an upstairs flat, and to save her legs, she gave me a key so that I could let myself in.

One day I was visiting and although the key fitted the lock OK, I had difficulty in opening the door. However, in trying to make an entry, I heard someone moaning, and so I forced the door and found Winnie unconscious behind the door. I immediately telephoned the Sussex Hospital, which was right bang opposite where Winnie lived, and within 5 minutes, a Doctor and two nurses appeared. Apparently Winnie was a regular visitor to the hospital and they knew she was an ex Matron, and in no time at all they had her in a private ward, giving her the treatment of which our Monarch would have been justifiably proud.

After 10 days they moved her on to a side ward to share with three other patients, and she promptly discharged herself, because she refused to share her living space with three old fogies!

There were times when I would take Winnie out for a ride round the beautiful Sussex villages in the Bentley. She was in her element because she was being driven in a vehicle fit for her station.

I used to park the Bentley in York Road, opposite the shop, in one of the free parking places. Some were out of bounds to allow for three point turns.

The Council employed a Traffic Warden to see fair play. He was a very nice man, a regular customer of mine, and so I got to know him well.

One Monday, I had just arrived from Camberley and parked in York Road, and I was walking down the hill towards the shop when I saw the Traffic Warden writing out a ticket.

He had his back to me, and I tapped him on his shoulder and said, "Have you booked any good numbers lately?" He continued to write, and without looking up he said, "I haven't booked DFM 808" which made me laugh because that was the number of my Bentley.

He had not only recognised my voice, but he remembered the number of my car, and for that I gave him 10 Brownie points!

One evening I was on my way to visit Winnie when I came across a man wrestling with a woman on the ground, and he was trying to force a Mars Bar between her lips.

"Help me", he said, which was not easy because she was throwing her arms and legs about and her skirt was virtually over her head. However she suddenly she stopped struggling as soon as she started to chew the Mars Bar. Together with her husband, I helped the young lady to her feet, when he then explained they were on a day visit to Brighton, and she was diabetic and had got out of her daily eating routine, and as a result had suffered a Diabetic Lapse, which, now I am a diabetic, I know as a 'hypo'. As soon as he had forced the Mars Bar between her teeth, her struggles stopped as quickly as they had begun.

He thanked me for my help, and they walked off hand in hand as if nothing had happened.

I was visiting Winnie one evening, and we were enjoying our glass of Port Wine, when the door opened and in walked a lady who turned out to be Winnie's daughter. Winnie was surprised but no more than I was because she had told me she had no relatives, and that she was alone in the world. She introduced me to her daughter, but I got a frosty reception, and it was obvious that Winnie having a boyfriend at 94 years of age did not meet with her daughter's approval! However I was able to make a quick exit, saying to Winnie that she must have a lot to talk about to her daughter.

Winnie's daughter was past middle age, and lived 50 miles away with her boyfriend. She stayed with Winnie over the weekend, and left on the Monday, but that was the last time I was to visit Winnie at her Flat. A few days later, one of her neighbours came and told me that she had been taken ill, and was in a rest home.

I used to visit her during visiting hours, and she was never her usual self, but when each time I left she would thank me for visiting her and order me in true Matron style by saying "Don't you ever forget me!"

In her younger days she had a horse called Rufus and she once had a very fine oil painting of him that she had commissioned which she gave to me.

I still have this painting, hanging in my office, and I look at it every day and remember what an amazing old lady she was.

* * *

29

Five Star Living

Both shops continued to be very busy, but I noticed Mary, our boss woman, was not as happy as was usually. I spoke to her husband, George, about it, and he confided in me that she was worried about the lure our open displays were to pickpockets, and it was keeping her awake at nights.

This problem was confirmed to me one evening when I was browsing in the Greeting Card section, and I noticed a man putting packets of silk stockings in the inside pocket of his jacket. He picked up a can of Coca Cola, and went to the till to pay. I followed him to the till, and when he volunteered to pay only for the Coca Cola, I challenged him and said, "But haven't you anything else to pay for?" The man said, "What's it to you?" I said, "Because this is my shop; what about these?" and I opened his jacket and took at least six packets of silk stockings out of his pocket. I noticed that Mary had shut the door, and was about to lock it, but I tore such a strip off in Airman's Air force language, and finished up by saying, "Now, get out, and never dare put a foot inside my shop again", and I bundled him out.

Mary thought I should have prosecuted the man, but I explained to her that it was just not worth it. It would get the shop a bad name, and the only people to gain would be the legal profession. As time went by I could see that Mary was making herself ill worrying about shoplifting, and as both she and George were getting near retirement age, I decided to sell.

I had both of them on a retirement plan, and so I bought a bookshop in Cheshunt in Hertfordshire for them to work at until they retired.

When they moved into the bookshop, they did not know what to do with their spare time! From managing a busy Newsagent from 0600 hours until 1900 hours, 7 days a week, to 0930 hours until 1700 hours for five and a half days a week, they thought they were working part time.

I spent the first six months with them until the organisation was right, during which time I was amazed at the number of new books published each month. It is impossible to stock the whole range of books, but we would always take an order to get any special book available which we could normally get within one week, whereas W H Smith's shop in Waltham Cross could not be bothered, and would send their customers to us.

We used to supply 25 local schools, and although the profit margin was much less than that of ordinary books, when schools ordered 100 of each title it was a nice little earner.

On one occasion Mary was taking an order, and the customer asked her if she could get a copy of Shaw's Pygmalion. Mary started to write the details down, and she wrote 'a copy of Pygmalion', and she then said, "Do you know the Author?" I was standing nearby and I jumped in and said, "Mary – I'll finish this order – be a good girl and make a cup of coffee?" thereby saving Mary from possible embarrassment. It is usual when customers order a particular book that they know the Title, the Author, and/or the Publisher, or any one of those three things accurately, to be able to trace the book required.

We only had a small section for greeting cards, and so we only had the best. Mary was in her element; she loved looking after that section, and it was always well stocked, and spic and span. Kay was very interested in the bookshop and quite often she would go with me and spend a pleasant day in Cheshunt. It was on one of these trips when she saw how well George and Mary had picked up the book trade, and she accused me of malingering, and so I decided to get a job!

As I had been responsible for the running of officers' messes for most of my service life, when I saw an advertisement for Receptionists for a five star hotel, which was shortly to be opened, I applied was invited to an interview.

I met a charming man, Michael Day, who was a Director of the hotel group. He was not the usual type of hard bitten businessman in an executive position; he was very friendly, about 50 years of age which was 10 years younger than me, and he was more interested in my Service career than talking about hotels. However, ultimately we got round to it, when he told me they were looking for much younger people with two or three languages for the Receptionists' jobs, and so I replied,

"That's OK, it was a brave try!"

But he went on to say, "There must be some other job you can do – do you know anything about stock control?"

"I used to lecture on RAF Stores and Equipment Accountancy – I could lay you on a Stock Control System." I replied.

"When can you start?" asked Michael.

"Now if you like" was my reply.

"Be here at 9.00 tomorrow Wing Commander!" he said.

And that's what happened. I turned up at the Howard Hotel, opposite the Temple Tube Station on the London Embankment in February 1975 and started work.

The hotel was in the process of being built on a two-acre site owned by the Duke of Norfolk, with a brand new 99-year lease. The shell of the hotel had been completed, but the interiors of the seven floors were in the process of being fitted out. The ground and first floors were more or less finished, but the contractors were working from the Basement completing the fixtures and fittings of the other floors. The main items of equipment had already been ordered, and they had started to arrive.

The Howard was part of a chain of seven hotels owned by David and Frederick Barclay. The stock control paper work used by the other hotels did not come up to RAF standards, and so I designed my own Stock Control Sheet, and had it printed.

I was given a conference room large enough to entertain 200 guests in which to receive the equipment, and as it arrived I unpacked everything, and if the items were sound, I laid them on the floor. Any damaged items I put to one side to be returned. I was given a coloured gentleman from Ghana to assist me in opening the packing cases and laying the equipment out, and in no time at all I had two gross of coffee pots, cups, and saucers laid out for display together with plates and dishes of all shapes and sizes, all of which I checked assiduously as if they were my own property.

My helper was a very intelligent man with a financial background, and he had been sent to our country to improve his vocabulary because on his return to his own country, he was to be promoted to a role where he would be dealing with financial matters on an international basis.   I liked him, and we got on well. He was keen to learn, and there were times when he would say, "Stop; what does that mean?" and if I had used an RAF expression or a local idiom, I would explain it to him in the Queens' English, and I began to realise when talking casually and not always articulating correctly, how difficult our language is to learn.

Equipment continued to arrive, including a full range of silverware. I knew how to handle silver from my RAF days, and having checked it all, I kept it in a special section under wraps because of its value.

The Head Chef arrived. He was tall, blond, and typical of the type of German that Hitler had wanted to breed. Michael, the Director, discovered that I was used to buying, and I was given the job of supplying the Chef's wishes, and I ended up buying all of the wet and dry food, and I was also put in charge of the Wine Store, which was a large room fitted out with racks to take 48 bottles in each column. On each column I labelled the name of the wine with best professional lettering, and although I say it myself, it looked quite impressive, and certainly fit for a five star hotel!

I trained my assistant how the stock control worked, and I put him in charge. A fortnight before we opened, a very large deep freeze arrived. It was beautifully packed, and I got the delivery people to put it in the kitchen, until it was decided where its final position would be. I duly signed for the article, unchecked, and awaited the return of the head chef who was working at one of our other hotels until it was nearer the opening time of the Howard.

When the Chef came to check that the kitchen was fully fitted and ready for opening, he came to me and said, "Where is the deep freeze?" I said, "It's in the packing case in the kitchen." "It's not there," he said, and so I went along to the kitchen, and lo and behold, someone had nicked it! That was one of the risks we had to take with contractors still working in the building. I reported the loss to Michael the Director, and he took over to claim on the insurance.

As the contractors completed each floor, the rooms started to be furnished. Each room had a refrigerator, in which were placed 30 bottles of drink, and as this came from my store I was put in charge of the 5 staff whose job it was to replenish the refrigerators of any drinks that had been consumed.

Each room also had its own television set, and these were installed a floor at a time. I was always properly dressed in black jacket, vest, and striped trousers so that I could go anywhere in the hotel, and one day when checking the room refrigerators, I noticed a T.V was missing on the second floor. By this time a General Manager had been appointed, and I made a written report about the T.V loss to him. No action was taken because I was told that the suppliers were still in the act of installing the sets, and it would be replaced.

However, a few days later I discovered another T.V had disappeared, and the first one still had not been replaced, and in contacting the Television suppliers, it was discovered that someone was nicking our T.V sets, and to cut a long story short, I was put in charge of security.

I was in my element and loving every minute at the Howard. I used to journey from Camberley to the Hotel every morning, getting there by 6.30 am, and would stay until 8 or 9 pm, or even later if the banqueting halls were being used.

On 1st April when we opened, we had 125 staff. We had a staff canteen and as I had plenty of experience in that type of catering, I noted that sometimes the food was not up the standard required.

And so, I mentioned this to Michael the Director, and reminded him that meals were part of the staff's wages. As a result, I was put in the charge of the Staff Canteen.

Therefore, every Friday, when I had a meeting with the head Chef to find out his future requirements, I would also agree with him a menu for the following week's Staff Canteen. When I had time I would eat there myself, and as the meals were to a predetermined menu, there were no more complaints.

As I was doing all of the buying, the Head Chef needed my cooperation for certain special items he might require at short notice. This was freely given and much appreciated by the Chef, and many were the times that he invited me into his Den, where the most delicious cheeses and biscuits were produced, for our mutual delight.

My first job every morning was the supervision of the cleanliness of the back of the house corridors, and these I had washed every day with disinfectant in the water.

By the time we opened, half of the crockery had been issued. Every room had been supplied with its own coffee and teapot, cups and saucers etc., and the Dining Room and bar had also been fully stocked, which left about half of the original stock in my store as a back up

A requisition chit had to be rendered every time new supplies were required, and I would only approve these if I thought it was necessary. In the beginning, the Restaurant kept ordering fresh cups and saucers etc, which I refused to action because I knew they had adequate supplies, and I would prove this to them by taking the Restaurant Manager and show him that his supplies were there, and just waiting to go through the Dishwasher!

The Restaurant staff thought I was a proper bastard, but as I had the backing of Michael, there was nothing they could do about it.

When the time came for our first Banquet, 10 cases of wine were ordered. I had a wonderful wine store, and I could meet most requisitions from stock, but even special items I could get within 24 hours. The Restaurant staff collected the 10 cases of wine, and the party was going with a swing. The food was superb, and the bar fully stocked, but in any case, I was there to supply any additional items that might be required. In my experience, when parties are held and free drinks are available, there are always people who drink to excess and make themselves ill, and I was on the lookout for those people. But, I was amazed! It was not the customers who were under the influence of drink; it was the waiters!

When collecting the empty glasses, they were drinking the dregs that had been left, and were walking around – sloshed! On these occasions extra waiters are required, and these we got from an agency, and it was these casual waiters who were misbehaving, and in two cases I noticed that each had a full bottle of wine when they left.

The next day I queried that procedure with Michael, and he said it was usual on such occasions for the Head Chef and the Restaurant Manager to be given a bottle of wine, but not any Tom, Dick or Harry. I thought, 'right monkey', and decided to do something about it.

A few days later we had another Banquet where 15 cases of wine had been ordered. The Restaurant Manager sent 2 Commis Waiters to collect the wine, and I gave them 4 bottles of white and 4 bottles of red, and sent them on their way.

I was immediately confronted by an irate Restaurant Manager who asked, "15 cases of wine had been ordered – why did you only send 4 bottles of each?"

I replied, "I'm in charge of stores – when you have used the bottles I have given you, bring back the empties and I will give you fresh bottles in exchange, because I am not going to have pissy casual waiters walking around with full bottles of our Customers' wine."

"Blimey!" he said, "But it is common practise after a successful Banquet for myself and the Head Chef to each have a bottle of wine."

"O.K." I said, "I'll make those arrangements."

Therefore, as the party was nearing its end, I approached the Host (who was well and truly away) and asked if everything had been to his satisfaction, and if so, would he agree to the Restaurant Manager and Head Chef having a bottle of wine each. To this he agreed, and suggested that I also take a bottle for myself, which I declined gracefully saying I preferred Coca Cola, amidst much laughter.

He was in such a state of happiness that if I had asked for a crate each, he would still have said yes.

So, in future, that was how all Banquets were conducted, and no more bottles of wine were stolen.

Being a five star hotel, we were open twenty-four hours a day. We had a skeleton staff of a Hall Porter, a Receptionist, a Room Service Manager, a Chef (any one of eight), and a Duty Manager to whom I would entrust the key to the wine store in case of need. On my arrival at 6.30 am every day I could tell if anyone had been in the Wine Store in my absence. Sometimes there was a requisition chit for an item, which was OK, but other times there was none, which made me feel uneasy.

As soon as I started to have concerns about the absence of chits, I would do a 100% check of the Wine Store, first thing every Monday morning. I was doing this one Monday morning with the help of a gorgeous Thai girl. I had the door open and who should pop in but David and Frederick Barclay.

"Is everything alright Bruce?" was David's opening gambit.

"Everything is fine Sir" I said, "By the way, we have been open three months now and we haven't sold a single bottle of Château Beuley".

"What is the price per bottle Bruce?"

"£14.50 a bottle Sir".

"That's the reason" said David.

"What shall I reduce it down to?" I asked

To my amazement David replied, "No, don't reduce it – you will never sell Château Beuley at £14.50 a bottle. Make it £24.50 a bottle."

I said, "You're joking Sir".

"No I'm not" was the reply. "Just alter all of the price lists and see what happens."

A few weeks later the Restaurant Manager gave me a chit for a bottle of Château Beuley. I said, "You know it's £24.50 a bottle?" "That's OK" was the reply.

An hour later he came back with another chit for a second bottle. "You are sure you know the price has gone up?" I said. "Don't worry, there are two young lads having lunch, and they're doing fine." I said, "They're going to bonk you; I'm coming to have a look at these two gentlemen." and off I went to the Dining Room, and there were these two lads, laughing and joking. I said, "I don't like the look of this – keep your eyes skinned – don't let them do a runner!" and I went back to work.

The Restaurant Manager always went for an afternoon break at 3.00 pm to his flat in High Holborn, and as I was in charge of security he would always come to see me before he took his leave, to show me that he was not absconding with any gear! So, on this occasion before he went for his break I said, "By the way – did those two lads pay up OK?" "They spent over £120.00 for lunch. One of them had over £1,000 in £50 notes in his back pocket – they gave me a £20 tip; I'm not complaining!"

Although my standard of living had changed a great deal considering my very humble beginnings, it always struck me as marvellous how the super rich ,whom we catered for, spent their money with such reckless abandon.

After the first week of opening, I did a physical check of the Wine Store and it proved that my Assistant's Stock Control system was working properly. There were just a few minor discrepancies, such as the loss of some large Havana Cigars and the odd miniature bottle of Whisky or Brandy, which we could trace back to the Night Duty Manager who had been entrusted with the Wine Store Key while I was off duty. These losses were written off, but reported to the General Manager for future reference.

The wages for the staff were done by a Junior Accountant from

Head Office every Thursday, and one week he fell ill, which put Michael the Director in a spin, until I volunteered to do it, and from then I did it every Thursday. I was given the Wages cheque and two bodyguards, and although it was obvious they were carrying the coinage, the paper money was distributed about my person, and the briefcase I was carrying was empty. It was a job I did willingly because I love counting money, and it was a nice break to get out of the Stores.

The accountancy details I was supplied with were always exact to the penny, which was proof that I hadn't made any errors. As a result of doing the wages, the Restaurant Manager approached me and asked if I would distribute the tips among his staff, because they did not trust one another, and they would like me to do it for them. I said, "You know I'm quite busy?" And the Manager trotted out the old maxim "if you want anything done, give it to a busy person!"

The division of the tips was 15% to the Restaurant Manager, 12% to the Head Waiter, 10% to the Assistant Restaurant Manager, and the rest split equally between the Waiters and Commis Waiters.

At 6.40 am one morning, the Head House Chambermaid came rushing into my office and in a panic, said, "Come quickly Mr. Gibson – there's an emergency!"

I was led in a trot to the Laundry room where I saw a chambermaid standing on a table holding her skirts around her knees, and pointing to something on the floor, and when I looked there was a solitary Cockroach. I immediately stamped on it, and peace was restored.

Apparently the Chambermaid had been unpacking stuff, which had been returned from the Laundry, and in taking out a sheet, the cockroach had fallen out, and from the reaction of the Chambermaid, one might have thought that the end of the World was nigh!

I drafted a letter of complaint for the General Manager to send to the Laundry stating that the Howard was a brand new five star hotel, and as such was free from insects and vermin, and that we wanted it to stay that way!

On another occasion, at 6.30 am, the Room Service Manager came with a chit for a bottle of Dimple Haig Whisky. A little later, the same man said they could not find the Night Cashier, and would I do an invoice for a customer who was anxious to check out and get away as I was the only one available who knew how to work the till. As I was doing this, detailing each item that was to be charged to his room account, I came across one bottle of Dimple Haig Whisky, at a cost of £13.40. I immediately queried this with the Room Service Manager and said, "You've made a mistake with this item – the correct price is £3.40". "Be that as it may" said the Manager, "At 6.30 am, its £13.40!"

The customer, on being presented with his Bill, did not bat an eyelid, but just produced a Credit Card, and thanked the Room Service Manager for his personal attention with a nice tip!

One of our customers had a suite of rooms on the top floor overlooking the Thames. He was an international financier who dealt with all of the five big banks. His permanent abode was in Geneva where he spent every weekend.

The General Manager's secretary typed all of his letters, and I was often called upon to print articles from the Financial Times for distribution to his Clients, and our Hall Porter made all of his travel arrangements. He truly was a wonderful, smooth operator! Every day, he would go into the Bar, and say "Good Morning", to the Spanish Head Barman; put a £1 coin on the bar counter, and leave. Many were the times that he would entertain his Clients to Luncheon, with drinks beforehand, and when he entered the bar with his Clients, no matter how busy the bar was, the Head Barman acted as if no one else existed. The Financier and his guests got the five star treatment.

Among the 125 members of staff, we had members from all of the five continents, and no matter what language a customer wished to use, we had a staff member who could communicate with them in their own language. However, it took some time before we could get staff of the right calibre to deal with the Hotel's expensive fixtures and fittings. Our Entrance Hall had matching pillars of marble from Italy, and in 1975 they cost one and a half million pounds.

I made a point of a daily inspection of the corridors, staff rooms, and the cubbyholes that contained the fire hoses. Firstly, to check for cleanliness and secondly, to check that no hotel property had been stashed away, waiting to be taken out of the hotel. I would do spot checks on some of the room refrigerators to see that they were being maintained correctly. These checks were necessary because items were being stolen, and as I was in charge of Security, I wanted to know on a daily basis what we were losing in the hope of catching the culprits. I had my suspicions who the thieves were, but I had no proof.

The windows of each of the corridors were hung with very expensive curtains, and one occasion a pair of these went missing. It transpired they had been thrown out of the window down into the courtyard, ready to be picked up later!

Within three months of opening, we had lost two gross of silver-plated coffee spoons. I reported this fact to Michael, and all he said was, "Yes Bruce, our guests nick them because they have the Hotel Crest on them, and they take them as a souvenir. Just order another two gross – our prices allow for such losses." I was flabbergasted at his casual remark at the loss of such expensive items. That made me even more determined to try and put a stop to the day-to-day 'pinchings'.

On one or two occasions, I had the feeling that the odd one or two of our ethnic staff were not acting naturally, and so I reported this fact to our General Manager at our weekly Heads of Department Meeting, (by now, I had been made Back of House Manager), and it was agreed to call the police. A few days later a detective called, and he was referred to me, and I showed him the list of items that I knew had been stolen, and I voiced my suspicions as to the possible culprits. The detective got himself a Search Warrant, and inspected the lodgings of some of our foreign nationals, and he found sheets, towels, pillow slips, knives, forks and spoons, and in one case a very expensive electric light shade.

Sadly to say the hotel refused to make an official complaint.

However, the culprits were sacked, and we informed the Home Office of their nefarious actions, and I was led to understand that they were deported.

Each room in the hotel had a different locking system, but it was necessary for the Head Chambermaid, Room Service Manager and myself to have a Master Key. Spares were kept in the Resident Director's safe, but somehow or other, someone got hold of the Master Key, because we were systematically losing the odd TV set. I solved that problem by having every Chubb lock in the hotel retumbled.

Sometimes in my peripatetic wanderings around the hotel I would find furniture had been moved from one room to another. If that piece of furniture was not replaced, and no complaint made of the shortage, it left that item wide open to be nicked at a future date. Therefore, I installed the system used in the Officers' Mess, whereby every furnished room had a Form, annotating the inventory of each room. This enabled missing items to be traced within seconds. When the chambermaids noticed that I was doing the odd check, they nicknamed me 'Bruce Hawk Eye.'

Most of the staff were honest and hard working. Some of the most attractive girls were from South America, Columbia, and Argentina, whilst the staff from Thailand had some of the most attractive ways. Every morning they would greet me with hands together as if in prayer and with a short bow as they said, "Good morning Mr. Gibson." Absolutely charming.

All staff were provided with hotel uniform, and the girls looked smashing. One day I was walking down The Strand, and a scruffy young female said to me, "Good afternoon Mr. Gibson"

"How do you do" I replied, and kept walking thinking nothing of it as the girl was a complete stranger to me.

The following morning in the staff canteen, one our gorgeous young receptionists in her smart red uniform said to me, "I saw you in the Strand yesterday afternoon, and you did not recognise me!" I said, "Was that you, Helen?" She said, "Yes!!" I apologised most profusely, but I couldn't say to her that I don't speak to scruffy individuals who look as if they're something the cat has dragged in!! She thought she was very 'with it' – whatever that means!!

Sarah was a lovely girl from Thailand, and she spoke several languages. She had previously been an airhostess, but her main job with us was as a Receptionist. After she had finished her stint at that, she used to come and work in my department because she was determined to find out all there was to know about hotels. The first thing I taught her was our stock control system, and I got her to work with my coloured assistant. Next, I got her to help replenish the drinks in the refrigerators in the bedrooms.

One day, I got her to do a spot check on some of the items in the stores, and she found a discrepancy with the stock control figure and the actual number we had in store. Together we re-checked the items, during the course of which I had to mention this to my Stock Control Clerk, and I discovered several chits were still waiting to be actioned. In effect, my assistant had fallen behind with his work, which I found unacceptable. I took him to task over this, and was gently and politely 'tearing him a strip off' when he interrupted me, and came out with the old coloured man's complaint that I was only going on at him because he was coloured.

This 'discussion' was taking place in the store room which had no windows, and that remark infuriated me, and so I promptly switched the light out, and then in airman's air force language, I completely slated him, and told him not to talk bullshit to me because now we were in the dark, and as far as he was concerned, I was the same colour as he was. This remark broke the tension and made him laugh when he realised that I had caught him out, and he promised not to get behind with his work again.

The Restaurant Staff, Manager and Waiters used to take their lunch at about 2.45 pm hours, after the Dining Room had been cleared, in a room adjoining the kitchen. When I had time, I would eat in the staff canteen, mainly to make sure the food produced was to the agreed menu, but occasionally I would eat with the waiters.

On one occasion I acted as the waiter. I took their orders and produced their requirements, and thought I was doing fine, but when at the end of the meal I asked the Head Waiter, "How am I doing?" and he replied, "Not bad; but no style," which cut me down to size amidst much laughter.

An accountant from Head Office used to attend two or three times a week to assure that all was well, and whom I got to know quite well.

He would do spot checks on the front office accounts and my storeroom, and he mentioned to me our telephone bill seemed a little high, and so we agreed to lock all telephones to prevent any misuse by staff. That reduced our bill considerably, but the he still wasn't happy.

One day I had some private business to do with Kay's brother who lived in Hertfordshire. It was quite late when I left Much Haddon, and as I was driving down the Embankment I decided to pop into the Howard, mainly to have a coffee. It was 2.00 am, the Link Man was outside; all was well and quiet as I went through the Entrance Hall and through the Head Porters Office, and to my surprise there was no telephone operator present, but a little Thai house chambermaid was on the telephone, talking to her mother at home in Thailand.

She did not see me, and so I waited several minutes until she finished her conversation, and when she replaced the receiver, I asked, "Where is the telephone operator?" and I was told that she had gone to have a coffee in the staff canteen.

This was the loophole that our accountant had been trying to find. Our telephone exchange operator was letting night staff have access to the telephone to make calls, world wide, for considerable lengths of time.

I left the accountant to take what action he felt right.

Our German Head Chef was a disciplinarian. All of his staff of 7 Chefs and Kitchen Orderlies were spotlessly clean, as was all of his equipment. At one of our weekly meetings he asked me to get some produce from a new Swedish supplier he knew of. The packaging of their goods was plain, with no expensive printing, just the name of the contents was shown on the label, but the goods inside were pricey, but superb – just the sort of gear a five star hotel needed.

I well remember one particular item, which were tins of peaches. They were huge – just 2 peaches in an A2 size tin. They were the size of Jaffa oranges!

One day, I heard a commotion in the Staff Canteen and I went to investigate. Our Head Chef had found one of his staff had helped himself to one of those tins of peaches for his desert. I thought the Head Chef was going to kill the culprit, because he said, "Those peaches were in my private Pantry – you're not permitted to enter there." But, the villain who apologised profusely for his misdemeanour and promised never to go into the Chef's Pantry again quickly resolved this altercation.

There was not a lot the Villain's boss could do after he had received a grovelling apology, but as he left he said, "Break that promise, and I'll grind up your nuts as an appetiser!"

The turnover of the 7 kitchen chefs was considerable. They were ordered about in such a dictatorial fashion. Foreign chefs accepted such autocratic behaviour, but English chefs would not succumb to such treatment, and generally after a week, they would give a week's notice, but the more truculent would just walk out and tell the Head Man to 'stuff his job'. However the attraction for a chef to work in a five star hotel was such that we were never short of staff. The snag I found with chefs generally was that they tended to drink too much. As part of their wages they were allowed 1 pint of alcohol a day; however our Head Chef's beverage was Perrier Water.

We were organised in such a way that Heads of Department were answerable to the General Manager, who was responsible for the smooth running of the hotel. To help him do this he had several Assistant Managers who were training to be General Managers, and it was their job to meet and greet guests on arrival, and to ensure their every wish was granted.

Our General Manager was charming, and he had come to us from the Savoy Hotel where he had been an Assistant Manager.

He had a large following from that establishment, and on taking up his new appointment with the Howard, he brought many long staying guests with him.

One lady guest was an American widow who had stayed at the Savoy for many years, and she came with our man because he ensured that she would get the Service that she demanded. Her basic order was that she be awakened every morning, at 10.00 am, with a cup of tea. One morning, our chambermaid took her a cup of tea a 9.55 am. Later that morning, the General Manager, the Head Housekeeper and the Room Service Manager were summoned to her presence, and were all reminded that her orders were a cup of tea at 10.00 am; not 5 minutes to 10, or 5 minutes past 10, and would they make a note that this morning's misdemeanour never happened again.

Every day a chauffeur driven Rolls Royce would appear at the front of the Hotel, just after 11.00 am, and would take this lady guest out into the country for a drive, and lunch somewhere, and she would be back at the hotel at about 3.00 pm for afternoon tea, which she took in her rooms, served by the Room Service Manager who was an experienced Turkish gentleman and who gave her the treatment.

The driver of the Rolls Royce was also the owner, and on one occasion when he was waiting for his customer, I got to chat him up, and discovered he was an ex Squadron Leader, and that he owned a small fleet of Rolls, but our guest always insisted that he drove her to wherever she wanted.

The weekly cost to this lady guest, or anyone similar living in a suite of rooms overlooking the Thames as a permanent domicile, was enormous, and I asked our General Manager why do they?

His reply was; "For several reasons. One, they like to live in London. Two, they have many friends whom they can entertain with the Room Service Manager looking after them. Three, we have 125 staff, and if the lady says 'Jump', we all jump. But above all, it is the security that a five star hotel provides."

As I was doing all of the buying, part of my job was to see the various representatives who were trying to sell us their wares. I always requested that they call before noon because lunch times were always a busy time for me.

One day we had a large lunch time Banquet, and I was dealing with a wine merchant, and as noon approached I was persistently interrupted by normal daily queries or requests, but the wine rep did not complain; he was just fascinated by the wide range of items I had to deal with. He said, "Is your day normally like this?" "Well – yes" I replied. "But that's why I like to see people like yourself before noon". "Good Lord!" he said, "I don't know how you cope!" But I thought nothing of it; it was part of usual routine that I had grown up with since the day we opened.

They were all common queries or requests that anyone with a basic knowledge of office routine or common sense could have answered, but the main ingredient of course was common sense. Since my father used to wake me as a child each morning at 6.30 am with his smoker's cough, I have always been an early riser.

From Camberley where I lived, which was about 35 miles from the hotel, I would always try to arrive just after 6.00 am. I had several means of transport.

I had a Bentley, a Chrysler, and old 8 cwt Ford Van which was a relic from the days when I had the shops, and Kay had a 1100 Princess Saloon which was like a little Rolls Royce. But mostly I chose to use the van. This was very convenient because frequently, when any of our chain of 7 Hotels ran out of any particular drink, I could supply them from my wine store, and I would deliver the goods in my van.

To help me do the buying I used to take the Grocer's Gazette each week, and one week I saw an advertisement for a partner in a Cash and Carry Warehouse. Therefore, I answered the advertisement and wrote asking for further details. These were returned to me, and the gist of the proposition was, a Cash and Carry Warehouse of some 40,000 square feet, supplying all of the Grocery Shops and businesses in the Southend on Sea area, and was owned by 2 Partners who wanted to retire.

They had a bright young man who had been taught to do the buying, and they proposed to sell him a half share in the business, and were looking for someone to buy the other half to join him. Also, the owners were prepared to work part time to ensure a smooth handover, and to ensure the new owners ran the business properly because they were prepared to let their protégée pay for his half share by monthly instalments.

After several visits, and going through the usual accountancy checks and legal details, I decided to become a half share partner in this Grocery Cash and Carry Warehouse.

Then it came to the time when I told Michael Day, the Director, that I was, with regret, planning to leave. I gave him a month's notice, and as he had previously been a Monk, he was quite philosophical about it.

During my notice period he was able to get someone to be in charge of stores, another person to do the buying and in charge of Stock Control, and a third person to be in charge of the wine store.

The remainder of my jobs were spread around the Trainee Managers. The accountant was recalled from the headquarters to do the wages and the waiters' tips, and so all was well and off I set, but before doing so, the staff gave me a farewell gift of a silver Parker Pen Set, which I have to this day, and which I treasure.

* * *

30

Warehouse Wisdom

The Warehouse was near where my sister Ellen lived with her husband Jock, and it was decided that I could live with them. At this time Ellen was still working in London, and she had to walk one and a half miles to Southend East Station every morning, with a repeat performance every evening.

She was an expert at knitting, and she would knit during the entire journey to Fenchurch Street and back. Jock used to leave for work before Ellen, and he went by car, so I used to take Ellen to the station on my way to work, where I would be in my office ready to commence work by 8.00 am.

Sometimes if I was not working late I used to pick Ellen up in the evenings to save her the long walk home. This arrangement worked well, and while she was getting our evening meal, I used to amuse myself by doing some gardening.

Ellen had a very colourful garden with a mass of Rhododendrons and the odd Hydrangea, which told me that she had acid soil, and which was also enjoyed by the Raspberry canes that she had. Once the meal was cooking, Ellen used to join me in the garden, and it was a time when we really got to know each other because for forty years, since I had left home at the age of 20, we had only met intermittently, and of course we had a great deal of catching up to do, and we had plenty of laughs.

Ellen enjoyed having me to live with her, and she and Jock showed me much love and kindness, but this was too good to last, and one day she confided in me that Jock would be much happier if I found myself somewhere else to live. The silly sod was jealous of our brother and sister relationship, but the last thing I wanted to do was cause a rift in my sister's marriage, and so I got myself some 'Digs'.

I settled in at the Warehouse with no trouble at all. Eddy Cummings was the name of my new partner, and he continued buying all of the Grocery gear, and I bought the Cigarettes and Tobacco, Confectionary and Stationery. Eddy controlled the Warehouse while I did the accounts. The two original partners by now were working part time, and their hours were so arranged that only one of them was present at the warehouse at a time.

Eddy was 30 years younger than me, along with most of the staff, but having spent the best years of my life in the Royal Air Force working with all age groups, I fitted in well. During lunchtimes I made it my business to get to know the staff, and they me, and it was our Forklift Driver, Mr. Hunt, who I recognised as a typical 'skiver', and he was the one I had to watch.

Doing the accounts and the odd bit of buying did not fully occupy my time, and so I would help out in the Warehouse. It was during these times that I found out that our Mr. Hunt was an old devil. In taking the pallets off the lorries, he would temporarily block the passageways before putting them in their final resting place, and sometimes by lunchtime, one couldn't even move in the Warehouse – and he would then go to lunch. During the afternoons he would, leisurely, unblock the warehouse passageways, but there were times when lorries arrived and had to be turned away because we had nowhere to put the gear.

This used to annoy Eddy, and so I decided to do something about it. I got our Mr. Hunt – who was a real expert – to teach me how to use the Forklift, and there were times when I used to unload lorries under the watchful eye of my Instructor until I became quite proficient. It was then that I put my newfound skill to work, for while our Skiver was at lunch, I would clear the blocked passageways so that they were ready for any new deliveries in the afternoon.

The female clerk in the cash desk was always busy taking money, and no one could beat me at that, and it was during those times, when I was helping out, that I got to know our Customers. They were mostly from General Stores, Hotels or Catering Establishments. One of them was an 18-year-old cockney boy named Glen, who was as bright as a button. He had a large van, but very little ready cash.

Our prices were keen; we worked on 2% net profit – we were made profitable by our vast turnover. Our main competitor was a firm called Nurdon & Peacock, who had a large chain of Cash & Carry Warehouses. They used to employ Grammar School boys in the evenings to do the pricing up of their goods, and quite often they would make errors which Glen would spot, and he would then come and tell Eddy.

Whenever this happened, and Nurden's price per pallet was cheaper than Eddy could buy from the manufacturer, Eddy would give Glen the cash to buy 8 pallets – the maximum quantity that Glen could fit in his van – and sell back to Glen 1 pallet at the same price on credit – and everyone was quite happy.

Eddy would also give Glen a special discount on goods that he bought from us for his trouble.

One day I was working in the office doing the VAT, and the telephone rang, and a lady's voice asked, "Is that Mr. Gibson?" I replied, "Yes", and the voice continued, "Have you a Forklift Driver by the name of Mr. Hunt working for you?" I said, "Yes". "Well, Mr. Gibson, Mr. Hunt has a room in his Council Flat full of your coffee and other goodies", and the phone went dead.

I had never had a more disturbing telephone call than that, and so, what was I going to do about it?

After a great deal of thought I decided not to tell my young partner because, at that stage, it was hearsay evidence, and I did not want to worry Eddy unduly. As a result I decided to watch Mr. Hunt very carefully, and try to find out what this was all about.

The following day I said to Eddy, "I've got a good idea what goes on in the Warehouse, but you haven't got a clue what goes on in the office upstairs. I suggest that we change jobs for a fortnight so that you can find out everything about our business." This was agreed, and of course my ploy was to watch Mr. Hunt.

I told Mr. Hunt that the job swap was to give me more practise working the Forklift under his supervision. He thought that this was a great idea. Not only was I doing the work for him, but he also loved 'balling me out' if I looked like I was making a mistake. Of course I insisted on putting each pallet in its rightful place, and not block the passageways, much to his chagrin, but there was nothing he could do about it.

One lunchtime I was on my own, moving some pallets of goods around, when a lorry driver came up to me and said, "Are you the Forklift Driver?" I said, "Yes". "I've got 24 cases of Andrex for you," he said. "Can I see them?" I asked.

He took me to his lorry, and there were 24 cases of Andrex that he had pinched by short delivering his customers. He asked, "Where do you want me to deliver them?" I said, "I don't want them – I don't deal in stolen property!" He said to me, "But you are the Forklift Driver aren't you?" I said, "Only at lunchtimes; I'm a Partner in this Warehouse; good day to you!"

The look of utter dismay on the driver's face was a picture, and as he turned and ran to his lorry, I could hear him say, "Oh!! Shit, shit, shit!!'"" and with his lorry tyres screeching, he disappeared down Victoria Avenue.

On another occasion, a delivery of Rowntrees products arrived just as Mr. Hunt was going to lunch, and I was about to take over. To my amazement, he delayed going to lunch and started to take six full pallets off the lorry, dumping them down for me to put away. But, I noticed on the delivery note that there was a seventh pallet containing mixed items. Mr. Hunt, in his hurry to go for his lunch, was about to sign for seven pallets when I said, "Hold on a minute – aren't you going to check that mixed pallet?" He replied, "No; that will be alright – Rowntrees are as good as gold". I said, "Right. Now you be as good as gold and go to lunch!!"

To the Rowntrees driver I said, "Strip that pallet down so that I can check it." That did not suit Mr. Hunt, and he went to the back of the Rowntrees lorry and I followed him, and as I did so I noticed that there was a tear in the plastic covering of our mixed pallet, and in the back of the lorry there were some loose packages which the driver had tried to kick out of view. I insisted on methodically checking our mixed pallet with great care, and found it to be short of several different packages, and being of a suspicions nature, I thought that some of our shortages were among the loose packages that the driver was trying to kick out of view. I said to the driver, "I will only sign for the six full pallets. You can take the mixed pallet with its shortages back to your depot."

I noticed that Mr. Hunt had still not gone to lunch, but was in a huddle with the Rowntrees driver, and I got the feeling that I had prevented a fiddle between them.

As a result of my action, the representative called to see me to enquire why I had returned the mixed pallet of goods. I explained my suspicions, and gave a repeat order of goods on the mixed pallet, and was told that I would get them by a special delivery. I said, "And make it with a special driver too, because I won't have that conniving driver you sent the last time on my premises again."

The special delivery arrived a couple of days later, but with the original driver. Fortunately I was still watching Mr. Hunt, and I was able to stop him from accepting the goods, and I told the driver to take the goods back.

That was the last time that driver came to our premises because I spoke to the Area Manager of Rowntrees and explained my grievance, and that solved my problem because the new driver was an ex Flight Sergeant in the RAF, and cordial relations were resumed.

The Flight Sergeant told me the old driver had been moved up north to Gateshead. That suited me fine because that was another one of Mr. Hunt's possible fiddles that I had cancelled out!

Just after that little episode with Rowntrees, they started a promotion to boost the sales of polo mints and refreshers. Each one of their customers was given a target figure to reach, and the Company that exceeded that figure the most would be the winner.

The prize was a holiday in Rome for two, staying in a five star hotel. That was of no interest to me, and so I just didn't bother, I just placed my usual order.

Surprise, surprise. The next time the Rep called, he told me we were doing well in the competition, and at that point we were lying second, and there were still three weeks of the promotion to go. Being a cynic, I always held the idea that the winners of such competitions were decided in advance, and in view of the recent rumpus we had experienced with the promoters, one could be led to believe that we had been chosen as the winners. But, I wasn't sure, and I had to make certain.

We had a customer named Freddie who was a market trader, and once again a cockney, and we liked one another and got on well. Quite often he would give me a couple of thousand pounds and would say, "Bruce, look after that for me and let me know when I've used it all up". He would call by every Monday to do his purchasing for the week ahead, and so the next Monday when he called, I took him up to my office and told him about the Polo and Refresher competition, and made him a proposition, which he seized upon with both hands. The idea was that I would supply him with those two particular items at the same cost to us so that he could have a trade up in the market. "Done", said Freddie, "I'll try a pallet of each."

He was back on Wednesday saying; "I've cleared those pallets in a couple of hours, selling six at a time! Can I please have three more pallets of each for next Monday?" I ordered enough pallets of Polos and Refreshers so that he could reap the benefit for the next three weeks.

I spoke to the Rowntrees Representative, telling him that since we were second in the competition, I had ordered 30 pallets of each item above our normal requirement, and that if we did not win the competition, I would know that he was either telling lies, or that there was a fiddle!

We won the competition, and Eddy and his wife had a nice

holiday in Rome.

Before the competition ended I decided to visit Romford Market where Freddie was operating to see him in action. When I got there I was absolutely astounded! There was a huge crowd around Freddie's stall, and he was dishing out the spiel, and he had three helpers dishing out the Polos etc, and taking the money. It took me quite a while to get to the front as I had to compete with his lady customers who were pushing one another to make sure they got some of Freddie's bargains, and ultimately, although I was no more than 4 feet away from him while he was spouting his sales talk, he was almost in a trance and he did not recognise me.

One of our specialities was cooked ham. We had a large boiler which took eight Hams, and we would put these in the boiler as we closed down at night, and the hams boiled all night and were cooked to perfection by the time we arrived the next morning.

Eddy taught me how to remove the Oyster bones, which was quite a skilful task, and one that I found very satisfying. It took me a long time however to get the knack because at the beginning Eddy could do three hams while I was still struggling to do my first.

Every six months we did a 100% stock check. We split the Warehouse up into sections, and each member of staff was given a section to count. My first stock take was done under the supervision of 'Dobby', who was one of the original partners, and he would secrete the odd package to make sure we had done our work efficiently.

There was a Mezzanine floor in one part of the warehouse and where the confectionary products were stored. One Monday morning when we opened up the warehouse, we noticed a terrific draft, and upon investigating we found one of the roof glass panels had been smashed, and someone had broken into the warehouse.

Our next-door neighbour had some workmen in and they had left their ladders unsecured, and over the weekend some person – or persons – unknown had used them to get on to our roof and make an entry through the glass panel. We got the impression that the rascals were juveniles because nothing had been stolen, but there were signs of a picnic where Mars Bars, Cadbury's chocolate and bottles of orange squash had been consumed.

We informed the police for insurance purposes, but even in the 1970's the Police did not want to know. All they said was that it had been partly our fault for not ensuring the ladders had been made secure.

One day when I was browsing through The Daily Telegraph I spotted that parts of Brazil had experienced a frost for the first time in donkeys years, and that the whole of the coffee crop had been lost. I drew Eddy's attention to that article, and said, "You know what that means, don't you? Coffee will become in short supply and it will pay us to stock up." Eddy, who was a super buyer, and the salesman, agreed. Our Coffee supplier was a man named Tony, and who was a 'one man band', and Eddy bought the whole of his stock.

After a week or so the price of coffee started to rise, and so Eddy repeated the previous procedure and cleared Tony out of coffee again. After a while the natural market forces came into play, and the price of coffee rose again, and finally rocketed. Tony ended up buying coffee – we made a killing, and Tony made a fortune, as within the area of the county of Essex that he supplied, he was the only holder.

One day Eddy came up to my office for his coffee break, during which he casually mentioned that Tony would like to buy my shares, and would I be interested?

I said, "Eddy, we have increased the turnover of our business considerably over the last couple of years since we took over – you know it would cost him? At this moment, the answer is No, but let me think about it,"

That weekend, as I was driving home to Camberley and was passing Heathrow Airport, as I approached a roundabout a young lady flagged me down.

I stopped and said; "I'm going to Camberley", and the gorgeous blond opened the door and said, "That'll do!"

I said to my hitchhiker, "Where do you want to go?" And she said, "Anywhere".

I tried to chat her up without success, and so I repeated that I was on my way to Camberley.

As we approached the last roundabout just before turning towards Staines, my blond job said, "Will you drop me off here?" and she got out.

I thought, what a funny lady, but aren't they all, and promptly forgot about it.

A few weeks later, Kay came to Southend by public transport to see Ellen and Jock and the Warehouse, and as we were driving home past Heathrow Airport, there was the same blond hitch hiking.

I said to Kay, "See that blond?"

And I related to her what had happened to me on a previous occasion, and that she had nothing to say for herself and had got out of the car at the next roundabout.

"You stupid clot" said Kay, "She's at it!"

"At it? At what?"

"Give me strength," said Kay, "She's a prostitute!"

"Oh!!" I said, much crestfallen. "I never thought of that!"

Once again Eddy mentioned that Tony was still interested and would like to buy me out. It was then that I realised that Tony was the same age as Eddy. I was twice Eddy's age, and that Eddy would prefer to have a partner younger than me, and so a deal was struck, and I made a handsome profit on the transaction.

* * *

31

Anyone for Camping?

B eing at a loose end, I answered an advertisement for a partner in a Camping Holiday Company. There were two partners, and they had started a Company called International Camping France but with insufficient capital. They had been operating in France for just over a year with 300 fully equipped tents, and they had debts to clear of £15,000 before they could proceed on to the second year. They had a camping site in the South of France which was on the beach, and which they rented from the local council of Hyère. It was a cheap self-catering holiday, but with six people in a tent, the profits were good.

I knew all about the attractions of the South of France. Gone were the days when it was considered only for the idle rich, and I discovered that families and friends had found camping holidays were well within their financial and travelling reach, and that holiday makers were flocking there in ever increasing numbers. And so, I became the Financial Director, and started work.

I helped with the design and copywriting of the brochure, and we started advertising in the National Press. The other two directors had previous experience with other camping companies, and they knew how to sell and successfully organise camping holidays, and in no time at all, applications started to come in for a copy of our brochure.

David Bavin, our Managing Director, was an excellent salesman and holiday bookings came rolling in with money up front, which gave us a very good cash flow. I had planning boards on the walls around our office, which held 'T Cards' so that I could see at a glance how many coach loads had been booked.

We had 200 four berth tents, and 100 six berth, and so it was possible to cater for 1400 campers per week. We rented a room at a hotel near Euston Station where campers assembled by noon each Friday, and where David met them along with our female director, Pat Pollard, who allocated them to the awaiting coaches, and off they would go on a 22 hour coach journey to our camp site at Hyère.

There our Camp Site Manager had a team of couriers to meet with them and show the campers to their tents. Coach companies catering for long distance travel had luxury coaches with reclining seats, and it was possible for campers to sleep most of their 800 mile journey, and so the first thing children wanted to do on arriving at our site was to go to the beach with Dad, but Mum had to stay and check the tent inventory! She had to forget what camping was like in Girl Guide days because living under canvas with us was a luxury.

The equipment supplied with each tent, which also included a free cooking pack, was: a camp Kitchen supplied with Cooker, Hanging Larder, Cutlery, Crockery, Teapot, Kettle, 3 Saucepans, Frying Pan, Chopping Board, Cooking Utensils, Mixing Bowl, Colander, Butter Dish, Egg Cups, Condiment Set, Dust Pan and Brush, Washing Up Bowl, Water Bucket, Water Carrier, Electric or Gas Light, a Mirror, Chairs, Table, Cool and Ice Packs, Pillows, and a Covered Foam Mattress.

Each tent had inner sleeping compartments, which could be zipped up to keep any insects at bay. Overall, no expense had been spared to give our Campers an enjoyable holiday and provide value for money. But, there is always someone to put the cat among the pigeons. I classified them as professional troublemakers. After their camping holiday these types would go through the brochure with a fine toothcomb, and find fault in any tiny detail of our copy, and verbally point out anything which, in their opinion, fell short of what we were claiming to offer, and they would want compensation, failing which they would sue.

Whether you win, lose or draw in a court case, the only people guaranteed to end up better off financially are the lawyers, and so we normally settled by offering the complainant a rebate on their next holiday.

Each coach had two drivers, and after the campers had been off loaded, the drivers had a 2 hour turn around period, during which they fed themselves and had a break before returning home with their coaches filled with campers who were returning home from their holiday.

At a pinch we could accommodate 1400 holidaymakers, but for comfort's sake, we kept the numbers down to 1200. This meant that for the first week our camp site was only half full, and the coaches would return to Euston half empty, likewise on the last week of the holiday period, the coaches went down to Hyère empty, and came back full. This might sound complicated, but this is how a campsite works.

On the last day of their holiday, all campers had to vacate their tent by 9.00 am to allow the couriers to get the tents 'ship shape and Bristol fashion' by noon, ready for the next coach loads.

There was a restaurant in close proximity to our site, which catered for our holidaymakers for entertainment in the evenings, and during the day we used to organise excursions to places such as St. Tropez, Cannes, Port Grimaud, or Monte Carlo. A Dutchman made our acquaintance and he was the representative of the owner of a Campsite in Argelès, and he wheedled his way into our confidence, saying that if we ever found that we had more holidaymakers than our Hyère site could handle, he could help us out with accommodation at Argelès.

This Dutchman called every week and became quite friendly. He would invite us out to lunch, but David and I were too busy booking holidays; however Pat went on a couple of occasions. I, being a season ticket holder with Tottenham Hotspurs Football Club, was able to get him tickets for football matches of his choice, and he became a regular member of our outfit, and to such an extent that David carried on selling, and we entered into a contract with the owners of the Argelès camp site to take 300 campers per week.

All we had to was sell the holidays, and deliver the campers to the Argelès site, and the owner would provide fully equipped tents and facilities similar to what we were offering at Hyère. Argelès was a huge campsite and had its own fully licensed restaurant. As is typical with the way all French campsites operated, we had to pay up front for that privilege.

All went well for the first few weeks of the season, but after a while the Dutchman on the Argelès site started to double sell tent spaces to passing trade holiday makers, and some of our customers from the Midlands were told on arriving at the Argelès site after a 22 hour coach trip, "There's your tent and equipment – you'll have to erect the tent yourselves."

That was not what our customers had paid their hard earned money for, and although they never actually knocked the Dutchman's block off, he was threatened with that, and much more drastic action, to such an extent the French Police became involved.

Pat Pollard, our female director, went to Argelès in an endeavour to sort things out and to try and placate our aggrieved holidaymakers. However, things did not improve. In fact, they got much, much worse, until one Thursday morning the French Police telephoned me and told me not to send any more holidaymakers down to the Argelès site, and if I did, they would refuse the holidaymakers to disembark and would send the coaches back to the U.K.

The next day, Friday, I had 300 campers – 5 coach loads – who were due to go to the Argelès site, and so I had just 24 hours to get reorganised. I managed to contact 298 of the prospective campers to tell them they were going to our other site at Hyère and not Argelès, so that it they wished, they could cancel their holiday and have their money back. The two campers who I was unable to contact had already started their holiday and were in Paris, and so there was nothing I could do about that.

David Bevan took off by motorcar to arrange for the 300 additional campers to be accommodated at Hyère. He did an excellent job, but it meant taking extra space at Hyère, for which the Council made us 'pay through the nose'. We also had to buy new tents and equipment etc. However, we had no cancellations, and everybody who had booked with us, whether it was originally at Hyère, or who were transferred from Argelès to Hyère, had a holiday.

Despite Pat's continuing presence at Argelès, things got worse, and ultimately the French Police had to put the Dutchman in gaol to allow matters to cool down. However, as far as our Company was concerned that action had an adverse effect as the Dutchman's girlfriend disappeared with the caravan in which they were cohabiting, together with all of the ready cash.

The Argelès campsite, together with the restaurant, was a thriving business, and which carried on working under new management, but despite Pat's efforts, the new Management had no authority to recompense us.

Ultimately the Dutchman's fraud cost our company over £200,000. I spent many weeks sorting out this mess, and had to pay many visits to the South of France, but I found out that everybody was trying to get rich quick, and their ethical standards were generally dodgy and not at all what I had been used to.

Hence I got out of the camping business, but at a great personal, financial loss.

During my travels to various camping sites I met a gentleman named Paul Drew. He was a retired schoolteacher, and he too had had enough of camping, and was trying his hand at development.

It transpired that he had some land in Tewkesbury, which had planning permission to build a public house. I casually mentioned that I had a friend who was a developer, and that it was a business where one had to have their wits about them.

Many months elapsed when suddenly, out of the blue; on 2nd December 1982 I had a telephone call from Paul. He was in dead stook. The land he had at Tewkesbury was mortgaged together with the house in which he was living, and the Lender was threatening to make him bankrupt and evict him. He would be totally destitute.

I said, "Paul – you've always given me the impression of affluence; surely you don't need me – you need to ring the Samaritans."

At that Paul burst into tears and cried like a water cart. In between deep sobs he said, "Don't be facetious Bruce, can you get your developer friend to help me to raise the cash so that I can pay off my mortgage and build the Pub?"

I said, "That's a tall order – why should I get my friend involved in your troubles?"

He said, "I will give you 10% of any money if you can help me raise sufficient money to build the Pub."

I replied, "Put that in writing, and I'll think about it."

In the meantime I spoke to my developer friend, Graham, and told him about Paul's planning permission to build a pub in Tewkesbury.

"Tewkesbury?" Graham said. "Tewkesbury floods. Don't touch it!"

"How do you know that?" I asked.

"Every developer worth his salt knows that Tewkesbury floods" was his reply.

However, after he had done his usual searches, he put me in touch with a Finance House, and after Paul had given me a guarantee in writing that he would pay me 10% of any money that I could raise, I ultimately got the Finance House to lend Paul £257,000 to build the pub.

Due to the knowledge that I had gained from the way the Howard Hotel bar had been run, I was able to give Paul much advice, and it was agreed that when the Public House was built at Tewkesbury, we would run it in partnership.

Because of the tendency of Tewkesbury to flood, the Council had insisted that the building should be put on stilts, but before this could happen, 20 foot deep piles had to be sunk into the River Avon before the platform could be built which was to support the stilts. Once the groundworks had been completed to the satisfaction of the Building Inspector, the pub grew quickly.

Although it was to be a Free house, the Representative of one of the big breweries who hoped to be our main supplier gave us some good advice as to where to buy the interior fixtures and fittings, and we spent many trips to London acquiring these.

I told Paul of some of the fiddles made by barmen, and talked him into having computerised optics for the serving of spirits.

The Clerk of Works was a chap named Alan Smith, and he was making such good progress, and as I was travelling daily from Camberley to Tewkesbury, Kay and I decided to move into the area. With the help of Paul, we found a house, and in October 1983 we moved in to our house in Ripple.

Our pub development was quite large, and overlooked the River Avon. The ground floor, which was of course on stilts, was the main drinking area and could comfortably hold 200 drinkers. The two floors above were designated for restaurants, and the top floor was for two, 2-bedroom flats, for staff accommodation.

Paul and I agreed to split the work. He was to concentrate on the building, and I was to fit the place out.

However one day, with the development nearing completion, I noticed that Paul was dealing with a firm's representative, and that side of the business fell into my province. When his meeting was over, I said to him, "that was my job – I should have been interviewing that Representative." Paul replied, "Bruce; there's been a change of plan; I've decided to run the pub on my own."

And this despite all of the help I had given him – I had raised the money to save him from Bankruptcy and to pay off his debts; I had saved his marriage; and yet he had reneged on our agreement. I thought that if that was the way in which he conducted his business, I did not want to have any part of it.

I therefore produced the letter that he had given me, where he had promised to pay me 10% of any monies raised, only to find the letter had been written on a Limited Company's Stationery with Paul as Managing Director, but the company itself was no longer in existence.

I had even done all of the Public Relations, including

arrangements for a grand opening with free beer for the first hour.

I must confess I was bitterly disappointed at our break up, and blamed myself in part for not getting our partnership legally binding.

The language I used to tell Paul what I thought of him would not be printable by any decent firm. Kay however agreed with me – if that was the way he did his business, I was well shot of him.

Once again however it was brought home to me what a sheltered life I had led during the best years of my life in the Royal Air Force, where Officers were men of integrity, and whose word one could trust.

The official Opening of the Pub was a resounding success – but this went to Paul's head. He never did any actual work, but was always present acting as 'Mine Host', and he would finish up under the influence of drink on a daily basis.

The computer Optics I had arranged to ensure a good stock control of spirits worked well, but too well for some members of the staff, and within 3 months someone stole the computer, which was never to be replaced.

Rowdy scenes were common place and quite often the Police were involved.

Had Paul honoured his verbal partnership with me, none of that would have happened, but it did, and I consider myself lucky to have had nothing to do with the running of such a depraved establishment.

* * *

32

Causing a Ripple..............

As a consequence of this failed venture Kay and I found ourselves living in Ripple; a small village of some 300 souls, and far away from all of our friends and business contacts. That was not totally true however as immediately opposite Hayes House where we live, resides a Wing Commander Trevor Thain and his wife, Eileen, with whom we had served in 1950 at RAF Manby when we were both on the Directing Staff of the Royal Air Force Flying College.

We moved into Hayes House, where we live to this day, on a Saturday, and the Vendor showed me a huge pile of logs to burn in the Hunter wood-burning Stove, which was in the Breakfast Room, saying that those would last me a year or two.

On our first full day in Ripple, which was a Sunday, I stoked up the Hunter Stove and set the chimney on fire!

Dense smoke billowed out across the whole village.

It was the most successful unplanned Public Relations exercise ever - the whole village, on our first full day in Ripple, learned that the Gibsons had arrived!

The local Fire Brigade, which was manned by volunteers from Upton on Severn, arrived quickly at the scene, and the fire was extinguished in no time.

The following day the Rector from Ripple Church, Jeffrey Green, called to welcome us to the village, and the day after he called and took me on his rounds, introducing me to several members of the Ripple congregation, where I was welcomed with open arms because I fitted in and could speak their language.

For all of my life, ever since my big sister Jess used to take Cyril and I to Sunday School, I have always attended Church and supported the local vicar. This background knowledge became invaluable during my service career when I always supported the Padré, and who would always be ready to hold my hand when I had to call on parents or wives to tell them their loved one had been killed or gone missing.

For a small village such as ours, Ripple Church is massive – this is because at one time it was a Minster, and the Benedictine Monks lived there.

It was at this time that my friend Graham, who was Chairman of BFT Ltd, called me to ask me to be his Personal Assistant to his Managing Director, who had been having some difficulties and which he knew that I would be able to solve.

BFT had a staff of 50, and was a Telex organisation. They were employed by all of the big national companies, sending Telex messages all over the world. They could send 1,000 telex messages worldwide to different addresses in 26 minutes. It operated 24 hours a day, 7 days a week.

Graham introduced me to the Managing Director who was a gentleman named Hal Martin, and I was told that my task would be that of trouble shooter, and as such I was free to operate wherever I thought it necessary. Hal was delighted to meet me, and over a coffee, he exuded charm to the extent that I put him in the classification of a smooth operator. During that period when we were getting to know each other, he said, "Bruce, there is something I've been wanting for a very long time – a hammer. There is an Army and Navy Store opposite; here's a £20.00 note, be a pal and go and buy me a hammer?!

I thought, what a funny thing to ask for, but as I had not started work, I went across the road and bought a hammer, which cost £5.00. I took the hammer to Hal together with the till receipt and £15.00 change, and he said, "No, that's OK, keep the change; there will be other things to buy in the near future."

Now, that's not the way to run a business. To spend Petty Cash with no records kept. I knew that when Kay was in charge of our accounts; she would never have let me get away with that. Every penny had to be documented. I remembered one occasion when she had been doing a Trial Balance prior to Audit, she had been sixpence out in her calculations, and at the end of the day she still hadn't found it, and so I gave her sixpence. "You stupid idiot (Idiot being her permanent sobriquet for me) – that makes me a shilling out now!"

And so now, I smelt a rat. My first job therefore as trouble shooter was to investigate the Petty Cash Account. My friend Graham was a very busy man, but as soon as I could button hole him, I asked him who was in charge of the Petty Cash Account, and he told me that it was the Accountant, a Mr. Norman Femur. I got him to introduce me to Norman as the new trouble shooter, and during our first conversation in Norman's office, we were interrupted by one of Graham's Directors who asked for £500.00 out of Petty Cash, and which Norman produced.

I immediately thought, 'right Monkey', and I went straight to Graham and told him, "One of your problems is the Petty Cash Account, and if you were to authorise the Accountant to hand over the Petty Cash Account to me, I might be able to put it on a more sound footing."

Graham sent for Norman, and instructed him to hand over the Petty Cash Account to me, together with any remaining cash. Norman gave me One Pound and 18 pence, and informed me the Ledger would follow as soon as he had brought it up to date.

I then put a notice on the Notice Board, informing all employees that I was now in charge of the Petty Cash Account, and I waited.

It was not long before a Salesman made his number with me, and asked for £50.00 from petty cash. I enquired, "May I ask what it is for?" and was told in a truculent manner, "That's my business!" "In that case," I said, "No! You can't have £50.00, because that's my business!"

The look of utter astonishment on the Salesman's face was worthy of an Oscar!

"Come off it Mr. Gibson – I need the money to take a client out to lunch; Norman always gives me the money up front."

I said, "but Norman is not in charge of the Petty Cash any more – take your client our for lunch, bring me a receipt, and if I think it is a cost that BFT should honour, I will give you the money to reimburse you. If I think it is not for BFT's benefit, then I won't!"

"Christ Almighty" was the reply. I said, "Well, that's a good start; but if you had listened to the Omnipotent Power in the first instance, you would not be standing in the embarrassing situation you are in now, and so, do as I say, and we will take it from there, but that is how the Petty Cash Account will be operated in the future"................

I heard no more from the Salesman, nor did I get a receipt for any business lunch.

I tried many times to get Norman to give me the Petty Cash Ledger, but each time without success, and so I started a new one, with the fifteen pounds change from the hammer operation, and the one pound and 18 pence from Norman, making a total of Sixteen pounds, three shillings, and seven pence

The Grapevine was working overtime for a while, until all of the staff knew of the new procedure, and also the name of the proper Bastard who was in charge!

Shortly after the afore mentioned occurrence, another Director, who had been on holiday when I joined the Company, tried it on, demanding £500.00 out of Petty Cash. I apologised most profusely, but informed him that the Petty Cash does not have £500 to hand over, and while I was in charge, never would have, because it does not operate in that way!

"What did you say your name was?" was the repartee.

I said, "I didn't say Sir, because you never asked, but I'm Bruce Gibson, and I'm the Personal Assistant to the Managing Director."

"We'll see about that" said the Director, and flounced off.

I heard no more about that incident, and neither did Hal Martin, but when I related that event to Graham, he said to me, "Good show Bruce; carry on the good work".

BFT had a female sales person who was good at her job, and quite pretty to boot! She would get into the office before any of the other sales staff, and would be on the telephone using a language which was totally foreign to me – about logging on, logging off, on line etc, - and which I found quite intriguing, and I made it my business to get to know her.

She often brought in sandwiches for breakfast and lunch, and it was during those times that I would find myself in her vicinity. We got on well, and although I was over 40 years older than her, she knew that I liked her.

One day she bought me a Petty Cash chit for travelling expenses to Birmingham, which included £30.00 for food.

She said, "Can I leave this with you to deal with?" I said, "Be my guest!" and off she went.

On perusing the petty cash chit that she had left with me, it annotated so much for breakfast, morning coffee, lunch, and an evening meal, and on top of that, fares for public transport. It was so outrageous that it made me laugh.

The next morning I trapped her at breakfast time when she was with her sandwiches, and I said, laughingly, "You're not telling me you spent £30.00 on food the day you went to Birmingham, for two reasons: firstly, you would not have had time to do any business; and secondly, if you ate like that on a regular basis, you would be as fat as a pregnant lady carrying triplets, instead of your sylph-like figure of seven stone!" which made her laugh, but she said, "We normally get £30.00 for expenses if we are away for a day." I said, "The amount is immaterial; you can have £130.00 if they are genuine expenses; I'll leave you your chit. Let me have another one of the actual expenses you incurred."

The new petty cash chit was for £20.00 less, and which I paid.

From my experience, 'new brooms sweep clean', but from day one, I stopped the Petty Cash fiddles, and the staff got the message about how that account would be operated in the future!

There were times when I had to visit firms of a similar nature, and I noticed the security of those firms was strict. Short of giving a DNA sample, identity was checked, time of arrival and departure recorded, a visitor tag had to be worn etc., and yet the BFT organisation, running 24 hours a day, people could come and go as they pleased.

I also noticed that for day workers who worked from 9.00 am to 5.00pm, time keeping was a bit slap happy. I spoke to Graham about the aforementioned facts, and also stated that in the event of fire, when the premises would have to be evacuated, it was essential to have records of all personnel who were present in the building at any one time. And so it was decided to keep a time-keeping book where all Directors and Staff could sign in on arrival, and out on departure. I put a notice on the Notice board stating the new procedure, stressing the importance that those facts were needed in the event of FIRE, and waited.

Every member of the staff who were good timekeepers accepted the new system. The only ones to complain were those who thought it was infra dig, and the skivers. The skivers I kept my beady eye on. One of those was the Accountant, who had still not passed on to me his Petty Cash Ledger in order to complete his handover to me, despite my many requests, with the excuse that he was far too busy.

He was a married man, but every morning he arrived with a female member of his staff, and I could tell from their body language and conversation that there was more between them besides space!! However, the lady part of the duo always displayed a friendly disposition towards me as well as every other member of the staff, but because Norman the Accountant always refused to sign in or out, she followed in his steps.

I had a desk just inside the entrance with the signature book on, and I made it my business to be at that desk every morning to welcome the day workers, and to remind those who were loath to sign in, the importance for security reasons, and in case of Fire, and in time I won everyone over apart from the truculent few who thought they were far too important to stoop so low!

The front door was always kept locked, and I noticed that most members of staff had a front door key to let themselves in. Those members who had to ring the front door bell to gain access I discovered had lost their keys, which I thought for security reasons, in particular at night, was most unsatisfactory.

A great deal of the work that BFT was doing had a security value, and so I decided to re-tumble the Chubb lock on the front door, and only issue keys to the night Telex staff. That caused a little concern among members of staff who had held a front door key for many years, but as I proved they could gain entry without their own key, the new system was accepted, and which had the Chairman's approval.

During my peripatetic wanderings around the large office block I discovered facilities were available for staff to make their own refreshments, tea, coffee etc, and that a member of staff would go to the Cash and Carry to provide the wherewithal to enable that to happen, and those items were purchased out of Petty Cash. I therefore decided to do a stock check. In doing that I found we had enough toilet rolls in stock to last 2 years, and 12 tins of Brasso which was used to keep the one and only brass nameplate on the front of the building in pristine order, and which measured just 12 inches by 9 inches! There was in my opinion therefore enough Brasso to last at least 10 years. I was not happy with that situation, and I volunteered to relieve that member of staff of that chore, which made a very happy bunny.

For the next few weeks I did a regular stock control, and I got the feeling that someone was nicking toilet rolls because we were using them at such a rate that even if a member of staff had permanent diarrhoea, we could not possibly use them at such a rate. Therefore I once more put my detective hat on and laid little traps.

I found the toilet rolls were disappearing during the night shift, and so it was the night staff that I kept a watch on, until finally one night I caught a telex operator putting a case of Andrex toilet rolls in the boot of his car, together with a couple of jars of coffee.

It was early morning, and just before the operator was due to finish his shift, I confronted him, and told him that those goods that he had just nicked had been specially marked by me, and if he did not want a police record, he would be well advised to put the goods back, which he did.

I then explained to him that I had been watching him for some time, and that his best plan would be to seek different employment because I would be leaning on him, and his life in future would not be as pleasant as it had been in the past. My words of wisdom had the desired effect because within a week, the culprit had resigned.

We had a little cockney girl who was our telephone operator, and she operated BFT's Switchboard a treat. She had a lovely smile in her voice, and she was everyone's friend. Her desk was just inside the door, and everyone who entered received a happy welcome. She also did typing in between calls, together with packing up any parcels that needed to be despatched.

Although she did her best, she was much better at Switchboard work than packaging.

Therefore, I would plan to see how she was getting on at 4.00 pm daily, when I would help her with her parcels. It was quite an enjoyable half hour, and I got the feeling that even some of the straightforward parcels had been left for me to do. Be that as it may, one day I was a little late, and I found her struggling with a very awkward package, but with my help we overcame the problem and she was so thankful she said, "Oh!! Mr. Gibson; you are kind to me – if you were 20 years younger I could fall for you!" But I made her laugh when I said, "If I were 50 years younger I'd take you up on that!!"

I made it obvious to Norman, the Accountant, that I was upset about not receiving the Petty Cash Ledger, and one morning he and his lady assistant turned up 10 minutes late, and as he brushed past me, I said to our Switchboard Operator, "Please sign Mr. Femur in".

He came rushing back and said, "I'm Norman Femur, I don't sign in"

I said, "I know, Femur, but security demands that you do so."

His girl friend said, "Leave it Norman!" which was yet another sign to me that their relationship was more than just shaking hands.

Our Chairman knew that I was not on the best terms with the Accountant, and I made it obvious to Norman that I was watching him when one day he had a day off, and after normal daily duty hours I suggested to our Chairman that he might like to examine some of the accountancy files.

As part of my security job I had a keyboard with duplicates of everything that locked, and on opening a four-drawer filing cabinet, we opened an Aladdin's Cave! Norman's part time hobby was in the pornographic business. We found copies of the monthly magazine, Forum, and similar publications, and letters galore from ladies who advertised in such publications, and Norman was offering them companionship on a Master Slave relationship, with quite a number of acceptances, and – surprise, surprise – his Accountancy girl friend was offering similar schemes to Lesbians!! I couldn't stop laughing for, although I knew such things went on, I had never come in contact until then with someone I thought I knew personally.

Graham also found things happening in Norman's accountancy procedures with which he did not approve, and the final outcome was that Norman and his girl friend were allowed to resign.....

Another chore that I took on was the Franking Machine to ensure that only BFT correspondence was franked. The Lewisham Post Office was large. It had thirteen serving positions, but rarely were there more than seven positions manned. Hence long queues would develop, and quite often up to 60 customers were waiting to be served. Then, suddenly, another position would open, and the smart Alecs at the end of some of the other queues would rush, making the Bible edict come true, that 'the first shall be last, and the last shall be first.'

That was very frustrating to customers who had been waiting a long time – me included – and so I wrote to the Postmaster stressing that his lining up procedures left much to be desired, but nothing happened. I wrote several times without any change.

I thought, 'Right Monkey' and so I wrote again, but at that time I indicated that a copy was to be sent to the Postmaster General. Of course, at that stage I did not send a copy to his boss, in fact, there was no need to, because within a week the 'Crocodile system' of lining up was installed, which was what I had wanted in the first place!

However, the Post Office was nearly 40 feet long, with an entrance/exit at each end, but one of those entrance/exits was closed with the new lining up system. That to me was not good enough, and so once again I wrote to the Post Master requesting that both entrances and exits be opened. The Post Master had never acknowledged any of my communications, and so after a fortnight, remembering how many letters I had written to him previously and the time wasted thereof, I then wrote to the Chief Fireman who covered the Lewisham area, pointing out that most times there were over sixty customers waiting to be served and the fire hazard that had been caused by closing one exit. Within 48 hours the Chief Fire Officer wrote, thanking me for my letter and my public spirit, and both doors were opened forthwith.

Bobby Sharp's remark once more sprang to mind – 'its not what you know, but who you know that counts'!

Near to where BFT had their offices, there was a street market that operated daily. It was a very busy market, and it was possible at times to get some good bargains.

One day as I was going to market, I noticed a huge Greengrocer stacking up a pile of 56lb bags of potatoes, and I noticed he was wearing earrings in both of his ears, and a gold chain around his neck.

He looked so feminine as to make me smile, and he said, "What are you laughing at?" to which I replied, "I think you look very pretty.!" "I'll knock your F****** block off" he said, to which I replied, "Maybe you could, but I still think you look very pretty!"

"F*** off" the Greengrocer said, as I laughingly went on my travels.

During one lunch break, I wandered across the road to the Army & Navy Stores. It was an intriguing building made up of many smaller premises which had been joined together.

It was early December, and I was on the ground floor where there was a Seasonal Grotto. I was obviously looking spare because a charming young lady assistant said, "Can I help you Sir?" She was gorgeous, and so I decided that I'd have some of that! And so I said, "Well – I've really come to see Father Christmas because I want to give him my list of things that I would like in my stocking."

"Oh!! I am sorry Sir" said the shop assistant, "But Father Christmas is at lunch, but if you leave me your list, I will give it to him." I replied, "But I did want to see Santa Claus personally; can you tell me when he will be back from lunch, and will you also be around?"

"Wing Commander Gibson, you naughty man, you are having me on! My mother works for your firm across the road, and I know all about you!" was her response.

"Oh! Do you?" I said, "May I wish you the compliments of the season" as I slunk off with what little dignity I could muster!

BFT had on its staff a mature lady whose job it was as a telephonist to acquire new clients. She had all of the qualities that such a job required, including the ability to accept refusals with grace and charm, but it could be very soul destroying.

A few days after my Army and Navy episode, I was passing the time of day with her when she said, "I hear you've been chatting up my daughter in the Army and Navy Stores?"

"Oh!!" I said, "I can see where she gets her good looks and charm from. May I congratulate you; you've done a fine job."

"Thank you very much" she responded, "My daughter is all there – she know's what's what!"

That remark reminded me of a Max Miller story which is worth recording:

There was a newly married couple, and the man's workmates were ribbing him, saying things such as; 'Now you're a married man, you know what's what!' The newly married man did not know what that meant, and he kept repeating to himself, "Now I am married, I know what's what." Any how, that night his wife had gone to bed, and after he had got undressed, he turned the light out, and being in new surroundings, he was fumbling about in the dark, and he suddenly touched something soft, and he said, "What's that?", and his wife replied, "What's what?", and there it was – it had been on the mantelpiece all the time!

Max Miller was known as the 'Cheeky Chappie', and he had a wonderful repertoire of funny stories. His timing was perfect, and he always had his audiences waiting for his next word, which is the aim of every comedienne, but not easy to achieve.

This book of the first 72 years of my life is supposed to be a happy book, but if the reader disagrees – well, the joke's on me.

More of Bruce's adventures in the next volume!

* * *

ACKNOWLEDGEMENTS

As a nonagenarian, I have thoroughly enjoyed
writing about the best bits of my life.

It has been made possible by the goading of my
God-daughter, Heather; my beloved sister, Betty,
and my friends, especially Graham Martin and
my new found friend, Melissa, who has typed,
formatted, edited and proof read the book.

If some of my present day friends and acquaintances
find some bits a little coarse,
all I can say is, it is a case of horses for courses!
But that is how we were.

BIBLIOGRAPHY

Customs of the Services
By Group Captain H. Stradling O.B.E.

Fifty Years a Borough – 1880 – 1836
The Story of West Ham
By Donald McDougall

Chronicle of the 20th Century
As conceived and co-ordinated by
Jacques Legrand